COMPARATIVE PERSPECTIVES ON REVENUE LAW

Dedicated to the work of John Tiley, the premier tax academic in the UK for more than two decades, this volume of essays focuses on two themes that, among others, inspire the writings of Tiley. The first of these themes, tax avoidance, involves using tax law in a manner that is contrary to legislative intent. The second theme, taxation of the family, involves proper identification of the tax subject and is therefore one of the fundamental structural features of income tax. Drawing on historical precedent, academic excellence and personal experience, the importance of Tiley's contribution to the tax field is identified through contributions by some of the world's most influential tax writers.

COMPARATIVE PERSPECTIVES ON REVENUE LAW

Essays in honour of John Tiley

Edited by

JOHN AVERY JONES, PETER HARRIS
AND DAVID OLIVER

CAMBRIDGE
UNIVERSITY PRESS

CAMBRIDGE UNIVERSITY PRESS

Cambridge, New York, Melbourne, Madrid, Cape Town, Singapore, São Paulo, Delhi

Cambridge University Press
The Edinburgh Building, Cambridge CB2 8RU, UK

Published in the United States of America by Cambridge University Press, New York

www.cambridge.org
Information on this title: www.cambridge.org/9780521887779

First published 2008

Printed in the United Kingdom at the University Press, Cambridge

A catalogue record for this publication is available from the British Library

Library of Congress Cataloging-in-Publication data

Comparative perspectives on revenue law : essays in honour of John Tiley / edited by
John Avery Jones, Peter Harris, and David Oliver.
p. cm.
Includes bibliographical references and index.
ISBN 978-0-521-88777-9 (hardback)
1. Taxation – Law and legislation – Great Britain.   2. Tax evasion – Great Britain.
3. Family – Taxation – Law and legislation – Great Britain.   I. Tiley, John.   II. Jones, John Avery,
1940–   III. Harris, Peter, 1964–   IV. Oliver, David (J. David B.)
KD5359.A2C66   2008
345.41′0233 – dc22   2008003212

ISBN 978-0-521-88777-9 hardback

CONTENTS

CONTRIBUTORS AND AFFILIATIONS

Brian J. Arnold
Goodmans LLP, Professor of Law Emeritus, University of Western Ontario, Canada

John F. Avery Jones CBE
Special Commissioner, UK

Philip Baker
QC, Gray's Inn Tax Chambers, London, UK

Martin Daunton
Professor of Economic History, University of Cambridge, Master of Trinity Hall, UK

Judith Freedman
KPMG Professor of Taxation Law, Oxford University, Joint Editor *British Tax Review*, UK

Malcolm Gammie
QC, Chambers of Lord Grabiner QC, London, UK

Peter Harris
Senior Lecturer, University of Cambridge, Fellow, Churchill College, UK

Erik M. Jensen
David L. Brennan Professor of Law, Case Western Reserve University, US

Martin J. McMahon, Jr.
Clarence J. TeSelle Professor of Law, Fredric G. Levin College of Law, University of Florida, US

David Oliver
Cambridge University, LSE, Joint Editor *British Tax Review*, UK

Wolfgang Schön
Director, Max Planck Institute for Intellectual Property, Competition
and Tax Law, Professor, Ludwig Maximilian University, Munich,
Germany

Richard J. Vann
Challis Professor of Law, University of Sydney, Australia

Graham Virgo
Professor of English Private Law, University of Cambridge, Fellow,
Downing College, UK

FOREWORD

DAVE HARTNETT

It is a real pleasure and a privilege to have prepared this foreword to a collection of essays honouring John Tiley as he nears retirement from the chair in Taxation Law at Cambridge University. The essays have been prepared by some of the most insightful writers on tax of recent times, all of them friends of John and some of them former students. In the paragraphs that follow I have described my personal experience of John, set out to say something about his achievements as one of the leading tax thinkers of modern times and then attempted to reveal something of the man that may not be readily apparent from his writings.

I first met John in the foyer of the Cambridge Law Faculty. As I walked in, he recognised me immediately – I still do not know how – and I realised that I was with the person who had been influencing my understanding of tax from the very first days of my career in the Inland Revenue.

In the second half of the 1970s, the Inland Revenue training regime for graduate entry tax inspectors was demanding, with a pass mark in internal examinations of 70 per cent. Tax cases had to be learnt by rote, which came hard after several years spent in research and university teaching. For a while, tax seemed a lot less stimulating than Cicero's speeches or letters. John's *Revenue Law* – essential reading for anyone with a serious interest in tax – changed all that. His ability to bring out the crucial importance of decided cases by reviewing their fit with precedent and his insights into the thinking of judges and the arguments of counsel, brought tax to life for me. Then there was his strong sense that tax should have a discernible structure and rationale, with his expectation that policy development should take that into account or risk creating a tax system without order. (More than once in recent years John has told me of his disappointment that tax policy changes in the UK and elsewhere have not always seemed to him to fit well with the established policy and legal framework and that they were supported by an inadequate explanation of why that should be so.)

I also discovered in *Revenue Law* a gentle irreverence and a sense of mischief when John wanted to suggest that judges, leading counsel, and even the UK's tax administration, were misguided in their arguments or conclusions. As I found my way in tax, and built up card indexes of cases – the nearest thing then to modern databases – I had three sections for each case: what the Inland Revenue told me to make of it, what I made of it for myself, and what *Revenue Law* taught me. Making sense of the three comments was rarely easy, but the *Revenue Law* element was often provocative and sometimes made me smile.

As I got to know John well and our friendship developed, I found there was a prescience in his suggestions and advice. He has long been concerned that tax administrations would get themselves into difficulty by becoming too dependent on sophisticated IT – his principal fear being that the IT would fail or that the confidentiality of taxpayers would be put at risk in ways that could not be immediately foreseen. The difficulties that arose with the IT supporting the implementation of tax credits in the UK and the growing global threat from identity fraud, often involving organised crime, have shown how right he was. His concerns about tax law research and teaching in universities in the UK have also been well founded and his imminent retirement is a timely reminder to all of us interested in tax law that we need to generate investment in tax in our universities. And his advice that tax law academics should play a greater part in the production of tax legislation – now happily addressed through his membership of the steering group overseeing the re-write of tax law in the UK – is being heard around the world.

John has not been alone in seeing the importance of tax academics, lawyers and practitioners (in the public and private sectors) getting together to share ideas and compare how taxes and their administration work. However, the seminar programmes he has organised in Cambridge in recent years have made a huge contribution to ensuring this happens. It is a mark of the esteem in which he is held that scholars, practitioners and tax officials of the highest standing from near and far have eagerly made their way to Queens' College to deliver stimulating and sometimes controversial seminars to audiences every bit as eager to be there.

The son of a distinguished tax inspector (who appears in *Revenue Law* through the decided case of *Grey v Tiley*), John was a scholar at Winchester and a student in Lincoln College, Oxford, where his tutor was Brian Simpson, a legal historian whose boundless curiosity and determination to establish not what a rule was but why it existed had a profound influence on him. This approach will be immediately recognised by those who know John in his teaching and public speaking. Academic posts at Oxford and Birmingham followed. In 1964 he published his first article – on the 'Rescue Principle' – arguing that a tortfeasor could owe a duty of care not just to the immediate victim but also to foreseeable rescuers. The courts have long adopted this principle and it led to John being known to his friends as 'the original two cake man'.

In 1967 John was awarded a fellowship at Queens' College, Cambridge, having been appointed to an assistant lectureship in the University. News of the fellowship reached Jillinda, John's wife, before he learnt of the lectureship, and when asked if she would arrange for him to telephone the College President the next day to say whether he would accept the fellowship, she explained that would not be easy as he was due to play cricket all day. Fortunately, nothing amiss came of this, not least because the President of Queens' was taken with the idea of John playing cricket, and for almost 41 years Queens' has been John's academic home and the place where *Revenue Law* and so much else that has informed and inspired the tax world has been produced.

Few could doubt that Queens' and John Tiley were made for each other. He has served in almost every college role and will be remembered by some as the 'grand inquisitor' in a BBC television programme about Cambridge life when he was admissions tutor. When he was Director of Studies in Law, he and Jillinda would entertain huge numbers of young men with voracious appetites – there were no young women in Queens' at the time. (He was a delighted admissions tutor when Queens' admitted women for the first time.) As Acting Bursar, he made some judicious purchases of land which in time generated a lot of money for the college. And at various times he has been both Vice-President and Acting President of Queens'. But perhaps most typical of the man, he has always been particularly caring of the college staff.

Famously, during a royal visit to Cambridge, the Duke of Edinburgh, passing the window of a room in the Old Schools where John was teaching, commented on the degree of hilarity being enjoyed by a class and queried what was happening inside. It was, of course, John bringing tax law to life for his students. Within the Law Faculty, John has been Director of the LLM course with particular responsibility for recruitment and care of the many overseas students and he has been Chairman of the Faculty. He was awarded his chair in 1991.

It is perhaps as a teacher of tax law that John has felt most fulfilled. He has influenced and shaped generations of students, many of them now in very senior positions in their firms or practices, members of the judiciary or government ministers, in the UK and all over the world. This collection of essays clearly demonstrates his influence as a writer and no more needs to be said here, though on a personal note I have been greatly heartened when he has mentioned with approval something he thought I had got right. And I have thought very carefully about issues he has said I have got wrong.

As Chairman of the Faculty, he introduced social events to bring people together where there had been none before. It was also John who led the Faculty as plans were laid for its new Norman Foster building. At the time, lectures mostly took place in the Old Schools and dons taught and worked from their college rooms. The Faculty had to raise the funds for the building to be erected on land given by Caius in exchange for the Old Squire Library behind the Senate House. There was much opposition to plans for centralisation of the Faculty and at times it appeared that the Faculty members really did not know what they wanted to do. John was very much in the middle of all this, steering the project to successful delivery while fronting to good effect the fundraising and handling some of the negotiations with the architects. Those who have used the building will know how well equipped it is and that it has the support staff needed to make it a special place to work.

The sense of a unified Faculty is widely credited to John, whose greatest achievement is seen by some as having ensured decent catering on site through a branch of Nadia's, the Cambridge bun and sandwich shop much beloved of students. When the Foster building was being planned and erected, most Faculty members said they did not want an office there. Today, the Faculty has a real focus and has grown to have a number of Centres which enable different groups to share ideas, host visitors and mount conferences. None of this would have been possible without the vision and team building which John masterminded. He is very proud to be the Director for the Centre for Tax Law and to be bringing to Cambridge in 2008 the conference of the European Association of Tax Law Professors.

John is very much a family man. Married to Jillinda, who is also a barrister and academic lawyer, they have three children of whom they are immensely proud. Interestingly, none of their children has followed them into law: the eldest is a chartered accountant and finance director in industry, the second a medical practitioner and the third an archae-ologist. They have travelled the world together, making many friends, in connection with John's sabbatical posts and lecturing engagements – first to Dalhousie University in Nova Scotia, and later to universities in the US,

New Zealand and Australia. John has a passion for boats and trains, once taking the family across Canada by train to Vancouver, then by plane to Auckland and then home by ship from Melbourne so that he could sail through the Panama Canal.

John is also passionate about most sports and is famed for watching any sport that involves a ball, whatever the time of day or night. He endeared himself to students at Case Western Reserve University in Cleveland with his knowledge of baseball and American football and confounded colleagues at Berkeley, California, where he was a visiting Professor, by making students laugh with his references to baseball and football in law lectures.

Music runs in the Tiley family. His tax inspector father was a gifted conductor and as a child John played the oboe, an instrument taken up later by his second son. As part of his preparation for retirement he has taken up the piano again and bought himself a new piano – a Steinway, because it sounds better. John also has a love of walking and in his youth walked all over Switzerland and Austria with his father and, more recently, has trekked in the Himalayas with his younger son. But it is Scotland and the island of Colonsay in the Hebrides for which he has a special fondness. Having read about the role of the forbears of the island's owner, Lord Strathcona, in building the Canadian Pacific railroad, John could not resist an advertisement placed in *The Times* for holiday cottages on Colonsay which said that most people would not like the place, because there was no entertainment and nothing to do. John just had to go, and he and Jillinda have been back nearly twenty times since.

The award of a CBE in the 2003 New Year's Honours List was fitting public recognition for John Tiley's service to tax law over many years. His family, friends and colleagues were delighted for him. What few may know, however, is that John attended the investiture ceremony carrying in his pocket the insignia of OBE awarded to his father, who would have been very proud of him.

It would be all too easy to conclude that John Tiley's abiding passion is for tax law but that does not quite capture the man. Like many fans of ball games, John will remember the description of football attributed to Bill Shankly, the former Liverpool manager:

> Some people believe football is a matter of life and death. I am very disappointed with that attitude. I can assure you it is much more important than that.

A more enigmatic comment on tax law can be found in *Revenue Law*:

Tax law provides us with a sharp instance of what some think life is all about – money, sex and power.

With a loving family, friends and colleagues who worship him, a huge range of interests and a global reputation in tax, life seems a bit more complex for John whose interests demonstrate a curiosity that knows no bounds.

Dave Hartnett CB
Acting Chairman,
HM Revenue & Customs, UK

FOREWORD

HUGH AULT

I was pleased and honoured to be asked to write a foreword to this collection of essays in honour of John Tiley, an old friend and respected colleague. Both the substance of the contributions in the collection and the status of the authors show the esteem in which the international tax community holds John.

It is appropriate that the title of the collection involves *comparative* perspectives on revenue law, as John's scholarship and academic activities were centred on comparative interests. He has been a visiting scholar at many foreign institutions, particularly in the US and France, and that experience gave a depth and substance to his comparative writing. In the other direction, he was the point of reference for all comparative work which deals with UK law. He was a welcoming host to many visiting scholars who made Cambridge a necessary stopping point in their scholarly travels. (And further he endeared himself to his international colleagues by writing a very useful essay on the double tax problems faced by travelling academics.)

John brought a unique style and approach to writing about tax law. As Brian Arnold puts it in the culinary metaphor with which he introduces his contribution to this collection, John Tiley is a 'master chef' when it comes to tax law scholarship. His offerings are many and varied and always have a special flavour. As an example, I can quote from his essay on the UK tax system in *Comparative Income Taxation*:

> History is all-important in the UK tax system. Thus since the UK tax system has been around since the Middle Ages, the tax year starts not at some arbitrary date in mid winter (such as January 1) but in the spring (April 6). As will be seen however in the later sections there are indications that some of the old pillars of the system (though not yet the start of the tax year) are under review or even redesign . . .
>
> (Tiley, 2004b, p. 115)

As the quoted passage shows, John's work combines wit, insight and a deep understanding of the historical roots of the tax system in its present manifestations.

John was fascinated with the problems of tax avoidance and the interpretation of tax statutes and several of the contributions in this volume reflect this interest, which goes back nearly 25 years. His works chronicle the twists and turns of the legal developments in this area, both in the UK and in other jurisdictions. The development of John's conclusions that, for the UK, there is 'no general overriding judicial anti-avoidance principle' and his general scepticism about the (undisciplined) use of the 'substance over form' doctrine in certain other jurisdictions make fascinating reading.

While I understand that John is retiring from his position in Cambridge, I am sure that he will not be 'retiring' from the intellectual conversation in the tax area to which he has contributed so much.

Hugh J. Ault,
Professor of Law, Boston College, US;
Senior Advisor, OECD, Paris, France

A comparison of statutory general anti-avoidance rules and judicial general anti-avoidance doctrines as a means of controlling tax avoidance: Which is better? (What would John Tiley think?)

BRIAN ARNOLD

Introduction

There is an inverse relationship between quantity and quality with respect to many things, including writing about tax avoidance. Everyone working in the tax area has views about tax avoidance and almost everyone, it seems, feels an irresistible urge to inflict these views on others. Most of the writing on tax avoidance is in the nature of fast food: quickly prepared, consumed, digested and forgotten – and, if consumed in excessive quantities, dangerous to your (mental) health. In a fast-food world, master chefs are revered and celebrated. Professor John Tiley is a master chef with respect to offerings about tax avoidance. His writings about controlling tax avoidance constitute the fine-dining experience, the Michelin three-star restaurant in a world of greasy spoons, chains and all-you-can-eat buffets. It is fitting that we celebrate his contributions.

The subject of my paper is a comparison of a statutory general anti-avoidance rule and judicial general anti-avoidance doctrines as methods of controlling tax avoidance. The paper assumes, fairly I think, that specific statutory anti-avoidance rules and limited judicial anti-avoidance doctrines such as sham are necessary but not even nearly sufficient to deal effectively with tax avoidance. The issue can be framed in a number of ways. Often in the context of a particular country, it takes the form of the question: is a statutory GAAR necessary? The issue was put this way in Canada in the mid-1980s when the GAAR was adopted and it has been put that way in the UK since the *Ramsay* case in 1981.

Other people, especially Tiley, are much more qualified than me to opine about whether the UK should adopt a GAAR. Instead, in this paper

I want to emulate Tiley and approach the issue from a comparative perspective. Comparative analysis has been a prominent feature of Tiley's writing on tax avoidance over his career. The subject lends itself to comparative treatment because some countries (notably the UK and the US) have vigorous judicial anti-avoidance doctrines and no statutory GAAR, while other countries with similar legal traditions (Australia, Canada, New Zealand and South Africa) have enacted statutory GAARs.

The organisation of the paper is straightforward. It commences with a background section dealing with some preliminary issues relating to the broader context in which anti-avoidance rules operate that are essential to an understanding of both judicial doctrines and statutory GAARs. The two following sections describe statutory GAARs and judicial anti-avoidance doctrines from a general perspective. I have avoided detailed descriptions and analysis of the anti-avoidance measures of specific countries because of space restrictions and the availability of this material elsewhere. These two sections are followed by an assessment of the two methods of controlling tax avoidance and a brief comparison of the seemingly similar situations in Canada under its statutory GAAR and the UK with its judicial approach.

1.1 Background – preliminary matters

Introduction

One typical aspect of Tiley's writings on tax avoidance that I especially value is the care with which he situates the discussion of the most recent case or statutory provision in a broader context – and for him that context is very broad indeed.

In a short article published in 1985,[1] soon after the *Ramsay*[2] and *Furniss v Dawson*[3] cases, Tiley reminds everyone, but in particular, panicking practitioners, that –

> these decisions represent a classic example of legal development; there is nothing unusual about the way the need for change has come about nor about the way in which the change was made and it is suggested that history may also warn us to avoid jumping to solutions.[4]

---

[1] Tiley (1985a).   [2] *Ramsay v IRC* [1982] AC 300 (HL).
[3] *Furniss v Dawson* [1984] AC 474 (HL).   [4] Tiley (1985a, p. 19).

He placed the decisions in the broader context of the law generally;[5] in the historical context of parallel developments in the law of negligence and the rule against perpetuities; and in the comparative context.[6] In a 2004 article, he wisely advises us to 'bypass the judicial rhetoric in particular cases and ask what the judges have actually done'.[7] At the same time, he admonishes the judges for forgetting that '[t]heir words are pored over not just for the fun of gazing at entrails but in order to give advice about what those very judges might do next.'[8]

In the chapter of his textbook[9] dealing with 'The Control of Tax Avoidance', before discussing the UK case law, which is the central focus of the chapter, he usefully sets the stage by identifying eleven ways in which legislatures can control tax avoidance and discussing the advantages and disadvantages of anti-avoidance legislation. That chapter also discusses the experience of several countries (European, Commonwealth and the US) with statutory general anti-avoidance rules and the aspects of a tax system related to the need for and structure of a GAAR (information disclosure rules and the availability of a clearance or advance rulings procedure). It also demonstrates an appreciation of history, with references to statutory GAARs in the UK excess profits tax during the Second World War. Thus, anti-avoidance rules and doctrines are always portrayed by Tiley as an integral part of the tax system.

The starting point: the Duke of Westminster

As noted above, Tiley is especially sensitive to the influence of history on tax law.[10] It is no surprise, therefore, that his analysis of anti-avoidance doctrines in the UK and other Commonwealth countries usually commences with the seminal *Duke of Westminster* case.[11] He cites the case not only for the obvious point that the House of Lords affirmed the right of taxpayers to arrange their affairs to minimise tax, but also for the more subtle and arguably more influential point that the courts cannot tax on

---

[5] 'New tax cases represent tax law joining this mainstream of judicial thinking not departing from it.' *Ibid.*

[6] 'The United Kingdom is now closer to the mainstream of legal experience in other countries.' *Ibid.*

[7] Tiley (2004a, p. 328).   [8] Tiley (2001, p. 158).   [9] Tiley (2005b).

[10] See, for example, his lecture reproduced in Tiley (1998a), which describes developments in the UK personal income tax since 1968.

[11] *IRC v Duke of Westminster* [1936] AC 1 (HL). For example, see Tiley (2005b, pp. 105–7) and Tiley (2004b, p. 133).

the basis of economic substance but must respect the legal rights and obligations created by the parties:

> The doctrine emerging from the *Westminster* case is that taxpayers and the Revenue are bound by the legal results which the parties have achieved – even though this may be inconvenient for the Revenue. The court cannot disregard those facts just because of the tax avoidance purpose which may have led the parties to create those facts in the first place.[12]

However, the *Duke of Westminster* principle does not mean, as some have suggested, that the legal form of a transaction is conclusive. A court is not bound by the labels that the parties have attached to their transactions; it is entitled to examine all of the facts 'to discover the true character in tax law of the transaction entered into'.[13] This fundamental principle emerging from the *Duke of Westminster* case is not just trotted out in the interests of tradition. According to Tiley, it helps to explain the recent House of Lords jurisprudence on tax avoidance: 'All the cases in which the Revenue have succeeded under the Ramsay composite transaction rule . . . can be seen as examples of this rule.'[14] Moreover, the *Duke of Westminster* case is still 'absolutely correct' based on a rigorous legal analysis of the contractual relations between the Duke and his gardener.[15] Only by applying an economic substance approach such as the US business purpose test, is it possible to conclude that the gardener continued to receive his full wages after the Duke executed the deed to provide the gardener with an annuity equal to a portion of his wages.[16]

Questions of fact or rules of law?

One of the fundamental difficulties with judicial anti-avoidance doctrines is differentiating between those that relate merely to the ascertainment of the facts and those that establish rules of law applicable to the facts. Students of tax avoidance owe a debt to Tiley for illuminating this issue over twenty years ago, and it is worthwhile recapping his analysis here.

---

[12] Tiley (2005b, p. 106).   [13] *Ibid.*   [14] *Ibid.*, p. 107.   [15] Tiley (1988a, p. 81).

[16] An alternative possibility would be to treat the annuity as a sham because it was never intended that the contractual arrangements between the Duke and his gardener would be acted upon. It was understood that the gardener would not sue the Duke to obtain his full wages. And it is significant in this regard that the Duke entered into these arrangements only with long-term loyal employees.

In a section of a 1987 article[17] entitled 'Anatomy of a Tax Case', Tiley identifies nine levels of reasoning to explain how tax cases are decided. The first four levels relate to the determination of the facts:

- The basic facts or events (who did what to whom? when? etc.).
- The classification of the basic facts in terms of the private law (was a contract entered into? was the property sold? etc.).
- The classification of the private law results for tax purposes (for example, if employment income is a recognised category for tax purposes, is the private law contract one of employment or of service?).
- The rearrangement of the facts as determined under the previous three steps (the application of the step transaction doctrine: can transfers from A to B and B to C be treated as a transfer from A to C?).

The following levels of reasoning relate to the interpretation of the tax law and its application to the facts as determined under the first four levels:

- The interpretation of the words of the tax legislation (according to Tiley, this is where the US business purpose test becomes relevant: do the terms of the particular statutory provision require a transaction to be carried out with a business purpose in order to come within its terms?).
- The application of the provisions of the tax law as interpreted to the facts as determined (this issue is often treated as a question of fact in terms of reviewability by an appeal court, whereas issues of statutory construction are reviewable questions of law).
- The application of overarching principles of tax law, such as the principle that all income must have a source, and the distinction between capital and income.
- The application of anti-avoidance doctrines, which, unlike the general principles, occurs spasmodically and whose limits are difficult to define.
- Finally, the application of broad principles 'floating about in the legal ether'[18] which reflect notions about what the law should be and which often conflict (for example, everyone is entitled to arrange his or her affairs to minimise tax, and everyone should pay his or her fair share of tax).

One may quibble with Tiley's classification of these nine levels of reasoning.[19] But such quibbles miss the point. The purpose of the

---

[17] Tiley (1987, pp. 190–5).   [18] Tiley (1987, p. 194).
[19] There is some obvious overlap between some of the categories and the ordering of the various levels may not reflect how courts actually decide tax cases.

identification of the various levels of reasoning is not important in itself but as a means of obtaining a deeper understanding of judicial anti-avoidance rules and how they fit into legal reasoning about tax issues. In the absence of this understanding, commentary about the rules is condemned to be emotional ranting based on gut feelings about what is right or wrong. Tiley forces us – tax practitioners, scholars, students and judges – seriously to consider our thinking about judicial anti-avoidance doctrines so that they have intellectual coherence and credibility. He is fond of quoting Justice Learned Hand in dissent in the *Gilbert* case:

> To say it [the test] is whether the transaction has a 'substantive economic reality' or 'is in reality as it appears to be in form,' or is a 'sham' or a 'masquerade' or 'depends on the substance of the transaction'; all of them appear to me to leave the test undefined because they do not state the facts which are determinative.[20]

And as he puts it himself:

> What is vital is that the courts should be honest in their reasoning; invoking the will of the wisp of substance or reality is simply not intellectually sustainable.[21]

Interpretation and application

As Tiley often reminds us, it is important to distinguish between the judicial functions of interpretation and application.[22] Judicial decisions about the meaning of statutory provisions should be justified on the basis of prior case law, the purpose of the provisions or the consequences of competing interpretations. They should be internally consistent and capable of being followed in subsequent cases. Application, however, involves deciding whether the facts of the particular case in front of the court are within or outside the meaning of the relevant provisions as interpreted by the court. For this purpose, how the court determines or characterises the facts is critical. As discussed earlier, in determining the facts, the actual legal rights and obligations created by the parties must be respected, subject to narrow exceptions for sham and legal substance. Perhaps the best brief summary of the twofold challenge for courts was provided by Judge Ribeiro in the *Arrowtown*[23] case:

---

[20] *Gilbert v CIR* (1957) 248 F 2d 399 (2d Cir.) at p. 411.
[21] Tiley (1988a, p. 89).   [22] Tiley (2004a, p. 308).
[23] *Collector of Stamp Revenue v Arrowtown Assets Ltd* [2004] 1 HKLRD 77 (HKCA), quoted by Lord Nicholls in the House of Lords in *Barclays Mercantile v Mawson* [2004] UKHL 51 (HL) at para. 36.

> The ultimate question is whether the relevant statutory provisions, construed purposively, were intended to apply to the transaction, viewed realistically.

As the foregoing summary of Tiley's 'Anatomy of a Tax Case' shows, it is simplistic to differentiate only between the judicial functions of interpretation and application. And yet at times the courts of many countries seem to mix them up. As Tiley says, in his straightforward way, a court must 'determine the facts, interpret the law and apply that interpretation to the facts'.[24] He argues that much of the judicial confusion comes from the courts' framing their task in terms of determining 'the true character of the transactions'.[25] According to Tiley, 'the characterization of the facts in the case must come before the interpretation' and in this regard he and Lord Hoffmann (who delivered one of the major speeches in *MacNiven v Westmoreland*[26]) disagree 'on which is the cart and which is the horse'.[27] Extending the metaphor in typical witty fashion, he suggests that 'much time will have to be spent mucking out this particular stable yard'.[28]

The confusion between interpretation and application is evident in the *Westmoreland* case. Recognising that *Ramsay* is a principle of construction, Lord Hoffmann attempted to introduce a distinction between statutory language referring to legal concepts and commercial concepts and to limit the *Ramsay* principle to the latter. This distinction has since been resoundingly rejected by the House of Lords; quite rightly, because the distinction is unclear and diverts attention from the important issue – did Parliament intend the transaction in question to be covered by the statutory language used? In contrast, Lord Hutton considered that *Ramsay* required an element of artificiality. As a result, under this approach it would be necessary for the courts to distinguish between real amounts and contrived, unreal amounts. Once again, this distinction is unhelpful because it does not provide any test to distinguish between real and unreal amounts. To me, the issue in *Westmoreland* that the House of Lords

---

[24] Tiley (1987, p. 191).   [25] Tiley (2001, p. 158).
[26] *MacNiven v Westmoreland Investments Ltd* [2001] UKHL 6 (HL).
[27] Tiley (2001, p. 157).
[28] *Ibid.* My own view is that, while Tiley is generally correct that the facts come first in tax avoidance cases, the characterisation of the facts and the interpretation of the legislation are more integrated than separate in the analytical process. Judges do not interpret legislation in the abstract; they confront questions concerning the application of the legislation to a particular transaction or set of facts. The House of Lords recognised this in *Barclays Mercantile v Mawson* [2004] UKHL 51 at para. 32: 'Of course this does not mean that the courts have to put their reasoning into the straitjacket of first construing the statute in the abstract and then looking at the facts. It might be more convenient to analyse the facts and then ask whether they satisfy the requirements of the statute.'

did not confront was: did Parliament intend that payment of an amount which, in the circumstances, did not have to be made and which had no financial or commercial consequences for the parties, should generate tax consequences?

Tiley's prediction about the need to sort out the confusion between interpretation and application is equally accurate with respect to the Canadian GAAR. In the *Canada Trustco* case,[29] the Supreme Court of Canada adopted a two-stage approach to the application of s. 245(4) of the general anti-avoidance rule. Section 245(4) provides that an avoidance transaction is subject to the GAAR only if it constitutes a misuse or an abuse of the provisions of the Income Tax Act or other relevant tax legislation. According to the Supreme Court, a court must determine: first, the purpose of the statutory provisions that confer the tax benefit; and second, whether the avoidance transaction abuses or frustrates that purpose. According to the court, the first issue is a question of law but the second is a question of fact, with the result that the factual findings of the trial court should be accepted unless there is a palpable and overriding error.[30] The first issue involves the interpretation of the statute; the second issue involves the application of the statute to the transaction. The striking point is that the Supreme Court's approach to the issue of abuse under the GAAR is virtually identical to the House of Lords' approach in tax avoidance cases, despite the absence of a GAAR in the UK.[31]

The relationship between statutory interpretation and tax avoidance

Since all taxes are imposed by statute, all questions of tax are ultimately ones that involve the interpretation and application of the statute. The result in the *Duke of Westminster* case was as much a product of the literal interpretation of taxing statutes that prevailed at the time in the UK and Commonwealth countries as the result in the contemporary US case, *Gregory v Helvering*,[32] was a product of a more purposive approach to interpretation. It is not mere coincidence that the adoption of the *Ramsay* approach by the House of Lords in the 1980s was accompanied

---

[29] *The Queen v Canada Trustco Mortgage Company* [2005] SCC 54 (SCC).

[30] The second issue is clearly a mixed question of fact and law. Indeed, the question of whether a transaction is abusive is quintessentially a legal question, not a factual one. For a more detailed analysis see Arnold (2006a).

[31] This point is explored in more detail below.

[32] *Gregory v Helvering* (1934) 69 F 2d 809 (2d Cir.), affirmed (1935) 293 US 465 (USSC).

by a gradual shift to a more purposive approach to the interpretation of statutes in the UK. As Lord Steyn wrote in the *McGuckian* case:

> Towards the end of the last century Pollock characterised the approach of judges to statutory construction as follows – '. . . Parliament generally changes the law for the worse, and that the business of the judges is to keep the mischief of its interference within the narrowest possible bounds' (see Pollock *Essays in Jurisprudence and Ethics* (1882) p 85). Whatever the merits of this observation may have been when it was made, or even earlier in this century, it is demonstrably no longer true. During the last 30 years there has been a shift away from literalist to purposive methods of construction. Where there is no obvious meaning of a statutory provision the modern emphasis is on a contextual approach designed to identify the purpose of a statute and to give effect to it. But under the influence of the narrow *Duke of Westminster* doctrine, tax law remained remarkably resistant to the new non-formalist methods of interpretation. It was said that the taxpayer was entitled to stand on a literal construction of the words used regardless of the purpose of the statute (see *Pryce v Monmouthshire Canal and Rly Cos* (1879) 4 App Cas 197 at 202–203, *Cape Brandy Syndicate v IRC* [1921] 2 KB 64 at 71 and *IRC v Plummer* [1980] AC 896). Tax law was by and large left behind as some island of literal interpretation. The second problem was that in regard to tax avoidance schemes the courts regarded themselves as compelled to adopt a step by step analysis of such schemes, treating each step as a distinct transaction producing its own tax consequences. It was thought that if the steps were genuine, ie not sham or simulated documents or arrangements, the court was not entitled to go behind the form of the individual transactions. In combination those two features – literal interpretation of tax statutes and the formalistic insistence on examining steps in a composite scheme separately – allowed tax avoidance schemes to flourish to the detriment of the general body of taxpayers. The result was that the court appeared to be relegated to the role of a spectator concentrating on the individual moves in a highly skilled game: the court was mesmerised by the moves in the game and paid no regard to the strategy of the participants or the end result. The courts became habituated to this narrow view of their role.
>
> On both fronts the intellectual breakthrough came in 1981 in the *Ramsay* case, and notably in Lord Wilberforce's seminal speech which carried the agreement of Lord Russell of Killowen, Lord Roskill and Lord Bridge of Harwich. Lord Wilberforce restated the principle of statutory construction that a subject is only to be taxed upon clear words ([1982] AC 300 at 323). To the question 'What are "clear words"?' he gave the answer that the court is not confined to a literal interpretation. He added 'There may,

indeed should, be considered the context and scheme of the relevant Act as a whole, and its purpose may, indeed should, be regarded'. This sentence was critical. It marked the rejection by the House of pure literalism in the interpretation of tax statutes.[33]

Tiley's appreciation of the tax case law in a broader historical context of the development of legal principles generally allowed him to anticipate by many years the statutory interpretation underpinnings of the *Ramsay* case law recognised by Lord Steyn in 1997. In 1985 he wrote in response to the criticism of tax practitioners that the House of Lords did not interpret the statute in the *Ramsay* and *Furniss v Dawson* cases:

> To take the criticism on a more substantial level, it can be said that the courts *are* interpreting the statutes but are doing so in a more adventurous way. As one reads the speeches in *Ramsay* one expects at any moment to come across a paraphrase of Lord McNaughten's famous dictum on income tax, 'My Lords, capital gains tax is, if I may be pardoned for saying so, a tax on capital gains.' What one detects in the speeches is not just an exasperated impatience with avoidance schemes or oversubtle arguments but an increasing confidence in handling the relatively new capital gains tax and an invocation of overriding concepts such as gain. If it is so, we are at the start of an era of strong tax jurisprudence . . .[34]

As discussed in the preceding section, Tiley recognised early on that there are two intimately related things going on in tax avoidance cases. One is factual: the search for the relevant transaction. The other is interpretive: what does the statute require? In the UK, the US, and most of the other countries considered here, the interpretation of tax statutes is supposed to take account of the purpose of the relevant provisions. Although good in theory, a purposive approach raises several issues: how is the purpose of tax legislation to be determined, what is the role of legislative history and other extrinsic material, and what is the competence of non-specialist judges to determine the purpose of complex tax statutes? Where do judicial anti-avoidance doctrines fit into this matrix of determining the facts and interpreting the statute? In Tiley's seminal analysis of judicial anti-avoidance doctrines,[35] he identifies the UK sham doctrine as essentially factual: the label that the parties attach to a transaction will not be conclusive in determining the legal rights and obligations created by the parties. On the other hand, the US business purpose doctrine is

---

[33] *IRC v McGuckian* [1997] 3 All ER 817 (HL) at p. 824.
[34] Tiley (1985a, p. 24).   [35] Tiley (1987a), Tiley (1987b) and Tiley (1988a).

interpretive: certain statutory provisions apply only to transactions that have some business or commercial purpose (or, in its broadest form, some purpose other than the avoidance of tax).[36] According to Tiley, the business purpose doctrine is 'intellectually sustainable' because it states the facts that are determinative of the application of the rule. Thus, although a tax avoidance motive is initially irrelevant, it is reintroduced as part of the interpreted concept. Tiley, however, is very critical of the substance-over-form doctrine and its relationship to statutory interpretation:

> One wonders, what exactly is meant by the interpretation of the law – crucially, does this cover both the meaning of the words and their application to the facts presented in the case or only to one of these?[37]

He suggests that substance-over-form is often 'a rhetorical device having no doctrinal value at all' that is used to express disapproval of a transaction, although a limited form of the doctrine is viable.[38]

Two final aspects of the relationship between statutory interpretation and tax avoidance must be noted. First, on the one hand, if or to the extent that judicial anti-avoidance doctrines are interpretive in nature, they should operate equally to the benefit of taxpayers as to the tax authorities;[39] on the other hand, if they are overarching principles of tax law then presumably they should operate only to protect the tax base. Second, if judicial anti-avoidance doctrines are rooted in a purposive approach to statutory interpretation, then it is reasonable to expect the tax legislation to be drafted accordingly. Thus, Tiley has warned the House of Lords about adopting an American approach to interpretation of UK tax statutes that have not been drafted with that interpretative approach in mind.[40]

1.2 Statutory general anti-avoidance rules

Several countries have adopted statutory general anti-avoidance rules as a means of controlling tax avoidance. Some countries, like Australia, New Zealand and South Africa, have had statutory GAARs since their income tax legislation was first adopted; other countries, like Canada and Ireland,

---

[36] For an analysis of the US business purpose doctrine, see discussion in Chapter 3 below.
[37] Tiley (1987b, p. 226). The US substance over form jurisprudence is analysed in Chapter 3 below.
[38] Tiley (1987b, p. 228).   [39] Tiley (2004a, p. 328).   [40] Tiley (2001, p. 158).

have adopted their rules relatively recently. In most countries the adoption of a GAAR was a response to the proliferation of artificial tax shelters and the absence of any effective judicial control over tax avoidance. In these countries there appears to be a pattern of legislative dissatisfaction and frustration with the performance of the courts. On the other hand, in countries where the courts use judicial doctrines to strike down abusive tax avoidance arrangements, there is sometimes pressure from tax practitioners to enact a GAAR in order to limit the courts.

The fundamental point is that every country's experience with a GAAR is unique: a product of its tax system generally, its tax history, the effectiveness of its tax administration, the approach of its courts to statutory interpretation and tax avoidance, and the attitude of taxpayers, tax practitioners and the public to tax avoidance. That said, one country can learn from the experience of other countries as long as caution is exercised and, as Tiley has warned, we avoid the importation of 'bleeding chunks of alien doctrine'.[41]

To the extent that it is possible to generalise about statutory GAARs, it seems that there are usually two critical common elements:

1. The purpose (determined objectively) of the transaction or series of transactions in question.
2. Whether the results of the transaction or series in question are in accordance with the purpose of the tax legislation.

These two elements are present in the GAARs of Canada, Ireland, the Netherlands and South Africa. They also make up the test of treaty abuse, as expressed in the Commentary to Art. 1 of the OECD Model Treaty:

> A guiding principle is that the benefits of a double taxation convention should not be available where a main purpose for entering into certain transactions or arrangements was to secure a more favourable tax position and obtaining that more favourable treatment in these circumstances would be contrary to the object and purpose of the relevant provisions.[42]

Since no country expressed an observation on this statement, it must be viewed as representing the agreed position of all the member countries about the test for the abuse of tax treaties.

There is, of course, considerable variation in the way these two common elements are expressed in the various countries' GAARs. Some countries

---

[41] Tiley (1987a, p. 180).
[42] OECD (1992-) Commentary to Art. 1, para. 9.5, added in January 2003. See Arnold (2004).

use a sole or dominant purpose test, others use a main, primary, or principal purpose test, and still others use a one-of-the-main-purposes test.[43] The countries also deal quite differently with the application of the GAAR to a series of transactions. The second element – the determination of whether a transaction is in accordance with, or is contrary to, the scheme or purpose of the legislation – is often the key issue in the application of a GAAR. Importantly, it provides both recognition that not all tax-motivated transactions are abusive and the basis for distinguishing between acceptable and unacceptable tax avoidance. Obviously, this distinction is formulated differently in the countries' GAARs. In Canada and Ireland the distinction is framed in terms of transactions that result in a 'misuse or abuse' of the legislative provisions. Other countries, including Germany and Israel, make a distinction between 'artificial' or 'fictitious' transactions. The South African GAAR, which was substantially revised in 2006, distinguishes between permissible and 'impermissible' tax avoidance on the basis of three tests:

1. 'Abnormality' of the transaction.
2. Lack of commercial substance.
3. Does the transaction frustrate the legislative purpose?

The Netherlands and New Zealand also use a test based on the frustration of the legislative purpose although, as explained below, the New Zealand test is an administrative and judicial gloss on the wording of the GAAR. The frustration test is in essence similar to the misuse and abuse test used in the Canadian and Irish GAARs.[44] The important point, however, is that, with the exception of Australia, Hong Kong and New Zealand, all of the GAARs make the distinction in some fashion.

The Australian, Hong Kong and New Zealand GAARs are special because they contain no statutory exception for tax-motivated

---

[43] Australia (dominant purpose), Canada and Ireland (primary purpose), Hong Kong (sole or dominant purpose), Israel (one of the main purposes), New Zealand (one of its purposes), Sweden (main reason), South Africa (sole or main purpose).

[44] In *The Queen v Canada Trustco* [2005] SCC 54 at paras. 48–9 the Supreme Court of Canada interpreted the term 'abuse' to mean 'frustrate': '[T]he predominant issue . . . is what constitutes abusive tax avoidance . . . the central question is, having regard to the text, context and purpose of the provisions on which the taxpayer relies, whether the transaction frustrates or defeats the object, spirit or purpose of those provisions . . . While the Explanatory Notes use the phrase "exploit, misuse or frustrate," we understand those three terms to be synonymous, with their sense most adequately captured by the word "frustrate".' Since abuse and frustrate are synonymous, the use of the word 'frustrate' in preference to 'abuse', the term used by the statute, does not assist in advancing the analysis of the GAAR.

transactions that are acceptable. Under Part IVA of the Australian Income Tax Assessment Act 1936, any scheme, defined broadly, whose dominant purpose, taking into account eight listed factors (including the form and substance of the scheme, any change in the financial position of the taxpayer or any other person as a result of the scheme, the manner in which the scheme was carried out, and time period over which the scheme was carried out), is to obtain a tax benefit, broadly defined, is subject to the GAAR. The Hong Kong GAAR is similar. Neither the Australian nor the Hong Kong GAAR provides any exception for transactions that have the purpose and/or effect of avoiding tax but are consistent with the statutory scheme and purpose. As a result, it is hardly surprising that the Australian GAAR appears to be more effective than the GAARs of other countries.[45] In fact, the concern in Australia is that the GAAR is overly broad in scope and the only thing that appears to prevent its application to inoffensive transactions is the discretion of the tax authorities.

Under the New Zealand GAAR, a tax avoidance arrangement, broadly defined, is void against the tax authorities if one of its purposes or effects is tax avoidance, which is broadly defined. Despite the lack of any statutory exception to the New Zealand GAAR, the Inland Revenue has indicated in its administrative guidance that it will apply a 'scheme and purpose' approach to the application of the GAAR. Only if an arrangement whose purpose is the avoidance of tax frustrates rather than facilitates the underlying scheme and purpose of the relevant provisions will the GAAR apply.[46] Probably because of this implicit exception to the GAAR, which has been endorsed by the case law, the New Zealand GAAR has had mixed results. In the *Peterson* case,[47] decided by the Judicial Committee of the UK Privy Council acting as New Zealand's final court of appeal,[48] the GAAR was not applied to a rather clearly abusive film tax shelter because, according to the majority, the investors had suffered the economic burden of the full cost of their interests in the film. Two Law Lords delivered stinging minority speeches that rejected the majority's decision as inconsistent with the factual findings of the trial court and as failing to take

[45] The Australian GAAR has been applied successfully in three High Court decisions: *FCT v Spotless Services Ltd* (1996) 186 CLR 404 (HCA), *FCT v Consolidated Press Holdings Ltd* [2001] HCA 32 (HCA) and *FCT v Hart* [2004] HCA 26 (HCA). For a detailed analysis see Cooper (2006).

[46] Inland Revenue, Exposure Draft INA0009: Interpretation of Sections BG1 and GB1 of the Income Tax Act 2004. For a detailed analysis see Trombitas (2004) and Trombitas (2005).

[47] *Peterson v CIR* [2005] UKPC 5 (PC).

[48] Since 2005 the New Zealand Court of Appeal is the final court of appeal for New Zealand cases.

into account the non-recourse loan and the circular movement of the funds. In a more recent case,[49] the New Zealand Court of Appeal applied the GAAR to a forestry investment scheme whereby the investors claimed current deductions for expenses payable in fifty years.

In his writings, Tiley makes extensive references to the experience of countries with statutory GAARs, in particular Canada, Australia and New Zealand.[50] He cautions that cases from countries with a GAAR should not be relied on in the UK and further, that the debate about the adoption of a GAAR is only tangentially relevant to the UK tax avoidance case law.[51] Conversely, it is clear that several countries with a GAAR have rejected the UK *Ramsay* line of cases.[52]

1.3 Judicial anti-avoidance doctrines

Although the courts of many countries, including countries with statutory GAARs, have developed judicial doctrines for controlling tax avoidance, here only brief references will be made to the situations in the UK and the US about which Tiley has written extensively.

With respect to the UK, Tiley would be quick to emphasise that the UK case law has not created any judicial anti-avoidance doctrine because that is beyond the constitutional authority of the court and 'is in any case a very hazardous thing to do'.[53] Instead, the UK anti-avoidance case law is based on a contextual and purposive interpretation of tax law in the same manner as other areas of law.[54] Tiley describes the principle that has emerged from twenty years of case law as follows:

> [T]he underlying basis of statutory construction explains the legal authority for the principle but tells us nothing about its content. One might say that the content is that judges will intervene to stop avoidance where they think that the avoidance is stopping the tax system from working properly or sensibly; however, this formulation has plenty of abstract, value-laden and question-begging terms of its own.[55]

---

[49] *Accent Management Ltd v CIR* [2007] NZCA 230 (NZCA).
[50] See Tiley (2005b, p. 101) and Tiley (2004a).   [51] Tiley (2004a, pp. 326–7).
[52] Tiley (2004a, pp. 316–18).   [53] Tiley (2004a, p. 305).
[54] Note that Freedman suggests that the current UK case law is far from stable and '[I]t is not impossible that we shall see the reemergence of a *Ramsay* doctrine'. She also notes that aspects of *IRC v Scottish Provident Institution* [2004] UKHL 52 (HL) suggest an overarching rule of tax law rather than an interpretive approach. See Freedman (2005, p. 1042). For further consideration of this case see Chapter 2.
[55] Tiley (2004a, p. 308).

The result is 'less chaos, more uncertainty'.[56] The current question for the UK is whether, having clarified the underlying principle of the case law, it would be preferable to substitute a statutory GAAR. Before attempting to answer this question, or at least speculating as to how Tiley would answer it, it is useful to look briefly at the US judicial anti-avoidance doctrines.[57]

The US courts have developed a wide array of judicial anti-avoidance doctrines to combat tax avoidance, ranging from the narrow sham doctrine to the broad and vague concepts of business purpose and economic substance. The doctrines overlap significantly. Some of them, such as the business purpose test,[58] are based on statutory interpretation (some tax provisions are intended to apply only to transactions with an independent business purpose) while others, such as the doctrine of economic substance, appear to be overarching principles of tax law. This is not the place for a description and analysis of these doctrines. There is a vast US literature. Moreover, Tiley's writings on the US doctrines, although twenty years old, still provide an excellent overview, especially for non-Americans.[59]

Like the courts in the UK and Commonwealth countries, the US courts have clearly recognised the right of taxpayers to arrange their affairs to minimise tax.[60] Perhaps agreement on this fundamental point has recently led some UK judges to express considerable enthusiasm for the US approach.[61] However, as Tiley has warned on several occasions, there are serious problems with UK courts adopting American anti-avoidance doctrines.[62] Historically, the US courts have taken a fundamentally different approach to the interpretation and application of statutes, including tax statutes, from that of Commonwealth countries.[63] Thus, while UK

---

[56] Tiley (2005b, p. 122).   [57] For a detailed analysis of the US position see Chapter 3.

[58] See *Gregory v Helvering* (1934) 69 F 2d 809 (2d Cir.); affirmed (1935) 293 US 465 (USSC).

[59] See Tiley (1987a) and Tiley (1987b). See also Tiley and Jensen (1998).

[60] See *Gilbert v CIR* (1957) 248 F 2d 399 (2d Cir.).

[61] For example, in *Collector of Stamp Revenue v Arrowtown Assets Ltd* [2004] 1 HKLRD 77 (HKCA) at para. 109, Lord Millett writes: 'Both [propositions that courts can consider a series of transactions as a whole and that transactions without any business purpose or effect are ineffective for tax purposes] were inspired by the work of Judge Learned Hand in the United States and in particular his seminal judgment in *Helvering v Gregory* (1934) 69 F.2d 809. Before turning to the decisions in *Ramsay* and the cases which followed it, it is convenient to examine the US decisions to see the extent to which they are echoed in the development of the jurisprudence of the United Kingdom and should influence the future development of our own.'

[62] See Tiley (1987a), Tiley (1987b) and Tiley (2004a, pp. 325–6).

[63] See generally Ward, Avery Jones *et al.* (1985) and Ward & Cullity (1981).

and Commonwealth countries have traditionally interpreted tax statutes literally and have respected the legal rights and obligations created by the parties, US courts have interpreted statutes broadly in accordance with their purpose and have not hesitated to recharacterise the legal rights and obligations created by the parties. With respect to the latter point, the US approach is much more similar to the approach of some civil law countries that apply abuse of rights doctrines. Unlike the traditional English common law position that legal rights can be exercised irrespective of a person's motives, the civil law tradition is that legal rights cannot be exercised to the detriment of others. The recharacterisation of transactions by the courts is commonplace in the US. Thus, for example, debt can be, and is, recharacterised as equity and vice-versa. In other countries, this result can be accomplished only through statutory rules.

The current state of US case law on anti-avoidance is, in Tiley's words, 'something of a mess'.[64] Recently, the US Supreme Court has placed increasing emphasis on literal interpretation. The various Circuit courts have taken substantially different approaches to tax avoidance cases.[65] Tax shelters have flourished and several commentators have called for the economic substance doctrine to be codified. Further, the US Supreme Court has not heard a significant tax avoidance case for almost fifty years.

1.4 Assessment of judicial anti-avoidance doctrines and statutory GAARs

Unhappily, the result of all the comparative analyses of responses to tax avoidance is that '[N]o country seems to be at ease with its system'.[66] This is not surprising because, as Tiley explains –

> equity and certainty are in conflict. Tax equity demands that artificial tax avoidance schemes should be of no effect, yet certainty demands that the tax laws should be such that an individual can arrange his affairs in the expectation that he will or will not have to pay tax.[67]

Nevertheless, we can venture some general conclusions from an evaluation of judicial anti-avoidance doctrines and statutory GAARs. Later, I want to

---

[64] Tiley (2004a, p. 326).
[65] See, for example, *Long Term Capital Holdings v United States* (2004) 330 F Supp 2d 122 (D. Conn.); *Coltec Industries v United States* (2006) 454 F 3d 1340 (Fed. Cir.), cert. denied (2007) 127 S Ct 1261 (USSC); *Black & Decker Corp. v United States* (2006) 436 F 3d 431 (4th Cir.); and *TIFD III-E Inc. v United States* (2004) 342 F Supp 2d 94 (D. Conn.).
[66] Tiley (2005b, p. 101).   [67] Tiley (2005b, pp. 101–2).

comment briefly on the striking parallel between the Canadian experience with its GAAR and the UK situation without one.

First, with respect to complexity and certainty, there appears to be nothing inherently preferable in either approach. Judicial doctrines apply haphazardly in the US but the same is true with respect to the Australian, Canadian, and New Zealand GAARs.[68] In my opinion, the new South African GAAR is destined to suffer a long period of confusion. It may be thought that a well-drafted GAAR can provide more certainty than judicial anti-avoidance doctrines. Although no doubt there is some truth to this statement, most GAARs are broadly worded and use conclusory terms ('abusive', 'artificial', etc.) that require courts to give the rules content in much the same way as they develop judicial doctrines. Some legislatures have attempted to limit the flexibility accorded to the courts by a broadly worded GAAR. Thus, Australia, New Zealand, Hong Kong and Ireland have spelled out several factors that the courts are supposed to take into account for the purpose of determining whether a particular transaction is offensive. South Africa's new GAAR goes even further by spelling out in detailed rules some of the typical features of tax shelters, such as the circular flow of funds, the participation of accommodation parties, the absence of commercial or economic substance, and the participation of related parties. These attempts are likely to prove futile. Tax avoidance is too varied and dependent on constantly changing exogenous factors to be dealt with effectively with detailed rules. Otherwise, specific anti-avoidance rules would be a complete answer to tax avoidance. Also, both judicial doctrines and statutory GAARs can be overreaching and inappropriately deter legitimate commercial transactions. Under either approach, however, a measure of certainty can be provided by an advance rulings or clearance procedure whereby taxpayers can get binding guidance from the tax authorities as to the tax consequences of proposed transactions.

Second, both approaches inevitably rely on the competence of the judges to parse the tax legislation rigorously, to understand the tax system as a whole and the purpose of its constituent elements and, finally, to have an appreciation of sophisticated commercial transactions. Statutory GAARs tend to be broadly worded, with considerable scope for judges to interpret and apply the rule appropriately. Judicial doctrines, whether

---

[68] Notwithstanding the recent government success in cases under the Australian GAAR, the experience has been chequered; see Waincymer (1997). With respect to Canada, see Arnold (2006a), and with respect to New Zealand, see Dunbar (2006).

rooted in statutory construction or not, are entirely the creation and responsibility of the judges. Therefore, it should not be surprising if the results are similar under both approaches.

Third, there is no inherent inconsistency between judicial anti-avoidance doctrines, at least those of the UK variety, and statutory GAARs. Theoretically, a tax system might have both. Thus, in the *McGuckian* case,[69] Lord Cooke stated that the UK 'approach to the interpretation of taxing Acts does not depend on general anti-avoidance provisions such as are found in Australia. Rather, it is antecedent to or collateral with them.' However, in practice the two approaches do not seem to cohabit comfortably. The scope for broad judicial anti-avoidance doctrines in a country with a statutory GAAR should be limited to avoid overlap and confusion.

Fourth, in practice both approaches appear to be equally effective or ineffective. Both may have some *in terrorem* effect. Theoretically, however, there are or should be limits on what courts can do under the guise of interpretation. In contrast, the legislature is under no such limits. It can create a ferocious overarching statutory anti-avoidance rule, although it is likely to find that the courts strive to cut such a rule down to size.

Fifth, a statutory GAAR is likely to operate only prospectively, whereas a judicial decision has the effect of declaring what the law has always been and cannot operate only prospectively. This is a difficulty where the judicial doctrine is an overarching rule of law created by the court that taxpayers could not have reasonably predicted. Any taxpayers having engaged in similar transactions in prior years that are not yet statute barred would be potentially subject to the arguably retroactive application of the new rule. Any new (i.e., not knowable in advance) anti-avoidance rule, whether judicial or statutory, should apply only prospectively. This point is not as valid where the judicial doctrine is simply the application of a purposive approach to the construction of statutes.

Sixth, judicial anti-avoidance doctrines are arguably more flexible than a statutory GAAR. There are no constraints on the courts with respect to judicial doctrines, whether they are interpretive or substantive in nature. Judicial doctrines can be expanded or restricted by the judges to meet the changing needs of the tax system. This is less true, I think, of a statutory GAAR because once the legislature settles on a particular linguistic expression of the rule, taxpayers, tax advisers and courts are likely to focus on the particular formula of words used in the legislation rather than the

---

[69] *IRC v McGuckian* [1997] 3 All ER 817 (HL) at p. 830.

broader question of distinguishing between acceptable and unacceptable tax avoidance. However, this point should not be overstated because, as noted above, courts will usually have considerable flexibility under a statutory GAAR.

Seventh, a judicial anti-avoidance doctrine that is a rule of construction is potentially applicable to any transaction and any statutory provision because the question in every case is whether the legislature intended the relevant transaction to be covered by the relevant provision. Theoretically at least, a statutory GAAR is narrower in scope because it will apply only to those transactions that are defined to be offensive.

Eighth, judicial anti-avoidance doctrines do not get hung up on what I consider to be peripheral issues, such as the burden of proof, that are controversial under statutory GAARs.[70] In contrast, judicial anti-avoidance doctrines provide no guidance as to how the tax consequences of an ineffective transaction are to be determined. A statutory GAAR can spell these matters out in detail.

Ninth, a statutory GAAR can apply to transactions (for example, transactions that step up the cost of property or that generate loss carryforwards) that will generate tax benefits only in future years. In contrast, judicial anti-avoidance doctrines can be applied to transactions only in respect of which tax benefits have been claimed.

1.5 Similarity between the UK judicial anti-avoidance doctrines and the Canadian GAAR

The similarities between the UK and Canadian approaches to tax avoidance, in particular, in light of the 2005 decisions of the House of Lords in *Barclays Mercantile* and *Scottish Provident* and the Canadian Supreme Court in *Canada Trustco* and *Mathew*,[71] have been noted by both Freedman and Gammie.[72] As noted above, the UK approach is an interpretive one involving a determination of the purpose of the relevant legislation and the application of the legislation to the transaction to determine if it

---

[70] The burden of proof as to the purpose of a transaction and the purpose of the legislation was controversial in the recent consultations concerning the amendment of the GAAR in South Africa and in the debate in the United Kingdom in the late 1990s concerning the introduction of a GAAR.

[71] *Barclays Mercantile v Mawson* [2004] UKHL 51 (HL); *Scottish Provident Institution v IRC* [2004] UKHL 52 (HL); *The Queen v Canada Trustco Mortgage Company* [2005] SCC 54 (SCC); and *Mathew v Canada* [2005] SCC 55 (SCC).

[72] Freedman (2005) and Gammie (2005).

is within the statutory purpose. As the House of Lords stated in *Barclays Mercantile*:

> The essence of the new approach was to give the statutory provision a purposive construction in order to determine the nature of the transaction to which it was intended to apply and then to decide whether the actual transaction (which might involve considering the overall effect of a number of elements intended to operate together) answered to the statutory description.[73]

In contrast, the Canadian GAAR appears to be an overarching substantive rule of law since it is a statutory rule well within the competence of the legislature. However, in the *Canada Trustco* case the Supreme Court has, unwittingly,[74] turned the misuse and abuse test of the GAAR into a rule of construction. The court states:

> In summary, s. 245(4) imposes a two-part inquiry. The first step is to determine the object, spirit or purpose of the provisions of the Income Tax Act that are relied on for the tax benefit, having regard to the scheme of the Act, the relevant provisions and permissible extrinsic aids. The second step is to examine the factual context of a case in order to determine whether the avoidance transaction defeated or frustrated the object, spirit or purpose of the provisions in issue.[75]

In effect, the Canadian GAAR applies to transactions, alone or as part of a series, where the primary purpose is obtaining tax benefits if the result is inconsistent with the purpose of the relevant provisions conferring the benefits. If this is an accurate description of the GAAR as construed by the Supreme Court, the questions that arise are, why is it necessary and what does it add to the textual, contextual, and purposive approach to the interpretation of all statutes? Freedman raises these questions.[76] Gammie finds the similarity between the Canadian and UK situations unsurprising because the GAAR is 'after all, only another piece of legislation'.[77] He acknowledges that, in Canada, courts must consider the relationship between specific provisions and the GAAR, something the UK courts are not required to do. If, however, the Canadian GAAR is simply a rule of construction then there is no conflict between the GAAR and specific provisions and the role of the courts is the same in Canada and the UK.

---

[73] *Barclays Mercantile v Mawson* [2004] UKHL 51 (HL) at para. 32.
[74] Because there is no discussion in the case of whether the GAAR is or should be a rule of construction or a substantive rule.
[75] *The Queen v Canada Trustco Mortgage Company* [2005] SCC 54 (SCC) at para. 55.
[76] Freedman (2005, p. 1043).   [77] Gammie (2005, p. 1051).

There is some history here that provides some important assistance in understanding the issues even if it does not provide a complete explanation.[78] The Explanatory Notes to the GAAR indicate that the misuse and abuse test in sub-s. 245(4) is intended to be applied by reference to the object and spirit of the Income Tax Act:

> [T]ransactions that comply with the object and spirit of other provisions of the Act read as a whole will not be affected by the application of this general anti-avoidance rule.[79]

This approach to the meaning of misuse and abuse was confirmed in an article by the then Senior Assistant Deputy Minister of Finance:

> The application of subsection 245(4) should involve an analysis of the object and spirit of the provisions of the Act read as a whole in the context of each particular case. An attempt to define the object and spirit of the provisions . . . will be the key to a coherent solution of those cases where it is uncertain whether the proposed rule should apply.[80]

Although the Explanatory Notes refer to s. 245(4) as a limitation on the GAAR, the Senior Assistant Deputy Minister clarified that it was intended to operate as a rule of construction rather than a substantive exception to the GAAR.[81] This attempt to cast the misuse and abuse test as a rule of construction explains why the original version of sub-s. 245(4) applied 'for greater certainty'. This phrase was deleted in 2005 with retroactive effect.

When the Canadian GAAR was introduced in 1987–88 the modern purposive approach to the interpretation of tax statutes was quite new, having been articulated by the Supreme Court only three years previously in the *Stubart* case.[82] It was unclear at that time whether the courts would embrace that interpretive approach or whether it would be effective in preventing abusive tax avoidance schemes.[83] As a result, it may well be that the GAAR was necessary to require the courts to follow a purposive

---

[78] For a detailed analysis, see Arnold and Wilson (1988, pp. 1164–6).
[79] Canada (1988, section 245).   [80] Dodge (1988, p. 21).
[81] *Ibid.*: 'Subsection 245(4) does not create an alternative test with regard to the definition of avoidance transaction. Instead, it indicates the proper construction of section 245 with respect to transactions that appear to be tax-motivated but that, arguably, do not produce tax results that frustrate the intention of Parliament. Thus, subsection 245(4) is a complement to the non-tax purpose test and is consistent with the general approach of a modern, as opposed to a literal, interpretation of the Act.'
[82] *Stubart Investments Ltd v The Queen* [1984] 1 SCR 536 (SCC).
[83] See Dodge (1988, pp. 17–18).

interpretation of tax statutes, if only for the purpose of dealing with abusive tax avoidance. If so, it is fair to say that the original modest purpose of the GAAR has perhaps backfired. (The most that can be said as of 2007 is that the GAAR's modest objective has been matched by equally modest results.) There are several statements in the *Canada Trustco* case that suggest that, except where sub-s. 245(4) is invoked by the tax authorities, taxpayers are entitled to rely on the literal meaning of the provisions of taxing statutes.[84] Subsequent tax decisions of the Supreme Court provide support for this view.[85]

In hindsight, the adoption of the Canadian GAAR was necessary to introduce the non-tax purpose test and the concept of a series of transactions. Pre-GAAR case law was clear that in the absence of a specific statutory provision, the taxpayer's purpose in carrying out a transaction was irrelevant. Even if a transaction was entered into solely to get some tax advantage, that fact was not sufficient to deny the tax advantage if the transaction otherwise complied with the requirements of the statute.[86] Moreover, the Supreme Court had also made it clear that, in the absence of a specific statutory reference to a series of transactions, the tax consequences of a series had to be determined on the basis that the transactions were separate and independent.[87] In contrast, the UK House of Lords was able to reach the eminently sensible conclusions, without any guidance from the legislature, that some statutory provisions are intended to apply only to transactions that have some business, commercial, or non-tax purpose[88] and that a series of transactions (or a composite transaction) could be considered as an integrated whole.

Thus, Canada appears to be in the position of having a statutory GAAR that applies only in situations in which the transaction would probably not be effective, simply by interpreting the relevant provisions in accordance with their purpose. The UK appears to have arrived at the same position without the need for any statutory GAAR. Nevertheless, as discussed above, the Canadian GAAR was necessary because the Canadian Supreme Court did not arrive at the same conclusions as the UK House of

---

[84] See Arnold (2006a).

[85] See *Placer Dome v The Queen* [2006] SCC 20 (SCC) and *The Queen v Imperial Oil Ltd* [2006] SCC 46 (SCC). See generally, Arnold (2006b).

[86] See, for example, *Duha Printers (Western) Ltd v The Queen* [1998] 1 SCR 795 (SCC) and *Shell Canada Ltd v The Queen* [1999] 3 SCR 622 (SCC).

[87] *The Queen v Singleton* [2001] SCC 61 (SCC).

[88] As Justice Learned Hand said in *Gilbert v CIR* (1957) 248 F 2d 399 (2nd Cir.) at p. 411: 'we cannot suppose that it was part of the purpose of the Act to provide an escape from the liabilities it sought to impose.'

Lords in the absence of the GAAR. The pre-GAAR tax avoidance case law of the Supreme Court provides strong evidence that, in the absence of the GAAR, the Supreme Court would be encouraging tax avoidance schemes to flourish. Its well-established position was that taxpayers were entitled to do anything that was not specifically prohibited by statute.

Conclusion

What would John Tiley think about the question of whether a judicial anti-avoidance doctrine or a statutory general anti-avoidance rule is a better method for controlling tax avoidance? First, it is safe to say that, like the cautious scholar he is, Tiley would say, 'It depends'. The answer depends on the type of GAAR and judicial doctrine, as well as all of the relevant aspects of the tax and legal systems of the particular country. He would be sensitive to the context and recognise that different answers might be appropriate for different countries. As he says, if a GAAR were introduced in the UK and 'if the judges were to give it the strength with which the Australian High Court has endowed its version', the Revenue would be better off than it is under the existing UK case law.[89] That's a big 'if'. On the other hand, if the UK judges turn a GAAR into nothing more than a rule of construction, nothing will have changed, although it could take another twenty years for the courts to arrive at that conclusion. As a result, I suspect that in the context of the UK situation, Tiley would prefer to let the courts develop the law 'on a flexible and pragmatic case-by-case basis,'[90] rather than introduce a GAAR. He is sceptical about whether a statutory GAAR would be an improvement on the case law; and even if it is on paper, as Tiley perceptively notes:

> What is clear is that, once a GAAR is introduced, the players (government and taxpayers alike) are still at the mercy of the courts.[91]

[89] Tiley (2004a, p. 327).   [90] Tiley (2004a, p. 330).   [91] Tiley (2005b, p. 122).

The judicial approach to avoidance: some reflections on *BMBF* and *SPI*

MALCOLM GAMMIE

Introduction

More years ago that either us would probably wish to call to mind, John Tiley taught me matrimonial law at Cambridge. He was a new fellow at Queens' and as a then first year student at Sidney Sussex I have a favourable recollection of his lectures even though the elements of family law that he taught me have barely impinged upon my professional career (and thankfully not at all upon my private life).

In those days I suspect that neither of us knew more about tax than what little we gleaned from the leading cases that tax issues had provided in the field of equity and the law of trusts and in other branches of the law. At some stage, and no doubt by different means and for different reasons, we were both drawn into the murky and unprincipled world of taxation. From there Tiley has risen to become the UK's foremost tax law professor and I have had the great pleasure of coming to know him through our shared interest in the subject.

Within the tax field Tiley has sought in particular to cast light on the difficult topic of tax avoidance. Among his many contributions to the *British Tax Review* on that topic is an article on the development of the case law since *Ramsay*[1] and a case note on what have become known as the *BMBF* and *SPI* cases.[2] What emerges from these two cases, Tiley noted, is a process of cleansing in which excrescences (or even errors) are removed. Tiley summarises the position as follows:

> [We] are left with the simple fact that tax law is about interpreting statutes and that statutes should be interpreted purposively. There is less intellectual chaos since there is agreement on the basic principles. The full mantra is that the words must be interpreted purposively and in their context.

[1] Tiley (2004a).   [2] Tiley (2005a).

However, this does not produce certainty since it is in the nature of the questions of construction that there will be borderline cases about which people will have different views. *MacNiven* showed that there was no general overriding judicial anti-avoidance rule of law (or doctrine) to be applied like a principle of EC law. *Barclays Mercantile* shows that there is no general overriding judicial anti-avoidance approach to construction.

To that conclusion I have pleasure in contributing the following thoughts as explanation of the outcome of the *BMBF* and *SPI* decisions and why there is no general overriding judicial anti-avoidance approach to construction.

2.1 The *BMBF* decision

Between 1991 and 1993 Bord Gais Eireann ('BGE') built a high pressure natural gas pipeline from Moffat in Scotland to Ballough in the Republic of Ireland. The project was financed initially in its construction phase by various loans and with the assistance of a 35 per cent grant from the EEC. In the short term, such large infrastructure projects involved considerable expenditure (including the project's financing costs) that qualifies as an ordinary deduction in computing business profits for tax purposes. The problem is that projects of this type only become profitable in the long run. The solution to that dilemma is to sell the benefit of the current business expenses to someone who has the current taxable profits against which those expenses can be deducted.

BGE accordingly set about reducing its financial costs by entering into a finance lease with Barclays Mercantile Business Finance Ltd ('BMBF'). As matters stood in 1993, BGE was able to transfer the benefit of capital allowances for the expenditure on the pipeline to BMBF through the expedient of BGE selling the pipeline to BMBF and taking a lease-back of the pipeline. The lease terms took account of BMBF's ability to use the capital allowances immediately against the profits of the Barclay's group. BGE might have used the proceeds of selling the pipeline to repay some of its existing borrowings. Instead, it deposited the proceeds with another Barclay's group subsidiary and the deposit was, in effect, used to secure a guarantee that Barclays Bank provided of the lease rentals. The effect nevertheless was to reduce BGE's financial costs in much the same way as if it had borrowed on better terms from Barclays and had repaid its existing borrowings. The better financial terms that Barclays was able to offer as compared to BGE's existing borrowings, and therefore the saving that BGE achieved, reflected Barclays' ability to deduct the capital allowances immediately rather than at some future time, as in BGE's case.

This summary simplifies considerably the underlying facts of *Barclays Mercantile Business Finance Ltd v Mawson*[3] but aims to get at the heart of the matter. The essential question for which an answer was sought at each stage of the judicial process was whether these arrangements represented acceptable tax mitigation – accelerating business deductions by selling the benefit of the deductions to a third party bank – or unacceptable tax avoidance.

Expected benefit of finance leasing

Finance leasing as a method of selling business deductions from one business taxpayer to another was not entirely an open house in 1993. Section 75(1)(c) of the Capital Allowances Act 1990 provided at the time that –

> if it appears with respect to the sale, or with respect to transactions of which the sale is one, that the sole or main benefit which, but for this [provision], might have been expected to accrue to the parties or any of them was the obtaining of an allowance under this Part . . .

then allowances could be restricted in various ways.

To the uninitiated this might appear a complete answer on the basis that the sole benefit of BGE's sale and leaseback was to transfer entitlement to the tax allowances from BGE (which could not use them) to BMBF (which could). This provision of the Capital Allowances Act was not, however, devoid of authority. In *Barclays Mercantile Industrial Finance Ltd v Melluish*,[4] the Inland Revenue had raised and had lost this argument in a film leasing arrangement. Both the Commissioners and Vinelott J on appeal accepted in *BMI's* case that the main object of the taxpayer in selling the film to BMI was to recover the cost of making the film while ensuring that the taxpayer could distribute the film. The main object of BMI as finance lessor was to make a profit by acquiring and leasing the plant. Although BMI would not have been able to offer a lease back to the taxpayer at an acceptable rent unless it could obtain a capital allowance and unless it had the profits to absorb the allowances, BMI's object and

---

[3] [2004] UKHL 51 (HL).   [4] (1990) 63 TC 95 (Ch D).

purpose was to make a profit on a purchase and lease of the plant and not solely to obtain the capital allowance.[5]

Basis of lease finance

The Inland Revenue accepted in *BMBF* that if the transaction had comprised the sale by BGE of its pipeline to BMBF followed by BMBF leasing back the pipeline to BGE and no more, nothing would have stood in the way of BMBF's claim for allowances. The objection, however, arose from BGE depositing the sale proceeds as security to Barclay's guarantee of the lease rentals. This sufficed to persuade the Commissioners that the arrangement represented unacceptable tax avoidance, on the basis that –

> commercially driven finance leasing is designed to provide working capital to the lessee. But BGE could not get its hands on the money. It parted with a valuable asset allegedly for £91,292,000 but received no immediate benefit from the transaction. [BMBF] provided no finance to BGE simply because the amounts had to be deposited as part of the arrangements with Deepstream to be repaid only in accordance with the deposit agreement with Deepstream . . . In our judgment the purpose of the expenditure by BMBF on 31 December 1993 was not the acquisition of the pipeline but the obtaining of capital allowances which would result in ultimately a profit to BGE and fees payable to BMBF and BZW. The transaction had no commercial reality.

On appeal Park J agreed, saying that –

> a common kind of finance leasing [is where] the lessee already has the asset (an item of machinery or plant) but has paid for it with borrowed money on which it is paying full commercial rates of interest; it sells the asset to the leasing company and takes a finance lease-back at more favourable rates; it uses the purchase price to repay its borrowings. Another possibility is for the lessee to sell the asset and lease it back under a finance lease, and to use the purchase price, not to repay the existing borrowing incurred to acquire the asset, but for other purposes of the lessee's business. In all of those cases the finance lessor provides 'up-front' finance to the lessee, and the finance so provided is used in one way or another in the lessee's business. But in the transaction involved in the present case no up-front finance was provided. BGE already owned the pipeline and had paid for it with a loan

---

[5] *Ibid.* at pp. 132–3. The reasoning can be criticised as relying on the object or purpose of the parties rather than the expected benefit of the transaction but was not challenged in *BMBF*.

from a syndicate of banks. After the transaction BGE was still able to use the pipeline as before, though by then it did so by virtue of the lease, sub-lease and Transportation Agreement, and it still owed to the banks the money which it had borrowed. Nor was the £91 million available to BGE for it to use in any other way to finance transactions or activities of its business.

The Court of Appeal and the House of Lords disagreed, and rightly so. A moment's thought indicates that the benefit of finance leasing is founded upon the transfer of tax allowances from one taxpayer to another. The Commissioners and Vinelott J recognised in the *BMI* case that the terms that the finance lessor is able to offer are necessarily based upon the tax assumptions that the finance lessor can make. As the Commissioners in *BMBF* observed, BGE's ability to transfer the benefit of its tax allowances to BMBF offered BGE the opportunity to profit from its sale and lease back. In other words, BGE and BMBF shared the benefit of the tax allowances. Once that is noted, however, the idea that it is acceptable tax mitigation for BGE to take that profit provided it reduces its borrowing costs by repaying some of its existing borrowings but it is unacceptable tax avoidance if it uses its profit to subsidise (i.e. reduce) its existing borrowing costs lacks any rationale.

Source of avoidance

BMBF, and its 'sister case', *IRC v Scottish Provident Institution*,[6] represent the most recent 'restatement' by the House of Lords of the principle enunciated by the House in *W. T. Ramsay Ltd v IRC*.[7] The *Ramsay* principle, in common with most judicial anti-avoidance approaches, has proved troublesome since it was first devised: 'troublesome' in the sense that it has meant different things to different judges from the beginning. We do not have to look far for the reasons for this. Kay provided the reason in 1979:

> What is avoidance? There is a conventional distinction between illegal evasion and legal avoidance. The incidence of evasion is a function of the mechanisms by which tax is assessed and collected, and the extent to which they can be controlled or monitored: the incidence of avoidance is a function of the tax base and depends on the extent to which legislation is successful in expressing the underlying economic concepts. Avoidance depends on the base: evasion on the assessment procedures. There is an area that lies in between the two, and this is mainly where the tax treatment of some transaction depends on the reason for undertaking the transaction. This

---

[6] [2004] UKHL 52 (HL).   [7] [1982] AC 300 (HL).

is bound to prove difficult to police and offers scope for distorting and misrepresenting activities which gradually shade from tax avoidance into tax evasion. A tax system in which the burden of tax depends upon motive rather than verifiable and objective fact is not very satisfactory, but such provisions arise in two main areas: in relation to business expenses and fringe benefits, where the problem is unavoidable, and in cases where legislators unable to deal with avoidance in more appropriate ways, seek to inhibit it by passing laws which require taxpayers to observe the spirit as well as the letter of the code by means of very general anti-avoidance provisions. This means attempting to distinguish tax avoidance mechanisms from similar or identical actions which are bona fide commercial transactions.[8]

It is important to recognise that tax allowances for finance lessors are not an example of a business expense that gives rise to an unavoidable issue of tax motivation. The unavoidable problem of business expenses and fringe benefits to which Kay is referring is that of distinguishing the (non-deductible) private consumption element of expenses and benefits from the (deductible) business element, as reflected in the question whether an expense is incurred wholly and exclusively for the purposes of a trade. Capital allowances for finance lessors on the other hand falls into that (avoidable) category in which Parliament has to curb perceived avoidance by requiring owners and users of plant and machinery to demonstrate that their transaction is, in Vinelott J's words in *BMI*, 'not . . . to obtain [a capital] allowance' but rather to 'make a profit on a purchase and lease of the plant.[9]

That is obviously a question that is capable of more than one answer depending upon the particular judicial proclivities. In the light of *BMBF*, one might speculate on Park J's answer had he been elevated to the bench by 1990 or had *BMI* been represented by a less able advocate than Graham Aaronson. The fundamental difficulty of the anti-avoidance provision in issue in *BMI*, however, is in distinguishing a tax avoidance transaction from a bona fide commercial transaction when the commercial terms of every transaction will necessarily depend upon the effective transfer or not of tax allowances from one taxpayer to another. There is, in essence, no underlying principle to guide the judicial mind in arriving at a conclusion in such a case. Parliament allows one taxpayer to sell his tax allowances to another provided that the tax effect is not the only or main expected benefit, notwithstanding that it is precisely the expected tax effects of the transaction that leads the parties to contract as they do.

[8] Kay (1979, p. 354).   [9] (1990) 63 TC 95 (Ch D) at p. 133.

Legislative developments

Governments and revenue authorities rarely leave matters to the courts if revenue is at risk. Final judicial pronouncements take more time than any government or legislator can tolerate and are built on the uncertain foundations of changing judicial attitudes. Thus, by the time the Commissioners came to hear *BMBF*, the law had been changed (and had been re-written) to defeat for the future arrangements such as those entered into by *BMBF*. Under s. 225 of the Capital Allowances Act 2001, Parliament prescribed that allowances should not be given where the finance lease or any transaction or series of transactions of which it was part removed from the finance lessor the whole or the greater part of any risk of loss if payments were not made under the lease in accordance with their terms. It may perhaps have been with this change at the back of his mind that Park J had said:

> I accept that finance lessors always wish to limit the credit risk to which they are exposed. But there can be cases where the credit risk is so comprehensively eliminated that it becomes apparent, if one steps back and thinks about it, that the lessor has not really laid out its money on a leasing transaction at all.[10]

It is not at all clear, however, why (or what degree of) risk should distinguish legitimate tax mitigation from unacceptable tax avoidance that should be counteracted. As it is, the finance leasing provisions have been subject to wholesale reform in the Finance Act 2006 to remove entirely in many cases the scope to transfer the tax allowances from lessor to lessee. In the course of all these changes the provisions have become longer and more prescriptive as Parliament has wrestled with the dilemma of when to allow or not to allow tax allowances to be sold from one taxpayer to another.

Basic principles of the judicial approach

Given that Parliament, by neglect, ignorance or deliberate judgment, insists in many cases in enacting legislation to which there is little or no discernible principle, what (if any) should be the judicial response? In *BMBF* the House of Lords doubted that it could give definitive guidance but thought that it should be possible to achieve some clarity about basic principles. Thus:

[10] (2004) 76 TC 446 (Ch D) at para. 60.

The essence of the new approach was to give the statutory provision a purposive construction in order to determine the nature of the transaction
to which it was intended to apply and then to decide whether the actual
transaction (which might involve considering the overall effect of a number of elements intended to operate together) answered to the statutory
description. Of course this does not mean that the courts have to put their
reasoning into the straitjacket of first construing the statute in the abstract
and then looking at the facts. It might be more convenient to analyse the
facts and then ask whether they satisfy the requirements of the statute. But
however one approaches the matter, the question is always whether the relevant provision of statute, upon its true construction, applies to the facts
as found.[11]

On the other hand, the new approach does not mean that –

in the application of any taxing statute, transactions or elements of transactions which had no commercial purpose [are] to be disregarded . . . that is
going too far. It elides the two steps which are necessary in the application
of any statutory provision: first, to decide, on a purposive construction,
exactly what transaction will answer to the statutory description and secondly, to decide whether the transaction in question does so.[12]

In particular:

MacNiven shows the need to focus carefully upon the particular statutory
provision and to identify its requirements before one can decide whether
circular payments or elements inserted for the purpose of tax avoidance
should be disregarded or treated as irrelevant for the purposes of the
statute.[13]

Thus:

The present case, like MacNiven, illustrates the need for a close analysis of
what, on a purposive construction, the statute actually requires. The object
of granting the allowance is, as we have said, to provide a tax equivalent
to the normal accounting deduction from profits for the depreciation of
machinery and plant used for the purposes of a trade. Consistently with
this purpose, s 24(1) requires that a trader should have incurred capital
expenditure on the provision of machinery or plant for the purposes of
his trade. When the trade is finance leasing, this means that the capital
expenditure should have been incurred to acquire the machinery or plant
for the purpose of leasing it in the course of the trade. In such a case,
it is the lessor as owner who suffers the depreciation in the value of the

---

[11] [2004] UKHL 51 (HL) at para. 32.   [12] *Ibid.* at para. 36.   [13] *Ibid.* at para. 38.

plant and is therefore entitled to an allowance against the profits of his trade.[14]

These statutory requirements, as it seems to us, are in the case of a finance lease concerned entirely with the acts and purposes of the lessor. The Act says nothing about what the lessee should do with the purchase price, how he should find the money to pay the rent or how he should use the plant.[15]

If these are the basic principles of the judicial approach to tax avoidance, there is relatively little that is remarkable about them. What is more remarkable, however, is the way in which the House of Lords went on to analyse matters in *BMBF's* 'sister case', *Scottish Provident* ('*SPI*').

2.2 The *SPI* decision

SPI was heard at the same time as *BMBF* by the same panel of Law Lords and their decision in *SPI* was given immediately following that in *BMBF*. The arrangement in *SPI* appears from paras. 2 to 4 of the Lords' decision:

This appeal concerns an artificial scheme devised in 1995 to take advantage of a prospective change in the system of taxing gains on options to buy or sell bonds and government securities ('gilts'). Under the legislation then in force, the Scottish Provident Institution ('SPI'), as a mutual life office, was not liable to corporation tax on any gain realised on the grant or disposal of such an option. Under the system proposed in an Inland Revenue consultation document published in May 1995, all returns on such options would be treated as income and losses made on disposals would be allowable as income losses . . .

The central element of the scheme devised by Citibank International plc ('Citibank') to enable SPI take advantage of the change-over was extremely simple. During the old regime, SPI would grant Citibank an option ('the Citibank option') to buy short-dated gilts, at a price representing a heavy discount from market price, in return for a correspondingly large premium. The premium received on the grant of the option would not be taxable. After the new regime came into force, Citibank would exercise the option. SPI would have to sell the gilts at well below market price and would suffer an allowable loss.

If that was all there was to the transaction, there would also have been a risk that SPI or Citibank would have made a real commercial profit or loss. The premium would have been fixed by reference to the current market

---

[14] This obviously represents a lawyer's perspective on the matter rather than that of an accountant or economist.

[15] [2004] UKHL 51 (HL) at paras. 39–40.

price, but the possibility of a rise or fall in interest rates during the cur-
rency of the option created a commercial risk for one side or the other.
Neither side wanted to incur such a risk. The purpose of the transaction
was to create a tax loss, not a real loss or profit. The scheme therefore provided for Citibank's option to be matched by an option to buy the same
amount of gilts ('the SPI option') granted by Citibank to SPI. Premium and
option price were calculated to ensure that movements of money between
Citibank and SPI added up to the same amount, less a relatively small sum
for Citibank to retain as a fee. In addition, SPI agreed to pay Citibank
a success fee if the scheme worked, calculated as a percentage of the tax
saving.[16]

Here again that elusive concept of 'risk' enters the equation but on this
occasion the significant elimination of risk leads the House to conclude
that the sole purpose of the arrangement was to create a tax loss, not
a real profit or loss – as if the same considerations were not present in
BMBF – and therefore to characterise the scheme as 'artificial' – as if the
contractual arrangements lacked reality.

On the face of it, there appears to be an inconsistency here but that is
not necessarily so. The apparently pejorative description of the arrangement in *SPI* might just anticipate the outcome in that case, where the
decision went against SPI while BMBF succeeded. In the absence of statutory language to suggest that tax risk or tax motivation are relevant to
the judicial consideration of the legislation, we might expect that neither
count for more than to indicate the parties' reasons for transacting as they
did. In *BMBF's* case one may observe that the transaction was designed
to transfer the tax allowances from BGE to BMBF at a certain (low) level
of risk to BMBF. That remains a commercial transaction when the legislation permits such a transfer without referring to risk (i.e. what the
finance lessee does with the sale proceeds). In *SPI's* case one may observe
that a gilt option exercisable over a period of time ordinarily involves
commercial risk so that the removal of that risk through the creation of
a matching cross-option suggests that the options are not entered into as
part of a speculative commercial transaction but are designed to achieve
a particular outcome, in this case a favourable tax outcome.

In fact the option terms were structured to leave an element of risk
attaching to the options so that it was uncertain whether both options
would be exercised or not. This did not deter the House of Lords:

---

[16] [2004] UKHL 52 (HL) at paras. 2–4.

[T]he uncertainty arises from the fact that the parties have carefully chosen to fix the strike price for the SPI option at a level which gives rise to an outside chance that the option will not be exercised. There was no commercial reason for choosing a strike price of 90. From the point of view of the money passing (or rather, not passing), the scheme could just as well have fixed it at 80 and achieved the same tax saving by reducing the Citibank strike price to 60. It would all have come out in the wash. Thus the contingency upon which SPI rely for saying that there was no composite transaction was a part of that composite transaction; chosen not for any transaction. It is true that it created a real commercial risk, but the odds were favourable enough to make it a risk which the parties were willing to accept in the interests of the scheme.

We think that it would destroy the value of the *Ramsay* principle of construing provisions such as s 150A(1) of the 1994 Act as referring to the effect of composite transactions if their composite effect had to be disregarded simply because the parties had deliberately included a commercially irrelevant contingency, creating an acceptable risk that the scheme might not work as planned. We would be back in the world of artificial tax schemes, now equipped with anti-*Ramsay* devices. The composite effect of such a scheme should be considered as it was intended to operate and without regard to the possibility that, contrary to the intention and expectations of the parties, it might not work as planned.[17]

In other words, the agreed transaction terms did not have effect to displace the tax purpose of the transaction. Nevertheless, the fact that transactions are designed with tax in mind or serve a tax purpose and no commercial purpose does not suffice to strike them down without statutory language to that effect.

Having regard to its decision in *BMBF*, you would expect to see the House of Lords approach *SPI* with the basic principles of *BMBF* in mind and engage in 'a close analysis of what, on a purposive construction, the statute actually requires'. The House certainly identifies the relevant statutory provision and frames the point in terms of its construction. Thus:

SPI is entitled to treat the loss suffered on the exercise of the Citibank option as an income loss if the option was a 'qualifying contract' within the meaning of s 147(1) of the Finance Act 1994. Section 147A(1) (inserted by the Finance Act 1996) provides that a 'debt contract' is a qualifying contract if the company becomes subject to duties under the contract at any

---

[17] *Ibid.* at paras. 22–3.

time on or after 1 April 1996. By s 150A(1) (also inserted by the Finance Act 1996) a 'debt contract' is a contract under which a qualifying company (which means, with irrelevant exceptions, any company: see s 154(1)) 'as any entitlement . . . to become a party to a loan relationship'. A 'loan relationship' includes a government security. So the short question is whether the Citibank option gave it an entitlement to gilts.

That depends upon what the statute means by 'entitlement'. If one confines one's attention to the Citibank option, it certainly gave Citibank an entitlement, by exercise of the option, to the delivery of gilts. On the other hand, if the option formed part of a larger scheme by which Citibank's right to the gilts was bound to be cancelled by SPI's right to the same gilts, then it could be said that in a practical sense Citibank had no entitlement to gilts. Since the decision of this House in *W T Ramsay Ltd v Inland Revenue Commissioners* [1982] AC 300 it has been accepted that the language of a taxing statute will often have to be given a wide practical meaning of this sort which allows (and indeed requires) the Court to have regard to the whole of a series of transactions which were intended to have a commercial unity. Indeed, it is conceded by SPI that the Court is not confined to looking at the Citibank option in isolation. If the scheme amounted in practice to a single transaction, the Court should look at the scheme as a whole.[18]

In reality, however, these passages involve no proper analysis of the statutory provisions in issue or the scheme of the transitional provisions involved in implementing the loan relationships legislation. It certainly makes no attempt to put the relevant statutory provisions within the broader legislative context of those provisions. The House of Lords may have felt able to short circuit matters by relying on the fact that the taxpayer had conceded that its scheme would fail if the two options involved could be regarded as a composite transaction. The House's conclusion that they had to be looked at together was its reason for disagreeing with the conclusion reached by the Commissioners and the Court of Session. Even so, the generalisation involved in these short passages appears to contradict the approach espoused in *BMBF* of analysing the legislative context in order to reach a conclusion.

Abuse of law

Indeed, although nominally the House of Lords' decision in *SPI* turns on the construction of the word 'entitlement' in the context of the particular composite cross-option scheme, in many respects one might as easily

[18] *Ibid.* at paras. 18–19.

justify the decision by saying that the transaction between Citibank and SPI was self-evidently not one that Parliament had in mind when it enacted the provisions, just as the transaction in *Ramsay* was not what Parliament had in mind as within the scope of an allowable loss. Presented in that way, the transactions leave the realm of pure construction and might be said to come closer to the European concept of abuse of law, where the transactions fit the statutory language but the court concludes that they are not what the legislator had in mind – an abuse of statutory rights otherwise conferred.[19]

An absolute rejection of such an approach seems to come in *MacNiven v Westmoreland Investments Ltd*, when Lord Hoffmann said:

> Everyone agrees that *Ramsay* is a principle of construction. The House of Lords said so in *Inland Revenue Commissioners v. McGuckian* [1997] 1 WLR 991; 69 TC 1. But what is that principle? Mr. McCall formulated it as follows in his printed case:
> 'When a court is asked
>
> (i) to apply a statutory provision on which a taxpayer relies for the sake of establishing some tax advantage
> (ii) in circumstances where the transaction said to give rise to the tax advantage is, or forms part of, some pre-ordained, circular, self-cancelling transaction
> (iii) which transaction though accepted as perfectly genuine (i.e. not impeached as a sham) was undertaken for no commercial purpose other than the obtaining of the tax advantage in question
>
> then (unless there is something in the statutory provisions concerned to indicate that this rule should not be applied) there is a rule of construction that the condition laid down in the statute for the obtaining of the tax advantage has not been satisfied.'
>
> My Lords, I am bound to say that this does not look to me like a principle of construction at all. There is ultimately only one principle of construction, namely to ascertain what Parliament meant by using the language of the statute. All other 'principles of construction' can be no more than guides which past Judges have put forward, some more helpful or insightful than others, to assist in the task of interpretation. But Mr. McCall's formulation looks like an overriding legal principle, superimposed upon the whole of revenue law without regard to the language or purpose of any particular provision, save for the possibility of rebuttal by language which can be

---

[19] See Case C-255/02 *Halifax* [2006] ECR I-1609 (ECJ). This case and the European concept of abuse of law are discussed below in Chapter 4.

brought within his final parenthesis. This cannot be called a principle of construction except in the sense of some paramount provision subject to which everything else must be read, like s 2(2) of the European Communities Act 1972. But the courts have no constitutional authority to impose such an overlay upon the tax legislation and, as I hope to demonstrate, they have not attempted to do so.[20]

The reference to the European Communities Act takes on a different significance when considering whether and to what extent it is possible to import into English law jurisprudence via the EC Treaty or EC Directives a concept of abuse of law, such as that enunciated by the European Court in *Halifax*. The ECJ concluded in *Halifax* that –

> the Sixth Directive must be interpreted as precluding any right of a taxable person to deduct input VAT where the transactions from which that right derives constitute an abusive practice.
>
> For it to be found that an abusive practice exists, it is necessary, first, that the transactions concerned, notwithstanding formal application of the conditions laid down by the relevant provisions of the Sixth Directive and of national legislation transposing it, result in the accrual of a tax advantage the grant of which would be contrary to the purpose of those provisions. Second, it must also be apparent from a number of objective factors that the essential aim of the transactions concerned is to obtain a tax advantage.[21]

The ECJ went on to conclude that:

> It follows that transactions involved in an abusive practice must be redefined so as to re-establish the situation that would have prevailed in the absence of the transactions constituting that abusive practice.[22]

By contrast, the *Ramsay* principle accepts the legal characterisation of the transactions entered into while denying their tax effect on the basis that viewed realistically they do not fall within the language of the statute.[23]

Conclusion

The *Ramsay* principle and the European concept of abuse of law start from different places. In terms of basic analysis, they reflect different legal and constitutional perspectives of legislation and of the statutory rights and obligations that legislation confers.[24] Nevertheless, they are directed to

---

[20] [2001] UKHL 6 (HL) at paras. 28–9.   [21] [2006] ECR I-1609 (ECJ) at paras. 85–6.
[22] *Ibid.* at para. 94.   [23] See Gammie (2006).   [24] See Gammie (1997).

similar ends and we should not therefore be surprised if they can produce similar results. The fundamental analytical problem that each judicial approach encounters, however, is that where it must be deployed – to find and apply a principle (usually an economic principle) in determining the rights and obligations of taxpayers vis-à-vis the state – there is frequently no clear principle involved at all: the lack of clear principle being the source of the avoidance in the first place. In short, we might conclude that there are no satisfactory judicial solutions to avoidance because judicial intervention cannot supply a clear principle where none exists. This is, of course, excellent news for future generations of tax lawyers who wish to continue examining the judicial runes.

3

Comparing the application of judicial interpretative doctrines to revenue statutes on opposite sides of the pond

MARTIN McMAHON

Introduction

Both the UK and the US have extraordinarily detailed revenue laws, although they differ in structure. The UK income tax is schedular, while (with some exceptions) the US federal income tax tends to a global computation. In both countries, the complexity of the statutes, which is itself intended to reduce ambiguity and tax planning opportunities, in fact often gives rise to unintended tax planning schemes.

As John Tiley so cogently notes in his magnificent treatise, *Revenue Law*, '[n]o legislature can allow taxpayers to continue to arrange their affairs in such a way that the tax system becomes voluntary (pay the Revenue or pay an advisor) . . .'[1] Yet in both the US and the UK, the statutory pattern is such that taxpayers frequently arrange transactions to fit literally the statutory language with the goal of reducing the tax burden on the particular transaction or even to create an apparent loss that might be offset against income from other transactions in calculating their income tax liability. This behaviour creates a dilemma for the legislature, the tax administrators, and the courts, because, as Tiley also notes –

> [t]ax equity demands that artificial tax avoidance schemes should be of no effect, yet certainty demands that the tax laws should be such that an individual can arrange his affairs in the expectation that he will or will not have to pay tax.[2]

The judiciary in both the UK and the US must constantly grapple with this tension in interpreting and applying the revenue laws. As Lord Tomlin in *Inland Revenue Commissioners v Duke of Westminster* said:

[1] Tiley (2005b, p. 96).   [2] Tiley (2005b, pp. 101–2).

Every man is entitled, if he can, to order his affairs so that the tax attaching under the appropriate Acts is less than it otherwise would be. If he succeeds in ordering them so as to secure this result, then, however unappreciative the Commissioners of Inland Revenue or his fellow taxpayers may be of his ingenuity, he cannot be compelled to pay an increased tax.[3]

In the same year as the House of Lords decided the *Duke of Westminster* case, in a similar vein, in *Gregory v Helvering* the US Supreme Court stated: '[t]he legal right of a taxpayer to decrease the amount of what otherwise would be his taxes, or altogether avoid them, by means which the law permits, cannot be doubted.'[4]

An even more famous statement of this principle was articulated by Justice Learned Hand in the decision of the Second Circuit Court of Appeals in the *Gregory* case before it was reviewed by the Supreme Court:

[A] transaction, otherwise within an exception of the tax law, does not lose its immunity, because it is actuated by a desire to avoid, or, if one choose, to evade, taxation. Any one may so arrange his affairs that his taxes shall be as low as possible; he is not bound to choose that pattern which will best pay the Treasury; there is not even a patriotic duty to increase one's taxes.[5]

What distinguishes the *Gregory* case from the *Duke of Westminster* case is the remainder of the analysis. While the Duke of Westminster prevailed, Mrs Gregory lost, because the court concluded:

The whole undertaking, though conducted according to the terms of [the statutory provision], was in fact an elaborate and devious form of conveyance masquerading as a corporate reorganization, and nothing else. The rule which excludes from consideration the motive of tax avoidance is not pertinent to the situation, because the transaction upon its face lies outside the plain intent of the statute. To hold otherwise would be to exalt artifice above reality and to deprive the statutory provision in question of all serious purpose.[6]

That is the true teaching of the *Gregory* case. Thus, the *Gregory* case often is cited as the seminal case in the application of a number of judicial interpretative and anti-abuse doctrines in the US. These doctrines play a critical role in understanding and applying the US revenue statutes. As Tiley has observed:

---

[3] [1936] AC 1 (HL) at pp. 19–20.   [4] (1935) 293 US 465 (USSC) at p. 469.
[5] *Helvering v Gregory* (1934) 69 F 2d 809 (2nd Cir.) at p. 810.
[6] *Gregory v Helvering* (1935) 293 US 465 (USSC) at p. 470.

United States courts have been much more willing than United Kingdom courts to develop some general tax jurisprudence or overriding principles that can be plucked from the sky to solve problems. The development of such doctrines has not been part of the United Kingdom tax tradition but there is far more of it than is generally admitted.[7]

This essay will compare the application to the revenue laws of judicial interpretative doctrines in the UK and the US and will consider Tiley's work in this area in light of recent developments. We will discover that while there are certain similarities in the UK and the US, the differences are substantial. To some extent, these differences are, as Tiley has explained, attributable to differing judicial approaches – the key difference has lain in the approach to statutes as sources of law and the much greater rule-formality in the UK system[8] – and to the differing intellectual and administrative structures of the two tax systems.[9] They are also attributable, however, as Tiley has further pointed out, to the greater frequency with which the US Congress reacts to tax avoidance schemes by enacting targeted statutory provisions to defeat tax avoidance schemes. Thus, 'schemes which have been explored in . . . Ramsay cases would not have been attempted in the United States'.[10]

3.1 Interpretative doctrines

Purposivism versus literalism

Tiley has described the current view of the UK courts as requiring that 'the words of the statute must be interpreted in their context and with an eye to the purpose of the provision'.[11] He concludes that this approach derives from the decision of the House of Lords in *MacNiven v Westmoreland Investments Ltd*,[12] where –

> [b]y freeing the taxpayer from some arguments based on the composite transaction doctrine, Lord Hoffmann has reinforced and developed what Lord Cooke and Lord Steyn said in *McGuckian* – all issues of construction are now to be looked at in their statutory context but are to be addressed purposively.[13]

He finds that the recent decisions in *Barclays Mercantile Business Finance Ltd v Mawson*[14] and *Scottish Provident Institution v Inland Revenue*

---

[7] Tiley (1987a, p. 188).   [8] Tiley and Jensen (1998, p. 162).   [9] Tiley (1987a).
[10] Tiley and Jensen (1998, p. 161).   [11] Tiley (2005b, p. 103).   [12] [2001] UKHL 6 (HL).
[13] Tiley (2001, p. 157).   [14] [2004] UKHL 51 (HL).

Commissioners[15] cement the requirement that tax statutes be interpreted purposively.[16] Historically, this description of judicial interpretative style applied likewise to the US judiciary. Purposivism was long dominant in Supreme Court tax jurisprudence.[17] *Gregory* is just one example. In the 1984 case of *Commissioner v Engle*, the Supreme Court reasoned that –

> the true meaning of a single section of a statute in a setting as complex as that of the revenue acts, however precise its language, cannot be ascertained if it be considered apart from related sections, or if the mind be isolated from the history of the income tax legislation of which it is an integral part.[18]

More recently, however, the Supreme Court has expressed favour for a literal application of the words of a provision in isolation, without regard to whether the construction is consonant with the overall statutory scheme or congressional purpose in enacting the statutory words. In *Gitlitz v Commissioner*,[19] the Supreme Court dismissed the government's argument that a literal interpretation would give the taxpayers an unwarranted double benefit: 'Because the Code's plain text permits the taxpayers here to

---

[15] [2004] UKHL 52 (HL).   [16] Tiley (2005a).

[17] See, for example, *Lucas v Earl* (1930) 281 US 111 (USSC) (developing the assignment of income doctrine); *Pinellas Ice & Cold Storage Co. v Commissioner* (1933) 287 US 462 (USSC) (denying tax-free status to merger involving only short term notes even though it literally complied with statutory requirement that was silent regarding consideration); and *Corn Products Refining Co. v Commissioner* (1955) 350 US 46 (USSC) (denying capital asset status to corn futures sold by a manufacturer for whom corn itself was 'inventory', even though the statute, while expressly excluding 'inventory' from the classes of property constituting capital assets, did not expressly exclude futures contracts to acquire such inventory). But see *Vulcan Materials Co. v Commissioner* (1991) 96 TC 410 (USTC), affirmed (1992) 959 F 2d 973 (11th Cir.) ('[if] statutory provisions . . . are unambiguous, we are not permitted, except in rare and unusual situations, to depart from the statutory language'); and *Apple Computer, Inc. v Commissioner* (1992) 98 TC 232 (USTC) (at p. 241: 'In construing a statute, we must first look to the plain language used by Congress. If the language of the statute is unambiguous, it is conclusive unless there is a "clearly expressed legislative intent to the contrary"', quoting *United States v Hurt* (1986) 795 F 2d 765 (9th Cir.) at p. 770).

[18] (1984) 464 US 206 (USSC) at p. 223 (quoting *Helvering v Morgan's Inc.* (1934) 293 US 121 (USSC) at p. 126). See also *UNUM Corp. v United States* (1997) 130 F 3d 501 (1st Cir.), cert. denied (1998) 525 US 810 (USSC) (at p. 507: 'courts must "not look merely to a particular clause in which general words may be used, but . . . take in connection with it the whole statute (or statutes on the same subject) and the objects and policy of the law, as indicated by its various provisions, and give to it such a construction as will carry into execution the will of the Legislature, as thus ascertained, according to its true intent and meaning"', quoting *Helvering v New York Trust Co.* (1934) 292 US 455 (USSC)).

[19] (2001) 531 US 206 (USSC).

receive these benefits, we need not address this policy concern.'[20] Many lower courts nevertheless continue to look to the statute's purpose.[21] Thus, courts often view their objective as determining 'Congress's intent', as explained by the Tax Court in one case:

> Our principal objective in interpreting any statute is to determine Congress' intent in using the statutory language being construed . . . Moreover, where the statute is ambiguous, we may look to its legislative history and to the reason for its enactment . . . In addition, we may seek out any reliable evidence as to the legislative purpose even where the statute is clear . . . As the Supreme Court summarized in Commissioner v. Engle . . .
>   Our duty then is 'to find that interpretation which can most fairly be said to be imbedded in the statute, in the sense of being most harmonious with its scheme and with the general purposes that Congress manifested.' . . . The circumstances of the enactment of particular legislation may be particularly relevant to this inquiry . . .[22]

On other occasions, however, the courts apply the literal language of the Internal Revenue Code without regard to congressional intent. For example, in *United States v Farley* the Court of Appeals for the Third Circuit stated: 'Although one could argue that the outcome mandated by the statutory language was not the outcome intended by Congress, we have nevertheless found that the language is clear and unambiguous.'[23] Thus, in this respect Tiley's observation that 'the US case law is in something of a mess'[24] is quite accurate. The battle between the 'purposive' and 'literalist' schools of statutory interpretation is a wide-ranging conflict in the US law generally, particularly in the tax law, and there is no clearly dominant school of thought.

Substance versus form

Tiley has fairly described the *Duke of Westminster* doctrine as requiring 'that taxpayers and the Revenue are bound by the legal results which the parties have achieved – even though this may be inconvenient for the

---

[20] *Ibid.* at p. 220.
[21] See, for example, *Andantech LLC v Commissioner* (2002) TC Memo. 2002–97 (striking down a complex corporate tax shelter); affirmed and remanded (2003) 331 F 3d 972 (DC Cir.).
[22] *Norfolk Southern Corp. v Commissioner* (1995) 104 TC 13 (USTC), modified on other grounds, (1995) 104 TC 417, affirmed (1998) 140 F 3d 240 (4th Cir.), cert. denied (1998) 525 US 1000 (USSC).
[23] (2000) 202 F 3d 198 (3rd Cir.).   [24] Tiley (2004a, p. 326).

Revenue', and he also notes that a sometimes proffered formulation – 'the court must look to the form of the transaction and not its substance' – is 'misleading'.[25] He concludes that the proper articulation of the doctrine is 'that the court must look at the substance of the matter in order to determine the true tax consequences of the transaction in the legal form adopted by the parties.'[26] This explanation finds support in Lord Bridge's speech in *Furniss v Dawson*, where he said:

> When one moves, however, from a single transaction to a series of interdependent transactions designed to produce a given result, it is, in my opinion, perfectly legitimate to draw a distinction between the substance and the form of the composite transaction without in any way suggesting that any of the single transactions which make up the whole are other than genuine.[27]

However, Lord Bridge's articulation of 'substance over form' in *Furniss v Dawson* is facially limited to cases involving the composite transaction doctrine, an analogue of the US step transaction doctrine, and does not apply to 'recharacterise' a single transaction as something other than that which it is in form, while Tiley's articulation does permit such an application.

The US judicial 'substance over form' doctrine is somewhat similar to the composite transaction doctrine, but it is also much broader. One Court of Appeals has called the substance over form principle 'the cornerstone of sound taxation'.[28] Nevertheless, a fundamental principle of US tax law is that the actual legal rights and liabilities established by the form of the taxpayer's transaction will be respected.[29] The proper characterisation of the transaction for tax purposes, however, is determined by the manner in which the tax law characterises the bundles of rights and obligations.[30] This characterisation issue probably arises most frequently with respect to whether a transaction that is in form a lease will be characterised

---

[25] Tiley (2005b, p. 106).
[26] See also Tiley (1987b, p. 227) ('the United Kingdom tax cases show that many issues are, with the acceptance of all parties, treated as matters of substance and not form').
[27] [1984] 1 AC 474 (HL) at p. 517.
[28] *Weinert's Estate v Commissioner* (1961) 294 F 2d 750 (5th Cir.) at p. 755.
[29] See *Tribune Company v Commissioner* (2005) 125 TC 110 (USTC) (at p. 198: '[W]e need not "substitute [the Commissioner's] version" for "what actually transpired." We deal only with what actually transpired and give effect to the legal documentation of the ... transaction, with key points emphasized by the terms of the documents and the statements made by [taxpayer's] representatives about what was accomplished in the ... transaction.').
[30] See Bittker, McMahon and Zelenak (2002, para. 1.02).

as a purchase and sale, and whether a sale and leaseback transaction will be treated as exactly that for tax purposes or instead recharacterised as a financing arrangement.[31] These cases frequently involve complex transactions and the resolution of the issue is highly dependent on the specific facts of the case.[32] The application of the substance over form doctrine to these transactions, however, remains fundamentally similar to the way Tiley has described the application of the UK substance over form doctrine, even though with respect to this particular issue, the UK follows a formalistic approach based on the House of Lords decision in *Helby v Matthews*.[33] But, as Tiley has observed, the broader substance over form doctrine applied in the US – to which he concludes UK courts are unlikely to be receptive – sometimes can be invoked to recast a transaction that produces a particular tax result in the form in it actually occurred as taking a different form with an identical substantive result, but with a different tax result.[34]

In *Heller v Commissioner*,[35] the shareholders of a Delaware corporation organised a California corporation, to which they contributed borrowed cash in exchange for the stock. The California corporation then borrowed additional cash and purchased the assets of the Delaware corporation, which paid its existing indebtedness and distributed the balance of the cash to its shareholders in liquidation. The taxpayer/shareholder, whose basis in the stock of the Delaware corporation exceeded the liquidating distribution, claimed a deductible loss on the liquidation. The Commissioner disallowed the loss, asserting that the series of steps was in fact a single transaction which was a reorganisation under the statutory predecessors of Internal Revenue Code s. 368(a)(1)(D) or s. 368(a)(1)(F) and that, accordingly, no loss was recognised. The shareholder argued that even if the transaction had the same result as a reorganisation, there had been no exchange of stock for stock as required by the predecessor of s. 354(a)(1). Notwithstanding the absence of the form of an exchange of stock, the Tax Court held for the Commissioner, reasoning as follows:

> In determining the substance of a transaction it is proper to consider the situation as it existed at the beginning and end of the series of steps as well as the object sought to be accomplished, the means employed, and the relation between the various steps . . .

---

[31] *Ibid.*, para. 28.06.
[32] Compare *Helvering v F&R Lazarus & Co.* (1939) 308 US 252 (USSC) (sale and leaseback 'was in reality a mortgage') with *Frank Lyon Co. v United States* (1978) 435 US 561 (USSC) (substance of the transaction accorded with its form, and the lessor was the true owner).
[33] [1895] AC 471 (HL). See Tiley (1988a, pp. 101–2).   [34] Tiley (1987b, p. 231).
[35] (1943) 2 TC 371 (USTC), affirmed (1945) 147 F 2d 376 (9th Cir.).

Petitioner and two others, the stockholders and directors of the Delaware corporation, decided to have the business, assets, and liabilities of that company taken over by a new California corporation. The desired end was accomplished by a series of steps, all of which were planned in advance . . . The net result was that petitioner and the other two stockholders had substituted their interest in the Delaware corporation for substantially the same interest in the California corporation. The nonrecognition of gain or loss provisions of the statute are 'intended to apply to cases where a corporation in form transfers its property, but in substance it or its stockholders retain the same or practically the same interest after the transfer.'

The result achieved under the plan could have been accomplished by having the California corporation acquire the assets of the Delaware corporation for its stock, and by having the latter distribute the stock to its stockholders in complete liquidation. Petitioner and his associates apparently chose the longer route, hoping that they might thereby become entitled to a loss deduction . . . The effect of all the steps taken was that petitioner made an exchange of stock of one corporation for stock of another pursuant to a plan of reorganization.[36]

In contrast, there are many instances when form, and form alone, controls. Compare another case decided a decade after *Heller*. In *Granite Trust Co. v United States*,[37] Granite Trust Co. owned a controlled subsidiary the stock of which had depreciated in value. To avoid non-recognition of the loss under the 1939 Code predecessor of current Internal Revenue Code s. 332 (which provides for non-recognition of gain or loss upon the liquidation of an 80 per cent controlled subsidiary), after the plan of liquidation of the subsidiary was adopted, Granite Trust Co. sold sufficient stock of the subsidiary to cause its ownership of the subsidiary to fall below the 80 per cent ownership requisite for non-recognition. The Commissioner of Internal Revenue argued that the transfers should have been ignored and the loss disallowed. The Court of Appeals for the First Circuit, however, found the stock transfers to be real in substance, not just form, and gave effect to them. The court stated:

As for the Commissioner's 'end-result' argument, the very terms of [s. 332(b)] make it evident that it is not an 'end-result' provision, but rather one which prescribes specific conditions for the nonrecognition of realized gains or losses, conditions which if not strictly met, make the section inapplicable . . .

In the present case the question is whether or not there actually were sales. Why the parties may wish to enter into a sale is one thing, but that is

---

[36] (1943) 2 TC 371 (USTC) at pp. 383–4.   [37] (1956) 238 F 2d 670 (1st Cir.).

irrelevant under the *Gregory* case so long as the consummated agreement was no different from what it purported to be.

... We find no basis on which to vitiate the purported sales, for the record is absolutely devoid of any evidence indicating an understanding by the parties to the transfers that any interest in the stock transferred was to be retained by the taxpayer ...

... To strike down these sales on the alleged defect that they took place between friends and for tax motives would only tend to promote duplicity and result in extensive litigation as taxpayers led courts into hair-splitting investigations to decide when a sale was not a sale. It is no answer to argue that, under Gregory v. Helvering, there is an inescapable judicial duty to examine into the actuality of purported corporate reorganizations, for that was a special sort of transaction whose bona fides could readily be ascertained by inquiring whether the ephemeral new corporation was in fact transacting business, or whether there was in fact a continuance of the proprietary interests under an altered corporate form ...

In short, though the facts in this case show a tax avoidance, they also show legal transactions not fictitious or so lacking in substance as to be anything different from what they purported to be, and we believe they must be given effect in the administration of [s. 332(b)] as well as for all other purposes.[38]

In contrast to the result in *Granite Trust Co.*, as applied in *Heller*, the substance over form doctrine resulted in the taxpayer being taxed as if he had effected a transaction to the same end in a form different than the form adopted. Tiley is sceptical of such applications of the doctrine: 'To argue that what the taxpayer had done should be equated with what she had not done ... creates a logical minefield.'[39]

Heller, however, might not be a paradigmatic application of substance over form. Much more recently, in *Esmark, Inc. v Commissioner*,[40] the taxpayer structured as a distribution what was in essence the sale of appreciated stock of a subsidiary, in order to take advantage of the pre-1986 rules under which corporations were generally not taxed on distributions of appreciated assets. Distilled to its essential facts, the 'purchaser' of the subsidiary first acquired stock of the taxpayer, a publicly traded corporation, through stock market acquisitions. After the 'purchaser' had acquired the stock of the taxpayer, the taxpayer corporation redeemed the purchaser's stock in the taxpayer in exchange for the stock of the subsidiary. The Tax Court rejected the IRS's claim that the transaction should

---

[38] (1956) 238 F 2d 670 (1st Cir.) at pp. 675–8.   [39] Tiley (1987b, p. 233).
[40] (1988) 90 TC 171 (USTC), affirmed (1989) 886 F 2d 1318 (7th Cir.).

be recast as a sale of the stock of the subsidiary, the proceeds of which was used by the taxpayer to retire some of its outstanding stock, because the IRS's proposed recasting did not reduce the number of steps, nor was its approach any more natural than the steps actually taken by the taxpayer. Thus, Tiley was right on the mark when he observed regarding the various judicial doctrines, that 'few are more insidiously attractive and yet at the same time more elusive than the doctrine that one should tax by reference to substance rather than form'.[41] He was also right on the mark when he wrote:

> What one is left with is the fact, however artificial, that there are two ways of doing things and that there can be no room to invoke the doctrine of substance over form in such a situation. This can be rationalised by saying that the choice of which of these two routes to take is a matter for the taxpayer, an implied election which the system allows, or by saying that where the facts have to fit one category or the other . . . one cannot reclassify the facts since the matter is one of legal substance and not mere form.[42]

Clearly, the substance over form doctrine should not constitute an untrammelled power in the revenue authorities or the courts to recast a complex transaction with particular starting and ending points as a differently structured, but equally complex, transaction with identical starting and ending points but a less advantageous tax result.

Step transaction doctrine

The step transaction doctrine is probably the most frequently applied tax law-specific US judicial statutory interpretative doctrine.[43] The classic articulation of the step transaction doctrine is found in *Minnesota Tea Co. v Helvering*: 'A given result at the end of a straight path is not made a different result because reached by following a devious path.'[44] When this judicial doctrine is applied, the tax treatment of several transactions is determined by examining their overall effect rather than giving effect to each of the several transactions in sequence. The US step transaction

---

[41] Tiley (1987b, p. 226).   [42] Tiley (1987b, p. 234).
[43] Tiley has masterfully captured the essence of the US step transaction doctrine and the difficulties in its application in Tiley (1987b, pp. 235–44).
[44] (1938) 302 US 609 (USSC) at p. 613. See also *Del Commercial Properties, Inc. v Commissioner* (2001) 251 F 3d 210 (DC Cir.) (at p. 213: 'a particular step in a transaction is disregarded for tax purposes if the taxpayer could have achieved its objective more directly, but instead included the step for no other purpose than to avoid U.S. taxes').

doctrine is closely related to, and quite possibly merely a subset of, the substance over form doctrine. Thus described, the step transaction doctrine is
somewhat similar to Lord Brightman's application of the *Ramsay* principle
in *Furniss v Dawson*,[45] but as will be shown, the US step transaction
doctrine is somewhat broader than Lord Brightman's application of the
Ramsay principle in *Furniss v Dawson*, because the latter requires that
'there be steps inserted which have no commercial (business) purpose
apart from the avoidance of a liability to tax'.[46]

The US step transaction doctrine is not merely an anti-abuse doctrine.
It is pervasively applied, and it can be applied at the behest of either
the Commissioner of Internal Revenue or the taxpayer (in contrast to
the UK practice that the composite transaction doctrine will be applied
only at the behest of the Revenue[47]), and does not require that one or
more intermediate steps have no business purpose.[48] Indeed, it often is
applied where the intermediate steps have a non-tax business purpose,
particularly with respect to finding that a series of transactions constitute
a tax-free corporate reorganisation.[49] Thus, unlike the UK composite
transaction doctrine, it is not 'an amalgam of a business purpose test
and a step transaction doctrine'.[50] Application of the step transaction
doctrine does not presuppose that the taxpayer's desired treatment will
be set aside. Sometimes its application produces an unfavourable result for
the taxpayer; other times its application produces a taxpayer favourable
result.[51] The step transaction doctrine is applied as an interpretative tool

---

[45] [1984] AC 474 (HL). This point is made in Tiley (1987a, pp. 182–3).

[46] [1984] AC 474 (HL) at p. 527.

[47] *Whittles v Uniholdings Ltd (No. 3)* [1996] STC 914 (CA), discussed in Tiley and Jensen
(1998, pp. 178–9). However, Tiley has argued that, after the decisions in *Barclays
Mercantile v Mawson* [2004] UKHL 51 (HL) and *Scottish Provident Institution v IRC*
[2004] UKHL 52 (HL), the taxpayer ought to be able to assert the composite transaction
doctrine; Tiley (2005a, p. 279).

[48] Some US cases hold that the taxpayer is bound to the form that he has chosen, but the
decisions are decidedly mixed in result. See Bittker, McMahon and Zelenak (2002, para.
1.03[6]).

[49] See, for example, Revenue Ruling 2001–26, 2001–1 CB 1297; Revenue Ruling 2001–46,
2001–2 CB 223.

[50] Tiley (1987b, p. 244).

[51] Compare *J. E. Seagram Corp. v Commissioner* (1995) 104 TC 75 (USTC) (applying the
step transaction doctrine to find that taxpayer disposed of stock pursuant to a tax-free
corporate reorganisation and thus could not recognise a realised loss) with *King Enterprises,
Inc. v United States* (1969) 418 F 2d 511 (Ct. Cl.) (applying step transaction doctrine
at taxpayer's behest to characterise a taxable sale and purchase of stock followed by an
upstream merger of the new wholly owned subsidiary into its parent as a tax-free corporate
reorganisation).

to identify the view of the facts to which the statute will be applied. To apply Tiley's hierarchical levels of analysis as set forth in 'Judicial Anti-Avoidance Doctrines, the US Alternatives – Part 1',[52] the step transaction doctrine generally is applied at Level 4 of the analysis.

In some cases, however, the form of a multi-step transaction will be allowed to control and separate tax consequences will be accorded to each of the constituent steps in the overall transaction. Predicting when the step transaction doctrine will be applied is difficult. This prediction is made even more difficult because there exist three variations of the step trans-action doctrine, which, generally speaking, the courts apply according to the circumstances of the case or the predilections of the court. The three principal tests are based on 'binding commitment', 'interdependence' and 'end result'.[53]

Under the binding commitment test, transactions are treated as steps of a single transaction if the parties were legally obligated to complete all of the transactions.[54] Absent a binding commitment, i.e., a contractual obligation, the separate transactions will not be integrated into a single transaction. This version of the test might be comparable to the analysis in *Campbell v IRC*.[55] This variation of the US step transaction doctrine is most often applied when the taxpayer seeks to invoke the doctrine. When the government seeks to invoke the step transaction doctrine, the analysis rarely stops with a failure to meet the binding commitment test.[56] As the court observed in *King Enterprises, Inc. v United States*, 'the step transaction doctrine would be a dead letter if restricted to situations where the parties were *bound* to take certain steps'.[57]

---

[52] Tiley (1987a, p. 192).

[53] See, for example, *Kornfeld v Commissioner* (1998) 137 F 3d 1231 (10th Cir.), cert. denied (1998) 525 US 872 (USSC); and *American Bantam Car Co. v Commissioner* (1948) 11 TC 397 (USTC); affirmed (1949) 177 F 2d 513 (3rd Cir.).

[54] See *Commissioner v Gordon* (1968) 391 US 83 (USSC) (exclusively applying this test to decline to treat distribution by a corporation to its shareholder of options to purchase the stock of a subsidiary and the subsequent sale of stock on exercise of the options as a distribution of the stock).

[55] [1970] AC 77 (HL); discussed in Tiley (1987b, p. 235).

[56] See, for example, *Kornfeld v Commissioner* (1998) 137 F 3d 1231 (10th Cir.), cert. denied (1998) 525 US 872 (USSC) (applying other tests to collapse steps even though there was not a binding commitment); *Associated Wholesale Grocers, Inc. v United States* (1991) 927 F 2d 1517 (10th Cir.) (applying other tests even though there was not a binding commitment); *True v United States* (1999) 190 F 3d 1165 (10th Cir.) (applying end result and interdependence tests at behest of Commissioner and declining to apply the binding commitment test for which the taxpayer argued).

[57] (1969) 418 F 2d 511 (Ct. Cl.) at p. 518 (emphasis in original).

The 'interdependence' test is met if the steps were 'so interdependent that the legal relations created by one transaction would have been fruitless without a completion of the series'.[58] This version of the step transaction doctrine is more akin to the application of the *Ramsay* principle in *Piggot v Staines Investment Co. Ltd.*[59]

McDonald's Restaurants of Illinois, Inc. v Commissioner[60] illustrates the application of the interdependence variant of the step transaction doctrine. McDonald's acquired a number of corporations that owned franchised McDonald's restaurants in a merger in which it gave the shareholders of the acquired corporations (the Garb-Stern group) McDonald's common stock. Pursuant to the merger agreement, McDonald's facilitated the subsequent sale on the New York Stock Exchange of the McDonald's stock acquired by the shareholders in the merger. As argued by the taxpayer – McDonald's Corporation – the step transaction doctrine was applied to treat the transaction as a cash merger, taxed as a sale and purchase, rather than a tax-free reorganisation. McDonald's thus received a stepped-up purchase price basis in the assets of the acquired corporations. The Tax Court held that the merger and the subsequent stock sale should not be integrated to deny tax-free reorganisation status and treat the overall transaction as a cash merger:

> In the present case, the two transactions were independent. The merger transaction did not require or commit the Garb-Stern group to sell their McDonald's stock. At the time of the merger, there was no assurance that the Garb-Stern group would sell. The decision to sell or to retain the McDonald's stock rested solely in the hands of the Garb-Stern group. They had unfettered discretion, within the constraints of the securities laws, to do with those shares as they wished. The fact that the Garb-Stern group intended to sell their stock and eventually sold it at the earliest possible moment should not obscure the discretionary nature of the sale.[61]

However, the Court of Appeals reversed the Tax Court's decision, reasoning that the original stock for stock merger would not have occurred without the guarantees of saleability. The Garb-Stern group insisted on this point in the negotiations and in the terms of the agreement, and had

---

[58] *American Bantam Car Co. v Commissioner* (1948) 11 TC 397 (USTC) at p. 405, affirmed (1949) 177 F 2d 513 (3rd Cir.) (declining to apply this test to combine formation of corporation followed closely by issuance of preferred stock).
[59] [1995] STC 114 (Ch D), discussed in Tiley (1995).
[60] (1982) 688 F 2d 520 (7th Cir.), reversing (1981) 76 TC 972 (USTC).
[61] (1981) 76 TC 972 (USTC) at pp. 998–9.

a one-time right to force registration – and hence sale – under the agreement: 'The very detail of the provisions about how McDonald's would ensure free transferability of the Garb-Stern group's McDonald's stock shows that they were the quid pro quo of the merger agreement.'[62] Thus, whether steps are mutually interdependent often is in the eyes of the beholder. This conclusion is confirmed by the Tax Court's decision five years later in *Penrod v Commissioner*, where on nearly identical facts the Tax Court again refused to integrate the merger and subsequent stock sale, finding that 'the Penrods did not intend to sell their McDonald's stock and that therefore the step transaction doctrine is not applicable under either the interdependence test or the end result test'.[63] The holding of the Tax Court in *Penrod* is based on reasoning similar to that applied in *Craven v White*,[64] where the transactions were not integrated under the *Ramsay* doctrine.[65]

The 'end result' test amalgamates into a single transaction separate events that were intended from the outset to be component parts of reaching a particular result. This version of the step transaction doctrine can be very difficult to apply to an arm's-length transaction where the transaction should be characterised symmetrically, because it raises the important question of 'whose intent controls'. A juxtaposition of two cases reaching analytically conflicting results illustrates the problem.

In *King Enterprises, Inc. v United States*,[66] Minute Maid Corporation acquired all of the stock of Tenco, Inc. for cash, notes, and stock, in a transaction which, standing alone, constituted a taxable sale and purchase of the stock of Tenco. After the acquisition, the Minute Maid board of directors approved a merger of Tenco into Minute Maid, which was consummated soon thereafter. The Tenco shareholders argued that the court should apply the step transaction doctrine to integrate the two transactions and treat the overall transaction as a statutory merger qualifying as a tax-free reorganisation under Code s. 368(a)(1)(A), except to the extent gain was required to be recognised with respect to the cash and notes. Because there was not a binding commitment, i.e., a contract, requiring that Tenco be merged into Minute Maid following the stock purchase, and the stock purchase certainly would not have been fruitless but for the subsequent merger, the variation of the step transaction doctrine that could be applied to integrate the transactions was the end result version. Despite the absence of any pre-acquisition expression to the Tenco shareholders

---

[62] (1982) 688 F 2d 520 (7th Cir.) at p. 525.   [63] (1987) 88 TC 1415 (USTC) at p. 1434.
[64] [1989] AC 398 (HL).   [65] See Tiley (1989).   [66] (1969) 418 F 2d 511 (Ct. Cl.).

of Minute Maid's intent subsequently to effectuate the merger, the court integrated the two transactions under that test, concluding that –

> [t]he operative facts in this case clearly justify the inference that the merger of Tenco into Minute Maid was the intended result of the transaction in question from the outset, the initial exchange of stock constituting a mere transitory step.[67]

This result is quite odd because, under the court's reasoning, the tax treatment of the shareholders of Tenco, the sellers, turned on transactions under the unilateral control of the purchaser of the stock, of which the selling taxpayer had no knowledge until after the fact, and with respect to which, therefore, they could not conceivably have had any intent.[68]

Compare the result and reasoning in *King Enterprises*, with the result and reasoning in *Bruce v Helvering*.[69] In *Bruce*, the taxpayer sold 200 shares of stock of E. E. Bruce & Co. to the Churchill Drug Co. for cash. On the same day, immediately following the sale, Churchill proposed to acquired all of the remaining outstanding shares of Bruce & Co. from the taxpayer and the other shareholders in exchange for its stock. The receipt of the offer following the initial sale was the first time the taxpayer had any indication of the full extent of Churchill's acquisition plans. The taxpayer accepted the offer on the same day, and within four months Churchill had acquired all of the outstanding shares of Bruce & Co. There was no doubt that the stock acquisitions following the taxpayer's initial sale of 200 shares were pursuant to a tax-free reorganisation under s. 112(c)(1) of the Revenue Act of 1928, and that the taxpayer had exchanged 500 shares of Bruce & Co. for stock of Churchill pursuant to the reorganisation. The Commissioner asserted that the initial disposition of the 200 shares of stock sold for cash should be integrated with the later transactions as part of the reorganisation for purposes of computing the amount of gain to be recognised by the taxpayer as a result of the receipt of Churchill stock and cash in exchange for 700 shares of Bruce & Co. The taxpayer argued that sale of 200 shares for cash and the subsequent exchange of 500 shares for Churchill stock were separate transactions, and that therefore the gain to be recognised as a result of the receipt of cash was to be calculated only with respect to the appreciation in the 200 shares and not with respect to

---

[67] (1969) 418 F 2d 511 (Ct. Cl.) at p. 519.
[68] Indeed, Tiley has described the *King Enterprises* opinion as 'an interesting example of the end result test in action and perhaps a rather generous interpretation of the facts'. Tiley (1988b, p. 132).
[69] (1935) 76 F 2d 442 (DC Cir.).

the appreciation in the full 700 shares. The court concluded that there was no basis for integrating the two transactions. Although Churchill Drug Co. might have intended from the outset to acquire all of the stock of Bruce & Co., the taxpayer had first entered into a binding contract only for the sale of 200 shares. Only after the contract had been completed did Churchill Drug Co. propose to acquire the taxpayer's remaining shares in exchange for its stock.

Bruce thus clearly stands for the proposition that the undisclosed unilateral intent of the counter-party to a transaction should not be a factor in integrating a later transaction with an earlier transaction for purposes of determining the tax consequences to the taxpayer of the earlier transaction. *King Enterprises* just as surely stands for the contrary proposition, and the reasoning and results in the cases are irreconcilable.

There is an interesting observation to be made about the differences between the US step transaction doctrine and the UK composite transaction doctrine, as the latter has evolved. In one respect the US step transaction doctrine might be narrower than the UK composite transaction doctrine. Tiley has noted that the decision in *Barclays Mercantile Business Finance Ltd v Mawson*[70] approves the conclusion of court in *Collector of Stamp Revenue v Arrowtown Assets Ltd*,[71] that the *Ramsay* principle can apply to ascertain the true nature of the transaction, even if the series of transactions was not preordained.[72] As discussed above, however, the US step transaction doctrine will be invoked only where, under whichever of the standards the court chooses to apply, completion of the entire series of transactions was preordained. If a subsequent step is not preordained, even under the fairly relaxed intent/end result standard, the subsequent step will not be integrated with the earlier steps.

3.2 Anti-abuse doctrines

Unlike the UK, the US has overarching judicial anti-abuse doctrines that go beyond principles of statutory construction. In contrast to interpretative doctrines such as substance over form or the step transaction doctrine, which are applied to clarify the view of the facts to which the statute should be applied, these anti-abuse doctrines are applied after the facts have been determined and the statutory language itself has been construed. These doctrines, the most important of which are the business purpose doctrine

---

[70] [2004] UKHL 51 (HL).   [71] [2004] 1 HKLRD 77 (HKCA).
[72] Tiley (2005a, pp. 277–8).

and the economic substance doctrine, deny the tax treatment sought by the taxpayer for a transaction (or series of transactions) that after application of the relevant interpretative doctrines has been determined to meet the statutory requirements to obtain the result sought by the taxpayer. Because business purpose and economic substance are doctrines of application, rather than interpretation, to apply Tiley's hierarchical levels of analysis as set forth in 'Judicial Anti-Avoidance Doctrines, the US Alternatives – Part 1', both doctrines generally are applied at Level 8 of the analysis.[73]

Business purpose doctrine

The business purpose doctrine traces its origins to *Gregory v Helvering*.[74] In that case, a corporation (United Mortgage), which was wholly owned by Gregory, owned stock of another corporation (Monitor Securities), which a third corporation desired to purchase. A sale of the Monitor Securities stock by United Mortgage followed by a distribution of the proceeds would have resulted in tax at both the corporate level (gain on sale) and shareholder level (dividend). A straightforward distribution of the Monitor Securities stock to Gregory followed by a sale by Gregory would have avoided the corporate level tax (under the law as it then stood), but would have been taxable to Gregory as a dividend. To attempt to achieve a result whereby Gregory would recognise a capital gain rather than a dividend (capital gain at that time being taxed at rates lower than dividends), the Monitor Securities stock was transferred to a newly created corporation (Averill), all of the stock of which was issued to Gregory. Averill then liquidated, distributing the Monitor Securities stock to Gregory, who then sold the stock. Under the statutory predecessors of ss. 355 and 368(a)(1), taken literally, the formation of Averill was a tax-free corporate reorganisation, and the trial court held that 'a statute so meticulously drafted must be interpreted as a literal expression of the taxing policy'.[75] Thus, Averill's existence was respected, and the only gain recognised was the capital gain recognised by Gregory upon the liquidation of Averill. Although the subsequent sale of the United Mortgage stock was a taxable event, no gain was realised, because as a result of the liquidation Gregory took a cost basis in the United Mortgage stock equal to its fair market value. The Supreme Court held that the transaction did not qualify as a

---

[73] Tiley (1987a, p. 194).   [74] (1935) 293 US 465 (USSC).
[75] (1932) 27 BTA 223 (USBTA) at p. 225.

'reorganisation' because the transaction was 'a mere device which put on the form of a corporate reorganisation as a disguise for concealing its real character', which was not to reorganise the business, but rather to transfer the original corporation's assets to the shareholder.[76] Although the Gregory court itself did not utilise the term 'business purpose' or explicitly ground its reasoning in the lack of business purpose for the convoluted series of transactions, later cases read it as so doing. For example, Judge Learned Hand later summarised the import of *Gregory* as follows:

> The doctrine of *Gregory v. Helvering* . . . means that in construing words of a tax statute which describe commercial or industrial transactions we are to understand them to refer to transactions entered upon for commercial or industrial purposes and not to include transactions entered upon for no other motive but to escape taxation.[77]

Note, however, that this formulation of the test requires that the transaction has no purpose apart from tax reduction for it to fail to produce the tax consequences expected under a literal application of the statute for lack of business purpose.

Although the business purpose doctrine originated in an interpretation of the corporate reorganisation statutes, over the years the business purpose requirement has evolved to become an implied requirement of many other statutory provisions. Two relevant cases, both involving deductions for interest payments, illustrate the development and application of the doctrine.

Twenty-five years after deciding *Gregory*, the Supreme Court handed down another landmark case in *Knetsch v United States*,[78] in which the taxpayer sought an interest deduction. The taxpayer purchased a number of single-premium, thirty-year annuity contracts, financed by a nominal down payment in cash and a non-recourse loan secured by the contracts for the balance, the interest on which was paid partly in cash and partly by borrowing against the increasing cash value of the contracts.[79] Over a period of years, the taxpayer paid substantial amounts to the insurance company because the interest payable on the debt (3.5 per cent) exceeded

---

[76] (1935) 293 US 465 (USSC) at p. 469.
[77] *Commissioner v Transport Trading & Terminal Corp.* (1949) 176 F 2d 570 (2nd Cir.) at p. 572, cert. denied (1950) 338 US 955 (USSC).
[78] (1960) 364 US 361 (USSC).
[79] Section 264(a)(2), precluding the deduction of interest on debts incurred or continued to purchase or carry single-premium annuity contracts, was not applicable to the years before the Court in *Knetsch*.

the rate of growth in the cash value of the contracts (2.5 per cent annually). Despite these payments, because the cash surrender value of the contracts to the taxpayer (i.e., the excess of the cash value of the contracts over the escalating debt) could not exceed $1,000, the annuity to be received when the contracts matured would be insignificant. Thus, the taxpayer's out-of-pocket expenses were obviously incurred in the hope of getting tax deductions under s. 163(a) that would be worth more than their cost. Knetsch's transaction met every literal requirement of the Code for the tax treatment he sought – deductibility of his interest payments. Nevertheless, the Supreme Court denied the interest deduction because:

> Knetsch's transaction . . . did 'not appreciably affect his beneficial interest except to reduce his tax . . .' [T]here was nothing of substance to be realised by Knetsch from this transaction beyond a tax deduction.[80]

As is true in so many US cases, the court did not stop with the application of only one of the possible interpretative doctrines. Rather, the court went on also to find that the indebtedness involved in the case was a 'sham', because it lacked any non-tax substance. After examining the before-tax cash flow of the transaction, the court concluded that the negative cash flow to Knetsch was no more than a 'fee' paid by him to the insurance company in exchange for the 'facade' of debt. In essence, Knetsch's transaction just wasn't the type of transaction to which the statutory rules were intended to apply.

The other illustrative case is the decision of the Court of Appeals for the Second Circuit in *Goldstein v Commissioner*,[81] another case denying the taxpayer an interest deduction. Goldstein realised an unusually large amount of windfall income and sought to create a substantial interest deduction to partially offset the gain. She borrowed approximately $950,000 to finance the purchase of $1 million of Treasury bonds (which were pledged as collateral for the loans) and she paid about $81,000 of prepaid interest. If the plan worked, the taxpayer would have reduced her current income by a large amount while increasing future income over a number of years by a somewhat lesser aggregate amount, but she would have realised a greater amount after tax by avoiding the impact of the then steeply progressive marginal tax rates through this 'self-help averaging device'.[82] The interest expenses would be more than offset by

---

[80] (1960) 364 US 361 (USSC) at p. 366.
[81] (1966) 364 F 2d 734 (2nd Cir.), cert. denied (1967) 385 US 1005 (USSC).
[82] The scheme in *Goldstein* now is statutorily foreclosed by Internal Revenue Code, s. 461(g).

the anticipated tax savings. Thus, a transaction that resulted in an economic loss before taxes would be profitable after taxes, if the sought-for tax consequences were allowed.

In this instance, the court was unwilling to describe the borrowing transaction as a 'sham' and acknowledged that it created a genuine indebtedness, but nevertheless disallowed a deduction for interest paid on the debt because it was contracted solely to generate the deduction itself. The court reasoned as follows:

> Section 163(a) . . . does not permit a deduction for interest paid or accrued in loan arrangements, like those now before us, that can not with reason be said to have purpose, substance, or utility apart from their anticipated tax consequences . . . Section 163(a) should be construed to permit the deductibility of interest when a taxpayer has borrowed funds and incurred an obligation to pay interest in order to engage in what with reason can be termed purposive activity, even though he decided to borrow in order to gain an interest deduction rather than to finance the activity in some other way. In other words, the interest deduction should be permitted whenever it can be said that the taxpayer's desire to secure an interest deduction is only one of mixed motives that prompts the taxpayer to borrow funds; or, put a third way, the deduction is proper if there is some substance to the loan arrangement beyond the taxpayer's desire to secure the deduction . . .
>
> [T]his provision should not be construed to permit an interest deduction when it objectively appears that a taxpayer has borrowed funds in order to engage in a transaction that has no substance or purpose aside from the taxpayer's desire to obtain the tax benefit of an interest deduction . . .[83]

Thus, *Goldstein*, even more so than *Knetsch*, stands for the proposition that a transaction that creates real legal obligations but has no business or profit-seeking motive (apart from the desired tax benefits) should not be permitted to result in tax savings.

As noted in the preceding excerpt from *Goldstein*, the business purpose doctrine does not prohibit all tax planning. As the Eleventh Circuit explained in *United Parcel Service v Commissioner*: 'A "business purpose" does not mean a reason for a transaction that is free of tax considerations . . . To conclude otherwise would prohibit tax planning.'[84]

The UK does not have any judicial doctrine closely analogous to the US business purpose doctrine,[85] whether the US doctrine is viewed as

---

[83] (1966) 364 F 2d 734 (2nd Cir.) at p. 741.
[84] (2001) 254 F 3d 1014 (11th Cir.) at p. 1019.   [85] See Tiley (1989).

applying to 'shams', as might be said if *Knetsch* is read narrowly, or more generally to any transaction that served no purpose aside from tax savings even though the legal and economic effects of the transaction were quite real, as in *Goldstein*. Lord Hoffmann's speech in *MacNiven v Westmoreland Investments Ltd*[86] rejected the inclusion of any 'business purpose' doctrine as part of the composite transaction approach: 'If a transaction falls within the legal description, it makes no difference that it has no business purpose. Having a business purpose is not part of the relevant concept.'[87]

As Tiley has explained in his works, the UK version of a 'sham' transaction is quite narrow.[88] He compares a passage from the opinion of Lord Diplock in *Snook v London and West Riding Investments Ltd*,[89] which he describes as 'definitive', with a different formulation by Lord Devlin in *Campbell Discount Ltd v Bridge*.[90] Lord Diplock's formulation of the concept of 'sham' in *Snook v London and West Riding Investments Ltd* takes the term to mean –

> acts done or documents executed by the parties to the 'sham' which are intended by them to give to third parties or to the court the appearance of creating between the parties legal rights or obligations different from the actual legal rights and obligations (if any) which the parties intended to create.[91]

Lord Devlin's formulation in *Campbell Discount Ltd v Bridge* suggests that –

> when a court of law finds that the words which the parties have used in a written agreement are not genuine, and are not designed to express the real nature of the transaction but for some ulterior purpose to disguise it, the court will go behind the sham front to get at the reality.[92]

Tiley reasons that, '[i]n the first version the doctrine of the sham means nothing more than that the label given by the parties to a transaction is not conclusive in determining the legal rights created by the parties', but that 'the second version can be made to express a wider doctrine based on a contrast between the "words used" and the "real nature" which would make it practically identical with the rule that there are circumstances in which the courts will look at the substance of a transaction rather than its form.' Tiley concludes that –

---

[86] [2001] UKHL 6 (HL).   [87] [2001] UKHL 6 (HL) at para. 58.
[88] Tiley (1987a, pp. 107–8).   [89] [1967] 2 QB 786 (CA).   [90] [1962] AC 600 (HL).
[91] [1967] 2 QB 786 (CA) at p. 802.   [92] [1962] AC 600 (HL) at p. 634.

[t]his reading is probably unjustified since it ignores the stress placed by Lord Devlin on the ulterior purpose of the transaction. These elements make the doctrine far closer to fraud and it is probably the well known reluctance of judges to brand parties as guilty of fraud that inhibits the development of the doctrine in the United Kingdom.[93]

Economic substance doctrine

The most potent and most unpredictable judicial interpretative doctrine in the Internal Revenue Service's quiver of arrows to fight tax avoidance schemes is the economic substance doctrine. The economic substance doctrine usually is said to have originated in the Supreme Court's 1978 decision in *Frank Lyon Co. v United States*,[94] but as the doctrine has evolved in the lower courts, it in some ways builds on the *Knetsch* legal sham and *Goldstein* purposive activity variants of the business purpose doctrine. Thus, one court has described the role of the economic substance doctrine as follows:

> The economic substance doctrine represents a judicial effort to enforce the statutory purpose of the tax code. From its inception, the economic substance doctrine has been used to prevent taxpayers from subverting the legislative purpose of the tax code by engaging in transactions that are fictitious or lack economic reality simply to reap a tax benefit. In this regard, the economic substance doctrine is not unlike other canons of construction that are employed in circumstances where the literal terms of a statute can undermine the ultimate purpose of the statute.[95]

Frank Lyon Co. involved a complex three-party transaction, involving a bank (Worthen) that needed a new building, but which it could not finance by a conventional mortgage loan because of state and federal banking restrictions, an unrelated business (Frank Lyon Co., the taxpayer), which was the purchaser/lessor in a sale and leaseback of the building constructed by Worthen, and the institutional lender (New York Life Insurance Co.) that financed the transaction. The question before the court was whether Frank Lyon Co. was the true owner of the building, and thus entitled to claim depreciation and interest deductions, or whether, alternatively, Worthen was the true owner of the building, and Frank Lyon Co. was simply a financial intermediary.

---

[93] Tiley (1987a, p. 196).   [94] (1978) 435 US 561 (USSC).
[95] *Coltec Industries, Inc. v United States* (2006) 454 F 3d 1340 (Fed. Cir.) at pp. 1353–4; cert. denied (2007) 127 S Ct 1261.

In deciding in the taxpayer's favour, the court stressed the factual nature of the judicial inquiry and in response to the government's arguments as follows:

> [W]here . . . there is a genuine multiple-party transaction with economic substance which is compelled or encouraged by business or regulatory realities, is imbued with tax-independent considerations, and is not shaped solely by tax-avoidance features that have meaningless labels attached, the Government should honor the allocation of rights and duties effectuated by the parties.[96]

This sentence at the same time says a lot and says very little, and what it says is ambiguous at that. To start, nothing in the court's analysis of the case preceding this portentous passage discussed at all the non-tax 'business or regulatory realities' that led Frank Lyon Co. to engage in the transaction.

The only party with a readily apparent non-tax business purpose for entering into the transaction was Worthen, whose tax consequences were not in question in the case. Perhaps more importantly, however, the passage does not tell us when the tax consequences of a transaction will not be those derived from a straightforward application of the statutory rules to the allocation of rights and duties facially established by the agreement of the parties, it only tells us when the expected tax consequences will be assigned – when the transaction (1) has 'economic substance' and (2) 'is imbued with tax-independent considerations, is not shaped solely by tax-avoidance features'. Furthermore, the decision itself tells us very little about what constitutes 'economic substance', and it tells us nothing at all about how to deal with cases that are shaped overwhelmingly by 'tax-avoidance' but which have a peppercorn of 'tax-independent considerations', largely as window dressing.

Since the decision in *Frank Lyon*, the courts have struggled with whether the test is 'disjunctive' or 'conjunctive'. Some circuit courts of appeal have adopted the conjunctive view under which a transaction is found to have economic substance, and the tax benefits thus will be allowed only if there *both* (1) has been a change in taxpayer's economic position *and* (2) is a non-tax business purpose for the transaction,[97] while others have adopted

[96] (1978) 435 US 561 (USSC) at pp. 583–4.
[97] See, for example, *In re CM Holdings, Inc.* (2002) 301 F 3d 96 (3rd Cir.) at pp. 105–6; *ASA Investerings Partnership v Commissioner* (2000) 201 F 3d 505 (DC Cir.) at p. 513, cert. denied (2000) 531 US 871 (USSC); *Pasternak v Commissioner* (1993) 990 F 2d 893 (6th Cir.) at p. 898; *Compaq Computer Corp. v Commissioner* (1999) 113 TC 214, reversed (2001) 277 F 3d 778 (5th Cir.).

the disjunctive view under which a transaction is found to have economic substance, and the tax benefits thus will be allowed as long as there is *either* (1) a change in taxpayer's economic position *or* (2) a non-tax business purpose.[98] Nevertheless, any dispute over whether the proper test is 'disjunctive' or 'conjunctive' is largely a tempest in a teapot. No case applying the disjunctive test has ever held that the taxpayer would be accorded the sought-after tax consequences on the grounds that either there had been a change in the taxpayer's economic position despite there being no non-tax business purpose for the transaction or that despite there being no change in the taxpayer's economic position there was a non-tax business purpose for the transaction.[99] Conversely, no case expressly purporting to apply the conjunctive test has ever held that the taxpayer would not be accorded the sought-after tax consequences because although there had been a change in the taxpayer's economic position, there was no non-tax business purpose for the transaction, or that although there was a non-tax business purpose for the transaction there was no change in the taxpayer's economic position. Nevertheless, it is important to note a significant difference between the two prongs of the economic substance test. While the taxpayer's subjective motivation may be pertinent to the existence of a non-tax business purpose versus solely a tax avoidance purpose, the objective reality of the transaction is salient in determining whether the transaction itself has any substance.[100]

The recent decision in *Coltec Industries, Inc. v United States*[101] is an important application of the economic substance doctrine, and is one that illustrates that the Supreme Court's application of the doctrine in *Frank Lyon Co.* is a bit crabbed and dated. *Coltec* involved a transaction that was a tax-free incorporation under s. 351, in which one corporation,

---

[98] See, for example, *Rice's Toyota World v Commissioner* (1985) 752 F 2d 89 (4th Cir.) at pp. 91–2; *Compaq Computer Corp. v Commissioner* (2001) 277 F 3d 778 (5th Cir.) at p. 781, reversing (1999) 113 TC 214; *ACM Partnership v Commissioner* (1998) 157 F 3d 231 (3rd Cir.), cert. denied (1999) 526 US 1017 (USSC).

[99] Depending on how the transactions are analysed, both *Compaq Computer Corp. v Commissioner* (2001) 277 F 3d 778 (5th Cir.) at p. 781, reversing (1999) 113 TC 214, and *IES Industries, Inc. v United States* (2001) 253 F 3d 350 (8th Cir.) at p. 354, involving cross-border dividend stripping shelters, might have objectively affected the taxpayer's net economic position, legal relations or non-tax business interests in a meaningful way apart from taxes without having a business purpose. In both of those cases the appellate court found the economic substance test to have been satisfied.

[100] See, for example, *Black & Decker Corp. v United States* (2006) 436 F 3d 431 (4th Cir.) at pp. 441–2; *Dow Chemical Co. v United States* (2006) 435 F 3d 595 (6th Cir.) at p. 599; *In re CM Holdings, Inc.* (2002) 301 F 3d 96 (3rd Cir.) at p. 103.

[101] (2004) 62 Fed Cl 716 (Ct. Cl.), reversed (2006) 454 F 3d 1340 (Fed. Cir.), cert. denied (2007) 127 S Ct 1261 (USSC).

Garlock, contributed to another corporation, Garrison, cash, a $375 million promissory note from a related corporation (Stemco), and certain other property. In connection with the transfer Garrison assumed $371.2 million of Garlock's contingent liabilities for asbestos product liability damage claims (neither of the events necessary to establish the fact of the liability had occurred, i.e., the filing of a lawsuit asserting a claim and an adjudication of liability). Shortly thereafter, Garlock sold a significant number of the shares of Garrison and claimed approximately $370 million of losses, having determined the basis of the Garrison stock with reference to an exchanged basis under s. 358 that was not reduced to reflect the assumption of the contingent asbestos liabilities. Since the liabilities were contingent and would have been deductible by the transferor upon payment, the Court of Claims held that the liabilities were within those described in ss. 357(c)(3)(A) and 358(d)(2), and thus neither s. 357(c)(1), requiring the recognition of gain to the extent that the amount of liabilities exceeds the basis of the contributed assets, nor s. 358(d)(1), requiring a reduction of the transferred basis assigned to the stock, applied. Therefore, Garlock's basis in Garrison properly was the exchanged basis of the transferred property, unreduced by the amount of liabilities assumed by Garrison, and the loss was allowed. However, the Court of Appeals reversed the trial court's decision and entered a judgment for the government, notwithstanding that the appellate court '[found] nothing in the literal terms of the statute that required Garlock to reduce its basis in the stock by the amount of liabilities assumed by Garrison', because the transaction lacked economic substance.[102]

One of the important questions in *Coltec* was which aspects of the multi-step transaction were to be tested against the economic substance doctrine. Analysing prior precedents from other courts of appeals, the court concluded that 'the transaction to be analyzed is the one that gave rise to the alleged tax benefit'. Otherwise, 'all manner of intermediate transfers could lay claim to "business purpose" simply by showing some factual connection, no matter how remote, to an otherwise legitimate transaction existing at the end of the line'.[103]

---

[102] (2006) 454 F 3d 1340 (Fed. Cir.) at p. 3147. After the transaction in *Coltec* occurred, but before the case was decided, Congress enacted s. 358(h), which, generally speaking, reduces the basis of the stock received in such a transaction to its fair market value, thus foreclosing any possibility of such a transaction post-dating the statutory change successfully reducing taxes.

[103] (2006) 454 F 3d 1340 (Fed. Cir.) at p. 1356 (quoting *Basic Inc. v United States* (1977) 549 F 2d 740 (Ct.Cl.) at p. 745).

Applying these principles to the facts, the court concluded that the economic substance test had not been satisfied:

> Looking at the transaction objectively, there is no basis in reality for the idea that a corporation can avoid exposure for past acts by transferring liabilities to a subsidiary . . . [E]ven Coltec concedes that Garrison's assumption of Garlock's asbestos liabilities did not actually shield Garlock or Coltec from direct liability . . . We therefore see nothing indicating that the transfer of liabilities in exchange for the note effected any real change in the 'flow of economic benefits,' provided any real 'opportunity to make a profit,' or 'appreciably affected' Coltec's beneficial interests aside from creating a tax advantage . . . Garrison's assumption of Garlock's liabilities in exchange for the Stemco note served no purpose other than to artificially inflate Garlock's basis in its Garrison stock. That transaction must be disregarded for tax purposes. When that transaction is disregarded, the basis in the Garrison stock is unaffected by the Stemco note/assumed liability exchange.[104]

It is important to note that, unlike the Supreme Court in *Frank Lyon*, which found a 'business purpose' in the benefit to the taxpayer's counter-party in the transaction without looking to the taxpayer's purpose, the *Coltec* court, like other lower courts since *Frank Lyon*, more properly looked to the taxpayer's business purpose for entering into the transaction, and focused on the precise technical origin of the tax benefit to determine whether the particular step that invoked a particular statutory rule served a business purpose and appreciably changed the taxpayer's position.

On the other hand, *Compaq Computer Corp. v Commissioner* illustrates how elusive the search for economic substance can be, and thus how unpredictable the application of the economic substance doctrine can be.[105] In 1992, shortly after Compaq recognised a $232 million long-term capital gain on the sale of a subsidiary, an investment firm, Twenty-First Securities Corp., contacted the Compaq treasury department (which focused primarily on capital preservation, typically investing in overnight deposits, Eurodollars, commercial paper and tax-exempt obligations) to suggest that Compaq take advantage of an American Depository Receipt arbitrage transaction to reduce its resulting tax liability. The transaction involved the purchase, for next day settlement, of $888 million of Royal Dutch Shell ADRs, cum dividend, followed immediately by sales, with settlement in five days, of those ADRs, ex dividend, for $868 million.

---

[104] (2006) 454 F 3d 1340 (Fed. Cir.) at pp. 1359–60.
[105] (2001) 277 F 3d 778 (5th Cir.), reversing (1999) 113 TC 214.

Compaq then carried back $20 million of loss against the previously recognised gain. It also claimed a $3.4 million foreign tax credit for taxes withheld from the $22.5 million dividend received. The net cash flow from the transaction without regard to US tax consequences was a $1.5 million loss. Compaq did not perform a cash flow analysis or investigate the investment, shredded the spreadsheet provided by the promoter, and did not disclose any communications indicating any reliance on the advice of its tax department or counsel.

The Tax Court applied the economic substance doctrine and denied the loss deduction, holding that the business purpose requirement of the economic substance doctrine is only satisfied when 'the transaction [is] rationally related to a useful nontax purpose that is plausible in light of the taxpayer's conduct and . . . economic situation'.[106]

The Court of Appeals for the Fifth Circuit reversed, holding for the taxpayer because it found that the taxpayer had made a pre-tax profit and that the transaction thus had economic substance. Consistent with the dictum in *Gregory*, the court concluded that the taxpayer's motive to reduce taxes did not vitiate a business purpose to earn a pre-tax profit: 'even assuming that Compaq sought primarily to get otherwise unavailable tax benefits in order to offset unrelated tax liabilities and unrelated capital gains, this need not invalidate the transaction.' The court reasoned as follows:

> [T]he evidence shows that Compaq actually and legitimately also sought the (pre-tax) $1.9 million profit it would get from the Royal Dutch dividend of approximately $22.5 million less the $20.7 million or so in capital losses that Compaq would incur from the sale of the ADRs ex dividend . . .
>
> [T]he ADR transaction had both a reasonable possibility of profit attended by a real risk of loss and an adequate non-tax business purpose. The transaction was not a mere formality or artifice but occurred in a real market subject to real risks. And, as has been discussed, the transaction gave rise to a real profit whether one looks at the transaction prior to the imposition of tax or afterwards.[107]

What the Court of Appeals for the Fifth Circuit either did not understand or was unwilling to acknowledge is that its pre-tax profit analysis was an erroneous artificial construct. In contrast, the Tax Court recognised that the transaction was not economically viable in the absence of the US tax

---

[106] (1999) 113 TC 214 at p. 224.   [107] (2001) 277 F 3d 778 (5th Cir.) at p. 788.

consequences of both the deduction for Compaq's capital loss on resale of the ADRs and the US foreign tax credit.[108] Aside from the tax consequences (and assuming the price would have been the same, which it would not have been), Compaq purchased and sold the ADRs at a loss of approximately $19 million, to acquire a dividend of $22,500,000. Compaq's investment in ADRs produced a pre-tax profit, however, only if the Netherlands withholding tax on the dividends was included in Compaq's profit. Assuming that there were no taxes (neither Netherlands nor US), as the Fifth Circuit did, the *Compaq* transaction, if it could have been effected at the same pricing, would have produced a positive cash flow. But the tax climate affected the pricing of the ADRs involved in the transaction, which was effected privately while the stock markets were closed. The price at which Compaq bought the ADRs was discounted by the amount of the Netherlands tax, because the seller was an entity (for example, a tax exempt entity) that could not use the US foreign tax credit. Compaq purchased the dividend for its after-tax value to the seller. The 'economic profit' from the transaction that was critical to the Court of Appeals' analysis, thus was entirely attributable to the discounted market price of the ADRs, which in turn was entirely attributable to the anticipated tax consequences.[109]

Notwithstanding the taxpayer's victory in *Compaq*, the record otherwise shows an impressive string of government victories in cases asserting that the economic substance doctrine should be applied to deny taxpayers tax benefits that the court concluded otherwise were allowable under the statutory pattern as applied to complex, contrived transactions motivated by tax avoidance.[110] The economic substance doctrine has emerged as the most powerful and, for now, possibly most frequently asserted general overriding judicial anti-avoidance doctrine, although one must recognise its limitations compared to a vigorous statutory GAAR. Once must always

[108] In 1997, after the year in question in *Compaq*, Congress amended s. 901(k) to increase to at least sixteen days the amount of time an ADR must be held within a thirty-day period that includes the dividend record date in order for the foreign taxes paid on the dividend to qualify for the foreign tax credit.
[109] For a more complete discussion, see McDaniel, McMahon, Simmons and Abreu (2004, pp. 1332–5).
[110] See, for example, *Winn-Dixie Stores Inc. v Commissioner* (1999) 113 TC 254 (USTC), affirmed (2001) 254 F 3d 1313 (11th Cir.) (per curiam) (denying interest deductions in a leveraged COLI tax shelter), cert. denied (2002) 535 US 986 (USSC); *Dow Chemical Co. v United States* (2006) 435 F 3d 595 (6th Cir.), cert. denied (2007) 127 S Ct 1251 (USSC) (COLI tax shelter); *Black & Decker Corp. v United States* (2006) 436 F 3d 431 (4th Cir.) at pp. 441–2 (*Coltec*-like transaction); *In re CM Holdings, Inc.* (2002) 301 F 3d 96 (3rd Cir.) at p. 103 (COLI tax shelter).

remember that, even in its most vigorous incarnation, the economic substance doctrine does not deny the sought-after tax benefits merely because the taxpayer motivation overwhelmingly was tax avoidance. Any non-tax business purpose for the transaction will preserve the tax benefits against government challenge.

Nevertheless, the UK has no judicial anti-avoidance doctrine approaching the breadth and vigour of the US economic substance doctrine. The case that might have come closest to the US economic substance doctrine is the House of Lords decision in *Ensign Tanker (Leasing) Ltd v Stokes*,[111] but this judgment is not certain and the distance is significant.[112] The result, but probably not the reasoning, in *IRC v Burmah Oil*[113] is consistent with the US economic substance doctrine.[114] However, the US economic substance doctrine is more akin to the 'fiscal nullity' doctrine rejected by the UK courts in *Whittles v Uniholdings Ltd*[115] and *MacNiven v Westmoreland Investments Ltd*.[116] No case better demonstrates the differences in the approaches than *MacNiven*. A similar circular preordained cash flow to pay interest to a lender has been struck down by the US courts, on the rationale that there was no 'payment', even though unlike in *MacNiven*, the lender was neither tax-exempt nor related to the taxpayer.[117]

Barclays Mercantile Business Finance Ltd v Mawson[118] also illustrates these differences. The sale and leaseback transaction that was respected in *Barclays*, with the result that the taxpayer/lessor was allowed the claimed capital cost allowances, was similar in many ways to the transaction involved in the US Supreme Court decision in *Frank Lyon Co.*, discussed previously. From that starting point one would be tempted to conclude that the UK and US doctrines do not differ so much. But *Frank Lyon Co.* is often viewed as erroneously decided, and has been accurately described as 'having more meaning for its rhetoric than for its facts'.[119] Capital cost recovery allowances to lessors in similar transactions have been disallowed with some frequency in the US. One such case is *Rice's Toyota World, Inc. v Commissioner*.[120] In *Rice's Toyota World* the taxpayer bought a computer and leased it back to the seller (a tax shelter promoter), who immediately

---

[111] [1992] 1 AC 655 (HL), discussed in Tiley and Jensen (1998, pp 163–75) (noting that the US has specific statutory rules to deal with the issue there presented).
[112] See Tiley (1992).   [113] [1982] STC 30 (HL).   [114] See Tiley (1988a, pp. 89–91).
[115] [1996] STC 914 (CA).   [116] [2001] UKHL 6 (HL), discussed in Tiley (2001).
[117] *Battlestein v Internal Revenue Service* (1980) 631 F 2d 1182 (5th Cir.), cert. denied (1981) 451 US 938 (USSC).
[118] [2004] UKHL 51 (HL).   [119] Sheppard (2007, p. 737). See also Wolfman (1981).
[120] (1985) 752 F 2d 89 (4th Cir.).

subleased the computer to the intended user. The taxpayer paid no cash in the purchase but gave the promoter a small recourse note and a large non-recourse note. The Fourth Circuit Court of Appeals disallowed the deductions claimed by the taxpayer for depreciation of the computer and for interest on the non-recourse note, because the transaction was motivated solely by tax considerations, and lacked economic substance since there was no reasonable possibility of profit.

A similar result was reached much more recently in *BB&T Corp. v United States*,[121] which involved a lease-in-lease-out transaction of wood pulp factory equipment, in which the taxpayer claimed deductions for advance rental payments. Although the court did not expressly acknowledge that it was applying the economic substance doctrine, instead relying on substance over form and step transaction analyses, its reasoning was not inconsistent with the economic substance doctrine. The court found that because for the term of the lease the counter-party (Sodra) in substance retained all of the rights in the equipment that it previously possessed, and BB & T bore no real risk of loss of its initial investment, BB & T acquired only a future interest in the equipment that would mature only if Sodra elected not to exercise its (fully funded) option to purchase BB & T's interest in the head lease. Thus, BB & T's payments to Sodra were not 'rent payments', and the deduction was disallowed. Furthermore, the taxpayer's claimed interest deductions with respect to a non-recourse loan in connection with the transaction were disallowed because after disregarding intermediate steps that served no business purpose, all that really occurred was a circular funds transfer without any genuine indebtedness. So, in the end, at least in these cases, we see a significant difference between the US economic substance doctrine, whatever it might be termed in a particular case, and the UK *Ramsay* approach.

Tiley has summarised the result of the synthesis of the UK *Ramsay* line of cases – which he has labelled the 'new approach' because it goes beyond merely the composite transaction doctrine[122] – after the recent decisions in *Barclays Mercantile Business Finance Ltd v Mawson*[123] and *Scottish Provident Institution v Inland Revenue Commissioners*:[124]

> The cases beginning with *Ramsay* are now mere examples of points of construction on which people may, presumably, have different views . . .
> [T]he *Ramsay* doctrine [has] been applied in at least four different contexts:

---

[121] (2007) 99 AFTR 2d 2007–376 (MDNC).   [122] See Tiley (2004a, p. 305).
[123] [2004] UKHL 51 (HL).   [124] [2004] UKHL 52 (HL).

(a) to ascertain whether a series of self-cancelling, pre-ordained transactions, effected solely to generate an allowable loss for capital gains tax
purposes, were to be respected for the purposes of capital gains tax
legislation or not (*Ramsay*);
(b) to ascertain the true parties and the true dealing in a transaction (*Furniss
v Dawson and Craven v White*);
(c) to ascertain the true nature of a receipt in the hands of a taxpayer (*IRC
v McGuckian*);
(d) to ascertain the true nature of instruments issued solely for tax avoidance purposes (*Arrowtown*).[125]

He then observes further that 'in (d) the notion of a preordained series of
transactions was irrelevant',[126] and he wonders whether –

> now that *Ramsay* in its more extreme forms has been brought to heel, it
> makes sense actually to talk about cases being avoidance cases. The clue
> here may be the observation of Park J., before going on to apply the *Ramsay*
> doctrine to the facts before him, that *Barclays Mercantile* was not a tax
> avoidance scheme. So 'avoidance' becomes a fifth wheel on the coach.[127]

Based on the cases read as a whole, the fairest general conclusion is that
unlike in the US, in the UK '[t]he courts have no power to strike down
[tax] avoidance schemes'.[128] But it is not true that courts in the US have
an absolutely unlimited power to strike down tax avoidance schemes. The
fairest summary of the role and scope of the economic substance doctrine
might be found in the recent *Coltec* decision:

> The economic substance doctrine represents a judicial effort to enforce
> the statutory purpose of the tax code. From its inception, the economic
> substance doctrine has been used to prevent taxpayers from subverting
> the legislative purpose of the tax code by engaging in transactions that are
> fictitious or lack economic reality simply to reap a tax benefit. In this regard,
> the economic substance doctrine is not unlike other canons of construction
> that are employed in circumstances where the literal terms of a statute can
> undermine the ultimate purpose of the statute.[129]

So understood and limited, the US economic substance doctrine might
not be as completely alien to UK jurisprudence as it is sometimes thought

---

[125] Tiley (2005a, p. 277).   [126] Tiley (2005a, p. 278).   [127] Tiley (2005a, p. 280).
[128] Tiley (2004b, p. 134) and Tiley (2004a, p. 304) ('the UK courts have no power to strike
down a transaction merely because it is motivated by tax avoidance purposes; the UK
courts have no power to reconstruct a transaction merely because it is entered into for
tax avoidance purposes').
[129] *Coltec Industries v United States* (2004) 62 Fed Cl 716 (Ct. Cl.), reversed (2006) 454 F 3d
1340 (Fed. Cir.) at pp. 1353–4, cert. denied (2007) 127 S Ct 1261 (USSC).

to be. Having said that, however, one must take heed of another highly insightful warning from Tiley regarding the import of tax avoidance cases:

> We should also look at what the judges have actually done, their reasons, stated and unstated, for doing so, remembering the particular factual background against which the words are used. We must distinguish reason from rhetoric and must avoid the trap of thinking that a test used in one situation has to become the equivalent of a statutory provision to be applied in another.[130]

Looking at what has actually occurred in the cases, who won and who lost, in the UK courts and in the US courts, we are back to finding significant differences.

Conclusion

As has been seen, the US and UK approaches to the use of non-statutory judicial doctrines in interpreting and applying the revenue laws so as to curb tax avoidance have much in common and at the same time are quite different. In one respect, Tiley's description of the UK approach serves equally well to describe the US approach – 'there is no fundamental principle about avoidance but rather a set of (sometimes conflicting) judicial attitudes or approaches which they bring with them as they consider the continuum of cases from sensible planning to outrageous schemes'.[131] The tax jurisprudence in both countries shares a 'purposive' approach to statutory interpretation and an expansive view of the facts to which the law is to be applied, although the US 'substance over form' and 'step transaction' doctrines are much more vigorously applied than the UK 'composite transaction doctrine' and '*Ramsay* approach'.

The judicial views on opposite sides of the pond, however, are separated by a wide and deep sea when we turn to true judicial anti-abuse doctrines.[132] The US approach is more expansive than the UK approach. Notwithstanding the enactment of an army of targeted statutory rules designed to curb specific tax avoidance transactions, the US courts vigorously apply the non-statutory 'business purpose' and 'economic substance' doctrines as overarching standards to deny tax benefits otherwise allowable under the statute, to curb what the courts consider to be abusive tax avoidance transactions. As a result, it is likely that in the US there is less certainty than in the UK regarding the tax consequences of aggressive transactions that are close to the edge.

[130] Tiley (2004a, p. 304).   [131] Tiley (2004a, p. 331).
[132] See Tiley and Jensen (1998, pp. 164–85).

The more cautious UK approach, with its greater certainty, finds favour with Tiley.[133] He has concluded that 'the United States authorities should not be followed',[134] warning that even a substance over form 'approach is logically justifiable only so long as the legal system tells the taxpayer and the Revenue authorities when one rule is superior to the other'.[135] Tiley further opines that, '[f]or all their invocation of substance the United States cases do not convince. The problem is not just what is meant by form and substance but why it is that substance should be preferred to form . . .'[136] This philosophy is reflected in his approval of the result, if not all of the reasoning, in *MacNiven*,[137] a case which, as noted earlier, would have been decided in favour of the Revenue rather than the tax-payer if US interpretative doctrines had applied. This difference reflects that his scholarship has 'highlight[ed] the necessity for clear and intel-lectually sustainable rules of law and the dangers of vague invocations of "substance" and "reality"',[138] as well as his wariness of the courts rechar-acterising facts.[139]

Tiley is also less sanguine about the broad application of a step (US parlance) or composite (UK parlance) transaction doctrine than almost any US tax academic. In the US, the application of the step transaction doctrine to determine the specific facts to which the revenue laws should be applied, without regard to whether tax avoidance is in the air, is well accepted by tax practitioners, revenue administrators, the courts, and tax academics, although conclusions about the details of its application to particular fact patterns may well differ. Tiley, in contrast, finds merit in the more limited application of the UK composite transaction doctrine after *Furniss v Dawson*:

> The present United Kingdom approach stemming from the speech of Lord Brightman is an amalgam of a business purpose test and a step transaction doctrine – transactions are to be linked only when there is no business pur-pose – and this provides a workable but limited weapon against avoidance. If the courts do not contain the doctrine within some such form they are heading for a quagmire of unprincipled decision making . . .'[140]

---

[133] Tiley (2004a, p. 326) ('the US case law is in something of a mess').
[134] Tiley (1989, p. 26).   [135] Tiley (1987b, p. 231).
[136] Tiley (1988b, p. 139).   [137] Tiley (2001).
[138] Tiley (1988a, p. 103). Nevertheless, in Tiley (1988b, p. 135) he suggested that the UK might want to consider adopting some of the flexibility, along with the accompanying uncertainty, that some of the US judicial doctrines provide.
[139] Tiley (1988b, pp. 142–3).   [140] Tiley (1987b, p. 244).

On the other hand, Tiley has endorsed a general business purpose doctrine, along the lines of the US application in *Knetsch*, concluding that –

> a doctrine that a transaction will be given legal effect only if some purpose other than tax saving can be deduced . . . is defensible . . . in the sense that where the taxpayer invokes a particular provision it is open to the courts to hold that the particular provision is not a mechanical rule but requires a particular purpose other than the saving of tax to be shown by the taxpayer.[141]

Despite his acceptance of the potential wisdom in a limited 'business purpose' doctrine, Tiley nevertheless does not find favour with a 'fiscal nullity' doctrine, analogous to the US economic substance doctrine.[142] In that judgment, he is joined by many tax experts in the US,[143] and even the Chief Counsel of the Internal Revenue Service cautions that –

> the economic substance doctrine will not be used as a general anti-abuse rule to be asserted every time the IRS confronts a tax shelter transaction it simply does not like . . . [it] should be used only in those cases where the tax result produced by the transaction is not in accord with the Congressional intent and economic reality.[144]

Thus restricted, even the US economic substance doctrine might be more in line with Tiley's view of the proper application of the 'new approach' in the UK.

My own view is that, however accurate Tiley's view of the appropriate application in the UK of judicial anti–avoidance doctrines might be, in the US vigorous judicial anti-avoidance doctrines play an important role. In the context of the US tax system and style of tax practice, judicial anti-avoidance doctrines that provide non-statutory standards that trump the bright-line rules in the statute are necessary and appropriate to curb the zeal of taxpayers and their tax advisors in structuring artificial transactions designed to produce little other than tax benefits. To expect that the statute (and/or Treasury regulations) could be crafted to foreclose abusive tax-motivated transactions with exacting specificity is to expect too much. First, despite the extraordinary detail of the US tax statutes, most statutory provisions are designed to deal with common day-to-day business transactions. Although the US tax statutes are replete with statutory anti-avoidance rules, to build specific anti-abuse rules into each

---

[141] Tiley (1988b, p. 142).   [142] Tiley (2004a, pp. 325–6).
[143] See, for example, Silverman, Lerner and Kidder (2006).   [144] Korb (2007).

and every statutory section would inordinately complicate the language and structure of the tax statutes. Second, narrowly targeted responses to tax avoidance transactions inevitably can have only partial success. Savvy lawyers and accountants will plan around narrowly targeted statutory anti-abuse rules, and greater specificity will breed new statutory anomalies to be exploited. The legislature and revenue authorities simply cannot keep pace on a prospective basis with the army of tax experts continuously engaged in the never-ending design of new tax avoidance transactions.

4

Abuse of rights and European tax law

WOLFGANG SCHÖN

Introduction

The author's personal relationship with John Tiley begins with the reading of his writings on tax avoidance some twenty years ago. Having returned to Germany from a three-month stint with City law firm Herbert Smith, I felt the necessity to keep my knowledge of UK law (and – even more important for a continental lawyer – of English legal terminology) updated. Respectfully, I resorted to the *British Tax Review* and the first piece I ever read in this prestigious journal was Tiley's masterly analysis of common law cases on tax avoidance.[1] I got stuck with the writer and his topic (and the journal) immediately and followed his work (at least insofar as it was published in sources available on the other side of the Channel) during the following years. The first time I started to build my own thoughts on these writings occurred in 1995, when I gave a lecture on tax avoidance and EC law at Bonn University which ventured to set out a common understanding of tax avoidance both from a comparative view of Member States' legal approaches to tax planning and from an autonomous interpretation of EC law.[2] Seven years later, I added a second piece to this mosaic which dealt with the concept of abuse in the ECJ's company law cases.[3] Unfortunately, these presentations were not published in English.

Against this background I regard it to be a lucky hint of providence that the publishers of this book in honour of Tiley proposed to take on the topic of abuse of rights in EC tax law again. I am fully aware of the fact that the following analysis will not be able to compete with the singular composition of elegance, irony and understatement which we find in Tiley's own writings. Moreover, it will not match his ability to *distinguish* the relevant cases with comparable sensitivity. Nevertheless, as he will not

---

[1] Tiley (1987a), Tiley (1987b), Tiley (1988a) and Tiley (1988b).
[2] Schön (1996).   [3] Schön (2002).

expect that degree of refinement in a German lawyer, I will go *in medias res* right now.

4.1 The two levels of legislation

The relevant situations

Any substantive analysis of the 'abuse of law' in the field of EC law has to be aware of the fact that *abuse of rights* can occur at different levels of legislation. In this respect we have to distinguish between the concept of abuse within the framework of primary and secondary EC law, on the one hand, and domestic rules and concepts of tax avoidance, which are tested as to their conformity with EC law, on the other hand.[4] To make things even more complicated, these two perspectives mix whenever the admissibility of a domestic anti-abuse provision depends on its compatibility with an anti-abuse concept at the level of EC law. For further analysis, the following situations have to be taken into account:

- Secondary EC law – in most cases a directive – contains a specific anti-abuse provision. The Member States have implemented the directive in their domestic law. In these cases the compatibility of domestic anti-abuse rules with Community law depends on the interpretation of the anti-abuse provision of the directive by the court. There have been several cases in this respect, starting with *Denkavit* (Art. 3 para. 2, Parent-Subsidiary Directive)[5] and *Leur-Bloem* (Art. 11, Merger-Directive).[6]
- Secondary EC law contains substantive rules which allegedly have been abused by the taxpayer but are not protected by a specific anti-abuse provision. In these cases the compatibility of domestic anti-abuse rules depends on the question whether EC law accepts a general notion of abuse – either by way of purposive interpretation of secondary EC law or as a general concept of EC law. This question has been discussed by the Court since *Meilicke* in 1992 (on the Second Company Law Directive)[7] and has been answered in the affirmative in *Halifax* in 2006 (regarding the Sixth VAT Directive).[8] The Court even went so far to assume that such a general notion of abuse of rights could be relied upon even if we

---

[4] Vanistendael (2006, p. 192).   [5] Case C-283/94 et al. *Denkavit* [1996] ECR I-5063 (ECJ).
[6] Case C-28/95 *Leur–Bloem* [1997] ECR I-4161 (ECJ).
[7] Case C-83/91 *Meilicke* [1992] ECR I-4871 (AG) at paras. 17–21; see also McCarthy (2007, pp. 162–4).
[8] Case C-255/02 *Halifax* [2006] ECR I-1609 (ECJ); see also Case C-32/03 *I/S Fini H* [2005] ECR I-1599 (ECJ).

find a specific anti-abuse provision in the framework of the directive, which – for procedural reasons – was not invoked in the respective case.

• Domestic law contains an anti-abuse provision which denies national treatment to cross-border situations. Such provision has to be examined as to its compatibility with the fundamental freedoms. This topic has been dealt with in ECJ case law quite frequently. As the judicature stands, two interrelated issues have to be addressed: Do the fundamental freedoms protect the transaction chosen by the taxpayer in the first place? And, if this is answered in the affirmative, does the fight against tax avoidance justify the measure taken by the domestic legislator or judge? There are many examples for this kind of test available in the judicature of the Court. Among the best-known cases with UK backgrounds which were recently decided we find *Marks & Spencer* (on cross-border loss compensation),[9] *Cadbury Schweppes* (on CFC legislation)[10] and *Test Claimants in the Thin Cap Group Litigation* (on thin capitalisation).[11]

The relationship between EC law and domestic law

This two-level approach has some specific consequences from the perspective of the application of domestic tax law. To start with, domestic law is not applicable in cases covered by EC law, insofar as it transgresses the boundaries of the concept of abuse under EC law. In this respect, the taxpayer can rely on the framework established under Community law. While it is clear that the fundamental freedoms confer individual rights on the taxpayers,[12] also directives in the tax sector can be invoked in most cases, as they tend to provide for individual entitlements of the taxpayer vis-à-vis the state, which do not leave much discretion to the national legislator.[13] On the other hand, when it comes to the application of domestic anti-abuse provisions which do not fall under the control of the fundamental freedoms (e.g. because they do not distinguish between domestic and cross-border cases) and which do not affect an area of taxation which has been harmonised so far, the Member States are free to employ anti-avoidance concepts which reach beyond the concept of anti-abuse under EC law.

---

[9] Case C-446/03 *Marks & Spencer v Halsey* [2005] ECR I-10837 (ECJ).
[10] Case C-196/04 *Cadbury Schweppes* [2006] ECR I-7995 (ECJ).
[11] Case C-524/04 *Test Claimants in the Thin Cap Group Litigation* [2007] ECR 00 (ECJ).
[12] Case 2/74 *Reyners* [1974] ECR 631 (ECJ) at paras. 24–8.
[13] See Case C-283/94 et al. *Denkavit* [1996] ECR I-5063 (ECJ) at paras. 37–40.

While the taxpayer will in most cases be entitled to rely on EC law against domestic legislation, one should not forget that EC law working to the detriment of the taxpayer is – as a rule – not self-executing. Therefore, insofar as domestic law does not contain an anti-abuse concept at all (or a concept which is more liberal towards the taxpayer than EC law requires), EC law does not step in automatically.[14] To give some examples: if EC law entitles Member States to legislate against the (ab)use of controlled foreign companies under an anti-abuse concept or allows them to introduce thin-capitalisation provisions for the same reason, this leeway for legislation does not affect taxpayers at all, as long as the domestic legislator does not enact provisions which are admissible under the EC concept. Moreover, if and so far as domestic legislation (e.g. UK tax law) does not contain a general anti-abuse rule, EC law does not step in and provide for such a remedy in favour of the tax administration. Community law lays down the boundaries for domestic anti-abuse provisions but does not render their enactment superfluous.

The only (apparent) exception from this rule refers to the necessity to interpret domestic legislation in accordance with EC legislation if domestic tax law is ambiguous on this point. Again, the *Halifax* case is of high relevance. In its judgment, the ECJ has decided that under a general concept of 'abuse of rights' some tax planning is disregarded when it comes to the application of the Sixth VAT Directive.[15] In Germany, the Federal Tax Court has made clear in a judgment that it will apply in such cases the German GAAR (s. 42 of the *Abgabenordnung*), which will be interpreted in accordance with the ECJ's definition of 'abuse of rights'.[16] In Belgium, the Parliament has enacted the anti-abuse rule for the VAT sector following the ECJ's line of reasoning.[17] In the UK, there seems to reign the perception that no statutory implementation is necessary.[18] But the transformation of the *Halifax* decision's merits into domestic law depends on the leeway of UK judges to interpret the British VAT Act 1994 in accordance with the directive (as interpreted by the ECJ). This leeway is not defined by EC law but by the division of powers between Parliament and the judiciary under the unwritten constitution of the UK. If and so far as UK domestic law does not empower the courts to re-characterise

---

[14] Case C-321/05 *Kofoed* [2007] ECR 00 (ECJ) at paras. 40–7.
[15] Case C-255/02 *Halifax* [2006] ECR I-1609 (ECJ) at paras. 67–86.
[16] *Bundesfinanzhof* judgment of 9 November 2006 V R 43/04, 56 Umsatzsteuer-Rundschau (2007) p. 111.
[17] Degadt and van Hoorebeke (2006); for a thorough analysis of this methodological problem see Baltus (2006, p. 348 *et seq.*).
[18] Tailby (2006); Moss and Gillham (2006, p. 5).

particular transactions, EC law is not in the position to overcome this obstacle. The consequence would be that the UK Parliament would be the right institution to implement the ECJ's interpretation of the Sixth VAT Directive including the general anti-abuse concept into English law.

4.2 Principles of 'abuse of rights' under EC law

The locus of the 'abuse of rights' doctrine

The concept of tax avoidance and the application of the 'abuse of rights' doctrine in this context have been discussed in many jurisdictions for decades.[19] The practical part of this debate is devoted to the factual borderline between illegal (tax evasion), abusive (tax avoidance) and acceptable (tax planning) behaviour. From an academic point of view, most writings concern the legal requirements for the application of a doctrine on abuse of rights. While some stress the effectiveness of purposive construction in the fight against tax avoidance, others acknowledge some value-added in a statutory general anti-avoidance rule.[20] The Court has made clear in a strand of judgments which covers many areas of EC law, including taxation, that the application of an anti-abuse doctrine under Community law is deeply related to the aims and goals of the abused or circumvented Community law provisions themselves.[21] It is the purpose of a provision which is essential in order to ascertain which transactions are called abusive and which are not. In this vein, AG Maduro has – in one of the most recent extensive analyses of this point – made clear that the application of the anti-abuse doctrine finds its foundation in the 'interpretation in conformity with the purpose and objectives of Community law'.[22] This holds true both in the field of primary law – most notably the fundamental freedoms – and of secondary law – in particular with reference to the directives in the tax sector.

As the purpose of a legal rule is of paramount importance for the recognition of abuse and circumvention, the specific aims and objectives

---

[19] For a recent treatment in different jurisdictions see: Harris (2007a); Harris (2007b); Leclercq (2007); Locher (2007); Pedroli (2007); and the general report of Zimmer (2002) and the many National Reports in International Fiscal Association (2002). Also see the discussion in Chapter 1.

[20] For the British debate, see Freedman (2004a); Gammie (2006); Hoffmann (2005); and Tiley (2004a).

[21] For example, Case C-436/00 *X and Y* [2002] ECR I-10829 (ECJ) at para. 42; Case C-196/04 *Cadbury Schweppes* [2006] ECR I-7995 (ECJ) at para. 52.

[22] Case C-255/02 *Halifax* [2006] ECR I-1751 (AG) at para. 65; for a seminal analysis of the Court's judicature see Neville Brown (1994).

of Community law give some particular nuances to the European debate. Against this background, it seems advisable to highlight some of the major features of EC law in general as they have been laid down in primary and secondary Community law and as they have been elaborated by the European Court of Justice.

The effectiveness of EC law

The first core element of legal interpretation in the judicature of the European Court of Justice which has to be taken into account refers to the necessity to safeguard the effectiveness and even-handed application of Community law.[23] From its very beginning, the Court has made clear that EC law has to be given *effet utile*, i.e. effective application in order to pursue the goals of the EC Treaty and secondary law.[24] As the scope of the fundamental freedoms and the effectiveness of the harmonisation efforts of directives shall not be undermined by domestic law, any leeway given to domestic legislation in the framework of anti-abuse legislation shall be reduced to a minimum.[25]

In our context, the Court is aware of the danger that domestic legislators might use the general notion of tax avoidance as a means to justify legislative protectionism or to dispense itself from the necessity to implement EC directives in full. This has some practical consequences. First, it seems to be clear that the concept of anti-abuse is handled quite restrictively in areas where the compatibility of domestic anti-abuse provisions has to be tested against primary or secondary EC law.[26] This has led to the assumption that abuse of rights requires an examination of the specific situation the taxpayer is in and does not give way to 'shot gun' provisions.[27] One might also conveniently assume that the tendency of the Court to restrict the application of anti-abuse rules to 'wholly artificial arrangements'[28]

[23] Case C-255/02 *Halifax* [2006] ECR I-1751 (AG) at para. 65.
[24] Case 41/74 *van Duyn* [1974] ECR 337 (ECJ) at para. 12.
[25] Case C-255/02 *Halifax* [2006] ECR I-1751 (AG) at paras. 65 and 89.
[26] Case C-283/94 et al. *Denkavit* [1996] ECR I-5063 (ECJ) at para. 26; Case C-28/95 *Leur-Bloem* [1997] ECR I-4161 (ECJ) at para. 40.
[27] Case C-324/00 *Lankhorst-Hohorst* [2002] ECR I-11779 (ECJ) at para. 37; Case C-28/95 *Leur-Bloem* [1997] ECR I-4161 (ECJ) at paras. 41 and 44; Case C-436/00 *X and Y* [2002] ECR I-10829 (ECJ) at para. 42.
[28] Case C-264/96 *ICI* [1998] ECR I-4695 (ECJ) at para. 26; Case C-196/04 *Cadbury Schweppes* [2006] ECR I-7995 (ECJ) at para. 51; Case C-324/00 *Lankhorst-Hohorst* [2002] ECR I-11779 (ECJ) at para. 37; Case C-524/04 *Test Claimants in the Thin Cap Group Litigation* [2007] ECR 00 (ECJ) at para. 72.

has to be understood in the same vein. On the other hand, in order to avoid uncontrolled discretion for domestic tax authorities when the existence of abuse has to be ascertained, the criteria laid down for abuse of rights must be 'objective', i.e. 'verifiable' for third parties.[29] When it comes to the application of domestic procedures on evidence, the effectiveness of Community law enforcement has to be guaranteed.[30] Again, the aim of the ECJ is to minimise the effect anti-abuse rules might have on the effectiveness of EC law and to limit hidden protectionism coming under the disguise of 'anti-avoidance' rules.

On the other hand, the Court is much more at ease when it comes to the application of anti-abuse concepts within the framework of EC law itself.[31] Insofar as EC law as such – either in the context of a specific anti-avoidance rule or as a general concept of law – refers to anti-abuse as a limit to the taxpayer's entitlements, the effectiveness of EC law requires an even-handed application of a given rule or concept but not necessarily a very restricted interpretation. Therefore, in *Halifax* the Court did not hesitate to apply a pretty broad anti-abuse concept to the Sixth VAT Directive – as long as it is handled evenly across the European Union.[32] Moreover, some of the anti-abuse provisions which we find in secondary EC law do not even fulfil the requirements which the Court has laid down for domestic legislation which is tested under the fundamental freedoms. To give an example, Art. 3(2) of the Parent-Subsidiary Directive provides that the benefits of this directive cannot be invoked by the taxpayer for dividend payments if the minimum holding period of two years is not fulfilled.[33] Such a blunt two-year rule would surely not be accepted by the Court if proposed by domestic legislators because it would not take into account the particularities of a case, would not require the 'artificial nature' of a

---

[29] Case C-524/04 *Test Claimants in the Thin Cap Group Litigation* [2007] ECR 00 (ECJ) at para. 81; Case C-255/02 *Halifax* [2006] ECR I-1751 (AG) at paras. 65 and 89.

[30] Case C-255/02 *Halifax* [2006] ECR I-1609 (ECJ) at para. 76; Case C-110/99 *Emsland-Stärke* [2000] ECR I-11569 (ECJ) at para. 54.

[31] It should be noted, however, that the Court does not cleanly distinguish between cases where domestic anti-abuse provisions are tested and cases where the anti-abuse doctrine is immediately applied to EC law (see for example Case C-478/98 *Commission v. Belgium* [2000] ECR I-7589 (ECJ) at para. 45).

[32] See Case C-255/02 *Halifax* [2006] ECR I-1751 (AG) at para. 79: 'Moreover, the application of this Community principle of interpretation fully respects the objective of uniform application of VAT rules in all Member States that underlies the procedural conditions and limits on the adoption of national measures designed to prevent certain types of tax evasion or avoidance imposed by Article 27.' See also Lang (2006, p. 179) and Vanistendael (2006, p. 195).

[33] See Case C-283/94 et al. *Denkavit* [1996] ECR I-5063 (ECJ) at paras. 23–36.

transaction and does not give the taxpayer the right to prove the genuine economic substance of the transaction. Nevertheless, as it stands, the European legislator has more leeway to shape anti-abuse provisions than the national legislator who seeks to free itself from the requirements of EC law by invoking abusive situations.

The aim to establish the internal market

The necessity to effectuate the provisions of the EC Treaty and of secondary EC law is not an end in itself. These provisions have been introduced to further the paramount goal of the Treaty, i.e. the establishment of an internal market (Arts. 3(c) and 14, EC Treaty). This market is meant to ensure optimal allocation of resources within the European Union (Art. 98, EC Treaty). Therefore, it requires a free flow of persons, goods, services and capital within the territory of the European Union (and in many situations even beyond).[34] Against this background, it will be up to the individual citizen to decide what to produce and what to consume and how to organise one's affairs. This includes the freedom to set up companies, to establish branches and to choose the most efficient organisational and legal structure for business entities and to allocate assets, personnel and risks to the respective entities.[35] The functioning of the internal market requires this fundamental freedom of choice.

This freedom of choice lies at the heart of many of the provisions which we find in primary and secondary EC law. The fundamental freedoms are meant to ensure that the choice between domestic and cross-border investment is not distorted by domestic law, including tax law. Therefore, also the concept of anti-avoidance shall not be employed in order to create new distortions which are not in line with the free flow of resources envisaged by the internal market[36]. Moreover, the directives of the European Community in the framework of tax legislation are meant to support this basic freedom: The Parent-Subsidiary Directive and the Interest-Royalty Directive have been enacted in order to relieve the payment of dividends, interest and royalties in cross-border groups of companies from a distorting withholding tax; the Merger Directive has been conceived in order to pull down tax barriers to cross-border restructurings of international

---

[34] Schön (2000, p. 91).   [35] Schön (2006a).
[36] Case C-436/00 *X and Y* [2002] ECR I-10829 (ECJ) at para. 42; Case C-196/04 *Cadbury Schweppes* [2006] ECR I-7995 (ECJ) at para. 52; Vanistendael (2006, p. 194).

enterprises. These directives are built on the assumption that the freedom to organise a business cross-border rather than domestically shall not be subject to obstacles in the tax area.[37] Therefore, anti-abuse provisions under these directives have to be interpreted narrowly in order to enhance the tax framework for cross-border restructurings.

A similar reference to the aims of the internal market is made in the directives on VAT which try to establish 'neutrality' as to the production and consumption of goods and services within the territory of the European Union.[38] Again, the concept of neutrality is equivalent to freedom of choice – the taxpayer will be entitled to arrange his or her affairs the way he or she sees fit without any distortions from the tax side. Any 'transactions which are carried out in the context of normal commercial operations'[39] shall be recognised, as the VAT rules must be 'defined in such a way as not to affect legitimate trade'.[40] If and so far as this choice is treated as abusive this decision has to be justified in the light of the aims of the internal market.

This last remark leads us back to the heart of the tax avoidance problem. The economic theory which is the cornerstone of the internal market (including the fundamental freedoms and secondary EC tax law) aims at an effective freedom of choice for the taxpayer. This means that the choice of the taxpayer to arrange his (or her) affairs is in general protected under EC law. Any restriction to this freedom which might lead to a distortion of this choice and thus impedes the free flow of goods and services which is meant to enhance the allocation of resources within the European Union is in general forbidden under EC law.

---

[37] Case C-283/94 et al. *Denkavit* [1996] ECR I-5063 (ECJ) at para. 22 (Parent-Subsidiary Directive); Case C-28/95 *Leur-Bloem* [1997] ECR I-4161 (ECJ) at para. 45 (Merger Directive): 'Such an interpretation is consistent with the aims both of the Directive and of Article 11 thereof. According to the first recital of its preamble, the aim of the Directive is to introduce tax rules which are neutral from the point of view of competition in order to allow enterprises to adapt themselves to the requirements of the common market, to increase their productivity and to improve their competitive strength at the international level. That same recital also states that mergers, divisions, transfers of assets and exchanges of shares concerning companies of different Member States ought not to be hampered by restrictions, disadvantages or distortions arising in particular from the tax provisions of the Member States. It is only when the planned operation has as its objective tax evasion or tax avoidance that, according to Article 11 and the last recital of the preamble to the Directive, the Member States may refuse to apply the Directive.'

[38] Case C-255/02 *Halifax* [2006] ECR I-1609 (ECJ) at para. 78.

[39] Case C-255/02 *Halifax* [2006] ECR I-1609 (ECJ) at para. 69.

[40] Case C-255/02 *Halifax* [2006] ECR I-1751 (AG) at para. 86.

4.3 Abuse of rights in the field of the fundamental freedoms

Against this background, the analysis of abuse of rights under EC law can be reformulated as the question of which choices by the taxpayer can be disregarded and which choices have to be respected when it comes to the application of tax law. This holds specifically true in the area of the fundamental freedoms, where the basic liberty of the European citizens refers to the decision to arrange commercial affairs either in a domestic setting or at the cross-border level. What does this basic choice mean for the application of abuse of rights in tax matters?

No free choice of applicable law

In this respect, the Court has made clear in matters of company law that the citizens of the European Union have the fundamental right to choose which legal order shall apply to his or her economic activities. In the field of company law, the Court has ruled in *Centros*,[41] *Überseering*[42] and *Inspire Art*[43] that economic agents are free to set up a company wherever in Europe they want and to carry on a business under the legal order governing this company. It is not regarded as abusive to set up a company in the UK which is not meant to do any business in the UK; to the contrary, the Court regards this choice of the applicable law to be at the core of the freedom of establishment as protected under Arts. 43 and 48 of the EC Treaty.

In the field of tax law, nobody would expect the internal market to simply provide for a free choice for taxpayers to opt for the most agreeable tax environment. The sovereignty of Member States in tax matters includes their entitlement to define a taxable event by compulsory provisions. Taxation is as a matter of principle not subject to menu-like check-the-box procedures but refers to the statutory nexus as provided by citizenship, residence or economic activity. The fundamental freedoms do not protect the taxpayer's wish to simply elect the relevant tax law for his or her tax assessment. Otherwise, the 'balanced allocation of taxing powers' in the European Union would be endangered.

The Court has accepted the necessity to defend national tax jurisdiction against mere options of taxation in *Marks & Spencer*[44] and, recently, in

---

[41] Case C-212/97 *Centros* [1999] ECR I-1459 (ECJ) at paras. 23–7.
[42] Case C-208/00 *Überseering* [2002] ECR I-9919 (ECJ) at paras. 78–82.
[43] Case C-167/01 *Inspire Art* [2003] ECR I-10155 (ECJ) at paras. 95–105.
[44] Case C-446/03 *Marks & Spencer v Halsey* [2005] ECR I-10837 (ECJ) at para. 51.

Oy AA.[45] In these cases, the ECJ did not support the taxpayer's choice to allocate a given amount of losses freely among companies of a group, thus enabling the parent company to 'use' the losses – irrespective of their territorial origin – in the jurisdiction where the tax level is the highest. It cannot be accepted that groups of companies could 'choose freely the Member State in which the profits of the subsidiary are taxed'.[46] They shall not be enabled 'to transfer their profits and losses from one Member State to another to suit their convenience',[47] e.g. by 'merely adjusting the accounts'.[48] To put it the other way round: as long as Member States have the power to define the taxable event and the taxable person, the taxpayer is not in the position to opt-out and submit himself to another tax jurisdiction.

Free choice of nexus to a jurisdiction

The Court has decided quite frequently that the taxpayer may choose to disrupt nexus and to transfer his or her residence and/or economic activities to another state.[49] The result will be that the taxable event will not occur any more in the home state but in the host state. The Court has made clear, from the beginning of its judicature in direct tax matters, that simple loss of revenue stemming from such relocation does not justify any tax-driven legislative obstacle against free movement of goods, services, persons and capital within the European Union.[50] There is no circumvention if taxes are not paid in the home state but in the host state.[51]

From the point of view of abusive behaviour, it is important to notice that the taxpayer will even be free to relocate economic activities to another Member State with the explicit aim of enjoying the lower tax burden which does exist there.[52] A taxpayer may move his residence to the UK or transfer

---

[45] Case C-231/04 *Oy AA* [2007] ECR 00 (ECJ) at para. 55.
[46] Case C-231/04 *Oy AA* [2007] ECR 00 (ECJ) at para. 56.
[47] Case C-196/04 *Cadbury Schweppes* [2006] ECR I-7995 (AG) at para. 102.
[48] Case C-196/04 *Cadbury Schweppes* [2006] ECR I-7995 (AG) at para. 108.
[49] Case C-9/02 *Hughes de Lasteyrie de Saillant* [2004] ECR I-2409 (ECJ) at para. 51 (transfer of residence by an individual); Case C-436/00 *X and Y* [2002] ECR I-10829 (ECJ) at para. 44 (transfer of shares abroad); Case C-264/96 *ICI* [1998] ECR I-4695 (ECJ) at para. 26 (setting-up of foreign subsidiary); Case C-324/00 *Lankhorst-Hohorst* [2002] ECR I-11779 (ECJ) at para. 37 (setting-up of foreign subsidiary).
[50] Case C-264/96 *ICI* [1998] ECR I-4695 (ECJ) at para. 28.
[51] Case C-264/96 *ICI* [1998] ECR I-4695 (ECJ) at para. 26; Case C-324/00 *Lankhorst-Hohorst* [2002] ECR I-11779 (ECJ) at para. 37.
[52] Case C-196/04 *Cadbury Schweppes* [2006] ECR I-7995 (ECJ) at paras. 36 and 49; Leclercq (2007, p. 242); Vinther and Werlauff (2006).

a factory to Estonia simply in order to save taxes. As the intention of this move seems to be specifically aimed at tax avoidance, this needs further clarification.

This topic is deeply intertwined with the concept of tax competition between Member States. The goal of the internal market is to set up an area where goods, services, persons and capital can float around in search of the location where they can be employed in the most useful fashion.[53] The outcome of this search was originally meant to follow from the geographical and economic benefits of this location but not from any advantageous tax treatment or other regulatory disparities. The disparities between the tax treatments of economic activities in different countries were regarded as a political obstacle to this ideal market and should be abolished over time by way of harmonisation. Against this background, one might contend that a Member State should have the power to take defensive measures against the relocation of economic activities to other Member States which are simply aimed at tax arbitrage.

In recent decades, however, another view of tax harmonisation has emerged. Tax disparities are regarded to be an expression of sound 'tax competition' which is accepted by the rules of the internal market as long as Member States have not found consensus on an instrument of tax harmonisation. Moreover, tax competition can prove to be beneficial as it exerts a useful pressure on governments to cut back superfluous public expenditure and to offer economic agents an attractive 'cost-benefit-package'. If Member State A succeeds in offering the same amount of public goods to its taxpayers for less tax money, the choice of citizens and businesses from Member State B to join the community of taxpayers in Member State A and to enjoy the good housekeeping of this state can lead to overall efficiency, thus feeding to the optimal allocation of resources as envisaged by the internal market. As EC law wants (or at least accepts) this to happen, no Member State is entitled to prevent its own citizens and businesses from reaping the benefits of tax competition.[54] As tax competition presupposes that citizens allocate their economic activities with a view to the tax burden they face in different jurisdictions, the intention of a taxpayer to save taxes by moving his residence or his economic activities to another Member State cannot be retaliated under the heading of tax avoidance or abusive behaviour. Moreover, no Member State is entitled

---

[53] Schön (2000, p. 92).
[54] Case C-196/04 *Cadbury Schweppes* [2006] ECR I-7995 (AG) at paras. 55, 51, 109 and 116; Case C-524/04 *Test Claimants in the Thin Cap Group Litigation* [2007] ECR 00 (AG) at para. 63; Douma and Engelen (2006, p. 439).

to levy (discriminatory) compensatory taxes which are meant to offset the tax benefits enjoyed in another country.[55] This point has been made quite explicitly by AG Léger in the *Cadbury Schweppes* litigation:

> I do not believe that the fact that a parent company establishes a subsidiary in another Member State for the avowed purpose of enjoying the more favourable tax regime in that State constitutes, in itself, an abuse of freedom of establishment.[56]

This leads to the additional problem of whether Member States have the power to introduce obstacles to cross-border activities whenever the tax disparity between Member States amounts to 'harmful tax competition', as defined by the OECD[57] and the EC[58] in their respective statements on this issue. Again, the application of any anti-abuse doctrine or provision is subject to the institutional framework of the European Union. In the past, extreme expressions of 'harmful tax competition' have been addressed either by application of Community State Aid rules[59] or by political consensus in the form of 'soft law', such as the 'Code of Conduct' from 1997.[60] Against this background, Advocate-Generals Geelhoed[61], Léger[62] and Mengozzi[63] have pointed out that Member States are not in the position to act unilaterally against 'harmful tax competition'. If this is true, the simple fact that the taxpayer arranges his or her affairs to move from a high-tax state to a low-tax state does not in itself justify the application of anti-abuse provisions in the losing Member State even if the tax benefits offered by the host state can substantively be regarded as elements of harmful tax competition.[64]

'Wholly artificial arrangements'

The foregoing analysis has shown that the relevant borderline between respected and disregarded choices runs somewhere between the opposing poles of choice of law on the one hand and choice of nexus on the other.

---

[55] Case C-294/97 *Eurowings* [1999] ECR I-7449 (ECJ) at para. 44.
[56] Case C-196/04 *Cadbury Schweppes* [2006] ECR I-7995 (AG) at para. 40.
[57] OECD (1998).
[58] European Commission (1997). For a recent overview see Bridgland (2006).
[59] Schön (2006b, pp. 275–6).   [60] European Commission (1997).
[61] Case C-524/04 *Test Claimants in the Thin Cap Group Litigation* [2007] ECR 00 (AG) at para. 64.
[62] Case C-196/04 *Cadbury Schweppes* [2006] ECR I-7995 (AG) at paras. 56–8.
[63] Case C-298/05 *Container Columbus Services* [2007] ECR 0 (AG) at paras. 161–200.
[64] Vinther and Werlauff (2006, pp. 385–6).

The main challenge posed by the concept of abuse of law is to examine the grey area where small or irregular economic activity exists but does not suffice to justify the application of substantive Community law, in particular the fundamental freedoms. In the judicature of the Court, these situations have been described as 'wholly artificial arrangements' where the legal reality of the transactions is not in doubt (otherwise they would be qualified as mere 'sham') but where the economic substance is largely missing. In order to assess the scope of the notion of 'wholly artificial arrangements', it is necessary to take a closer look at different groups of cases.

U-turn transactions

The first category of cases concerns situations where economic activity exists which has no enduring character but is cancelled out in a second step. The ECJ had to deal with this kind of 'U-turn transaction'[65] quite often when parties set up an international operation in order to cater to their home market. In the seminal case *van Binsbergen*,[66] a Dutch lawyer set up an office in Belgium only in order to get easier access to the courts in the Netherlands. In other cases, export and ensuing import of goods was used to take advantage of beneficial rules which were applicable to cross-border sales.[67] The Court has declared these transactions to be abusive and not covered by the fundamental freedoms (or relevant secondary law).

A case in point from the tax perspective is *Hughes de Lasteyrie de Saillant*.[68] French law provided for an exit tax on unrealised capital gains in shareholdings if taxpayers left the country only to sell the shares abroad and to return to France afterwards. The Court accepted the view that this sort of behaviour might amount to abuse and thus be counteracted by domestic legislation.[69] The French rule, however, did not pass the test of proportionality: as the exit tax was levied without any examination of the particular circumstances if the taxpayer returned within a five-year period the Court held that this was not narrowly focused on U-turn transactions but could also cover situations where a real shift of residence was achieved but – due to changed circumstances – later revoked.

---

[65] Case C-255/02 *Halifax* [2006] ECR I-1751 (AG) at para. 66.
[66] Case 33/74 *van Binsbergen* [1974] ECR 1299 (ECJ) at para. 13.
[67] See (among others) Case C-8/92 *General Milk Products* [1993] ECR I-779 (ECJ); Case C-110/99 *Emsland-Stärke* [2000] ECR I-11569 (ECJ).
[68] Case C-9/02 *Hughes de Lasteyrie de Saillant* [2004] ECR I-2409 (ECJ).
[69] Case C-9/02 *Hughes de Lasteyrie de Saillant* [2004] ECR I-2409 (ECJ) at para. 54.

This case clearly shows the meaning of abuse in the context of the fundamental freedoms: as the optimal allocation of resources within the internal market will be enhanced, any effective relocation of goods, services, persons and capital will be protected. This means that any transactions executed in the course of normal commercial relationships fall under the scope of the internal market.[70] Such relocation does simply not occur if the transaction is cancelled out immediately after it has been executed. Therefore, the acknowledgement that U-turn arrangements do not fall under the protection of the fundamental freedoms is related to the basic goal of the internal market to enhance the framework for genuine economic choices taken by economic subjects. Again, abuse of law and purposive interpretation meet each other.

Company formation

A special case concerns company formations. This is due to the legal framework EC company law provides for the recognition of companies.[71] Under the rules of the First Directive on European Company Law from 1968, a company registered under the laws of a Member State cannot be declared void because it has been set up for fraudulent or other legally doubtful purposes. Legal certainty requires that a company which has come into existence and entered into contractual and other obligations shall not disappear before the eyes of its creditors and other trading partners. Therefore, the formation of a company in a foreign country is as a rule accepted under European law and leads to a genuine cross-border situation. Again, even tax law is not in the position to dispute the legal existence of the company, the property it has acquired and the liabilities it is subject to. Moreover, the simple fact that a company has been set up in order to save taxes is not giving way to the application of anti-abuse rules in itself. No anti-abuse rules may be applied where 'despite the existence of tax motives, the incorporation of a CFC reflects economic reality'.[72]

Against this background, it is not easy to ascertain whether the setting-up of a company can be disregarded under the concept of abuse for tax purposes at all. To be sure, tax legislation is not obliged to follow company law insofar as the jurisdiction to tax is at stake: while company law rules

---

[70] Case C-8/92 *General Milk Products* [1993] ECR I-779 (ECJ) at para. 21.
[71] See Schön (2002, p. 1292).
[72] Case C-196/04 *Cadbury Schweppes* [2006] ECR I-7995 (ECJ) at para. 65.

are dependent on the place of incorporation, tax rules tend to look at the place of management instead. Therefore, the simple establishment of a 'letter-box' company in Member State A, which is managed out of Member State B, does not call into question Member State B's jurisdiction to tax the profits of this company and therefore does not require the application of some abuse of rights concept.

The main field of application for the abuse of law doctrine is CFC-legislation which provides for a 'look-through' approach with regard to foreign-based companies engaged in certain activities. In this context, the Court has reiterated its formula that 'wholly artificial arrangements' are not protected against discriminating tax provisions.[73] But what does this mean? Against the background that CFC legislation only makes sense where the foreign subsidiary is not subject to domestic corporate income tax, we have to ask whether a company which is legally registered and effectively managed abroad can still be 'artificial' in the sense of the ECJ judicature.

Taking into account the basic goal of the fundamental freedoms to enhance mutual penetration of markets within the European Union, the decisive 'test' should be whether the company is integrated in the market of its host country at all. This has been made clear by the Court as early as 1991 in the famous *Factortame* litigation.[74] In *Cadbury Schweppes* the Court described the scope of Art. 43 EC as covering the 'actual pursuit of an economic activity through a fixed establishment for an indefinite period'.[75] The subsidiary has to 'participate, on a stable and continuing basis, in the economic life of a Member State'.[76] Taking a closer look, such 'integration' can be twofold. A first test would require the company to supply goods or services or capital to the market of the country where it is located.[77] Under this test, an 'artificial arrangement' could be ascertained if the company only caters to markets outside its country of registration, e.g. a service company providing services only to the parent company or a holding company investing only in international securities. Yet this test is incomplete, as it does not take into account the economic impact of a company as a customer to domestic business. If the examined subsidiary rents out premises in its host country and hires employees among the

---

[73] Case C-196/04 *Cadbury Schweppes* [2006] ECR I-7995 (ECJ) at para. 55 and [2006] ECR I-7995 (AG) at para. 108.
[74] Case C-221/89 *Factortame* [1991] ECR I-3905 (ECJ) at para. 20.
[75] Case C-196/04 *Cadbury Schweppes* [2006] ECR I-7995 (ECJ) at paras. 54 and 66.
[76] Case C-196/04 *Cadbury Schweppes* [2006] ECR I-7995 (ECJ) at para. 53.
[77] Simpson (2006, pp. 682–3).

inhabitants of this country, it uses economic resources available in this country and thus effectuates the integration into a foreign market which is required to get protected under the rules of the internal market. In this vein, the Court stresses the necessity that the subsidiary has got 'premises, staff and equipment',[78] even if the object of the company is to supply intra-group services to the parent company which is located in another jurisdiction.

If we accept that the prerequisite of market integration is fulfilled if a company uses resources available in its state of registration, it will be extremely hard to find a company which can be called 'artificial' although it has its effective management (and thus office space and at least one employee – the company's director) in the country of registration. The debate in recent literature, how many fax machines and secretaries you need to be fully established under Art. 43 of the EC Treaty,[79] shows that the 'artificiality' test does not lead us anywhere. It should be accepted that the tax concept of 'effective management' suffices to prove that a foreign-based company is not an 'artificial arrangement' in this sense.[80]

Recharacterisation of contractual obligations

A second area of 'choice' refers to the contractual obligations which a taxpayer enters into. Depending on the nature of these obligations, the tax consequences may differ. A case in point is 'thin capitalisation', where a foreign parent company decides to grant a loan to its domestic subsidiary rather than contributing equity. As the payment of interest is regarded as deductible cost while the payment of dividends is subject to corporate income tax at the level of the subsidiary, this might lead to a shift of revenue from the Member State where the subsidiary is located to the Member State where the parent company is resident.

As a rule, the choice between debt and equity evolves from the concept that any economic agent is free to arrange his or her economic affairs within the European Union. As this choice may affect the efficiency

---

[78] Case C-196/04 *Cadbury Schweppes* [2006] ECR I-7995 (ECJ) at para. 67.
[79] Leclercq (2007, p. 243) wants to consider the 'proportionality' between the services provided and the resources used by the subsidiary.
[80] In this respect, the remark by the Court that 'letter-box' companies could be disregarded as abusive (Case C-196/04 *Cadbury Schweppes* [2006] ECR I-7995 (ECJ) at para. 68) is not very helpful, as these companies can be tackled without having resort to CFC legislation; see also Leclercq (2007, p. 243).

of a firm's financial structure, thus leading to a better allocation of resources within the European Union, it is in general protected under the fundamental freedoms.[81] Therefore, a Member State is not in the position simply to recharacterise debt contracts as equity contributions (unless the same recharacterisation does apply to domestic loan arrangements).[82] Against this background, the Court has – in *Test Claimants in the Thin Cap Group Litigation* – asked whether such a shareholder loan arrangement can be regarded as a wholly artificial arrangement in the abovementioned sense.[83] If so, the interest payments would be regarded to be 'in reality profit distributions'.[84] The Court reiterates the distinction explained above, i.e. that while such arrangements are in general recognised as valid, the taxpayer is not in the position to simply opt for a jurisdiction and therefore the 'economic reality' of the arrangement has to be examined.

As we have seen before, this test requires that the contractual arrangement between the parties can be regarded as valid commercial activity under the protection of the internal market. Therefore, it has to be entered as 'under normal competitive conditions',[85] i.e. it has to meet the arm's-length standard.[86] As the arm's-length test refers to the contractual situation which would have arisen under free competition between independent economic agents (this is actually the translation of 'arm's-length' given in the German version of the judgment) the ECJ regards any deviant agreement between parent and subsidiary to be not in line with the efficiency criteria of the internal market. To put it another way, as a loan agreement which does not meet the arm's-length standard does not contribute to the efficient allocation of resources (in this case capital) which will be enhanced by the free play of the market forces, it is regarded as artificial and not protected under the fundamental freedoms of the EC Treaty. Any Member State is free to re-characterise such debt as equity under its thin-capitalisation rules.

---

[81] Case C-524/04 *Test Claimants in the Thin Cap Group Litigation* [2007] ECR 00 (AG) at para. 66.

[82] Case C-324/00 *Lankhorst-Hohorst* [2002] ECR I-11779 (ECJ) at para. 37.

[83] Case C-524/04 *Test Claimants in the Thin Cap Group Litigation* [2007] ECR 00 (ECJ) at para. 74.

[84] *Ibid.*, at para. 64.

[85] Case C-196/04 *Cadbury Schweppes* [2006] ECR I-7995 (AG) at para. 108 (for services provided by a subsidiary to the parent company).

[86] Case C-524/04 *Test Claimants in the Thin Cap Group Litigation* [2007] ECR 00 (ECJ) paras. 80–92.

Relevance of the taxpayer's intention

Having recognised that the taxpayer's intention to save taxes is no valid argument when it comes to the justification of Member States' legislation against abusive practices in cross-border transactions, one can reach the provisional conclusion that the taxpayer's state of mind is in general without any relevance for the application of the fundamental freedoms. Only the question of whether there is genuine economic activity taking place may be put forward in order to find out whether a cross-border transaction is protected by the relevant provisions of the EC Treaty. If there are, however, 'wholly artificial arrangements' to be found, a Member State is entitled to disregard them by applying the doctrine or specific provisions against abusive behaviour of taxpayers.

Nevertheless, there may be a few situations where the subjective element does play a limited role. This is the case if a transaction was started bona fide by the taxpayer but had to be aborted after a short time or – for some other reason – does not meet the criteria of regular commercial transactions. If this is the case, the taxpayer must be in the position to prove that there were valid commercial reasons for the apparently artificial arrangement.[87] Therefore, we have two cases to distinguish: if there is a valid commercial activity, the taxpayer's intention is irrelevant; if there is no arm's-length transaction at hand, the taxpayer is still in the position to prove that he or she acted in good faith, i.e. intended to pursue a genuine economic activity. This becomes clear when we look at the goal of the internal market to extend the scope of 'choices' available to the taxpayer. The acknowledgement of these choices should not depend on the fact whether they are successful or not but on the bona fide character of the choice to enter into genuine commercial transactions.

4.4 Abuse of rights in the field of tax directives

Relevance of free choice in secondary EC law

We have seen in the foregoing analysis that the fundamental freedoms prevent a Member State from applying anti-abuse doctrines or provisions in order to fight the relocation of economic activities to other Member States, even if the taxpayer's explicit goal is to get rid of taxation in his or her home state. This is due to the fact that while the taxpayer is not in the position simply to elect the applicable tax law, he or she may shift genuine

---

[87] *Ibid.*, at para. 82.

economic activities to another jurisdiction in order to enjoy beneficial tax treatment.

Also in the area of tax directives the concept of abuse can be defined by reference to the range of choices a taxpayer is entitled to use. This has been laid out in clear words by AG Poiares Maduro in the *Halifax* case, concerning input VAT. In his elaborate opinion, AG Poiares Maduro refers to what he calls the 'objective element' of abusive behaviour:

> It is in fact a teleological element whereby the purpose and objectives of the Community rules allegedly being abused are compared with the purpose and results achieved by the activity at issue. This second element is important, not only because it provides the standard upon which the purpose and results of the activity in question are to be assessed. *It also provides a safeguard for those instances where the sole purpose of the activity might be to diminish tax liability but where that purpose is actually a result of a choice between different tax regimes that the Community legislature intended to leave open.* Therefore, where there is no contradiction between recognition of the claim made by the taxable person and the aims and results pursued by the legal provision invoked, no abuse can be asserted.[88]

Again, it is recognised that there are choices between different tax regimes 'that the Community legislature intended to leave open' and others which are not. Therefore, we have to ascertain for each and every provision of secondary EC law whether it was enacted to give a certain option to the taxpayer or whether the right he or she claims runs afoul of the aims and results of the directive. Moreover, the Court in *Halifax* accepted the view that –

> the Sixth Directive does not require him [the taxpayer] to choose the one [transaction] which involves paying the highest amount of VAT. On the contrary, as the Advocate General observed in para 85 of his opinion, taxpayers may choose to structure their business so as to limit their tax liability.[89]

We can safely assume that this holds true for other directives in the tax area as well: tax planning as such is a legitimate aim but which has to be achieved by legitimate tools.[90] But where does the train stop?

In the *Halifax* case the question was whether a tax-exempt entity, which was not entitled to claim refunds for input VAT, could achieve this result by an intermediate subsidiary which was meant to supply taxable services

---

[88] Case C-255/02 *Halifax* [2006] ECR I-1751 (AG) at para. 88.
[89] Case C-255/02 *Halifax* [2006] ECR I-1609 (ECJ) at para. 73.
[90] Makkus & de Preter (2006, p. 17); Ridsdale (2006, p. 11).

to the tax-exempt entity and to claim large upfront input VAT deductions for its investments. AG Poiares Maduro and the Court did not accept this arrangement to be recognised as one possible 'choice' which a person can make in order to gain tax benefits. A similar case in point is *Leur-Bloem*, which deals with the benefits of the Merger Directive. This directive aims at facilitating cross-border restructurings of enterprises by doing away with capital gains taxation on particular types of mergers, divisions, transfers of assets and exchanges of shares. When this directive was implemented in the Netherlands, its scope was extended to regular domestic cases but not to companies which did not carry on any business. This restriction was tested against Art. 11 of the Merger Directive, which provides that:

> A Member State may refuse to apply or withdraw the benefit . . . where it appears that the merger, division, transfer of assets or exchange of shares:
>
> (a) has as its principal objective or as one of its principal objectives tax evasion or tax avoidance; the fact that one of the operations referred to in Article 1 is not carried out for valid commercial reasons such as the restructuring or rationalization of the activities of the companies participating in the operation may constitute a presumption that the operation has tax evasion or tax avoidance as its principal objective or as one of its principal objectives . . .

While the Court held that the general denial of the directive's capital gains treatment for non-active companies was exceeding the situation covered by Art. 11, it gave some hints as to the interpretation of this provision in other cases. On the one hand, it made clear that tax-driven restructurings can fall under the scope of the Merger Directive.[91] Therefore, the simple aim to save taxes by restructuring the enterprise does not immediately lead to an application of Art. 11. On the other hand, the Court reached the conclusion that a merger with an inactive company which was only executed in order to achieve a horizontal setting-off of losses was not a 'valid commercial reason' under Art. 11 of the Merger Directive.[92] Therefore, the domestic legislator was entitled to exclude such merger from the benefits of the directive, i.e. the relief from capital gains taxation.

As the diversity of the provisions which we find in secondary EC law is quite large, so are the 'choices' granted to taxpayers and the scope of their freedom has to be ascertained in each and every case. Of course, the liberty granted to the taxpayer will be more extensive when directives aim

---

[91] Case C-28/95 *Leur-Bloem* [1997] ECR I-4161 (ECJ) at para. 36.
[92] *Ibid.*, at paras. 46–8.

at facilitating cross-border economic activities, which is specifically true in the field of direct taxation covered by the Parent-Subsidiary Directive, the Merger Directive and the Interest-Royalty-Directive.[93] On the other hand, in the field of VAT and specific consumption taxes, EC law tries to establish a whole tax system which has to be protected against abusive behaviour and where a 'level playing-field' for economic operators urges for broad-based taxation of goods and services. Therefore, the freedom of choice might be more restricted in this area.[94]

Moreover, unlike in the area of fundamental freedoms, where only 'wholly artificial arrangements' can be treated as abusive, the Court has accepted in *Halifax* that also genuine economic activities which have been arranged in order to achieve some beneficial tax result may be disregarded under an anti-abuse doctrine.[95] In this case, the interposition of a subsidiary which was established in order to supply taxable services and to deduct corresponding input VAT was not a 'sham' and it was not devoid of any economic reality. Yet it was an arrangement which did not follow ordinary commercial behaviour and was thus disregarded for VAT purposes.

Intention to save taxes

While the Court has made clear, in the context of the fundamental freedoms, that the taxpayer's intention to save taxes by relocating resources to other Member States is protected by EC law, the same cannot be said when it comes to the application of the tax provisions enshrined in the tax directives of the European Community.[96] As has been said above, not all tax-driven activity is covered by the benefits enshrined in tax directives. To the contrary, outside the area of the fundamental freedoms the aim to save taxes is of high importance for the application of the anti-abuse doctrine. This is due to the fact that the concept of tax competition is restricted to

---

[93] Rousselle & Liebman (2006).   [94] Vanistendael (2006, p. 195).
[95] Case C-255/02 [2006] ECR I-1609 (ECJ). The Court is not unambiguous on this point. While it recognises the chosen transactions as genuine 'economic activity' under Art. 4 of the Sixth Directive (at paras. 48–60) it requests the national court to 'determine the real substance and significance of the transactions concerned' in order to assess the abusive character of the transaction: 'In so doing, it may take account of the purely artificial nature of those transactions and the links of a legal, economic and/or personal nature between the operators involved in the scheme for reduction of the tax burden' (at para. 81). One cannot hide the feeling that the Court did not exactly know what sort of test the national judge would have to apply.
[96] Lang (2006, p. 279); Vanistendael (2006, p. 195); for the opposite view see Douma and Engelen (2006, p. 440).

the choice of nexus in international tax affairs; it does not cover all sorts of tax-saving devices within a certain tax jurisdiction. Seeking tax arbitrage is only legitimate 'where that purpose is actually a result of the choice between different tax regimes that the Community legislation intended to leave open'.[97]

According to this concept, the Court held in *Leur Bloem* that it is necessary for the enjoyment of the directive's benefits that the taxpayer has acted in order to pursue a genuine commercial aim.[98] A similar stance was taken by the Court in *Emsland-Stärke*, which does not explicitly refer to direct or indirect tax but rather to premiums paid in the agricultural sector. In this judgment the Court held that a subjective element is necessary to establish abuse, i.e. 'the intention to obtain an advantage from Community rules by creating artificially the conditions laid down for obtaining it'.[99] In *Halifax*, which dealt with deductibility of input VAT, the Court finally made clear that the taxpayer's intention to save taxes lies at the heart of the concept of abuse in the area of tax directives. According to the ECJ, 'it must be apparent from a number of objective factors that the essential aim of the transactions concerned is to obtain a tax advantage'.[100]

According AG Poiares Maduro, this subjective element has to be distinguished as follows: as it may prove to be unhelpful to examine the taxable person's 'state of mind', one should rather resort to the question of whether 'the relevant economic activity carried out has no other objective explanation than to create that claim against the tax authorities'.[101] That purpose – AG Poiares Maduro writes – 'which must not be confused with the subjective intention of the participants in those activities – is to be objectively determined on the basis of any other economic justification for the activity than that of creating a tax advantage'.[102] By this distinction, AG Poiares Maduro tries to come to terms with the (somewhat hypothetical) situation that a taxpayer acts upon the advice of another person (who has tax advantages in mind) but is not aware of the tax consequences

[97] Case C-255/02 *Halifax* [2006] ECR I-1751 (AG) at para. 88.
[98] Case C-28/95 *Leur-Bloem* [1997] ECR I-4161 (ECJ) at paras. 39–45.
[99] Case C-110/99 *Emsland-Stärke* [2000] ECR I-11569 (ECJ) at para. 53.
[100] Case C-255/02 *Halifax* [2006] ECR I-1609 (ECJ) at para. 75; for a critical assessment of the practical merits of this advice see de la Feria (2006a, pp. 30–2); moreover, it is widely discusses whether the Court wanted to introduce a distinction between the 'sole' purpose and the 'essential' purpose of a transaction (de la Feria (2006b, pp. 122–3); Makkus and de Preter (2006, p. 16); Vanistendael (2006, p. 195)). Again, the author's impression is that the Court did not mint its words in such a sophisticated manner as to justify these fine lines.
[101] Case C-255/02 *Halifax* [2006] ECR I-1751 (AG) at para. 86.
[102] Case C-255/02 *Halifax* [2006] ECR I-1751 (AG) at para. 87.

himself. Yet this – rather far-fetched – distinction should not divert our eyes from the fact that in 99 per cent of the relevant cases we are looking for the aims and motives of the taxpayer him- or herself when we try to ascertain whether this subjective element is given with respect to the taxpayer's transactions. Therefore, one should not in principle deviate from the basic assumption that abusive behaviour in the area of tax directives requires an intention to save taxes as opposed to valid commercial reasons which are accepted for the transactions executed by the taxpayer and his contractual partners.

Conclusion

The foregoing analysis has attempted to improve our perception of the way the European Court of Justice employs the concept of anti-abuse doctrine in tax cases. In order to identify the underlying theory we have focused on the topic of 'choice', i.e. we have examined the hitherto published cases according to the question of which choices are accepted and which choices are disregarded under primary and secondary EC law. In the field of the fundamental freedoms it seems to be clear that, while there is no simple 'choice of law' for taxpayers, the freedom to shift economic activities between Member States is undisputed and cannot be counteracted by relying on anti-abuse provisions or concepts. Therefore, only 'wholly artificial arrangements', where no real economic activity is executed, can be regarded as abusive as they are not covered by the fundamental freedoms at all.

In the field of secondary EC law, the application of anti-abuse concepts depends on the range of choices which is left to the taxpayer under the relevant provisions of directives in the tax sector. While the tax directives in the field of direct taxation show a tendency to extend the liberty of the taxpayer and plead therefore for a narrow notion of anti-abuse, the directives in the field of indirect taxation try to establish a fully equipped tax system and are therefore more easily accessible for the application of broad based anti-abuse concepts. Not only wholly artificial arrangements but those transactions which are executed with the intention to save taxes but are not fully covered by the 'freedom of choice' granted by Community legislation can be disregarded under this broader concept. Nevertheless, the Court does fully accept the existence of tax planning as such: 'Taxpayers may choose to structure their business so as to limit their tax liability.'[103]

[103] Case C-255/02 *Halifax* [2006] ECR I-1609 (ECJ) at para. 73.

5

The US legislative and regulatory approach to tax avoidance

ERIK M. JENSEN

Introduction

It is risky, foolhardy even, to contribute an essay on anti-avoidance issues to a collection honouring John Tiley. No one deserves to be honoured more than John, of course, and anti-avoidance doctrine is one of his specialties. But what can I write that he does not already know or that he could not say more elegantly?

In fact, Tiley knows more than I do about everything (except maybe – *maybe* – baseball), and that includes American tax law. In a project Tiley undertook while visiting Case Western Reserve University in 1985–86, he studied anti-avoidance doctrines developed by US courts. In the resulting trilogy of articles in the *British Tax Review*, Tiley not only educated British lawyers about US law (and argued against unthinking importation of that law into the UK); he also forced those of us in the colonies to reconsider our instinct that substance should generally trump form.[1] The US and the UK have different views about the relative importance of substance and form,[2] and John was unconvinced that his home country had the worse of the arguments.

In Chapter 3 of this volume, Marty McMahon discusses the evolution of judicial anti-avoidance theory. I will make reference along the way to the judiciary, which has played such an important role in American anti-avoidance jurisprudence, but the focus of this essay is different. I examine statutory and regulatory developments that are changing American anti-avoidance law – with the hope that *something* here is new to Tiley.[3]

---

[1] Tiley (1987a); Tiley (1987b); Tiley (1988a); and Tiley (1988b).

[2] See Atiyah and Summers (1987, p. 3) (arguing that 'the English legal system inclines to the greater use of formal reasons, while the American system inclines to the greater use of reasons of substance').

[3] It will not all be new. I was lucky enough to join John on an article, Tiley and Jensen (1998), which discussed some non-judicial responses to avoidance.

After a look at the nature of tax shelters, I discuss several statutory and regulatory methods of dealing with them: statutes or regulations aimed at particular problems of abuse; 'outcomes-oriented' legislation intended to deal with wider patterns of behaviour; codification of an 'economic substance' or other general anti-avoidance doctrine; imposition of anti-abuse doctrines through regulations; disclosure of potentially abusive transactions; and creation of national standards that govern tax professionals' advice.

Each of these methods has merit, in some circumstances, but our expectations should be realistic. Abusive behaviour can at best be controlled; it cannot be eliminated. (In fact, it has been suggested that 'shutting down shelters actually feeds the shelter market because it creates a demand for the services of tax shelter providers'.[4]) Moreover, no one method will by itself bring abusive behaviour to acceptable levels, even temporarily. Flexibility is going to work better than rigidity in attacking shelters, and a combination of methods will work better than a single one. Each method, standing alone, is imperfect, but each might contribute to a broad-based offensive against shelters.

5.1 The tax shelter problem

Tax shelters are once again (or is it still?) a problem in the US. (Not everyone would agree that 'tax shelter' is the best term to use in a general discussion of tax avoidance, but I am anticipatorily going to ignore catcalls and use it anyway.) For present purposes, I intend 'tax shelter' to be understood in a flexible way, to refer to transactions with claimed tax benefits that are highly questionable when measured against congressional intentions and basic good sense (but with sufficient supporting authority that fraud is not involved). I do not limit the term to transactions marketed to multiple persons.

Bankman has provided a working definition that is useful but not perfect: a shelter is a –

(1) tax motivated; (2) transaction unrelated to a taxpayer's normal business operations; that (3) under a literal reading of some relevant authority; (4) produces a loss for tax purposes in excess of economic loss; (5) in a manner inconsistent with legislative intent or purpose . . .[5]

---

[4] Weisbach (2001, p. 78).   [5] Bankman (2004, p. 925).

Such a transaction ought to be considered a shelter, without a doubt, but why focus on transactions intended to create losses, and not on ones structured to avoid or defer income recognition,[6] to convert ordinary income into capital gain, or to achieve any other favourable tax treatment – if relevant authority is being interpreted hyper-technically 'in a manner inconsistent with legislative intent or purpose'?

Disagreement at the margins, however, should not obscure general agreement about the core characteristics of abusive behaviour. The typical shelter, broadly understood, has little or no motivation behind it other than hoped-for tax benefits. As Graetz pithily puts it, a shelter is 'a deal done by very smart people that, absent tax considerations, would be very stupid'.[7]

Moreover, although the typical shelter relies on legitimate authority, the authority is usually read in a mindlessly literal way[8] – to achieve results that seem (and probably are) too good to be true when measured against congressional intentions.[9] (For present purposes, I do not consider taking advantage of authority in a way that *is* consistent 'with legislative intent' – for example, using accelerated depreciation schedules – to be 'shelter' behaviour, regardless of how amazingly good the tax results might seem to be.[10]) Tax planning, which requires close reading of the Internal Revenue Code, is usually considered necessary in American society,[11] but, whatever the rest of the world thinks, mindlessness is not. (Canellos says shelters disparage 'the intellectual foundations of principled and creative tax practice'.[12]) It is probably unfair to blame shelters on 'textualism', a

---

[6] See Schizer (2006, p. 334) (including 'transactions that rely on a strained reading of the relevant tax provisions . . . to avoid including otherwise taxable income, and the like').

[7] Quoted in Herman (1999).

[8] The authority may be garbled as well. See Schizer (2006, p. 334) (arguing that shelters 'exploit poorly drafted statutes and regulations').

[9] See United States (2005, p. 2) (noting '[r]ecent tax avoidance transactions have relied upon the interaction of highly technical tax law provisions to produce tax consequences not intended by Congress'); Schler (2002, p. 327) (defining shelters as 'transactions that violate the intent of the Code and the regulations').

[10] See Gunn (2001, p. 174) (noting 'very favorable tax results, results that may seem too good to be true, are sometimes required by the language and purposes of particular statutory provisions') (footnote omitted).

[11] 'Congress sometimes intends to encourage [tax planning]': Galle (2006, p. 381) (footnote omitted), but not always. Reading statutes hyper-technically is justified by citing cases that have blessed planning. For example, *Gregory v Helvering* (1934) 69 F 2d 809 (2nd Cir.) at p. 810 (Hand, J.) ('Any one may so arrange his affairs that his taxes shall be as low as possible . . .'), affirmed (1935) 293 US 465 (USSC). But see Weisbach (2002, p. 222) ('[Tax planning] is almost always positively bad for society – it is worse than worthless').

[12] Canellos (2001, p. 49).

defensible method of statutory interpretation, but the perception that prominent jurists have been applying textualism in an extreme form may have added legitimacy to the shelter phenomenon.[13]

Finally, the typical shelter depends for success on taxpayers being convinced that, because of the 'audit lottery' and associated effects, it is worthwhile taking a shot at claiming too-good-to-be-true results. Maybe the taxpayer will not be audited; or any audit will be cursory and uninformed;[14] or, for a large taxpayer with a massive tax return, questionable transactions will be lost in the mass of material. Even if a suspect transaction is picked up, well-heeled taxpayers often can outgun governmental legal teams.[15] And penalties that are unlikely to be imposed do not help.[16] Besides – here is a real killer – this audit and penalty stuff does not matter much if a transaction is deemed legitimate. As Weisbach has emphasised, many shelters 'work', in the sense that taxpayers can convince decision-makers that hyper-technical interpretations are justified.[17]

I just described characteristics of a 'typical' shelter, but I intend to define shelters for purposes of this discussion in a way that does not depend on bright-line, formalistic tests. So please read what I write taking into account the most important words in an American tax lawyer's vocabulary: generally, usually, typically, ordinarily.[18] There are always exceptions to general propositions.

For an example of a tax shelter, consider the widely noted case of *Black & Decker Corp. v United States*,[19] where the claimed tax results depended on special treatment of contingent liabilities. In 1998 Black & Decker ('BXD') created a new corporation, Black & Decker Healthcare Management, Inc. ('BDHMI'), and transferred $561 million in cash, together with $560 million in contingent employee healthcare claims, for all the stock. Under American corporate tax law, the formation of the corporation was tax-free. If the liabilities had to be taken into account in determining B&D's basis in the BDHMI stock,[20] however, that basis would have been only

---

[13] See Galle (2006, p. 359).

[14] Schizer (2006, p. 335) (noting shelters 'take advantage of poor auditing').

[15] Schizer (2006, p. 335).

[16] Taxpayers 'choose avoidance and evasion strategies based on expected rather than nominal sanctions'. Raskolnikov (2006, p. 569).

[17] Weisbach (2001, p. 78).

[18] My wife, a tax professional and another Tiley fan, had a colleague who would greet her with 'Hello generally, Helen'.

[19] (2004) 340 F Supp 2d 621 (D. Md.), reversed and remanded (2006) 436 F 3d 431 (4th Cir.).

[20] For non-American readers: Gain is the difference between amount realised and asset 'basis', generally the cost of acquisition. For example, if a person pays $10 for a share of stock and

$1 million (that is, $561 million less $560 million),[21] a figure equivalent to the net value contributed.

B&D in effect took the position that the obligations were too contingent to be treated as liabilities for purposes of the basis rules. As a result, B&D said its basis in the $1 million worth of BDHMI stock was $561 million, the amount of cash transferred, unaffected by future obligations. When B&D sold the stock for $1 million, it claimed a $560 million loss, a result the government challenged.

There should have been a serious dispute about the meaning of 'liability' in the relevant provisions,[22] but, without discussing the Code, the trial judge in 2004 accepted B&D's interpretation and granted its motion for summary judgment. B&D had conceded that tax avoidance was its only purpose in putting the deal together, but the judge found enough economic substance for the transaction to be honoured: BDHMI became responsible for the healthcare claims, had employees, and so on.[23]

B&D was right that, for some purposes, such an obligation would not be treated as a 'liability'. But in this case the technical argument – a *hyper-technical* argument – trumped good sense. The obligations were real enough to affect the net value of what B&D had transferred, as the sales price for the stock indicated, but, under B&D's theory, the effect was dramatically to accelerate deductions attributable to the contingent claims.[24]

Whether the grant of summary judgment was consistent with 'legislative intent or purpose' depends on what that phrase means, of course. The average Congressman – indeed, the above-average Congressman – is clueless about corporate taxation; in that respect, there was no legislative intent. Nevertheless, I am confident that, *if* Congress had been able to focus on such a transaction, and had it in fact done so, it would not have intended the result reached by the judge. As a matter of first principles, the result was absurd.

later sells it for $15, the gain is $5. However, the Code includes rules providing for bases other than cost, generally when property is acquired in non-taxable transactions.

[21] Incorporation transactions are tax-free if the requirements of Code, s. 351 are satisfied, but gain not recognised must be reflected in a lower-than-cost basis in stock received. If liabilities are transferred, basis must be reduced by the amount of liabilities to ensure that gain does not permanently disappear from the system. See IRC, s. 358(d)(1).

[22] See IRC, ss. 357 (especially 357(c)(3)) and 358(d).

[23] *Black & Decker Corp. v United States* (2004) 340 F Supp 2d 621 (D. Md.) at p. 624.

[24] Furthermore, *BDHMI* was apparently taking deductions as the claims were satisfied, effectively giving two taxpayers the benefit of deductions from the contingent claims.

The trial court's decision did not stand, for which we can be grateful, but it took a while for good sense to re-enter the system. On appeal in 2006, the Fourth Circuit spelled out and accepted B&D's hyper-technical basis analysis, but remanded the case to reconsider application of the sham transaction doctrine.[25] Before the trial on remand began, B&D, recognising that it was probably fighting a losing battle, accepted a settlement offer from the government.[26] In a reasonable world – with statutory, regulatory, and judicial doctrines lined up to prevent bizarre results – B&D's argument would have been a clear loser to begin with, with little to discuss. But it was not a clear loser, and that is why there is a lot to discuss.

Another case worth mention as a test for anti-avoidance doctrine is *Cottage Savings Association v Commissioner*,[27] decided by the Supreme Court in 1991. The *Cottage Savings* deal is often not thought of as a shelter, but, as Weisbach writes, '[a]bsolutely nothing happened except for tax'.[28] In that respect, this was a shelter par excellence.

The taxpayer, a savings and loan association, was holding bundles of low interest home mortgages in a market with rising interest rates. Unlike the typical shelter, Cottage Savings had suffered real economic losses. In the US system, however, decline in value does not create a deductible loss; something else (a 'realisation' event, like a sale) must occur. In an attempt to create a tax loss, Cottage Savings exchanged bundles of 90 per cent participation interests in mortgages for other, almost identical bundles. The new bundles were secured by different homes and the obligors were different, but the bundles relinquished and the bundles received were economically fungible.

The exchange was carefully structured, with the help of bank regulators (who modified applicable accounting rules), to avoid a financial account-ing loss, which might have required shutting Cottage Savings down. The goal was simple: to permit S&Ls to recognise losses for tax purposes, without having to do so for financial accounting purposes.

Cottage Savings' position was not abusive if the test is divergence between economic and tax positions. But if the appropriate baseline is that losses cannot be recognised until a realisation event has occurred, the exchange provided a weak foundation for a deduction.

The government reasonably argued, to no avail, that the exchange was a non-event for tax purposes. In large part, however, the government

---

[25] See *Black & Decker Corp. v United States* (2006) 436 F 3d 431 (4th Cir.) at pp. 441–3.
[26] See Stratton (2007).   [27] (1991) 499 US 554 (USSC).   [28] Weisbach (2001, p. 75).

was trapped by its own regulations, read in a hyper-technical way. The relinquished and replacement participation interests were deemed to be materially different because they embodied 'legally distinct entitlements': the different obligors and the different homes securing the loans.[29] The result, a striking loss for the government, was, for Cottage Savings, too good to be true.

Any method proposed to attack tax shelters should take cases like *Black & Decker* and *Cottage Savings* into account. Some absurd results are to be expected in a complex tax system, but how do we generally prevent results that, while tenuously supported by a serious legal argument, are nonetheless bizarre? And how do we do so without causing serious damage to legitimate business activity?

Those are questions Congress and the Internal Revenue Service must constantly wrestle with. And those questions are addressed in the rest of this essay, as I survey several statutory and regulatory methods to counter shelters.

5.2 Targeted legislation

If statutes or regulations are being read hyper-technically, one possible remedy is to amend the authority to clarify that offending interpretations are impermissible. Congress does this occasionally. To deal with contingent liability transactions like *Black & Decker*, which had become widespread, Congress modified the stock basis rule to provide that 'the term "liability" shall include any fixed or contingent obligation to make payment, without regard to whether the obligation is otherwise taken into account for purposes of this title'.[30] Problem solved – until a smart person finds a way around the amended statute.

But targeted legislation will not work, even in the short run, in many cases. Modification of the regulation involved in *Cottage Savings* might change the result in later, similar cases, but with the risk that transactions involving exchanges of fungible assets when *gain* recognition is at issue could fall on the tax-free side of the line. From the government's

[29] *Cottage Savings Association v Commissioner* (1991) 499 US 554 (USSC) at pp. 566–7. Treasury Regulation § 1.1001–1(a) states that, unless otherwise provided, 'gain or loss realized from . . . the exchange of property for other property differing materially either in kind or in extent is treated as income or as loss sustained'.

[30] IRC, s. 358(h)(1) and (3). The change was made in 2000, and was not applicable to the *Black & Decker* transaction. Had it applied, B&D's basis in the BDHMI stock would have been $1 million.

standpoint, a technical change to fix the *Cottage Savings* problem might have been worse than doing nothing.

To be sure, some abusive arrangements can be controlled, if not stopped, by targeted legislation. For example, taxpayers in the US historically used contributions to and distributions from partnerships to disguise sales of property. Suppose a taxpayer is holding a parcel of real estate that is worth $20,000 but which he acquired for only $5,000. If he sells the property for $20,000, he would pay tax on $15,000 of gain. But suppose he instead contributes the parcel to a partnership and later receives a distribution of $20,000 in cash. Contributions to and distributions from partnerships are generally non-taxable events. If each step were analysed alone, the taxpayer would receive the economic benefit, but not the tax liability, from the 'disguised' sale.[31]

Disguising a sale using a partnership was never the norm,[32] but the potential for abuse was there and disguised sales structured for tax purposes used to be common. In 1986 legislation, however, Congress set out circumstances in which a contribution and distribution would be re-characterised as a sale of all or part of the contributed property. Taxpayers were put on notice that step-transaction principles *had* to be applied to determine if the two transfers, 'when viewed together, [were] properly characterised as a sale or exchange of property'.[33] Subsequent regulations provided rules as to when a contribution and a distribution were to be 'viewed together'.[34]

The 1986 legislation was largely successful on the disguised sale issue, but targeted statutes of that sort can go only so far. At best, they react to specific events and apply only to specific sorts of transactions and, by the time Congress realises a barn door is open, the horse is across the state line.[35] (One argument in favour of a disclosure regime is to help the government react faster.) Furthermore, targeted statutes typically have only prospective effect, doing nothing about transactions already under

---

[31] A distribution of cash *is* taxable to the extent it exceeds a partner's basis in his partnership interest. See IRC, s. 731(a)(1). For my example to be potentially tax-free, assume the partner has a basis of at least $20,000 before the distribution.

[32] The formal results were not all positive. If the transaction were not a sale, the partnership would take the property with a basis of $5,000, not $20,000. See IRC, s. 723.

[33] IRC, s. 707(a)(2)(B).   [34] See Treasury Regulation §§ 1.707–3 – 1.707–6.

[35] When an open door is discovered, quick statutory action is unlikely in the US. Even if one political party controls the presidency and both houses of Congress, which is often not the case, party discipline is weak.

contract or already consummated.[36] And new statutory language invites new hyper-technical interpretation.[37] As Ginsburg predicted, in his *Law of Moses' Rod*, '[E]very stick crafted to beat on the head of a taxpayer will, sooner or later, metamorphose into a large green snake and bite the Commissioner [of Internal Revenue] on the hind part'.[38] Changing statutory language can breed, rather than deter, tax avoidance.

5.3 Outcomes-oriented legislation

In some circumstances, a congressional response more promising than targeted legislation of the sort described above is to go after broad categories of behaviour based on outcomes rather than the technical details of, or the motivations behind, transactions. This strategy is illustrated by the oxymoronic passive activity loss ('PAL') rules, enacted in 1986 and directed at the then prevalent shelters marketed to individual investors.

The typical investment structure was a limited partnership engaged in a business intended to generate losses (through accelerated depreciation and the like) that purely passive investors (lawyers, doctors and other high-income folk) could use to offset income from other sources. The fact that the same structure was used for many different types of shelters (real estate, movie production, research and development) gave congressional draftsmen something to aim at. In that respect, the PAL rules are another example of targeted legislation, although the nature of the target is different from what I described earlier.

Complex in form – s. 469 of the Code goes on and on – the PAL rules actually operate in a simple way. Losses from a trade or business in which a taxpayer does not materially participate (a 'passive activity') – a category that generally includes a limited partnership interest – can be used only to offset income from other passive activities.[39] The losses cannot be used

---

[36] Regulatory agencies can act faster, but here too remedies are usually prospective. For example, on 31 May 2007, the Internal Revenue Service announced it would issue regulations, effective that day, dealing with stock repurchases made by foreign subsidiaries of US corporations in triangular mergers – treating funds used as subject to US taxation because of deemed repatriation to the US. Notice 2007–48, 2007–25 IRB 1428. The Notice responded to an IBM announcement, *two days* earlier, that it had effected a $12.5 billion repurchase. IBM saved $1.6 billion that would have been due had the deal proceeded under the new rules. See Bulkeley (2007).

[37] A statute with only prospective effect also invites the argument that Congress implicitly blessed transactions arranged before the effective date.

[38] Ginsburg (1985, p. 100).   [39] IRC, s. 469(a)(1), (d)(1) and (h)(2).

against income from practising medicine or law, for example. Nor can they be used to offset income not attributable to the taxpayer's trade or business, like dividends and interest.[40] By restricting their utility, s. 469 makes losses from passive activities less valuable than had been true in the past and therefore makes investing in loss-generating passive activities less attractive. The PAL rules took away the benefit of the shelters, and the shelters largely disappeared.

The PAL rules worked in an imaginative and administrable way. Yin praises how the rules do not require many difficult judgment calls. Section 469 –

> is not concerned with whether the taxpayer's activities are undertaken for valid business purposes or tax avoidance purposes, or with any other particular motive or intent. It is not concerned with how the amount of tax savings resulting from a transaction compares to its pre-tax economic return. Section 469 operates to prohibit or constrain certain outcomes, however they may be achieved and for whatever reason.[41]

The PAL rules earned a high grade for predictability of application.

Section 469 is not above criticism, however. The complex provision simplified the world by eliminating shelters of a particular sort, but it can affect other transactions as well; its complexity is not of purely historical interest. For example, suppose a passive investor puts real dollars into a business that will, in its early stages, generate losses – as new enterprises generally do. It is hard to see anything automatically wrong with deducting out-of-pocket outlays connected to business activity,[42] but s. 469 covers this behaviour. The investor will be able to currently deduct losses from his investment only to the extent he has income from other passive activities. Any effective anti-avoidance doctrine, codified or not, will reach some behaviour that ought to be favoured,[43] but s. 469 might go too far.

In addition, because shelter planners work around the law as it exists, s. 469 does not reach new versions of shelters. Since 1986 the tax shelter problem in the US has shifted to different sorts of transactions (e.g., basis

---

[40] That income may be attributable to *someone's* trade or business, but an investor (e.g., a shareholder in a corporation) is not treated as being engaged in a trade or business by reason of his investment. This most passive of all income was intentionally not treated as income from a passive activity. IRC, s. 469(e)(1).

[41] Yin (2001, p. 219).

[42] If outlays are capital expenditures, related to a hoped-for future income stream, they should not be currently deductible. But that issue is independent of s. 469.

[43] Contrast Weisbach (2001, p. 82) ('[I]f strong anti-shelter doctrines do catch a few transactions that we might otherwise allow, it is hard to see the harm').

or income shifting using tax-indifferent parties) entered into by different sorts of taxpayers, including corporations, and the PAL rules do not speak to those shelters.

It might be that another form of outcomes-oriented legislation could help with new shelters, and some possibilities have been suggested. For example, Chirelstein and Zelenak have proposed rules emphasising outcomes, actual or foreseeable, rather than economic substance or taxpayer motive:

> (1) No deduction shall be allowed for losses substantially in excess of any measurable reduction in the taxpayer's net worth, and (2) no deduction or exclusion from gross income shall be allowed through the allocation of noneconomic income to a tax-indifferent party.[44]

These proposed rules are intended to be bright-line tests, not standards or principles to guide decision-makers.

Gunn has found in the partnership anti-abuse regulation, which I will discuss presently, a meritorious standard that also would look to outcomes. It would deny 'a tax result that no sensible legislator would have approved of if the transaction had been called to the legislator's attention when the statute was drafted'[45] – regardless of motive, economic substance, or anything else. It would be difficult to enact a statute in that form – would Congress acknowledge it cannot think of everything and that 'sensible legislator' is not redundant? – but perhaps it could provide that results inconsistent with legislative intent are not to be honoured.

Conceptually, those positions have much to commend them. If either Chirelstein-Zelenak or Gunn were enacted, courts reluctant or unwilling to apply anti-avoidance doctrines would have no choice but to apply the new outcomes test. Furthermore, either standard, properly applied, would lead to the right result in a case like *Black & Decker*: no loss on sale of the BDHMI stock.

No test is perfect by itself, however, and Chirelstein and Zelenak recognise that their rules would not change the result in *Cottage Savings*, where real economic losses were involved.[46] And, although I assume Gunn's 'sensible legislator' would condemn *Cottage Savings*, I could be wrong, given sympathy for the S&L industry.

---

[44] Chirelstein and Zelenak (2005, pp. 1952–3) (footnotes omitted).
[45] Gunn (2001, p. 160).
[46] Chirelstein and Zelenak (2005, pp. 1960–1). Chirelstein and Zelenak question, however, whether the *Cottage Savings* transaction should be considered a shelter in the first place.

It is also the case that the positives Yin saw in the PAL rules are absent from the proposals. Neither would call traditional tax planning into question, but uncertainty in application would be great.[47] Measures of 'net worth' or 'noneconomic income' cannot be scientifically precise. (I am not sure that *science* can be scientifically precise.) And trying to discern what a sensible legislator would have thought, had she been thinking about a matter, has its own difficulties. Maybe they can be overcome: some cases are easy, and perhaps anti-abuse rules should not apply where more than one result is intellectually defensible. But we need to recognise that these suggestions would not be self-executing in codified form.

In any event, the Chirelstein-Zelenak proposal comes from fuzzy-headed academics, which means it has no prospect of being enacted. And Gunn's interpretation, another academic product, will also not reach the halls of Congress.

These suggestions might make more sense as interpretive standards than as codified rules. And that brings me to a new set of issues: whether codification of general anti-avoidance doctrines is desirable in the US.

5.4 Codifying anti-avoidance doctrines

Drafting carefully tailored, substantive provisions that will put a dent into tax-shelter activity has always been difficult, which is why general anti-avoidance doctrines have attracted new interest as statutory fixes.[48] Over ten years ago, Gustafson wrote that 'Congress has never seriously considered and no administration has proposed the adoption of a general anti-avoidance or anti-abuse rule that would apply to all situations'.[49] That is still generally true, but the Democratic Congress may be moving to codify an economic substance doctrine.[50]

It is not as though anti-avoidance doctrines are new to the US (as Tiley, better than anyone else, knows). It has been understood forever that the Internal Revenue Code is to be enforced with the aid of several overlapping judicial doctrines: substance-over-form (the substance, not form, of

[47] Yin (2001, p. 220).
[48] See Chapter 1 for a consideration of statutory general anti-avoidance rules.
[49] Gustafson (1997, p. 350). Anti-avoidance doctrines have been codified to deal with particular situations. See, for example, IRC, s. 269 (denying deductions and credits for corporate acquisitions if the 'principal purpose . . . is evasion or avoidance of Federal income tax').
[50] See Tax Analysts (2007). (When I was double-checking these footnotes, I discovered, to my surprise, that Tax Analysts had removed the cited item from its database, noting that 'the information at this cite was not intended for publication'. I assume that means the tax counsel's comments, which were accurately recorded, were off the record.)

a transaction should determine tax consequences[51]); step transaction (formally discrete, but substantively related, steps should be collapsed into one transaction to determine results); sham transaction (a transaction having no purpose other than achieving particular tax results should be disregarded[52]); business purpose (a transaction that in form is business-related should not be honoured if it lacks a non-tax, business purpose[53]); and economic substance (a transaction lacking substance should not be honoured, determined by looking to both motive and changes in economic position[54]).[55]

Bits and pieces of these ideas have appeared in statutes and regulations directed at particular problems, like the disguised sale statute described earlier. None of these doctrines, however, has been codified in a generally applicable way.

What might codification look like?

No proposal has yet received congressional approval, but the points most likely to be codified are two. A transaction would be treated as having economic substance only if: (1) 'the transaction changes in a meaningful way (apart from Federal tax effects) the taxpayer's economic position'; and (2) 'the taxpayer has a substantial non-tax purpose for entering into such transaction and the transaction is a reasonable means of accomplishing such purpose'.[56]

One proposal with those elements, and a twist, fell by the wayside in deliberations on 2004 tax legislation. The two-tiered doctrine would have applied only if a court first determined that the doctrine was 'relevant' to the transaction.[57] That would have made it easy for a court to avoid economic substance analysis, if it wished, by determining that the analysis was irrelevant.

---

[51] Substance-over-form language is pervasive in American jurisprudence, but on many issues it is accepted that form controls. See, for example, Revenue Ruling 84–111, 1984–2 CB 88 (holding that tax results of incorporating a partnership are governed by form).

[52] See *Knetsch v United States* (1960) 364 US 361 (USSC).

[53] See *Gregory v Helvering* (1935) 293 US 465 (USSC).

[54] See, for example, *ACM Partnership v Commissioner* (1998) 157 F 3d 231 (3rd Cir.), cert. denied (1999) 526 US 1017 (USSC).

[55] See Chapter 3 for a detailed consideration of these doctrines.

[56] See American Bar Association Section of Taxation (2007, p. 390) (critiquing doctrine as legislatively proposed in 2005).

[57] See United States (2004, pp. 445–52).

A 2005 proposal prepared by staff of the Joint Committee on Taxation recommended applying two-tiered economic substance analysis to transactions 'having any of six characteristics present in many tax shelters'. The list is a catalogue of potentially abusive deals:

> The six types of transactions to which the proposal applies are transactions: 1) in which the taxpayer holds offsetting positions which substantially reduce the risk of loss and tax benefits would result from differing tax treatment of the positions; 2) which are structured to result in a disparity between basis and fair market value which creates or increases a loss or reduces a gain; 3) which are structured to create or increase a gain in any asset any portion of which would not be recognised for Federal income tax purposes if the asset were sold at fair market value by the taxpayer (or a related person); 4) which are structured to result in income for Federal income tax purposes to a tax indifferent party for any period which is materially in excess of any economic income to such party with respect to the transaction for such period; 5) in which the taxpayer disposes of certain property which the taxpayer held at risk for a period of less than 45 days; or 6) which are structured to result in a deduction or loss which is otherwise allowable for Federal tax purposes but not for financial accounting purposes.[58]

Under the staff proposal, taxpayers would have to demonstrate economic substance for a suspect transaction. Others would be subject to traditional methods of scrutiny.

At the time of writing, summer 2007, it is impossible to know whether codification will occur, and, if it does, what will be included. It would be surprising, however, if any codification did not encompass at least some of these points.

Is codification desirable?

In a system that prides itself on not being formalistic, codification might seem silly. Whether economic substance is a statutory requirement or not, the Internal Revenue Service can invoke anti-avoidance doctrines, and courts can apply them.

Several arguments have nonetheless been advanced to support codification. Aprill notes the positive effect codification could have on the Service: 'Codifying these standards . . . will give administrative officers

---

[58] United States (2005, p. 3, footnote 3).

greater ability to attack taxpayer transactions.'[59] Courts are limited to resolving disputes, and are constrained by the adversarial nature of the disputes, but the Service fights shelters on an everyday basis. Yes, it can invoke judicially created doctrines anyway – this is not an either/or question – but, in the allocation of authority between courts and agencies, codification is arguably a point in the *Service's* favour.[60]

Codification would strengthen *courts'* application of the doctrines as well. Because of uncertainty about judicial authority, the use by some judges of hyper-technical versions of textualism to interpret statutes, and many other reasons, not all American courts apply the doctrines. Some judges are gung ho, but others are bewildered or openly hostile.[61] (Although reversed on appeal, several courts have concluded they had no authority to apply anti-avoidance principles.[62]) But if Congress tells the judiciary it must apply an economic substance test – if a textualist is told she should not apply textualism in interpreting statutes[63] – even a reluctant judge will have to go through the motions.[64]

The case for codification is not one-sided, however. Sceptics, including Bush administration officials and many commentators from the academy and the bar, advance a number of propositions that go beyond redundancy (i.e., that the doctrines already exist, so what's the point?). Some complain about 'the ambiguous and untrustworthy application' of economic substance doctrine, whether or not codified.[65] The American Bar Association Section of Taxation says other mechanisms work better:

---

[59] Aprill (2001, p. 20). (She is not writing about the proposal that would have applied to courts only. See discussion above.)

[60] Moreover, if the Service makes a fact-dependent determination about economic substance, a reviewing court would generally apply an 'abuse of discretion' standard. See Aprill (2001, pp. 20–2).

[61] See Chirelstein and Zelenak (2005, pp. 1946–7). Reluctance to conclude that a technically structured transaction does not work is understandable, particularly if judges are not tax experts. Judicial inconsistency is exacerbated by the multiple fora in which cases may be brought – Tax Court, Court of Federal Claims, federal district court – and the many appellate courts add to doctrinal confusion.

[62] See, for example, *Coltec Industries v United States* (2004) 62 Fed Cl 716 (Ct. Cl.), reversed (2006) 454 F 3d 1340 (Fed. Cir.).

[63] See Galle (2006, p. 372).

[64] Of course, it might not matter. Chirelstein and Zelenak note that 'although codification would prevent a court from concluding that the doctrine does not exist, courts would remain free to conclude that the doctrine is not relevant in particular situations. And even when they did find the doctrine relevant, courts would remain free to find meaningful changes in economic positions and substantial nontax purposes in highly dubious circumstances.' Chirelstein and Zelenak (2005, p. 1950).

[65] *Ibid.*, p. 1948.

The legislative and regulatory actions imposing greater transparency are having the intended effect of limiting aggressive transactions while at the same time allowing taxpayers to engage in tax planning to minimise their taxes legally.[66]

Most important, many sceptics (including this author) are concerned that codification could *hinder* the fight against shelters by taking away flexibility. Judicial doctrines evolve to deal with changing circumstances and to adapt to new hyper-technical readings of statutes.[67] Codifying economic substance would make the doctrine rule-like, and shelter architects would have new language to work around.[68] Define 'economic substance' rigidly, and imaginative architects can provide for the minimum of substance required by the statute.[69]

Reflecting the Bush administration's hostility to codification, a Service official noted that, if the economic substance or business purpose doctrine had been codified in 1935, when *Gregory v Helvering*[70] was decided, the doctrine would have been inadequate to deal with later generations of abusive activity: 'Given the imagination and energy with which tax shelters seem to be evolving . . . it's useful to let the organic nature of the economic substance doctrine also evolve.'[71] Although the government has had a mixed record in shelter litigation over the years, it has recently had a string of victories, and it has done so relying on uncodified doctrines.[72]

It is perhaps another way of making the same point to note the drafting difficulties in any codification project. I began this essay defining 'tax shelter' in a general way. A clear line between shelters and non-shelters, if I could have drawn one, would have defeated my purposes. The same problem exists in codifying 'economic substance'.

Anti-avoidance doctrines and uncertainty

Evolving doctrines mean fuzzy lines, and fuzzy lines, it is often argued, mean uncertainty. Is that true, and, even if it is, is uncertainty a bad thing?

---

[66] American Bar Association Section of Taxation (2007, p. 391).
[67] See, for example, Wolfman (2004, p. 445) (complaining that codifying a 'rigid or formulaic' version of economic substance would be constraining).
[68] See Bank (2001, p. 41) ('The adoption of more rules may be seen as an invitation to structure a transaction that strictly complies with the letter of such rules, but only loosely, if at all, comports with the underlying justification.').
[69] It might also be the case that codifying one anti-avoidance doctrine would imply that courts are not to apply others.
[70] (1935) 293 US 465 (USSC).   [71] Quoted in Glenn (2007, p. 888).
[72] See Simmonds (2007); Nutt (2007).

Uncertainty is an issue with any anti-abuse doctrine, of course, whether codified or not, and fuzziness does cause uncertainty in some situations. How could it not? Opponents of anti-avoidance doctrines have been condemning fuzziness and uncertainty for decades: who knows whether a court will determine that substance diverges from form, or that two formally distinct transactions are one? Who can tell how much economic substance is enough or what a good business purpose is? Although nothing can eliminate uncertainty, perhaps codification of economic substance could control it.

Uncertainty is a legitimate concern. Weisbach notes: 'If [anti-abuse provisions] are not more certain than other approaches to solving the rules/standards/complexity problem, they are undesirable . . . If they are more certain, they are desirable.'[73] Would uncertainty be so great that legitimate business activity would be deterred? Or would a carefully drafted doctrine miss some abusive behaviour? Ultimately, as Aprill writes –

> [d]eciding whether over-inclusion or under-inclusion produces the greatest danger is an empirical question – how many tax shelters and at what size would be stopped by codifying judicial doctrines versus how many legitimate transactions and at what size would be stopped by this codification . . .[74]

We just do not know: 'The effects of uncertainty are uncertain.'[75]

Although we have few data, uncertainty associated with judicial anti-avoidance doctrines may be more apparent than real. It does not affect the everyday practice of the vast majority of American tax professionals. And, even for those whose practices push envelopes, the difficulties may be manageable. Canellos notes that –

> [a]lthough in theory the line between a tax shelter and an aggressively structured real transaction may appear difficult to draw, in actuality the distinction is generally rather easy to establish . . . That is why it may be hard to define shelters legislatively . . . but so easy for courts to determine whether an actual transaction is a shelter.[76]

Practitioner Canellos's intuitions correspond to those of academics. Weisbach believes that 'tax lawyers are sufficiently trained and share a sufficiently common understanding of the tax law to be able to determine

---

[73] Weisbach (1999, p. 879). [74] Aprill (2001, p. 34) (footnote omitted).
[75] Weisbach (2002, p. 247). [76] Canellos (2001, pp. 53–4).

which transactions anti-abuse rules target and which they do not'.[77] Yes, poorly trained or inexperienced lawyers are going to feel uncomfortable with fuzziness, but they will get over it – or find another way to fill their days. Cooper came to the same conclusion about codified general anti-avoidance rules in other countries. Although many had worried about GAARs being '"loose canon[s]" on the tax ship of State, injuring friend and foe alike',[78] he concluded that 'the experience with a GAAR does not support the worst fears of tax advisors'.[79]

In fact, anti-avoidance doctrines can *support* simplification and certainty. No set of explicit rules can cover every conceivable transaction, and anti-avoidance doctrines can help avoid the proliferation of detailed (and therefore uncertain) rules drafted in response to particular abusive transactions.[80]

It is hard to imagine the American tax system relying only on substantive rules.[81] Try to mesh a multitude of bright-line, but transaction-specific, rules into a coherent whole, and the monster that is the Internal Revenue Code will grow several more heads. Surrey wrote in 1967:

> It is clear that [anti-avoidance provisions and doctrines] save the tax system from the far greater proliferation of detail that would be necessary if the tax avoider could succeed merely by bringing his scheme within the literal language of substantive provisions written to govern the everyday world.[82]

Besides, some uncertainty is valuable; it deters taxpayers from getting too close to abusive territory. Weisbach goes farther than I would in condoning *significant* uncertainty, but I accept his basic points:

> [W]e should have no presumption that reducing uncertainty . . . is a good thing . . . We cannot say that uncertainty is necessarily bad and cannot say that we should not impose significant uncertainty if it is needed to implement strong anti-shelter doctrines . . .[83]

In any event, no one in the US is considering having only a rules-based or only a standards-based system. A combination is inevitable,

---

[77] Weisbach (1999, p. 881) (footnote omitted) (citing Halperin (1995, p. 809)).
[78] Cooper (2001, p. 117).
[79] Cooper (2001, p. 117). GAARs have also 'not proved to be the panacea of revenue authorities', however; *Ibid.* See also the discussion above in Chapter 1.
[80] Weisbach (1999, p. 865) ('[R]ules must systematically be more complex than standards').
[81] It is, of course, also impossible to imagine the system relying only on general standards. See Weisbach (1999, p. 876).
[82] Surrey (1969, p. 707, n. 31) quoted in Weisbach (1999, p. 861).
[83] Weisbach (2001, p. 81).

with standards coming into play 'in situations where strict application of the rules produces perverse results'.[84] To the extent codification would limit desirable evolution of those standards, it should be
resisted.

5.5 Anti-avoidance doctrines and administrative action

Whether or not Congress acts, the Internal Revenue Service might be
able to codify aspects of anti-avoidance doctrines through regulations.
The Service probably does not have authority to issue a general anti-
avoidance rule that would apply across the board, and it has not tried to
do so. But it might have (or at least claim) authority to do so in particular
areas. That is what happened in the mid-1990s in partnership taxation.[85]

The first section in the subchapter of the Internal Revenue Code that
deals with partnerships – s. 701 – provides simply that: '[a] partnership
as such shall not be subject to the income tax imposed by this chapter.
Persons carrying on business as partners shall be liable for income tax
only in their separate or individual capacities.'[86]

No surprise there. It is a premise of American taxation that partnerships
are not income-taxpaying entities. Instead, items of income are treated
as earned by the partners and are taxed currently to them. Section 701
provides no details on the implementation of the principles of that section;
that is what the rest of subchapter K does.

In 1995, the Service finalised a so-called 'anti-abuse rule', in the form
of a regulation, under the authority of s. 701. In general, the regulation
provides that, for arrangements that are not 'consistent with the intent of
subchapter K', the Service has power to recast transactions, to treat persons
not as partners, and even, in egregious cases, to ignore the existence of a
partnership.[87]

The key concept, the 'intent of subchapter K', has three components:
that a partnership be bona fide and enter into transactions with a 'substantial business purpose'; that the form of any transaction satisfy substance-
over-form principles; and that, in general, the partnership operations
and the arrangements between partnership and partners properly reflect
income.[88] The regulation provides examples to illustrate arrangements

---

[84] *Ibid.*, p. 79.
[85] Because of limited liability companies, which generally combine corporate characteristics
with partnership tax treatment, partnership taxation may be more important today than
its sexier older brother, corporate taxation.
[86] IRC, s. 701.   [87] Treasury Regulation § 1.701–2(b).   [88] *Ibid.*, § 1.701–2(a).

that are abusive and others that are not. On the *who-could-have-thought-otherwise?* front, the use of a partnership, which avoids entity level tax and therefore almost certainly has tax avoidance as one of its purposes, is not ipso facto abusive. It is obviously consistent with the intent of subchapter K to use a partnership.[89]

The regulation contains a large amount of substance-over-form and other traditional anti-avoidance language. Because those powers were always available to taxing authorities, however, what, if anything, does codification add? For one thing, the regulation makes it clear that anti-avoidance doctrines are the law in partnership taxation, so that, as discussed earlier, judges reluctant to impose those doctrines now have authority to do so. And, even if it merely reinforces old law, the regulation could have an incremental deterrent effect on those contemplating aggressive planning.

But the regulation may add something substantive as well. The regulation says the doctrines that may be invoked by tax officials are not limited to the generally known ones,[90] and Gunn found a new anti-abuse standard in the 'intent of subchapter K':

> [a] transaction can be abusive without running afoul of any of the traditional anti-avoidance doctrines; that is, it can have a business purpose and substance, its substance and form can coincide, and yet it yields a tax result that no sensible legislator would have approved of if the transaction had been called to the legislator's attention when the statute was drafted.[91]

Much of the regulation is flawed, in Gunn's view, but the 'concept of "abuse", distinct from other anti-avoidance doctrines', is potentially powerful.[92]

---

[89] See *ibid.*, § 1.701–2(d), Ex. 1.

[90] See *ibid.*, § 1.701–2(i) and – 2(d), Ex. 11(ii) ('in addition to possibly challenging the transaction under applicable judicial principles and statutory authorities . . . the Commissioner can recast the transaction as appropriate under . . . this section'). As critics noted, this calls into question the Service's authority to issue the regulation. Section 701 delegates no explicit power to do so, and the regulation's principles have a tenuous connection to s. 701.

[91] Gunn (2001, p. 160).

[92] *Ibid.* Gunn provides an example in which S corporation rules lead to preposterous results. The case 'is abusive not because it calls for a bad interpretation of the relevant Code section (it does not), but because it seeks to use a Code section for a purpose its drafters could not plausibly be thought to have contemplated'. *Ibid.*, p. 163.

Gunn might be finding more than the drafters intended.[93] As Zelenak points out, although the regulation is titled an 'anti-abuse rule', neither 'abuse' nor 'abusive' is used in the text.[94] And the drafters emphasised that 'the fundamental principles reflected in the regulation are consistent with established legal doctrines'.[95]

Whether or not Gunn's principle really can be found in the regulation, or in other regulations projects, it is a wonderful concept that – one way or another – ought to be applied generally: no statutory system should ever be interpreted in a way that leads to absurd results unless the legislature clearly intended the absurdity.

5.6 Disclosure

If substantive disallowance rules augmented by anti-avoidance doctrines cannot prevent shelters, and that seems to be the case, it is not surprising that American attention has turned to a disclosure regime.[96] Indeed, some commentators, like Canellos, believe this is where efforts should be concentrated: 'The key to deterrence for all classes of tax shelters is reporting and penalties. To fight what amounts to audit lottery and to nip schemes in the bud, airtight, focused, prompt and efficient disclosure rules are required.'[97]

Although critics have concluded that disclosure is misguided (about which more presently), Gergen has argued that the strategy for deterring corporate tax shelters – 'monitoring tax shelter activity, blacklisting new shelters when they are identified, and pursuing users of blacklisted shelters through promoters of the shelters alongside more conventional audit techniques'[98] – can be effective. Tweaking is required as conditions change, to be sure, but disclosure can work.

The disclosure rules mandated by Congress and the Treasury have several goals. Two are compliance and deterrence, of course. And, if the

---

[93] He admits that '[o]nly three of the regulation['s] seven listed factors aim directly at abuse, as distinct from "substance over form" or mere suspicion'. Gunn (2001, p. 166) (footnote omitted).

[94] Zelenak (2001, p. 178). For that matter, it is more like a 'standard' than a 'rule'.

[95] Treasury Decision 8588 in Internal Revenue Service *Cumulative Bulletin*, Vol. 1995–1, p. 109 at p. 112.

[96] See generally Granwell and McGonigle (2006).

[97] Canellos (2001, pp. 67–70); see also Beale (2006, p. 612) ('Lack of disclosure is key to taxpayers' ability to exploit the audit lottery').

[98] Gergen (2002, p. 255).

mass of material sent to Washington can be sifted in a manageable way, disclosure can help authorities (particularly the Office of Tax Shelter Analysis, made up of experts 'dedicated to identifying and shutting down tax shelter transactions'[99]) learn about new avoidance strategies and act accordingly.

This is not the place for a line-by-line discussion of the rules, some of which I would probably get wrong anyway, but a few highlights are in order. (I will not discuss penalties for noncompliance,[100] but they are obviously an important part of the system.)

Participants: return disclosure. A taxpayer who participates in a 'reportable transaction', as defined below, is required to attach a form to its tax return describing, among other things, the –

> expected tax treatment and all potential tax benefits expected to result from the transaction, . . . any tax result protection . . ., [and] sufficient detail for the [Service] to be able to understand the tax structure of the reportable transaction and the identity of all parties involved.[101]

This increases the probability that a taxpayer who has engaged in a suspect transaction will have its return scrutinised and, if items relating to the transaction fail scrutiny, will be subject to penalties.

In addition, if taxpayers have to disclose questionable return positions, they are less likely to participate in reportable transactions to begin with. Disclosure is not an admission that a taxpayer's reporting of a transaction is wrong,[102] but it is like tattooing 'Audit me' on one's forehead or corporate logo (or so a participant might fear).

Material advisors. As a result of statutory changes in 2004, 'material advisors' also must disclose 'reportable transactions' about which they

---

[99] Morse (2006, p. 1002).

[100] See, for example, IRC, ss. 6707A (penalty for not disclosing reportable transaction on returns); 6707 (penalty on material advisors for not accurately disclosing reportable transaction); 6708 (penalty on material advisors for not maintaining or supplying investor lists); 6700 (penalty on promoters of abusive shelters); 6662(a) (accuracy-related penalty for understatements of tax liability); 6662A (accuracy-related penalty for understatements associated with reportable transactions); see also Wolfman, Holden and Harris (2006, pp. 25–33).

[101] Treasury Regulation § 1.6011–4(d) and see IRS Form 8886.

[102] 'The fact that a transaction is a reportable transaction shall not affect the legal determination of whether the taxpayer's treatment of the transaction is proper'. Treasury Regulation § 1.6011–4(a).

advise.[103] The term 'material advisor' is broadly defined. It includes any person 'who provides any material aid, assistance, or advice with regard to organizing, managing, promoting, selling, implementing, insuring, or carrying out any reportable transaction, and . . . who [as a result] directly or indirectly derives gross income' above a 'threshold amount'.[104] As with return disclosure, the transaction and its potential tax benefits must be described.[105]

List maintenance. An advisor is also required to maintain a list of those 'to whom [the] advisor acted as a material advisor with respect to such [reportable] transaction', and to provide the list to authorities 'upon written request'.[106] List maintenance is directed not so much at advisors (although penalties for non-compliance apply) as at potential shelter investors who are understandably leery of being on a list of that sort.

Reportable transactions. The taxpayer disclosure, material advisor reporting, and list maintenance obligations are all tied to the concept of 'reportable transaction'.[107] In broad outline, 'reportable transaction' encompasses five categories (often called 'filters'), which are not mutually exclusive:

1. 'Listed transactions': generally those labelled as tax avoidance transactions by the Internal Revenue Service in published notices, regulations, or other guidance. In effect, the Service tells the world it is sceptical (or more than sceptical) about the transactions. For example, in 2001 the Service listed contingent liability transactions that were similar to the one in *Black & Decker* and were not subject to the statutory fix.[108] Marketed products are almost certain to be listed; 'promotion' has been called a 'litmus test' for this purpose.[109]

---

[103] IRC, s. 6111. By requiring both taxpayers and material advisors to disclose the same transactions, the disclosure regime is 'redundant by design'. Granwell and McGonigle (2006, p. 173).

[104] IRC, s. 6111(b)(1)(A). That amount is $50,000 if 'substantially all of the tax benefits' from the reportable transaction go to natural persons, otherwise $250,000. IRC s. 6111(b)(1)(B).

[105] IRC s. 6111(a).   [106] IRC s. 6112(a) and (b)(1); Treasury Regulation § 301.6112–1.

[107] 'The term *transaction* includes all of the factual elements relevant to the expected tax treatment of any investment, entity, plan, or arrangement, and includes any series of steps carried out as part of a plan.' Treasury Regulation § 1.6011–4(b)(1).

[108] See Notice 2001–17 in Internal Revenue Service *Cumulative Bulletin*, Vol. 2001–1, p. 730.

[109] Morse (2006, p. 1004).

2. 'Confidential transactions': ones 'offered to a taxpayer under conditions of confidentiality and for which the taxpayer has paid an advisor a
   minimum fee' ($50,000 to $250,000, depending on type of taxpayer).[110]
   The concern is obvious: transactions kept secret in that way emit an
   odour.
3. 'Transactions with contractual protection': ones requiring that any
   adviser's fee be returned if all or part of the promised tax results do not
   materialise.[111] How confident should anyone be about the merits of a
   tax position if the adviser is on the hook like this?
4. 'Loss transactions': ones for which a taxpayer claims a loss above a
   threshold amount (e.g., $10 million in one year for a corporation).[112]
5. 'Transactions of interest': ones identified by the Service through published guidance as having the potential for tax avoidance or evasion but
   about which the government has insufficient information to conclude
   that the deals are in fact avoidance or evasion transactions.[113] This
   category, added by regulations finalised in late July 2007, supplements,
   and indeed strengthens, the listing procedure.

The five categories do not pick up every transaction that you or I might
find suspect,[114] of course, but they are a good start.[115] In particular, the
power to list a newly discovered transaction, or to denote a transaction
as one 'of interest', permits the government to act fast, without having
to wait to rule definitively on the merits. (A published notice listing a
transaction might include definitive, substantive analysis, as did the one

---

[110] Treasury Regulation § 1.6011–4(b)(3).   [111] *Ibid.*, § 1.6011–4(b)(4).
[112] *Ibid.*, § 1.6011–4(b)(5).
[113] *Ibid.*, § 1.6011–4(b)(6); see Treasury Decision 9350, dated 31 July 2007 in *Internal
Revenue Bulletin*, Vol. 2007, LEXIS 685 (announcing new final regulations that include
this category).
[114] Contrast- Harvard Law Review Association (2004, p. 2255) ('[T]hese . . . largely unrelated
filters . . . suggest[] that the IRS lacks a well-defined principle for distinguishing between
legitimate and illegitimate transactions').
[115] Transactions with large book-tax differences and those 'involving a brief asset holding period' (under forty-six days) were once reportable as well. The Service decided,
however, that a schedule accompanying corporate tax returns requires enough data
to make further disclosure on book-tax differences unnecessary. See Notice 2006–6
in *Internal Revenue Bulletin*, Vol. 2006–5, p. 385. Commentators convinced the Service that transactions involving brief holding periods did not need to be reported.
See Treasury Decision 9350 dated 31 July 2007 in *Internal Revenue Bulletin*, Vol. 2007,
LEXIS 685.

listing contingent liability transactions, but it need not do so.[116] Denoting a transaction as 'of interest' signals that the Service does not yet know enough to rule definitively.) The effect of listing is likely to be immediate on investors who are not already participating in such a transaction: they will have been warned that they should probably look elsewhere for tax thrills. The effect of denominating a transaction as 'of interest' may not be quite so stark, but it would deter most investors. (It would deter me.)

In the abstract, the deterrent effects of disclosure are obvious, but the system – inevitably? – does not work as smoothly as hoped.[117] And critics worry that the government will overemphasise disclosure to the exclusion of other methods. Weisbach has repeatedly stressed the need to reform substantive law. Requiring disclosure of a transaction that is deemed to meet legal requirements – like a *Black & Decker* deal (maybe) before Congress acted or a *Cottage Savings* deal today – seems pointless.[118]

Weisbach is right that disclosure by itself will not do the job, but he may underestimate its positive effects. Pearlman stresses the importance of 'tax return disclosure' because, he argues, many shelters do *not* 'work'.[119] Make taxpayers disclose suspect positions that might turn out to be losers, and disclosure can disinfect the system, without Congress's having to change substantive law.

Even if suspect transactions do 'work', not many taxpayers have a 'Bring it on!' attitude. Tell them disclosure is required, that the government is curious, and most will do tax planning in other ways. For example, disclosure directed at *promoted* shelters has largely shut those shelters down, whatever legal arguments might have been marshalled on their

---

[116] See Notice 2001–17 in Internal Revenue Service *Cumulative Bulletin*, Vol. 2001–1, p. 730 (providing alternative rationales for contingent liabilities reducing stock basis in a *Black & Decker*-like transaction).

[117] Schizer argues that advisors have an incentive to do no more than the minimum to avoid penalties. Moreover, '[t]he tax bar is highly motivated to undermine the effectiveness of [the disclosure] effort', Schizer (2006, p. 369), through, for example, interpreting 'reportable transaction' hyper-technically and burying the government in paper. *Ibid.*, p. 370.

[118] See, for example, Weisbach (2001, p. 78) ('Many of these transactions work under current law. [T]hey do not rely on the audit lottery. Disclosure and penalties would not stop them'). In its notice listing contingent liability shelters, however, the Service made it clear that, in its view, those transactions do *not* work. See Notice 2001–17 in Internal Revenue Service *Cumulative Bulletin*, Vol. 2001–1, p. 730.

[119] Pearlman (2002, pp. 292–3).

behalf.[120] (And Weisbach concedes disclosure's potential as a way to learn about new avoidance strategies.[121])

Two other sceptics, Chirelstein and Zelenak, argue that 'disclosure is not a solution' in part because 'the government has lost at least as many audited tax shelter cases as it has won'.[122] But the government's win-loss record in litigation, which has been improving anyway,[123] is not a good measure of disclosure's effect. A possibility of prevailing on the merits is not going to convince many taxpayers to go ahead with a transaction that must be disclosed. A 50 per cent chance of success in litigation for a transaction that might escape discovery is much more appealing than a 50 per cent chance of success for a transaction the government knows about. Disclosure increases the expected cost of any penalties, as well as the expected cost of defending questionable return positions.

I respect the critics who doubt the efficacy of disclosure, but I am convinced it is helping control abusive behaviour. Yes, complexity and costs of compliance remain concerns. Lawyers are making good livings deciphering disclosure rules – parsing the definition of 'minimum fee' or whatever – and that is not the best use of America's human capital.

One nevertheless hopes that, once the rules have become part of the landscape, compliance concerns will largely disappear. Determining whether a transaction is reportable is generally not going to be hard for most taxpayers and advisors. And the cost of planning around disclosure rules will itself be enough of a disincentive to deter some undesirable behaviour.

5.7 Improving advisors' behaviour

Another anti-avoidance mechanism in vogue is, in Lavoie's phrase, to 'co-opt[] the tax bar into dissuading corporate tax shelters'.[124] Congress long ago authorised the Secretary of the Treasury to 'regulate the practice of representatives of persons before the [Internal Revenue Service]',[125]

---

[120] See Morse (2006, p. 1003) ('[L]abeling promoted tax shelter transactions as deviant behavior has . . . translated into an anti-tax shelter compliance norm.'). High-profile prosecution of promoters has also obviously helped in the shutdown. See Granwell and McGonigle (2006, pp. 171–3).
[121] See Weisbach (2001, p. 78) ('The benefit of disclosure comes only if the government is willing to change, or at least clarify, the law.'); Weisbach (2002, p. 226).
[122] Chirelstein and Zelenak (2005, p. 1942).   [123] See Simmonds (2007, p. 913).
[124] Lavoie (2001, p. 43).   [125] United States Code, Title 31, s. 330(a)(1).

and regulations known as 'Circular 230' followed in 1966 – with many subsequent revisions, most recently in 2005.[126] 'Practice . . . before the . . . [Service]' is defined so broadly – including not only physical appearances, but also communications, preparing and filing documents, and other activities[127] – that complying with the requirements of Circular 230 is a *sine qua non* for a tax practitioner.[128]

For present purposes, the important parts of Circular 230 are the rules governing opinions that practitioners may give about tax shelters. (The term 'tax shelter' is no longer used in the regulations, but the idea survives in rules, promulgated in 2005, that govern 'covered opinions'.) Regulate the content of opinions and constrain the way potential investors can use those opinions, and shaky transactions may lose their underpinnings.

The bar is critical of Circular 230, in part because many of the rules are directed at the bar. And some of the criticism is justified. Well motivated though it is, Circular 230 contains a lot of regulatory overkill. Anyone receiving e-mails from American tax lawyers must chuckle at the attached disclaimers. Following a message like 'Lunch at 12:30?' comes the boilerplate – like 'IRS Circular 230 Notice: To comply with US Treasury regulations, we advise you that any US federal tax advice included in this communication is not intended or written to be used, and cannot be used, to avoid any US federal tax penalties or to promote, market, or recommend to another party any transaction or matter'.[129] All you want is a hamburger, and you get a lecture on Circular 230.

For clients (and others who might see an opinion, such as offerees of a marketed shelter), the big concern is protection against penalties. The risk of taking an aggressive position on one's tax return is not only that, if the position is disallowed, unpaid tax plus interest will be due; it is also that penalties might be imposed. Some penalties do not apply if a taxpayer can demonstrate it acted in 'good faith', with 'reasonable cause' for the return position,[130] but an opinion of counsel will provide penalty protection – 'reasonable cause' – only if Circular 230's requirements have been satisfied.

---

[126] The rules are found in Part 10 of Title 31 of the Code of Federal Regulations. I shall cite to Circular 230, rather than to CFR.

[127] Circular 230 § 10.2(d).

[128] Return preparation, which need not be done by lawyers, accountants, or enrolled agents, has its own set of rules. See Circular 230 §§ 10.7(e), 10.22(a), 10.34 and IRC, s. 6694.

[129] The disclaimers are intended to ensure that the e-mail is not a 'reliance opinion' or a 'marketed opinion', as defined below.

[130] See IRC, s. 6664(c)(1) and (d)(1).

For tax lawyers,[131] providing a rosy opinion about a shaky tax position was always risky – damage to reputation, possible malpractice, and the like – but Circular 230 increases the stakes. Violating Circular 230 can lead to the tax lawyer's losing practice privileges before the Service and to other sanctions.[132] (These rules are enforced by an Office of Professional Responsibility in the Treasury Department, which, in egregious cases, intends to pursue *public* disciplinary proceedings.[133]) Circular 230 also pushes firms to police themselves, providing for sanctioning bosses who do not adequately supervise their underlings.[134]

I cannot discuss all of Circular 230's particulars here, even if I wanted to.[135] The brief overview that follows should demonstrate why the rules can have significant effect on written advice about any tax shelter – the advice is likely to be a 'covered opinion' – but knowing the particulars is unnecessary to understand the underlying ideas. The content of documents, including e-mails, that provide tax advice is serious business under Circular 230. Because of Circular 230, lawyers should be much less willing than was true in the past to give disclaimer-free, favourable written advice about tax shelters. As a result, taxpayers are much less likely to get the opinions they require to take aggressive positions on their tax returns while avoiding penalty risk. No favourable opinion, no penalty protection, and, often therefore, no shelter.

Requirements for 'covered opinions'. If opinions are 'covered', they must satisfy requirements that make these opinions 'elaborate and expensive exercises':[136]

1. The lawyer must use reasonable efforts to identify and ascertain relevant facts; not base the opinion on unreasonable factual assumptions; and not base the opinion on any factual statement the lawyer knows (or should know) is incorrect or incomplete.[137]
2. He must relate applicable law to relevant facts; generally not assume favourable resolution of any significant tax issue or otherwise base the opinion on unreasonable assumptions, representations, or

---

[131] I will refer to lawyers, although the term 'practitioners' in Circular 230 includes accountants and others as well.
[132] See Circular 230 § 10.50; Morse (2006, pp. 991–2).   [133] See Morse (2006, p. 992).
[134] Circular 230 § 10.36.   [135] I don't.
[136] Morse (2006, p. 991). Written opinions that are not 'covered' must still satisfy some specific requirements, and in no event are lawyers to give written advice that takes audit-lottery possibilities into account. Circular 230 § 10.37.
[137] Circular 230 § 10.35(c)(1).

conclusions; and not include internally inconsistent analyses or conclusions in the opinion.[138]

3. He must generally consider *all* significant federal tax issues and provide a conclusion as to the likelihood that the taxpayer would prevail on the merits on each significant issue[139] (*not* taking audit-lottery considerations into account in the evaluation).[140]

4. He must provide an overall conclusion as to the federal tax treatment of the transaction, or, if that cannot be done, provide reasons why.[141]

If any covered opinion does not reach a more-likely-than-not conclusion (i.e., a confidence level of more than 50 per cent) for any significant tax issue, that fact must be disclosed prominently in the opinion. In addition, the opinion must prominently note that, for any such low-confidence issues, the opinion 'was not written, and cannot be used by the taxpayer, for the purpose of avoiding penalties that might be imposed on the taxpayer'.[142]

'*Covered opinion*'. Given those requirements, a covered opinion is obviously not something that should be dashed off over tea; it is supposed to be a painstaking exercise. And the term includes much more than the formal documents traditionally called legal opinions. It can include almost *any* written advice, including electronic communications,[143] relating to federal tax issues arising from three related, but different, types of transactions: (1) a 'listed' or substantially similar transaction, as the term was used in the disclosure discussion; (2) '[a]ny partnership or other entity, any investment plan or arrangement, the *principal purpose* of which is the avoidance or evasion of any tax imposed by the Internal Revenue Code'; and (3) a 'reliance opinion', a 'marketed opinion', or an opinion

---

[138] *Ibid.*, § 10.35(c)(2).

[139] *Ibid.*, § 10.35(c)(3). In some cases, a 'limited scope opinion' may address selected tax issues and make factual and legal assumptions that otherwise would not be permitted – assuming that appropriate disclosure is made about the opinion's limited scope. However, marketed opinions and opinions issued for listed transactions and for transactions where a principal purpose is tax avoidance or evasion can *never* be limited scope opinions. See *ibid.*, § 10.35(c)(3)(v) and (e)(3).

[140] *Ibid.*, § 10.35(c)(3)(iii). That is, it is not appropriate for a lawyer to give a *don't-worry-about-it* opinion to the effect that the auditing agent is unlikely to notice the suspect transaction.

[141] *Ibid.*, § 10.35(c)(4).   [142] See *ibid.*, § 10.35(e)(4).

[143] It is some small comfort to practitioners that *oral* communications are not covered (but oral advice would not provide penalty protection anyway). In addition, preliminary written advice to a client during an engagement is not 'covered' if the practitioner is expected later to provide written advice that will be a 'covered opinion'. *Ibid.*, § 10.35(b)(2)(ii)(A).

'subject to conditions of confidentiality' or 'subject to contractual pro-tection', if the opinion relates to '[a]ny partnership or other entity, any investment plan or arrangement' and a *significant purpose* (a lower stan-dard than the *principal purpose* test in category (2)) for the arrangement is tax avoidance or evasion.[144]

Breathe

That group of transactions includes almost anything that might be con-sidered a tax shelter. Remember that, although tax *evasion* is illegal, *avoidance* – planning in permissible ways to reduce one's tax bill – is not. Indeed, it is what tax professionals help their clients do.[145] If tax avoidance is at least a 'significant purpose' – and, for a shelter, that is obviously (and tautologically) the case – the rules applicable to covered opinions are going to apply.[146] So, for example, if a 'reliance opinion' – one that reaches a conclusion, at a confidence level of more than 50 per cent, that one or more significant tax issues would be resolved in the taxpayer's favour – is issued for a *significant purpose* transaction, that opinion is 'covered'.[147]

A 'marketed' opinion – one to be used by a person outside the firm in 'promoting, marketing, or recommending a partnership or other entity', etc. – is also going to be 'covered' if tax avoidance is at least a significant purpose for the transaction.[148] In addition to the other rules applicable to covered opinions, Circular 230 requires that any marketed opinion come to a more-likely-than-not conclusion (a more than 50 per cent likelihood of success) about *every* significant tax issue and about the overall tax effect of the transaction. In addition, a marketed opinion must include disclosures that it was written to support the marketing effort, and that recipients of the opinion should consult their own tax advisors about the transaction described.[149] High standards indeed.

Disclaimers. Circular 230 seems to provide a way around some of the stringent rules through disclaimers (as in the e-mails), but the benefits of disclaiming are chimerical. For example, written advice that includes

---

[144] *Ibid.*, § 10.35(b)(2)(i).
[145] Use of a partnership, say, which avoids entity-level taxation and permits pass-through of losses, presumably always has tax avoidance as at least a *significant* purpose, and in many cases it is the *principal* one.
[146] In both *Black & Decker* and *Cottage Savings*, for example, tax avoidance was the *only* purpose for the transactions.
[147] Circular 230 § 10.35(b)(2)(i) and (b)(4).   [148] *Ibid.*, § 10.35(b)(5)(i).
[149] *Ibid.*, § 10.35(c)(3)(iv), (c)(4)(ii) and (e)(2).

a disclaimer stating that the advice may not be used to protect against penalties does not count as a reliance opinion.[150] From the lawyer's standpoint, that seems to be good; the requirements for covered opinions might not have to be satisfied. But a taxpayer who is told that he is not entitled to rely on the opinion will not be in a good mood: the disclaimer works for Circular 230 purposes by making the opinion essentially worthless as penalty protection.

Similarly, what would otherwise be a *marketed* opinion will not be subject to the marketed-opinion rules if it contains a disclaimer – that it is not to be used for penalty protection, that the recipient should consult its own tax advisors, and so on.[151] The effect is that an opinion that will do no good in marketing anyway – because nobody can rely on it – need not be treated as a 'marketed opinion'. The opinion might be an interesting intellectual exercise, but, for penalty (and therefore marketing) purposes, it will not be worth the paper it is written on, or the electrons it is written with.

* * * * *

Circular 230's requirements are far-reaching, but this is not to say that favourable opinions will never again be issued for tax shelters. I think the result in *Cottage Savings* was too good to be true, but I would be willing to give an overwhelmingly favourable opinion about a similar transaction today. My opinion would be 'covered'; the 'principal', indeed the only, purpose of the transaction would be tax avoidance. But a very favourable opinion could be safely issued with a Supreme Court case directly on point. I might be bothered by the hyper-technical interpretation applied in *Cottage Savings*, but, if the court says the law is *X*, the law is *X*. Taxpayers are entitled to too-good-to-be-true results if that is what Congress intended (or is deemed to have intended).

In a high percentage of shelter situations, however, the Circular 230 rules should prevent lawyers from issuing unqualifiedly favourable opinions, and, without such opinions, proposed shelters will not proceed. If the Office of Professional Responsibility is able to meet its enforcement obligations, these rules have bite.

Conclusion: beyond the rules and a few final thoughts

If there is a lesson in all of this – and there is, of course – it is that no single method of attack on tax shelters is going to be successful. Give

---

[150] See *Ibid.*, § 10.35(b)(4)(ii).   [151] *Ibid.*, § 10.35(b)(5).

too much emphasis to economic substance alone, for example, and, as Weisbach argues, 'shelters themselves may get worse' in that they will become more exotic to satisfy the requirement.[152] But change substantive rules where appropriate, apply anti-avoidance doctrines forcefully, add in disclosure, make sure lawyers are not promising better tax results than are justified, and the system just might work – not perfectly, of course, but adequately.[153]

The precise mixture of governmental weapons used will have to vary over time because the shelter target is a moving one. Some smart people make sure of that. In an often-quoted line, Ginsburg said that '[t]he tax bar is the repository of the greatest ingenuity in America, and given the chance, those people will do you in'.[154] That is funny – and largely true.

'Ingenuity' is great, up to a point. It is generally better to have smart tax lawyers than dumb ones. But it is even better to have smart, honourable tax lawyers. We should not emphasise rules to such an extent that we ignore the professional norms that guided American tax lawyers for decades.

One of my colleagues claims that tax lawyers all work for the government. That is not true, of course, but tax lawyers are obligated to provide advice in a responsible way. It used to be understood, at the better law firms at least, that certain things were just not done. Certain types of transactions were not the sort that *professionals* worked on. If that understanding has changed, it needs to be resurrected. If it still exists at the better firms, as I think it does – it is one of the things that makes those firms 'better' – it needs to be preserved and extended.

Recent scholarship recognises the critical role of the tax lawyer as *lawyer* in curbing abusive behaviour – not because anything in Circular 230 applies, but because behaving responsibly and exercising good judgment are part of being a lawyer. Beale emphasises that 'the basic opinion practices [of Circular 230] (e.g., thorough consideration of law and facts, rejection of unrealistic assumptions) are not substantially different from that which has traditionally been considered good lawyering'.[155] Rostain argues that tax lawyers who have moved to accounting firms, which are technically not permitted to practise law,[156] might be less inclined to view

---

[152] Weisbach (2002, p. 237) (footnote omitted).
[153] I have largely ignored a factor that should not be ignored: the costs of implementing, and complying with, the various methods. In general, it makes no sense to spend $100 to bring in $99 in revenue. However, we do not yet have sufficient data to do informed cost-benefit analyses.
[154] United States (1982) (testimony of M. D. Ginsburg).   [155] Beale (2006, p. 619).
[156] What they do, however, often looks a lot like law practice.

themselves in a professionally appropriate way.[157] Canellos notes that, although many shelter 'professionals' are lawyers, they do not adhere to the standards that guide lawyers generally: 'The tax shelter professional is a different breed, by experience, temperament, reputation, and calling... Tax shelter professionals tend to be specialists rather than generalists and often suffer from the specialist's lack of judgment.'[158] And so on.

'Oh piffle', I hear some of you say. Encouraging tax lawyers to act as *lawyers*, as traditionally understood, is the equivalent of endorsing apple pie, motherhood and cricket. In this context, it also might seem otherworldly. Who am I, an academic not engaged in the practice of law, to imply that lawyers ought not to give opinions that depend only on hyper-technical readings of authority? After all, refusing to provide an opinion can have unhappy economic consequences for a lawyer, and the kids have to eat.

The disclosure rules and Circular 230 do not define honour, however, and acting honourably is what tax lawyers should be doing. This brings me back to the reason for this essay and this book. We are honouring an honourable man, John Tiley, the consummate tax lawyer and scholar. We know from John's life – which, I am sure, has at least another half century to go, with Mount Everest yet to be climbed! – that tax lawyers can in fact meet the highest possible standards, while being immersed in the nitty-gritty details of practice and scholarship. Piffle this is not.

---

[157] Rostain (2006, p. 120).   [158] Canellos (2001, p. 56).

6

The law of taxation and unjust enrichment

GRAHAM VIRGO

Introduction

My first piece of academic research on being appointed to a Lectureship in Taxation at Cambridge, where I taught with John Tiley, concerned the extent to which the law of taxation could be supplemented by the common law of unjust enrichment.[1] This was prompted by the decision of the House of Lords in *Woolwich Equitable Building Society v IRC*,[2] which recognised a common law right to restitution of taxes. Over the subsequent fifteen years, the law of unjust enrichment has developed dramatically, and one of the main contexts for that development has concerned the recovery of taxes which were not due to the Revenue. This has recently reached its highpoint in the context of the extensive litigation arising from the decision of the ECJ[3] that part of the UK tax legislation was discriminatory and consequently the national court had to provide remedies for those taxpayers who had paid taxes which were unlawfully paid to the Revenue. Now is an opportune time to review this litigation and to reassess the modern interrelationship between the law of unjust enrichment and the law of taxation.

At the heart of any claim for the restitution of taxes is the fundamental proposition that the state can only demand the payment of tax where it is lawfully authorised to do so.[4] The Revenue can be considered to have

---

[1] Virgo (1993).   [2] [1993] AC 70 (HL).
[3] Case C-410/98 *Metallgesellschaft; Hoechst* [2001] ECR I-1727 (ECJ).
[4] Bill of Rights 1689, Art. 4: 'levying money for or to the use of the Crown, by pretence of prerogative without grant of Parliament, for longer time, or in any other manner than the same is or shall be granted, is illegal.' See *Gosling v Veley* (1850) 12 QB 328 (Ex Ch) at p. 407 (Wilde CJ); *Attorney-General v Wilts United Dairies Ltd* (1922) 38 TLR 781 (HL) at p. 782 (Lord Buckmaster); *Congreve v Home Office* [1976] QB 629 (CA) at p. 652 (Lord Denning MR); *Woolwich Equitable Building Society v IRC* [1993] AC 70 (HL) at p. 177 (Lord Goff); *Kingstreet Investments Ltd v Province of New Brunswick* [2007] 1 SCR 3 (SCC)

received tax unlawfully for a variety of different reasons. For example, the money may have been paid pursuant to a statute which was invalid or a statutory provision may have been interpreted incorrectly or the tax assessment may simply have been mistaken, either by virtue of a mistake made by the Revenue or the taxpayer. In each case, because the Revenue has received tax which was not lawfully due to it, that tax ought to be repaid to the taxpayer. The crucial questions which need to be considered concern whether the modern law of unjust enrichment can provide an effective framework for the recovery of this money and, if it cannot, to what extent it should be reinterpreted or reformed to provide such a framework.

6.1 The relevance of the law of restitution

The nature of the law of restitution

The law of restitution is preferably defined as that body of law which is concerned with the award of a generic group of remedies which arise by operation of law to deprive the defendant of a gain rather than to compensate the claimant for loss suffered.[5] Although the matter remains controversial, the preferable view is that such remedies are triggered by three distinct principles.[6] One is the vindication of property rights, where the defendant has received property in which the claimant has retained or obtained a legal or equitable proprietary interest.[7] It is inconceivable that such a claim would arise in respect of a claim for the recovery of tax, since, where money is paid to discharge a tax liability, title to that money will pass even if the tax liability did not exist. This is supported by the decision of the House of Lords in *Westdeutsche Landesbank Girozentrale v Islington LBC*,[8] where banks paid money to public authorities in respect of interest rate swap transactions. These transactions were subsequently declared void, but this did not prevent title to the money from passing to the

---

at para. 40. Similarly, where a public authority pays money unlawfully it has a right to recover it: *Attorney-General v Wilts United Dairies Ltd* [1924] AC 318 (HL).

[5] See Lord Wright (1939, p. 36); *Kingstreet Investments Ltd v Province of New Brunswick* [2007] 1 SCR 3 (SCC) at para. 47.

[6] Virgo (2006, pp. 6–18).

[7] See *Foskett v McKeown* [2001] 1 AC 102 (HL) at p. 129 (Lord Millett).

[8] [1996] AC 669 (HL).

public authorities so that a restitutionary claim based on the vindication of property rights could not be established.[9]

Secondly, a restitutionary remedy may be available where the defendant has profited from the commission of a wrong, such as the commission of certain torts, equitable wrongs or, exceptionally, breach of contract. This type of claim could conceivably arise in the context of restitution of taxes which were not due, if it can be established that the unlawful demand for payment of taxes constitutes a wrong. There is no explicit evidence of such an approach being adopted in the case law, although, as will be seen later, such a claim might be more likely to succeed where the demand for tax infringes EC law.[10]

It is the third principle underpinning the law of restitution which has been of most significance to claims for the recovery of taxes which were not due. This is the unjust enrichment principle, which was formally recognised by the House of Lords in 1991,[11] but which has a much older pedigree.[12] Although 'unjust enrichment' has sometimes been used in a purely descriptive sense to describe a state of affairs where the defendant can be considered to have been enriched in circumstances of injustice, it is properly regarded as a substantive cause of action in its own right consisting of a formula, all elements of which need to be satisfied. This formula consists of four distinct elements:[13]

1. The defendant must have received an enrichment. This is easily established in respect of restitutionary claims to recover taxes which were not due, because the claimant will usually have paid money to the Revenue and, since this is the measure of enrichment, money is considered to be an incontrovertible benefit.[14]
2. The enrichment must have been received directly at the expense of the claimant. Again, this will easily be established as regards the payment of taxes which were not due, since usually the money purportedly

---

[9] A claim based on the vindication of equitable proprietary rights did not succeed either, primarily because the receipt of the money by the defendant could not be characterised as unconscionable to enable a constructive trust to be created. However, a claim based on unjust enrichment was successful.

[10] See discussion below.

[11] *Lipkin Gorman (a firm) v Karpnale Ltd* [1991] 2 AC 548 (HL).

[12] This can be traced back to *Moses v Macferlan* (1776) 2 Burr 1005 (KB) at p. 1012 (Lord Mansfield). See also *Fibrosa Spolka Akcyjna v Fairbairn Lawson Combe Barbour Ltd* [1943] AC 32 (HL) at p. 61 (Lord Wright).

[13] *Banque Financière de la Cité v Parc (Battersea) Ltd* [1999] 1 AC 221 (HL) at p. 227 (Lord Steyn).

[14] *BP Exploration Co (Libya) Ltd v Hunt* [1979] 1 WLR 783 (QBD) at p. 799 (Robert Goff J).

paid to discharge a tax liability will be paid directly by the claimant to the defendant tax authority. It has sometimes been suggested that the defendant's gain must correspond with the claimant's loss. This is unlikely to be an issue as regards the payment of taxes, since the claimant's loss will correspond with the Revenue's gain. Anyway, Lord Hope has recently rejected the principle that gain must coincide with loss[15] since the focus of a restitutionary claim is the defendant's gain and not the claimant's loss.

3. The enrichment must have been received in circumstances of injustice, meaning that the claim falls within one of the recognised grounds of restitution. This has been the most controversial part of the unjust enrichment claim in the context of taxation, since the established grounds of restitution have not always been readily applicable to the recovery of taxes which were not due.[16]

4. The defendant is not able to rely on a defence which defeats the claim. Whilst less controversial than the previous requirement, the identification and interpretation of defences has proved to be significant in the tax context.

Once the first three elements have been established and no defences operate to negate liability, a personal remedy will be awarded to enable the claimant to recover the value of the benefit which had been received by the defendant.[17]

The grounds of restitution

A number of grounds of restitution are recognised for the purposes of the law of unjust enrichment, some of which may be relevant to claims to recover taxes which were not due.

Mistake

One of the most significant grounds of restitution is that of mistake. Over 200 years ago this was recognised as operating where the claimant paid money to the defendant in the mistaken belief that he or she was liable

[15] *Sempra Metals Ltd v IRC* [2007] UKHL 34 (HL) at para. 31. See the further discussion of this case below.

[16] See discussion below.

[17] The determination of the appropriate remedy is sometimes considered to be a fifth question which needs to be examined. See *Lloyds Bank plc v Independent Insurance Co. Ltd* [2000] QB 110 (CA) at p. 123 (Waller LJ).

to pay the money.[18] Clearly this could be applicable where the claimant mistakenly believed that he or she was liable to pay tax to the Revenue. Today it is sufficient that the claimant's mistake was an operative cause of the payment being made,[19] which will also be satisfied where the claimant wrongly believes that there is a tax liability and paid the money to discharge it.

However, claims grounded on mistake were subject to a long-standing limitation that only mistakes of fact would ground a restitutionary claim and not mistakes of law.[20] A taxpayer may have made a mistake of fact where the mistake relates to the assessment of the tax. Where, however, the mistake relates to the very authority of the Revenue to demand payment this would constitute a mistake of law. However, the House of Lords in *Kleinwort Benson Ltd v Lincoln City Council*[21] abolished this mistake of law bar. Consequently, it has become much easier at common law to recover taxes which were not due.

There is an advantage in relying on the mistake ground, since this can result in a longer limitation period than the normal six-year limit in which the claimant can bring the claim. This arises by virtue of s. 32(1)(c) of the Limitation Act 1980, which states that, where an action involves relief from the consequences of mistake, time does not begin to run until the claimant discovered the mistake or could have done so through the exercise of reasonable diligence.[22]

With the abolition of the mistake of law bar and the advantage of the extended limitation period, it would seem that mistake is the ideal ground of restitution on which to rely when seeking to recover taxes which were not due. However, not every claim for the restitution of taxes can be founded on the mistake ground, because sometimes the claimant will simply not be mistaken in making the payment. This will be the case where the claimant knew that the tax was not due or suspected this.[23] Mere negligence on the part of the taxpayer, in the sense that the reasonable person would have realised that the tax was not due, will not, however, prevent the claimant from relying on the ground of mistake.[24]

[18] *Bilbie v Lumley* (1802) 2 East 649 (KB); *Kelly v Solari* (1841) 9 M and W 54 (Exch).
[19] *Barclays Bank v WJ Simms (Southern) Ltd* [1980] QB 677 (QBD).
[20] *Bilbie v Lumley* (1802) 2 East 649 (KB).   [21] [1999] 2 AC 349 (HL).
[22] Although this extension of the limitation period for taxes paid by mistake has been removed by s. 320 of the Finance Act 2004.
[23] See *Woolwich Equitable Building Society v IRC* [1993] AC 70 (HL), where the taxpayer suspected that the tax demanded by the Revenue might not be due but paid anyway because of the fear of adverse publicity if it was wrong.
[24] *Kelly v Solari* (1841) 9 M and W 54 (Exch).

Alternative grounds of restitution

Where the claimant cannot rely on mistake to recover tax which was not due, other orthodox grounds of restitution might be applicable. First, there is the ground of duress. This will apply where the defendant made an unlawful demand accompanied by a relevant threat, express or implied. Where the Revenue has demanded the payment of tax which was not due, this could be characterised as an unlawful demand. If it is accompanied by a threat against the person or a threat to seize goods, duress will be established. Since failure to pay tax may result in the defendant being imprisoned or fined, the demand to pay tax is accompanied by an implicit threat against the person or property and so duress could be established.[25]

Alternatively, where money has been paid on condition that an event will happen and the event does not occur, the money can be recovered on the ground of failure of consideration. This might be applicable as regards the recovery of taxes which were not due because the condition for the payment of the money is the discharge of liability to pay tax and, if there is no such liability, the condition will not be fulfilled. Here the ground of restitution is appropriately characterised as absence of consideration.[26]

Ultra vires demand

Since 1993, however, these alternative grounds of restitution have been of little significance as regards claims to recover taxes which were not due, because of the recognition of a new ground of restitution which is specifically concerned with the recovery of money from public authorities, such as the Revenue, when there was no authority for it to demand payment.

This independent ground of restitution was recognised by the House of Lords in *Woolwich Equitable Building Society v IRC*.[27] In this case the claimant building society had been assessed by the Revenue to pay tax by reference to regulations which were subsequently declared to be ultra vires. It followed that the claimant had paid £57 million more than was actually due. The Revenue repaid this money but refused to pay the interest claimed by the taxpayer from the date the Revenue had received the money until the regulations had been declared void.[28] This interest amounted to

---

[25] See *Maskell v Horner* [1915] 3 KB 106 (CA).
[26] See *Campbell v Hall* (1774) 1 Cowp 204 (KB): recovery of export duties which had been demanded without Parliamentary authority.
[27] [1993] AC 70 (HL).
[28] The Revenue conceded that it was liable to pay interest in respect of the period after the regulations had been declared to be void.

£6.73 million. It was held by the House of Lords that the Revenue was liable to pay this interest because it had been liable to repay the tax at common law from the moment of receipt by virtue of the unjust enrichment principle. The ground of restitution was not a mistake, but was held to be a new ground of restitution, namely that the Revenue had demanded an ultra vires payment and, for constitutional reasons, public authorities were not entitled to demand, receive or retain such payments. This principle was specifically recognised by Lord Goff as follows:

> money paid by a citizen to a public authority in the form of taxes or other levies paid pursuant to an *ultra vires* demand by the authority is *prima facie* recoverable by the citizen as of right.[29]

This constitutional justification for the recognition of this right to restitution has also been accepted by the Supreme Court of Canada in *Kingstreet Investments Ltd v Province of New Brunswick*.[30] The *Woolwich* principle has been recognised as applying only where there has been an unlawful demand for payment.[31] It is not confined to the recovery of taxes, but includes other levies paid to public authorities,[32] and applies even where the claimant is mistaken in paying the tax.[33] The limitation period for bringing claims founded on the *Woolwich* principle is restricted to six years, since the claim is not grounded on mistake to gain the benefit of the extended limitation period.[34]

Statutory routes to recovery

In addition to the common law route for recovery, there are also a variety of statutory mechanisms for the recovery of tax which was not due. If the statutory route for recovery applies then this will usually preclude

---

[29] [1993] AC 70 (HL) at p. 177.
[30] [2007] 1 SCR 3 (SCC), overruling the previous decision in *Air Canada v British Columbia* (1989) [1989] 1 SCR 1161 (SCC), which had rejected the right to recover taxes which were not due.
[31] *NEC Semi-Conductors v IRC* [2006] EWCA Civ 25 (CA) at para. 159 (Mummery LJ).
[32] *Waikato Regional Airport Ltd v AG* [2003] UKPC 50 (PC); *Deutsche Morgan Grenfell plc v IRC* [2006] UKHL 49 (HL) at para. 140 (Lord Walker).
[33] *Deutsche Morgan Grenfell plc v IRC* [2006] UKHL 49 (HL) at para. 13 (Lord Hoffmann).
[34] Although the better view is that, if the claimant was mistaken the extended limitation period should be available, even though it did not form part of the underlying cause of action. See discussion below.

reliance on the common law route,[35] although this is ultimately a matter of statutory construction.[36] Which statutory provision is relevant depends on the nature of the tax which is being sought to be recovered. The key provision is s. 33 of the Taxes Management Act 1970, which concerns the recovery of income tax and capital gains tax for which there has been an excessive assessment by reason of some error or mistake[37] in the tax return. That is why s. 33 was not applicable in Woolwich, because no valid assessment of tax liability had been made. Where s. 33 does apply, it excludes the common law restitutionary regime,[38] but there is no automatic right to restitution since the Revenue is empowered to award such relief as it believes is reasonable and just.[39] No relief is to be granted where the tax return was made in accordance with the practice which was generally prevailing when the return was made.[40] This effectively constitutes a bar to prevent unnecessary disruption of public finances by confining recovery to cases of individual error rather than where the error arose from the general practice adopted by the Revenue.

Separate provision is made for the recovery of corporation tax paid by mistake[41] and Value Added Tax.[42] The latter mechanism applies even if the tax has not been paid by mistake, it being sufficient that the money was not due. The limitation period for statutory claims involving the recovery of income tax, capital gains tax and corporation tax is limited to six years, whereas the limitation period for claims involving VAT is three years.[43]

---

[35] Autologic Holdings plc v IRC [2005] UKHL 54 (HL) at paras. 20 (Lord Nicholls) and 62 (Lord Millett). See also Value Added Tax Act 1994, s. 80(7); IRC v Total Network SL [2007] EWCA Civ 39 (CA) (the statutory scheme for the recovery of overpaid VAT credits displaced any common law remedy).

[36] Deutsche Morgan Grenfell Group plc v IRC [2006] UKHL 49 (HL) at para. 135 (Lord Walker).

[37] Including a mistake of law: Heastie v Veitch (1933) 18 TC 305 (CA).

[38] Deutsche Morgan Grenfell Group plc v IRC [2006] UKHL 49 (HL) at para. 135 (Lord Walker).

[39] Taxes Management Act 1970, s. 33(2).

[40] Ibid. Whether a defence of a settled view of the law is generally available is considered below.

[41] Finance Act 1998, Sch. 18, para. 51.

[42] Value Added Tax Act 1994, s. 80, as amended by the Finance Act 1997, ss. 46–7. Section 73(2) of the VATA 1994 provides a mechanism for the Revenue and Customs Commissioners to recover money wrongly paid by way of VAT credits, subject to a three-year limitation period which is extended to twenty years where the VAT credit was obtained dishonestly: IRC v Total Network SL [2007] EWCA Civ 39 (CA) at para. 24.

[43] Value Added Tax Act 1994, s. 80(4), as amended by the Finance Act 1997.

Potential defences

Claims for unjust enrichment are subject to a number of specific defences. Chief amongst these is the defence of change of position,[44] which arises in two forms. First, where the defendant has spent the enrichment which was received from the claimant other than in the course of ordinary expenditure and, secondly, where, in reliance on this receipt, the defendant has changed his or her position in some other way. Either form of the defence will only be applicable where the change of position was in good faith and the defendant was not a wrongdoer. Whether this defence would be available in respect of claims for recovery of tax will depend on the facts. There is certainly no reason in principle why the defence should not be available to the Revenue.[45] However, it will be difficult for the Revenue to show that the money which was received has been expended in extraordinary circumstances or that the receipt of the tax resulted in other expenditure being incurred which would not have happened but for the receipt of the tax payment from the claimant.[46] Further, it could legitimately be argued that the Revenue is a wrongdoer, since it will, by definition, have received the money unlawfully. This objection based on wrongdoing will be much easier to establish where the reason for the unlawful receipt is that it contravenes European Community law.[47]

It would appear, therefore, that the defence of change of position is unlikely to be of any real significance as regards restitutionary claims against the Revenue. This will also be true as regards the alternative defence of estoppel. This applies where the defendant has received an enrichment and suffers detriment by relying on a representation from the claimant that the enrichment was properly transferred.[48] It is inconceivable that a taxpayer would have made such a representation on which the Revenue could have relied, so the defence could not be made out.

So if neither of the key defences to unjust enrichment claims is likely to be available to the Revenue, the odds of recovery are clearly stacked in the claimant's favour. But bearing in mind that the Revenue is a public authority, should such a result be tolerated? Should special defences be formulated for the particular benefit of the Revenue, bearing in mind that

---

[44] Recognised in *Lipkin Gorman (a firm) v Karpnale Ltd* [1991] 2 AC 548 (HL) at p. 580 (Lord Goff).

[45] Its potential application was even acknowledged by the House of Lords in *Sempra Metals Ltd v IRC* [2007] UKHL 34 (HL) at para. 119 (Lord Nicholls).

[46] *Deutsche Morgan Grenfell Group plc v IRC* [2006] UKHL 49 (HL) at para. 145 (Lord Walker).

[47] See discussion below.   [48] *United Overseas Bank v Jiwani* [1976] 1 WLR 964 (QBD).

taxes benefit the wider community? Various defences peculiar to public authorities have been canvassed over the years, but few have received much support, largely because they lack sufficient clarity. For example, it has been suggested that a defence should be available where restitution would seriously disrupt public finances. This was rejected by the Law Commission[49] and has never received judicial support. Alternatively, it has been suggested that the Revenue should have a defence where tax has been paid at a time where there was a settled view of the law that the tax was lawfully due. Such a defence was canvassed by Lord Goff in *Kleinwort Benson Ltd. v Lincoln CC*.[50] However, such a defence would undermine the constitutional rationale of requiring restitution in the first place, namely that if the tax was not due then the money should not be retained. It would also be very difficult to determine when a particular view of the law could be regarded as settled. This defence was specifically not recognised by the House of Lords in *Deutsche Morgan Grenfell Group plc v IRC*.[51]

There is, however, one other defence of potential significance to claims for restitution against public authorities, known as the defence of passing on. Where this defence is recognised, it operates to reduce the defendant's liability to make restitution to the extent that the claimant passed the loss, which had been incurred by paying money to the defendant, on to a third party. So, for example, in the tax context the defence could potentially be available if the claimant paid tax to the Revenue but passed this on to third parties by increasing its prices. This defence is implicitly recognised by statute as regards the recovery of overpaid VAT. Section 80(3) of the Value Added Tax Act 1994[52] recognises a defence of unjust enrichment which applies where the consequence of recovering overpaid VAT will be to unjustly enrich the claimant. In *Customs and Excise Commissioners v McMasters Stores (Scotland) Ltd.*[53] it was recognised that two conditions are required to establish the defence, namely that the claimant would be enriched by the recovery of VAT and this recovery would be unjust because the taxpayer would be placed in a better position than he or she would have occupied had the tax not been paid, as will occur where the

---

[49] United Kingdom (1994).
[50] [1999] 2 AC 349 (HL) at p. 382. See Taxes Management Act 1970, s. 33 for the recognition of such a defence as part of a statutory restitutionary mechanism. See discussion above.
[51] [2006] UKHL 49 (HL) at paras. 18 (Lord Hoffmann) and 145 (Lord Walker).
[52] As amended by the Finance Act 1997, s. 46. See Chowdry (2004). See also Finance Act 1989, s. 29(3), which contains a similar defence in respect of the recovery of overpaid Excise Duty and Car Tax.
[53] [1995] STC 846 (Ct Sess).

taxpayer has passed on the burden of the tax to his or her customers. This will not, however, be an easy defence to establish. For example, it does not follow from the fact that the taxpayer has increased prices that the burden of any tax has been passed on, because a consequence of the increase in prices might be a fall in sales. This was recognised by the Court of Appeal in *Baines and Ernst Ltd v Customs and Excise Commissioners,*[54] where it had been argued by the Commissioners of Customs and Excise that the taxpayer had increased charges for its debt management services following its payment of VAT, whereas the taxpayer had argued that it would have charged the same rate for its services even if they had been exempt from the tax. The court affirmed that the burden of proving that loss had been passed on was borne by the Revenue. Having regard to all the evidence, it was concluded that the burden of the tax had not been passed on to customers and so the defence failed.[55]

Although the passing on defence is potentially available for certain statutory claims for restitution of tax, it remains controversial whether the defence is available where the common law route for restitution is being pursued. In some jurisdictions the defence has been explicitly rejected, notably Australia[56] and Canada.[57] As regard the UK, in *Marks and Spencer plc v Customs and Excise Commissioners*[58] Lord Walker did recognise the defence, although this was *obiter* and he incorrectly assumed that this was consistent with the approach adopted by the High Court of Australia. In fact, there is clear authority against the recognition of the defence at common law in England,[59] and this is consistent with the principle of unjust enrichment.[60] For that principle is concerned with identifying whether the defendant's benefit was obtained at the expense of the claimant. The 'at the expense of' requirement exists to establish a connection between the defendant's receipt and the claimant's loss, but there is no need to show that the defendant's gain corresponds precisely with the claimant's loss.[61]

---

[54] [2006] EWCA Civ 1040 (CA).
[55] The UK has made a reference to the ECJ (Case C/309/06) concerning whether the existence of the unjust enrichment defence is compatible with EC law: *Marks and Spencer plc v Commissioners of Customs and Excise* [2005] UKHL 53 (HL).
[56] *Roxborough v Rothmans of Pall Mall Australia Ltd* [2001] HCA 68 (HCA).
[57] *Kingstreet Investments Ltd v Province of New Brunswick* [2007] 1 SCR 3 (SCC).
[58] [2005] UKHL 53 (HL).
[59] *Kleinwort Benson Ltd v Birmingham CC* [1997] QB 380 (CA), although the court did leave open the possibility of the defence applying to claims for the recovery of taxes.
[60] See Rush (2006), whose thesis is that passing on should not be recognised as a defence to the unjust enrichment claim.
[61] This was explicitly recognised by Lord Hope in *Sempra Metals Ltd v IRC* [2007] UKHL 34 (HL) at para. 31.

Rather, the requirement exists to establish a causative link between the transfer from the claimant and the receipt by the defendant. Further, the liability of the defendant to make restitution crystallises at the time when all the elements of the unjust enrichment formula have been satisfied. Events affecting the claimant after this crystallisation are irrelevant.[62]

In the light of this, it does seem odd that the defence has been recognised by statute as regards claims for the recovery of certain taxes. This application of the defence might be justified, however, on the ground that where the claimant taxpayer can be proved to have passed on the burden of the tax to his or her customers, the claimant could be considered to have collected the tax from the customers on behalf of the tax authority. Consequently, it is permissible to treat the tax authority as having been enriched at the expense of the customers, because the claimant is simply acting as the agent for the authority, so the customers should be able to sue the tax authority directly for recovery of the tax which was not due. But even this justification of the defence cannot avoid the real difficulties of proof that the claimant's loss has been passed on.

Summary of the law

This review of the law of unjust enrichment suggests a rational and principled development of the rules concerning restitution of taxes. There are two routes available to the claimant taxpayer. First, the statutory route, which will usually prevail over the common law regime. Secondly, if the statutory route is unavailable, the claimant can rely on the unjust enrichment principle at common law. As regards grounds of restitution the claimant can rely on the *Woolwich* principle, which is dependent on the unlawfulness of the Revenue's demand for payment, or mistake of law. In many cases there will be nothing to choose between them. Sometimes, however, the *Woolwich* principle will be preferable where the claimant is unable to establish a mistake, and in other cases mistake of law will be preferable either because the Revenue has not made an unlawful demand (where, for example, the taxpayer's liability is simply less than the Revenue claimed[63] or the taxpayer has paid the tax as a result of a tax return rather

---

[62] Of course, events after receipt which affect the defendant may reduce or eliminate liability through the operation of the defence of change of position: see discussion above. But this defence goes to the heart of restitutionary liability, concerning the extent of the defendant's gain. The law of restitution is not concerned with the identification and compensation of the claimant's loss.

[63] *NEC Semi-Conductors Ltd v IRC* [2006] EWCA Civ 25 (CA) at para. 91 (Sedley LJ).

than a demand from the Revenue)[64] or because the longer limitation rule is potentially available for mistake claims.

The coherence and elegance of this restitutionary structure has, however, been tested through a series of cases concerning the recovery of taxes, the receipt of which infringed EC law. A number of test cases have examined fundamental issues involving the law of unjust enrichment, concerning both the specifics of restitution of taxes at common law and also, more generally, the function of the unjust enrichment principle as a whole.

6.2 Restitutionary claims for the use of money

The European Court of Justice

The trigger for a spate of cases concerning restitution of tax was the decision of the European Court of Justice in *Metallgesellschaft; Hoechst*,[65] where it was held that the denial of group income relief[66] to companies which had paid dividends to parents resident in a Member State other than the UK was discriminatory and unlawful.[67] Subsidiary companies had consequently paid Advance Corporation Tax to the Revenue in respect of dividends which they had paid to their parent companies,[68] whereas if they had paid the dividends to parent companies incorporated in the UK, they would have made a group income relief election which would have had the effect of delaying the payment of tax. The ECJ decided that the UK had to provide an effective remedy for those taxpayers which had been denied relief and which had paid tax prematurely. The ECJ left open the appropriate legal characterisation of the remedy, considering that this was a matter to be resolved by the national courts. In different parts of

---

[64] *Ibid.* at para. 146 (Mummery LJ).

[65] Case C-410/98 *Metallgesellschaft; Hoechst* [2001] ECR I-1727 (ECJ).

[66] Which was available under the Income and Corporation Taxes Act 1988, s. 247.

[67] See also Case C-446/04 *Test Claimants in the FII Group Litigation* [2006] ECR I-11753 (ECJ) (concerning discrimination in the operation of the franked investment income regime as regards the receipt by UK companies of dividends from non-resident companies). Contrast *Boake Allen Ltd v IRC* [2007] UKHL 25 (HL) (denial of group income relief to subsidiaries of parent companies which were not incorporated within the EC did not involve discrimination under double tax conventions and, even if it did, there was no remedy under domestic law because international treaties do not give rise to any rights in English domestic law unless they were incorporated by legislation, as the EC Treaty is by the European Communities Act 1972).

[68] The period of discrimination was from 1973 to 1999.

its judgment, the ECJ considered that the remedy could be compensation for damage caused by breach of Community law[69] or restitutionary,[70] although AG Fennelly preferred the latter analysis.

A number of test cases were identified by the English courts raising a variety of different legal issues arising from the decision of the ECJ, one of which was *Sempra Metals Ltd (formerly Metallgesellschaft Ltd) v IRC*[71] and another was *Deutsche Morgan Grenfell v IRC.*[72] Both of these cases have been of real significance to the development of the modern law of unjust enrichment.

The causes of action at common law

The claimant taxpayers had three different routes to establishing a claim against the Revenue, one in tort and two for restitution.

Tort

Rights conferred by the EC Treaty fall within s. 2(1) of the European Communities Act. Consequently, infringement of a right under the EC Treaty constitutes breach of a statutory duty in English law,[73] for which compensatory damages are available.[74] The discrimination in denying group income relief to companies with parents who were not resident in EU states contravened what is now Art. 43 of the EC Treaty, which guarantees freedom of establishment. The underlying cause of action here is the wrong and not unjust enrichment.[75] Although remedies to compensate for loss arising from the commission of a wrong are usually awarded, sometimes restitutionary remedies have been awarded to deprive the wrongdoer of any benefits obtained from the commission of the wrong.[76] The award of restitutionary remedies for wrongs tends, however, to be available only where the defendant has committed a property tort[77] and not for breach of statutory duty.

---

[69] Case C-410/98 *Metallgesellschaft; Hoechst* [2001] ECR I-1727 (ECJ) at para. 90.
[70] *Ibid.* at para. 82.   [71] [2007] UKHL 34 (HL).   [72] [2006] UKHL 49 (HL).
[73] *Garden Cottage Foods Ltd v Milk Marketing Board* [1984] 1 AC 130 (HL) at p. 141 (Lord Diplock).
[74] Case C-48/93 *Factortame* [1996] ECR I-1029 (ECJ).
[75] *NEC Semi-Conductors Ltd v IRC* [2006] EWCA Civ 25 (CA) at para. 95 (Sedley LJ). See also *Pirelli Cable Holding NV v Commissioners for Revenue and Customs* [2006] UKHL 4 (HL).
[76] See, for example, *Ministry of Defence v Ashman* [1993] 2 EGLR 102 (CA) (trespass to land).
[77] See Virgo (2006, pp. 465–75).

Unjust enrichment

It was recognised in *Sempra Metals Ltd*[78] that the claimant had two distinct claims for restitution in respect of the premature payment of tax. First, a claim to recover the tax itself. This claim could not be pursued, however, if the tax paid was eventually[79] set off against the claimant's mainstream corporation tax liability. Secondly, a claim in respect of the benefit obtained by the defendant in having the use of the money until it was set off against the claimant's corporation tax liability. As regards this second claim, the relevant cause of action was within the law of unjust enrichment and two grounds of restitution were potentially available, namely the *Woolwich* principle[80] and mistake of law. In some cases the taxes had been paid more than six years before the claim was brought, so that the claim was time barred unless the claimant could found the claim on a mistake of law, for which time would not begin to run until the mistake could reasonably have been discovered. Whether the claimant could elect to rely on mistake rather than the *Woolwich* principle was the key issue for the House of Lords in *Deutsche Morgan Grenfell*.

Deutsche Morgan Grenfell

Deutsche Morgan Grenfell had made three payments of Advance Corporation Tax without the benefit of group income relief in 1993, 1995 and 1996, which it claimed it would have elected had it been able to do so. It sought restitutionary relief in respect of the Revenue's use of each payment. The claims for restitution in respect of the second and third payments were made within the six-year limitation period, but the first payment was not. Deutsche Morgan Grenfell claimed a sum assessed by the application of a rate of interest, not as an ancillary remedy but as a measure of the principal sum which the claimant argued that the Revenue owed to it for the Revenue's use of the claimant's money.

The trial judge, Park J,[81] held that the claimant had made a mistake of law in failing to elect for group relief which should have been made available to it. Since it could found its claim on mistake, it followed that s. 32(1)(c) of the Limitation Act 1980 applied with the result that no part of

---

[78] [2007] UKHL 34 (HL) at para. 162 (Lord Walker).
[79] In *Sempra Metals Ltd v IRC* [2007] UKHL 34 (HL), set-off of one payment occurred up to ten years after payment to the Revenue, although the average period was eight years.
[80] The application of this principle in this context was doubted by Mummery LJ in *NEC Semi-Conductors v IRC* [2006] EWCA Civ 25 (CA) at para. 161.
[81] [2003] STC 1017 (Ch D). See Virgo (2004).

the action was time barred because the claimant could not have reasonably discovered the mistake of law before the ECJ had delivered judgement in *Metallgesellschaft*. The Court of Appeal reversed this decision.[82] It held that a fundamental distinction should be drawn between public and private law claims for restitution. The claim for recovery of tax fell within the public law regime and could only be recovered with reference either to a particular statutory regime or, if one was not available, the *Woolwich* principle at common law. Crucially, the ground of mistake of law was held only to be available for private law claims and so it followed that the extended limitation period was not available to the claimant.

The House of Lords reversed the decision of the Court of Appeal and reinstated that of Park J.[83] It followed that the claimant could ground its claim for restitution on the common law ground of mistake of law and so gain the benefit of the extended limitation period. It was held that the mistake was not discovered until the ECJ had given judgment[84] and so no part of the claim was time barred. This decision is much less significant as regards future claims for the recovery of taxes which were not due following the enactment of s. 320 of the Finance Act 2004, which retrospectively limits the limitation period for all claims for the recovery of taxes paid under a mistake of law to the usual six-year period.[85]

Although the result of the decision of the House of Lords is clear, there was significant disagreement between their Lordships as to some fundamental issues concerning the law of unjust enrichment, especially in the context of recovery of taxes.

Concurrent claims

It is an essential feature of the view of the majority that, if a statutory mechanism for the recovery of taxes is not available, the claimant has the choice of which ground of restitution to rely on for the purposes of establishing an unjust enrichment claim at common law. In particular, if the claimant can establish that the payment was made under a mistake, it is legitimate to rely on this ground to obtain the benefit of the extended limitation period even if other grounds of restitution are available. It was emphasised that concurrent claims involving either contract or tort are recognised,[86] so that a claimant can choose to sue either in contract or

---

[82] [2005] EWCA Civ. 78 (CA). See Virgo (2005).   [83] [2006] UKHL 49 (HL).
[84] *Ibid.* at para. 144 (Lord Walker).
[85] The provision arguably is invalid under EC law because no transitional period was included. See Chowdry (2005).
[86] *Henderson v Merrett Syndicates Ltd* [1995] 2 AC 145 (HL) at p. 193.

tort and also can choose between different torts, and such concurrence of claims should also be recognised within the law of unjust enrichment. Indeed, even in *Kleinwort Benson Ltd v Lincoln CC*,[87] Lord Goff had recognised that different grounds of restitution may be concurrently available in respect of the same claim. It is simply a matter for the claimant to choose which route is better; a decision which may legitimately be influenced by different rules as to the limitation period.

The public and private law distinction

The Court of Appeal's distinction between public and private law claims was controversial, both as regards how such a distinction should be drawn and as to why it is necessary to draw it at all. The rejection of such a distinction by the House of Lords is to be commended. The distinction was rejected on the technical ground that it arose from improper reliance on the dicta of Lord Goff in earlier cases,[88] which were taken out of context.[89]

However, the public law nature of the *Woolwich* ground of restitution does continue to be of significance. For example, it is clear that this ground of restitution is not available to recover money paid under a private law transaction. Further, the constitutional justification for the *Woolwich* ground has proved to be significant in other jurisdictions as a reason for recognising it as a distinct claim.[90] There might also be a case for developing different defences as regards claims against public authorities, although the House of Lords considered that this should be a matter for Parliament. It remains unclear, however, as to which defences ought to be recognised. The defence that tax was paid when there was a settled view as to the law was specifically not recognised by the House of Lords in *Deutsche Morgan Grenfell*.[91]

A further reason for distinguishing between public law and private law claims for restitution is because there appears to be a different procedure for recovery when the claimant seeks to recover taxes which were not due rather than money paid at private law. The appropriate procedure for

---

[87] [1999] 2 AC 349 (HL).

[88] Namely *Woolwich Equitable Building Society v IRC* [1993] AC 70 (HL) and *Kleinwort Benson Ltd v Lincoln CC* [1999] 2 AC 349 (HL).

[89] See, in particular, [2006] UKHL 49 (HL) at paras. 47 (Lord Hope) and 136 (Lord Walker).

[90] See especially *Kingstreet Investments Ltd v Province of New Brunswick* [2007] 1 SCR 3 (SCC).

[91] [2006] UKHL 49 (HL) at paras. 18 (Lord Hoffmann) and 145 (Lord Walker).

recovery of taxes was not at issue in *Deutsche Morgan Grenfell* because the ECJ had previously declared that the denial of relief was discriminatory and that a remedy should be awarded. So the only issue concerned the identification of an appropriate cause of action and determination of the appropriate remedy. Where, however, the validity of the tax has not yet been determined, it is first necessary to establish that the tax was not due. Three different procedural routes are available for this. First, the claimant can seek judicial review[92] of the validity of the tax demand and the underlying authority to demand payment. Such a claim can now include a claim for restitution,[93] although a restitutionary remedy cannot be sought by itself. It will, however, be sufficient that the claimant seeks restitution in conjunction with a declaration of invalidity of the demand for tax. Judicial review is subject to a three-month limitation period. Secondly, a dual procedure can be adopted whereby the claimant uses judicial review to challenge the validity of the demand and then seeks restitution in separate proceedings. This dual procedure was adopted in *Woolwich* itself. It too is subject to a three-month limitation period as regards the judicial review part of the process. Following the recognition that restitutionary remedies are available as part of judicial review, this dual procedure now seems unnecessary. Thirdly, it has been recognised that a single procedure for restitution in the High Court relying on the *Woolwich* principle can be pursued without prior judicial review proceedings.[94] This avoids the three-month limitation period for judicial review. This non-judicial review procedure has been criticised. In *Autologic Holdings plc v IRC*[95] the House of Lords held that it was an abuse of process to pursue a claim before the courts rather than by appealing to the Commissioners of the Inland Revenue. In *NEC Semi-Conductors v IRC* Sedley LJ emphasised that it was 'an abuse of process to ignore the primary mode of challenge provided by law [namely challenge by judicial review or through the statutory appeal mechanisms] and instead to bring an action which evades the controls on that mode'.[96] The validity of the non-judicial review mechanism remains unclear after the recent decisions of the House of Lords in

---

[92] There are also statutory appeal mechanisms for particular taxes. The decisions of appellate bodies are also open to judicial review.
[93] SI 1998/3132; Civil Procedure Rules, r. 54.3(2).
[94] *British Steel v CEC* [1997] 2 All ER 366 (CA).
[95] [2005] UKHL 54 (HL) at para. 13 (Lord Nicholls).
[96] [2006] EWCA Civ 25 (CA) at para. 97. This procedural question was not considered on appeal to the House of Lord: *Boake Allen Ltd v IRC* [2007] UKHL 25 (HL).

Deutsche Morgan Grenfell Group plc and *Sempra Metals Ltd*, which did not need to consider the matter. However, the recognition that the claimant taxpayer may rely on the ground of mistake of law to gain the benefit of the extended limitation period under the Limitation Act 1980 might suggest that there is no intrinsic objection to using the non-judicial review procedure.

The nature of mistake

A crucial issue in *Deutsche Morgan Grenfell* concerned whether the claimant had made a mistake in paying the tax to the Revenue and whether this mistake had caused the tax to be paid when it was. For if no operative mistake had been made then the extended limitation period would not be available. It was held by a majority that the claimant had indeed made a mistake of law. It was recognised, relying on *Kleinwort Benson Ltd v Lincoln CC*,[97] that judicial developments and changes in the law operate retrospectively, so that payments which were valid when they were made can be treated as having been mistaken in the light of subsequent interpretations of the law,[98] and this includes changes in the law through decisions of the ECJ. Consequently, the decision of the ECJ in *Metallgesellschaft Ltd* operated retrospectively, so that when the claimant paid the tax to the Revenue, it should have been able to claim group income relief and its failure to do so constituted a mistake. There was some disagreement amongst the judges as to whether the mistake related to the failure to make a group income election[99] or to the liability to pay ACT,[100] but ultimately nothing turned on this difference of opinion.

In the course of their Lordships' consideration of the ground of mistake, there was some significant analysis of what constitutes a mistake for the purposes of the law of unjust enrichment. It is clear that restitution will not be available to the claimant where he or she acted voluntarily in transferring a benefit to the defendant.[101] This will arise where the claimant knew all of the facts relating to the payment[102] or was suspicious

---

[97] [1999] 2 AC 349 (HL).
[98] Lord Hoffmann described this as a deemed mistake: [2006] UKHL 49 (HL) at para. 23. See generally Beatson (2006).
[99] [2006] UKHL 49 (HL) at paras. 62 (Lord Hope) and 88 (Lord Scott).
[100] *Ibid.* at para. 32 (Lord Hoffmann).
[101] *Kleinwort Benson Ltd v Lincoln CC* [1999] 2 AC 349 (HL) at p. 401 (Lord Hoffmann).
[102] *Brisbane v Dacres* (1813) 5 Taunt 143 (KB) at pp. 159–60; 128 ER 641 at pp. 647–8 (Gibbs. J); *Brennan v Bolt Burdon* [2004] EWCA Civ 1017 (CA) (mistakes of law).

about the circumstances.[103] But it is unclear why the claim will fail. Three distinct approaches were adopted in *Deutsche Morgan Grenfell*.[104]

Suspicion negates mistake. Lord Brown recognised that suspicion that a payment might not be due would negate a mistake.[105] Consequently, he considered that the claimant would not be mistaken once it was aware of a possibility that the payment of tax was not due, because, for example, the obligation to pay tax was subject to a serious legal challenge.[106] But it is unclear when a challenge will be serious. The emphasis on suspicion negating a mistake is, however, consistent with other decisions. For example, in *Rowe v Vale of White Horse DC*,[107] it was held that the claimant was not mistaken when it had made a conscious decision to provide sewerage services without charge until the legal position had been clarified, presumably because its suspicions that the services might be required to be provided gratuitously meant that it was not mistaken. Similarly, in *Brennan v Bolt Burdon*[108] it was held that the claimant's doubts about the proper interpretation of the law would not constitute a mistake of law. The court in that case also held that a claimant who ought to have known that a particular issue was about to be reconsidered on appeal could not be considered to be mistaken either. But this conclusion that negligence can negate a mistake surely goes too far. The long-standing rule is that a claimant should be able to rely on the ground of mistake even if the reasonable person would not have been mistaken.[109] Negligence on the part of the defendant in changing his or her position, in the sense that the reasonable person would have been aware of a possibility of a liability to make restitution, will not prevent the defendant from relying on that defence.[110] If the defendant can rely on the defence despite negligence, then surely it is only right that the claimant should be able to establish mistake despite negligence. It is only where the claimant was reckless, in

---

[103] *Kleinwort Benson Ltd v Lincoln CC* [1999] 2 AC 349 (HL) at p. 410 (Lord Hope); *Rowe v Vale of White Horse DC* [2003] EWHC 388 (Admin); *Brennan v Bolt Burdon* [2004] EWCA Civ 1017 (CA).

[104] In the end the majority concluded that the taxpayer did not suspect that the tax might not be due at the time of payment: [2006] UKHL 49 (HL) at paras. 29 (Lord Hoffmann) and 71 (Lord Hope).

[105] *Ibid.* at para. 162.

[106] Or a 'worthwhile' challenge (*ibid.*, para. 176), although this is not any clearer.

[107] [2003] EWHC 388 (Admin).   [108] [2004] EWCA Civ 1017 (CA).

[109] *Kelly v Solari* (1841) 9 M and W 54 (Exch).

[110] *Dextra Bank & Trust Company Ltd v Bank of Jamaica* [2001] UKPC 50 (PC); *Niru Battery Manufacturing Co v Milestone Trading Ltd* [2002] EWHC 1425 (Comm).

the sense that he or she was consciously aware of the possibility that the tax might not be due, that the claimant can be considered to be sufficiently suspicious so that he or she was not mistaken.

No liability if the claimant is a risk-taker. An alternative way of analysing the situation where a payer of tax was suspicious about the validity of the payment but who paid nonetheless, is not to deny that such a person is mistaken, but instead to conclude that their claim for restitution should fail because they can be considered to have taken the risk as to the validity of the payment. This was the approach advocated by Lord Hoffmann,[111] although he did not consider that doubts as to liability would necessarily mean that the claimant had taken the risk that the tax was due. Rather, he considered that whether the claimant was a risk-taker would depend on 'the objective circumstances surrounding the payment as they could reasonably have been known to both parties, including . . . the extent to which the law was known to be in doubt'.[112] This risk-taking analysis is an alternative way of explaining why the claimant in *Rowe v Vale of White Horse DC* was unsuccessful in its claim for restitution.

It is a fundamental principle of the law of restitution that any claim for restitution should fail where the claimant can be considered to have acted officiously or as a volunteer.[113] This will occur where the claimant can be considered to have taken the risk that the payment of money to the defendant might be invalid. Of course, it might be difficult as a matter of public policy and constitutional principle to conclude that a taxpayer, who has paid tax following a demand for payment from the Revenue, took the risk that there was no liability to discharge. In the tax context, at least, the risk should be borne by the Revenue, save perhaps where the mistake arose from errors made by the taxpayer.

A question of causation. Lord Hope suggested the taxpayer's suspicions concerning the legitimacy of the tax liability affected whether the payment could be considered to have been caused by the mistake.[114] According to this approach, it should be a question of fact and degree as to whether the mistake was operative or whether money was paid for other reasons, such as to avoid the coercive powers of the state,[115] or because the

---

[111] [2006] UKHL49 (HL) at para. 27.   [112] *Ibid.* at para. 28.
[113] *Falcke v Scottish Imperial Insurance* (1886) 34 Ch D 234 (CA) at p. 248 (Bowen LJ).
[114] [2006] UKHL 49 (HL) at para. 65.
[115] As in *Woolwich Equitable Building Society v IRC* [1993] AC 70 (HL) at pp. 198 (Lord Browne-Wilkinson) and 204 (Lord Slynn).

claimant had taken a calculated risk about the existence of a liability to pay money.[116]

Choosing the preferable analysis.   Which of these three approaches is to be preferred can be tested by reference to a hypothetical problem modelled on an example identified by some of the judges in *Deutsche Morgan Grenfell*.[117] What about the contestant on a quiz show who is given the million pound question and four possible answers? If the contestant eliminates answers A and C, but is unsure whether the correct answer is B or D, and incorrectly chooses B, is that contestant mistaken? Since the contestant has given the wrong answer he must have been mistaken, but this could not be a relevant mistake for the purposes of the law of restitution because he took a calculated risk. We could adopt a policy that risk-takers should not be deemed to be mistaken, but surely it is more sensible to say that this was not a causative mistake. The answer was given in circumstances where the contestant hoped that it was the right answer. It is that hope which prevents the mistake from being operative.

Of course, if the claimant is not mistaken but has paid tax which was not due then it will still be possible to obtain restitution at common law by virtue of the *Woolwich* principle, but without the benefit of the extended limitation period. Presumably, the fact that the claimant can be characterised as a risk-taker in paying the tax despite a suspicion that the tax was not due, will not bar the claim for restitution since the constitutional rationale which underpins the *Woolwich* principle should support restitution being granted regardless of the claimant's suspicions.

Money due

It is a fundamental feature of claims for restitution of tax that the tax was not lawfully owed to the Revenue. It was for this reason that Lord Scott dissented in *Deutsche Morgan Grenfell* on the ground that the claimant was liable to pay ACT to the Revenue so that the payment was lawfully due.[118] The majority considered that the tax was not due. Lord Scott's conclusion is immediately open to challenge because it would mean that the claimant would not have been entitled to a restitutionary remedy, but the ECJ in *Metallgesellschaft Ltd* had made it clear that the UK was required to provide an effective remedy for taxpayers. This objection could be dealt with by arguing that the claimant could still have brought a claim for the

---

[116] [2006] UKHL 49 (HL) at para. 175 (Lord Brown).
[117] *Ibid.* at paras. 26 (Lord Hoffmann) and 175 (Lord Brown).   [118] See Stevens (2005).

tort of breach of statutory duty for which a compensatory remedy would be available and which would not be affected by the fact that the tax was due; this would be irrelevant because the claim would be founded on the wrong of infringing EC law. Such a claim would, however, have been subject to the normal six-year limitation period and so would be statute barred. Also, could it really be concluded that the claimant had suffered loss even though the tax was owed to the Revenue and at the same time assert that the Revenue had not made a gain for the purposes of the law of unjust enrichment because the tax was due? The crucial issue, therefore, is to determine whether the tax was actually due to the Revenue at the time it was paid.

In analysing whether Lord Scott was correct, it is vital to remember the essential feature of the restitutionary claim. This was not a claim for recovery of the amount of tax which had been paid because, as was subsequently recognised in *Sempra Metals Ltd*,[119] the ACT which had been paid was eventually set off against mainstream corporation tax which was lawfully due, so the restitutionary liability was discharged because the tax was lawfully paid at that point. The claim was instead for the Revenue's use of the money from the period of payment until the point when the ACT was set off. During this period the Revenue's receipt was unlawful because the claimant has been unlawfully discriminated against by not being able to claim group income relief, which the claimant would have elected had it been able to do so.[120] The taxpayer's claim related simply to the early payment of tax in circumstances where the claimant would have wished to delay payment by means of the group income election.[121] If we focus on the entitlement of the Revenue to receive the money when it did, rather than on the language of whether the tax was actually due to the Revenue, it is much easier to understand why the Revenue was required to make restitution; because the Revenue obtained an unlawful timing advantage through premature payment of the tax.

The nature of the remedy: Sempra Metals

Once it had been accepted in *Deutsche Morgan Grenfell* that the claimant could rely on the ground of mistake of law it was able to obtain restitution from the Revenue. It was accepted by the Revenue that the appropriate

---

[119] [2007] UKHL 34 (HL).
[120] [2006] UKHL 49 (HL) at para. 7 (Lord Hoffmann). See also *Pirelli Cable Holding NV v Commissioners for Revenue and Customs* [2007] EWHC 583 (Ch).
[121] [2006] UKHL 49 (HL) at para. 5 (Lord Hoffmann).

mechanism for assessing this use value[122] of the money was by reference to interest. However, this claim for the use value of the money raised a number of difficulties, particularly as to whether the remedy should be characterised as restitutionary or whether it was in fact compensating the claimant for loss suffered. Another key issue concerned whether the appropriate type of interest was simple or compound and, if the latter, what the appropriate rate of interest should be. Some of the cases arising from the decision of the ECJ in *Metallgesellschaft Ltd* had considered that the remedy should be analysed as restitutionary,[123] whereas others treated it as compensatory,[124] although these differences are primarily explained by the nature of the pleadings and the focus of counsels' arguments. The matter has now been resolved by the House of Lords in *Sempra Metals Ltd*.[125]

Sempra Metals Ltd was formerly called *Metallgesellschaft Ltd*, which was one of the claimants to the original proceedings before the ECJ. The claimant taxpayer had amended its pleadings to claim restitution of the Revenue's enrichment from the use of the money it had paid and asserted that the appropriate method of valuing this enrichment was by reference to compound rather than simple interest.

Whether simple or compound interest could be awarded in claims for unjust enrichment was considered by the House of Lords in *Westdeutsche Landesbank Girozentrale v Islington LBC*,[126] where the majority held that compound interest could be awarded only in respect of equitable claims. The judgments of the two dissentients are, however, more persuasive. Lords Goff and Woolf asserted that, since the policy of the law of restitution

---

[122] Or 'time value', as Lord Hope described it in *Sempra Metals Ltd. v IRC* [2007] UKHL 34 (HL) at para. 10.

[123] *Sempra Metals Ltd v IRC* [2005] EWCA Civ 389 (CA); Case C-446/04 *Test Claimants in the FII Group Litigation* [2006] ECR I-11753 (ECJ) at para. 205; *NEC Semi-Conductors Ltd v IRC* [2006] EWCA Civ 25 (CA) at paras. 86 (Lloyd J), and 172 and 175 (Mummery LJ).

[124] *NEC Semi-Conductors Ltd v IRC* [2006] EWCA Civ 25 (CA) at para. 90 (Sedley LJ); *Boake Allen Ltd v IRC* [2007] UKHL 25 (HL) at para. 5 (Lord Hoffmann). See also *Pirelli Cable Holding NV v Commissioners for Revenue and Customs* [2006] UKHL 4 (HL) which held that the possibility of payment of a tax credit to a parent company resident in another EU member state should have a bearing on the 'compensation' available to the UK subsidiary in respect of unlawful ACT payments which had been made, because the tax credits affected the loss suffered by the group as a whole. See especially Lord Nicholls at para. 20. This compensation analysis can only be justified if the claim was founded on the tort of breach of EC law rather than the law of unjust enrichment. In the end, Rimer J held ([2007] EWHC 583 (Ch)) that the tax credit was not available to the parent and that it could not be compensated for what it had not lost.

[125] [2007] UKHL 34 (HL).   [126] [1996] AC 669 (HL).

was to remove benefits from the defendant, compound interest should be available in respect of all restitutionary claims, regardless of whether they arose at law or in equity.[127] The logic of this can be defended in the following way. If it can be shown that, had the defendant borrowed an amount equivalent to what he or she had received from the claimant then he or she would have paid compound interest to the lender, this should be used as the measure of the defendant's enrichment from the use of the money.[128] If the defendant would only have paid simple interest to a lender, it would be appropriate for the interest awarded to the claimant to be simple rather than compound.[129] Usually, however, the interest awarded in commercial transactions will be compound interest and so this would be appropriate in an unjust enrichment claim.

In *Sempra Metals Ltd* a majority affirmed that the appropriate measure of the Revenue's enrichment was compound interest.[130] The court went further and accepted that compound interest should be generally available as of right for unjust enrichment claims at common law.[131] All their Lordships considered that the taxpayer's claim was founded on unjust enrichment and so a restitutionary gain-based remedy would be appropriate, rather than a compensatory remedy which would have been available had the claim been founded on the Revenue's wrongdoing of demanding payment of tax prematurely and unlawfully. This emphasis on restitution is significant as regards the determination of the appropriate form of interest, since a compensatory remedy would be assessed by reference to what the claimant lost by not having the use of the money which had been paid to the Revenue, which would be measured either by

---

[127] *Ibid.* at pp. 696 (Lord Goff) and 736 (Lord Woolf).

[128] *Ibid.* at p. 719 (Lord Woolf). See also Hobhouse J in *Westdeutsche Landesbank Girozentrale v Islington LBC* [1994] 4 All ER 890 (CA) at p. 995; *Black v Davies* [2004] EWHC 1464 (QB) at para. 41 (McCombe J).

[129] [1996] AC 669 (HL) at p. 728 (Lord Woolf).

[130] Contrast *Kingstreet Investments Ltd v Province of New Brunswick* [2007] 1 SCR 3 (SCC), where the claimant had paid an unconstitutional direct tax which was to be repaid, but compound interest was not available because of the absence of any allegations about the defendant's wrongful conduct which warranted a moral sanction.

[131] So effectively overruling *Westdeutsche Landesbank Girozentrale v Islington* LBC [1996] AC 669 (HL); [2007] UKHL 34 (HL) at paras. 36 (Lord Hope) and 112 (Lord Nicholls). Lord Scott, at para. 153, was willing to recognise the award of compound interest as of right, but he dissented on the facts. Lord Walker, at para. 184, agreed to awarding a remedy with reference to compound interest, but as a matter of equitable discretion rather than as of right, although he accepted that the common law and equitable route lead to the same result on the facts of the case: para. 188. Lord Mance, at para. 236, was willing to award compound interest if the defendant had made a real gain, but again through discretionary equitable jurisdiction.

the cost of borrowing an equivalent amount or the loss of the opportunity to invest the money. A restitutionary remedy, on the other hand, would be assessed by reference to the defendant's benefit, typically what it had saved in not having to pay interest to borrow an equivalent amount of money. The vital link between the event of enrichment and the restitutionary response was consistently emphasised.[132]

Where the claimant has paid money too early and has a choice between suing in tort or in unjust enrichment, it may be preferable to pursue the latter route, and not just because of the advantage of the extended limitation period, but because assessing the defendant's benefit with reference to compound interest might give the claimant a potentially larger remedy, especially if the defendant would have been able only to borrow an equivalent amount of money at a higher interest rate than the claimant would have obtained had the claimant invested an equivalent amount. However, in some circumstances a compensatory remedy would be preferable[133] where the claimant's loss is greater than the defendant's gain. But this raises the important and difficult question of what was the defendant's gain in *Sempra Metals*?

There was a clear difference of opinion as to the appropriate method which should be adopted for identifying the defendant's gain. For Lords Scott and Mance, restitutionary relief should only be available where the defendant had obtained an 'actual benefit' and not where the benefit was 'assumed'.[134] For Lord Scott this meant that, if the Revenue had obtained interest on the money it had received, then this interest should be paid to the claimant.[135] Similarly, if the defendant could be shown to have decided not to borrow money from a third party because of the receipt of the tax from the claimant then the actual interest saved would be a real benefit.[136]

---

[132] [2007] UKHL 34 (HL) at para. 27 (Lord Hope): 'because the concept is one of enrichment not of damages, it determines the nature of the response'; Lord Nicholls (para. 66); Lord Scott (para. 132). But some infelicities of language did emerge involving confusion between loss and gain, e.g. Lord Hope (para. 35) and Lord Walker (para. 183). See especially Lord Scott, who suggested, at para. 143, that a claim for restitution was based on the loss of use of the money and not unjust enrichment. See also Lord Scott's analysis of restitution for wrongs at para. 146 and Lord Mance's reference to the restitutionary measure of 'damages' at para. 234.

[133] Indeed, compensatory damages would probably have been preferable for the claimant in *Sempra Metals* itself in the light of the conclusions about subjective devaluation, discussed below; but a tort claim would have been time-barred after six years.

[134] [2007] UKHL 34 (HL) at paras. 132 (Lord Scott) and 231 (Lord Mance).

[135] *Ibid.* at para. 132. Lord Mance rejected a claim to the interest received because it became the recipient's property: *ibid.*, para. 218.

[136] *Ibid.* at para. 143 (Lord Scott).

But the fact that the Revenue *could* have earned interest on the money, or saved interest by not having to borrow money from elsewhere, was not considered to be an enrichment, because it was not proved to be an actual benefit and the mere opportunity to use the money was not considered enough to constitute an enrichment. So, for example, if a defendant had received money which was not due to it and put that money in a box under a bed, there would have been no actual enrichment beyond the receipt of the money, since nothing else would have been gained or saved.

However, for Lords Hope, Nicholls and Walker, the Revenue had obtained a negative enrichment, in that it had the opportunity to use the money paid by the claimant rather than to borrow an equivalent amount from elsewhere. This opportunity to use the money was considered to be a real benefit,[137] albeit a non-money benefit.

The key difference between the majority and the minority on this point simply concerned whether a 'wholly conceptual benefit'[138] was enough to constitute an enrichment. Ultimately, this difference of approach turns on the use of assumptions about what the defendant did or failed to do following receipt of the money.[139] The judges in the majority were willing to infer that receipt of the money must have benefited the defendant. Surely it is appropriate to assume that a defendant who has received money did use that money. If the defendant did not do so then he or she should bear the burden of establishing that the money was not used, but was placed, for example, in a box under a bed or paid into a non-interest bearing current account. It is appropriate to place the burden for establishing this on the defendant, who is in the best position to know whether or not the money was used or relied on in any way.[140]

The majority accepted that the defendant could 'subjectively devalue' the benefit which it had received. This is a significant conclusion. The notion of 'subjective devaluation' has been used primarily by commentators to explain how an enrichment should be established. Enrichments should first be identified by reference to an objective market value. It is then open to the defendant to subjectively devalue this objective value by asserting that he or she did not value the benefit at all, or at least not to the extent of the objective value. This reliance on subjective devaluation will be defeated if the enrichment was incontrovertibly beneficial

---

[137] *Ibid.* at para. 66 (Lord Nicholls). It was described by Lord Hope (at para. 9) as a 'timing advantage' for the Revenue.
[138] *Ibid.* at para. 145 (Lord Scott).   [139] *Ibid.* at para. 233 (Lord Mance).
[140] *Ibid.* at para. 48 (Lord Hope).

or if the defendant had freely accepted it. The approach of the House of Lords in *Sempra Metals* is essentially consistent with this analysis. The claimant needed to establish that the defendant had received an objective enrichment and this could be shown by proving that the defendant had received money which was available for use for a period of time. It was presumed[141] that the government did rely on the receipt of money, in that if it had not had the money, it would have borrowed an equivalent amount. The objective value of this benefit was the reasonable cost of borrowing an equivalent amount of money to that paid by the taxpayer.[142] This was assessed by reference to the so-called conventional basis of 'the rates of interest generally prevailing on ordinary commercial borrowings during the relevant period'.[143] Commercial borrowings would incur compound interest and it was the saving of this which constituted the enrichment. However, it was open to the Revenue to assert that it did not value the use of the money so highly[144] and this it was able to do by showing that it would have been able to borrow the money at a rate which was less than the commercial rate. Consequently, the Revenue, whilst not able to deny that it had received a benefit of value, was able to assert that it did not value this benefit as much as the market value because it was able to borrow an equivalent amount at a cheaper rate. In other words, it subjectively devalued the benefit.[145]

Although Lord Nicholls did use the language of subjective devaluation to explain this result, he suggested that this might be characterised as part of the change of position defence.[146] But this was an inappropriate conclusion. Defences such as change of position are only available once the unjust enrichment claim has been established. The function of the defence is to show that the defendant is no longer enriched, either because the enrichment itself has been dissipated or the defendant has relied on the validity of receipt to change his or her position in some other way.[147] But in *Sempra Metals* the restitutionary claim was founded on the defendant's continuing benefit from the opportunity to use the money which it had received. This enrichment was benefiting the Revenue from the moment when the tax was paid until it was set off against mainstream corporation tax. Because the enrichment continued, the court was right to focus on identifying and valuing the enrichment rather than whether

---

[141] *Ibid.* at paras. 33 (Lord Hope), 102 (Lord Nicholls) and 180 (Lord Walker).
[142] *Ibid.* at para. 116 (Lord Nicholls).   [143] *Ibid.* at para. 13 (Lord Hope).
[144] *Ibid.* at para. 45 (Lord Hope). See also Lord Nicholls (para. 128).
[145] *Ibid.* at para. 119 (Lord Nicholls).   [146] *Ibid.*   [147] See discussion above.

the Revenue had any defence of change of position to reduce or eliminate the restitutionary claim.[148]

The decision of the House of Lords in *Sempra Metals* is of more general significance to the law of unjust enrichment. This is because the claim for the time value of money will be available for all unjust enrichment claims where money has been paid which was not due to the defendant. So, for example, any claimant who pays money by mistake has two restitutionary claims at common law,[149] one for the amount paid and one for the defendant's use value of that money.[150] It follows that in *Woolwich Equitable Building Society v IRC*,[151] a case which only concerned the award of interest when the tax had already been repaid by the Revenue, the claimant taxpayer should have been awarded compound interest, rather than the simple interest which was awarded, in respect of the period from original payment until repayment. This was a non-money benefit which was obtained at the expense of the claimant, because the use should have been the claimant's since the defendant should have repaid the money immediately he or she had received it.

There is one further issue concerning the award of interest in claims for unjust enrichment. It is clear that once a liability to make restitution has crystallised interest is payable in respect of the period from when liability accrues until that liability is discharged. This is interest arising on the debt owed by the defendant to the claimant. In *Sempra Metals* this was the period from when the ACT was set-off against mainstream corporation tax, at which point the unjust enrichment claim had crystallised, until the date when liability was discharged. The claimant had conceded that this interest should be awarded under the Supreme Court Act 1981, s. 35A(1).[152] This gives the court a discretion to award simple interest, the function of which appears to be to compensate the claimant for the loss suffered in not having the use of the money until the liability is discharged. However, Lord Nicholls did contemplate the possibility of compound interest being awarded at common law as a restitutionary remedy for the period from set-off until judgment because 'the Inland Revenue continued

---

[148] [2007] UKHL 34 (HL) at paras. 48 and 49 (Lord Hope) and 233 (Lord Mance).
[149] Assuming that this has not been excluded by any statutory regimes.
[150] A reference to the ECJ had been made by the Court of Appeal in *British Telecommunications plc v Commissioners for Revenue and Customs* (case C-185/06) as to whether European law governed recovery of taxes paid by mistake where there was no unlawful demand for payment and the remedies which would be available, but this reference was subsequently withdrawn.
[151] [1993] AC 70 (HL).   [152] [2007] UKHL 34 (HL) at para. 114 (Lord Nicholls).

to derive interest benefits from the benefits it had already obtained from having use of the ACT payments'.[153]

This raises an important issue about the award of restitutionary remedies, namely whether it is possible to award the claimant a remedy to deprive the defendant of a benefit which derives from the receipt of the enrichment, such as interest earned[154] on an investment or dividends obtained from the purchase of shares with the money paid by the claimant. It is undoubtedly the case that where the claimant brings a claim founded on the vindication of property rights, it is possible to recover all the proceeds of the enrichment.[155] Similarly, where the restitutionary claim is founded on wrongdoing, it is possible to recover indirect benefits.[156] In *Sempra Metals* Lord Walker accepted that indirect benefits could also be recovered in a claim for unjust enrichment:

> [I]ncome benefits are more accurately characterised as an integral part of the overall benefit obtained by a defendant who is unjustly enriched. Full restitution requires the whole benefit to be recouped by the enriched party . . .[157]

The better view, however, is that benefits which are obtained indirectly from the receipt of the enrichment are not received at the expense of the claimant and so cannot be recovered.[158]

As Lord Hope recognised in *Sempra Metals*, the court is not concerned with what the defendant did with the money after it had been received.[159] Claims for the use of the money is different because this is an enrichment which was received directly at the claimant's expense. Equally, claims for interest for the period from when the liability to make restitution arises until it is discharged should also be treated as a direct benefit to the defendant, because the defendant has the use of money which should have been paid to the claimant immediately the liability arose. This benefit is also obtained directly at the claimant's expense[160] and so it is appropriate to

---

[153] *Ibid.* at para. 129. See also Lord Walker, at para. 156, who described this as 'interest on restitution' rather than 'interest as restitution' which was what the appeal was about. Lord Hope did contemplate the award of compound interest on late payment of a debt, but he considered this to be compensating for loss suffered (para. 17).

[154] As was contemplated by Lord Scott, *ibid.* at para. 132. See discussion above.

[155] See *Foskett v McKeown* [2001] 1 AC 102 (HL).

[156] See *Attorney-General for Hong Kong v Reid* [1994] 1 AC 324 (PC).

[157] [2007] UKHL 34 (HL) at para. 178.

[158] See *Moses v Macferlan* (1760) 2 Burr 1005 (KB), where Lord Mansfield recognised that a defendant cannot be liable for more than the money received in an action for money had and received.

[159] [2007] UKHL 34 (HL) at para. 32.   [160] See also McInnes (2003, p. 704).

value this benefit with reference to compound interest on the assumption that this is what the defendant would have had to pay to borrow an equivalent amount of money.

The role of absence of basis

These two recent decisions of the House of Lords have shown that the common law of unjust enrichment still has a very important function in recovering taxes, and related non-money benefits, which were not due to the Revenue. An orthodox analysis of the unjust enrichment principle, with reference to recognised grounds of restitution, was adopted and in both cases restitutionary remedies were awarded. However, there is some evidence of a more radical approach emerging.

This new approach was advocated by Birks in his book *Unjust Enrichment*.[161] He advocated that the orthodox analysis of the law of unjust enrichment, which requires positive grounds of restitution to be established, should be rejected in favour of a continental European approach, whereby restitution would lie whenever there was an absence of basis for the defendant's receipt of an enrichment.[162] There would be a basis for receipt if the enrichment was transferred pursuant to a contract, gift or a compromise or, most importantly in the context of restitution of taxes, by virtue of a lawful statutory authority. Birks advocated a pyramidal structure to the law of unjust enrichment.[163] According to this analysis, the base of the pyramid consists of the recognised grounds of restitution which, if established, show that there was no basis for the defendant's enrichment which should then be characterised as unjust. So, even according to Birks's scheme, the recognised grounds of restitution would not be rejected completely.

This absence of basis approach would be potentially significant in the restitutionary cases arising from the decision of the ECJ in *Metallgesellschaft Ltd*, especially those claims which were time barred under the normal limitation period. An absence of basis for the payment of the tax

---

[161] First published in 2003, now see Birks (2005).
[162] This approach was specifically rejected by Lord Goff in *Woolwich Equitable Building Society v IRC* [1993] AC 70 (HL) at p. 172. Birks, however, considered the new approach to have been accepted implicitly by cases which had recognised that money paid pursuant to void interest rate swap transactions could be recovered simply because the transaction was void. See especially *Guinness, Mahon and Co. Ltd v Kensington and Chelsea Royal London Borough Council* [1999] QB 215 (CA).
[163] Birks (2005, p. 104).

could be identified because there was no lawful basis for the claimant to have paid the tax when it did, due to the decision of the ECJ declaring the denial of group income relief to be unlawful. There would consequently have been no need to identify a mistake in *Deutsche Morgan Grenfell* because restitution would lie whenever tax was paid which was not due. But the fact that mistake would not form part of the claim would have meant that the extended limitation period would not be applicable, save if it can be concluded that the extended limitation period was available even where mistake did not form part of the cause of action,[164] although this would be inconsistent with the decision of the Court of Appeal in *Deutsche Morgan Grenfell*.[165]

All of the judges in the House of Lords in *Deutsche Morgan Grenfell* analysed the unjust enrichment principle with reference to the need to establish positive grounds of restitution and none adopted the absence of basis analysis. However, Lord Walker did acknowledge the persuasiveness of Birks's approach.[166] But that approach has many flaws. The biggest problem with Birks's pyramidal analysis of unjust enrichment is that it suggests something elegant, when in fact it is unwieldy. The analogy with a pyramid is misplaced. The better analogy is with an iceberg, where nine-tenths of the object is below the surface. For focusing on absence of basis alone cannot be sufficient. Where there is a potential basis for a transfer, the grounds of restitution still need to be examined to determine whether there was in fact no basis, for example because of a mistake or because of an absence of authority to demand payment of tax within the *Woolwich* principle.

It is more logical and consistent with principle, as well as authority, to analyse the law of unjust enrichment linearly, by reference to the ortho-dox formula of unjust enrichment; namely enrichment, at the claimant's expense, a recognised ground of restitution and no defence to negate the claim. However, this orthodox analysis needs to be extended, since, once the ground of restitution has been identified, it is also necessary to consider whether there is any policy, rather than a defence, which should operate

---

[164] See *Deutsche Morgan Grenfell v IRC* [2006] UKHL 49 (HL) at paras. 22 (Lord Hoffmann) and 147 (Lord Walker); Edelman (2005).

[165] See also *Phillips-Higgins v Harper* [1954] 1 QB 411 (CA); *Deutsche Morgan Grenfell v IRC* [2006] UKHL 49 (HL) at para. 91 (Lord Scott).

[166] [2006] UKHL 49 (HL) at para. 158 (Lord Walker). Lord Hoffmann also made reference to this absence of basis analysis (para. 28). See also Lord Hope in *Sempra Metals Ltd v IRC* [2007] UKHL 34 (HL) at para. 25, who did refer to 'no legal ground' as the ground of restitution, although he had earlier accepted that the ground was mistake of law. Lord Mance left the point open (para. 192).

to bar the unjust enrichment claim. Such a policy would include that the defendant's receipt is lawful, as where the tax demand was authorised,[167] or that the claimant was a risk-taker who cannot then seek restitution.[168] This is consistent with the decision of the House of Lords in *Deutsche Morgan Grenfell* and with the principles which underpin the law of restitution. The operation of the bar of lawful receipt is illustrated by the first type of restitutionary claim which was recognised in *Sempra Metals*, namely a claim to recover the tax which had been paid to the Revenue, as opposed to a claim for the Revenue's use of the money. This first claim was properly not pursued because the ACT was subsequently set-off against the taxpayer's mainstream corporation tax liability, at which point the Revenue's receipt of the money became lawful.

Conclusion

In 1993 I argued that the law of taxation was not an island, a legal regime unto itself as some commentators and judges appeared to suggest, and that it was influenced and developed by other bodies of law, especially the common law of unjust enrichment. Over the subsequent years this has continued to be the case. However, just as significantly, there is sometimes a tendency for the law of unjust enrichment to be treated as an island, the inhabitants of which speak their own language and have little concern for the policies and principles elsewhere in the law.[169] The importance of not treating the law of unjust enrichment as an island is especially illustrated by claims for restitution of taxes, which have provided the context for rapid and significant development of the law of unjust enrichment. That development needs to proceed further. Whilst some may be willing to assert, as the Supreme Court of Canada has done,[170] that taxes which have been paid but which were not due should be repaid for constitutional reasons, or simply because there was no valid basis for the Revenue's receipt, in England at least there is still a legitimate role for the function

---

[167] In *Kingstreet Investments Ltd v Province of New Brunswick* [2007] 1 SCR 3 (SCC) the Supreme Court of Canada recognised that it was open to the state to suspend the declaration of invalidity and also to enact valid taxes and apply them retrospectively. In either case the tax demand would become authorised.

[168] Where a claim is grounded on mistake this risk-taking bar might be incorporated within the definition of a causative mistake, as was discussed above. Risk-taking should, however, remain a distinct bar for other grounds of restitution.

[169] As recognised by Sedley LJ in *NEC Semi-Conductors Ltd v IRC* [2006] EWCA Civ 25 (CA) at para. 101.

[170] *Kingstreet Investments Ltd v Province of New Brunswick* [2007] 1 SCR 3 (SCC).

and formula of the unjust enrichment principle. But the orthodox formula needs to become more sophisticated through clearer attention being given to the legitimacy of defences peculiar to public authorities. But when considering whether such defences should be recognised the rule of law and fundamental constitutional principle should never be ignored; receipt of tax which was not due cannot be countenanced. It is for the law of unjust enrichment to ensure that the rule of law is preserved and that taxes which were not due are returned to the taxpayer.

7

The history of royalties in tax treaties 1921–61: Why?

RICHARD VANN*

Introduction

John Tiley's breadth of interests and scholarship in matters of taxation is a disappearing art but makes it easy for friends to find starting points in his work for their own specialist eccentricities. History is fascinating to John and for a UK scholar working with the oldest income tax in the world, it is probably obligatory. Old income tax systems are generally schedular in nature and with schedules come many borderlines to draw; John has done his tours of duty surveying these borders, including the ones to be explored here.[1] More to the point, John always wants to ask not only what the law is and where it came from but 'Why?'. He has visited many other parts of the world in pursuit of solutions to why. Happily for me, his travels brought him to Sydney Law School to see our uncommon friend, Ross Parsons.[2]

So an international cocktail is appropriate to celebrate Tiley's work and this one will mix the history of the tax treaty rule on royalties up to the emergence of the modern form,[3] the borders of the provision and the fundamental question of 'Why?' we have it (viewed from an historical perspective). In the modern context of the Organisation for Economic

* The research for this paper has been supported by the Australian Research Council. I owe special thanks to Peter Harris, who provided the material from the OECD archives referred to under the heading OEEC Work and Treaty Practice as well as the model for this kind of work (Harris, 2000), and commented on a draft. Thanks also to John Avery Jones and Niv Tadmore for comments on and discussion of a draft.
[1] The borders here involve property and services and sale or use in the area of intangibles. Tiley (2005b) deals with the issues in several places but my favourite is on casual authorship at pp. 599–602, which involves many of the possibilities under Schedule D as well as CGT.
[2] In 2007, Tiley delivered the Ross Parsons lecture entitled 'Death, Taxes and Policy: Recent UK Experience'.
[3] Tiley has generally avoided the tax treaty area except as the necessary last (and least?) sections in textbooks, though he makes an exception when important matters are involved like taxation of travelling professors, Tiley (1990).

Cooperation and Development (OECD) *Model Tax Convention on Income and on Capital*,[4] with zero taxation at source on royalties, the 'Why?' is indeed a mystery. The work of the royalties article as it has been drafted at various times is already effectively covered by the modern forms of the business profits, capital gains and other income articles,[5] so why not abolish it like the OECD recently did for the article on independent personal services.[6]

For many such a suggestion may seem shocking – after all, the royalties article is often viewed as critical in modern policy and political debates on source taxation and the fair sharing of revenues among countries, especially for smaller and developing countries. A review of the history of the royalties article suggests, perhaps surprisingly, that its development was as much concerned with technical and structural tax treaty issues as with the broader issues. It is not the purpose of this chapter to take a position on the broader issues but rather to try to reconstruct the historical thinking that produced the modern form of the article.

7.1 Early League of Nations models and treaty practice

In brief,[7] the institutional history of tax treaty models during the period 1921–46 is that at the urging of the International Chamber of Commerce, the Financial Committee of the League of Nations in 1921 appointed four economists to study the problem of international double taxation that impeded the re-establishment of international trade and had emerged after World War I as a result of the introduction of increases in income tax by many countries during the war. Even before the report of the economists was received in 1923, the Financial Committee appointed a committee of seven technical experts to pursue the work that produced recommendations for drafting a model tax treaty in 1925. Following the recommendation of this group, a broader committee of government experts drawn from twenty-seven countries, including twenty-two European countries, was then appointed and produced the first models

---

[4] (OECD, 1992–). The various model treaties down the years are generally referred to by the organisation sponsoring them and the year they were produced without full title details.

[5] Without the royalties article, royalties and alienation of intellectual property will end up in one of these and they all provide for residence only taxation in the absence of a permanent establishment to which the royalties are connected, the same treatment as the royalties article.

[6] OECD (2000).

[7] The publications of the League of Nations relating to its meetings on tax treaties and its draft models are conveniently collected in United States (1962).

consisting of a 1927 draft and then three alternative models for bilateral income tax treaties in 1928 referred to as models 1a, 1b and 1c.

In turn, this committee recommended the setting up of a smaller permanent Fiscal Committee, which held a series of meetings between 1929 and 1939. It debated various tax treaty issues and developed model language for a variety of situations without, however, revisiting the models as a whole. Up to this time, all the meetings were in Geneva. The chaos in Europe caused by World War II meant that the final meetings of the Fiscal Committee were held in the Americas during the war and in London shortly after its conclusion, with different people and broader representation. Following these meetings, the Mexico and London models, which were the first comprehensive models for bilateral treaties since 1928 and represented the culmination of the League of Nations' work, were published in 1946.

There were some large international corporations operating in the 1920s and 1930s whose international trade was mainly in goods, especially raw materials and finished goods. International trade in services was then less important, though there were issues in some long-established service sectors such as banking and insurance. Technology-based services were in their infancy, but do get some passing mention in the work of the League of Nations (such as international telegraph corporations). However, many of the international tax problems of central Europe, where tax treaties had their main origins and where the League of Nations was based and so drew its main membership, concerned individuals who were employed or conducted businesses, including the provision of services and intellectual property, across borders.

Thus the development of the definition of permanent establishment (PE) was concerned as much with travelling salesman, professionals and small businesses as with large corporations. Even in the 1950s and 1960s, the Organisation for European Economic Cooperation (OEEC) and its successor the OECD felt it necessary to explain it was only after 'a good deal' of 'careful consideration' that no express provision was made in their new models for 'itinerant merchants, pedlars and watermen'.[8] In the League of Nations 1928 models, services were generally covered by the business profits article (income from 'any industrial, commercial or agricultural undertaking and from any other trades or professions') and so outside the employment context, only gave rise to source taxation if there

---

[8] OECD (1958) in United States (1962, p. 4491), OECD (1963), as reproduced in van Raad (1987, p. 36).

was a PE. Employment was taxable in a country if the services were rendered there, though it was recognised that countries may wish to include 'special clauses . . . to meet the case of persons working in the vicinity of the frontier or engaged in any itinerant occupation, employment or trade.' Such frontier worker provisions are still common in treaties between neighbouring European countries.

There was no express mention of intellectual property or royalties in the 1928 models and the committee of government experts that developed them expressly designated the topic of 'income derived from patents and authors' rights' for future consideration.[9] It was a close thing – we almost did not have the royalties article at all, which would have made this piece much shorter. There was debate in the 1929 Fiscal Committee meeting over whether the issue was already covered by the 1928 models, even though not expressly mentioned, involving possibly for the first time a debate over the different language versions of the models. On one side, it was said that model 1a implicitly covered the issue by the following language in the last article dealing with impersonal taxes and gave exclusive taxing rights to the country of residence:

> Annuities or income from other sources not referred to in the previous paragraphs shall be taxable in the State of fiscal domicile of the creditor of such income.

On the other side, it was argued there were several indications in the League documents that the English version of model 1a had mistranslated 'créances' (debts or financial claims) as 'sources' and that the model was not exhaustive of all kinds of income – in modern parlance there was no other income article.[10] Rather than decide the issue by semantics, the Committee sent out a questionnaire into how countries actually taxed such income.

At the 1930 meeting the Fiscal Committee, drawing on the results of the replies from twenty-one countries –

> adopted in first reading the following conclusions:
> The Committee did not wish to offer any opinion on the drafting . . . as it appears in draft 1a . . .

[9] United States (1962, pp. 4188–9). For a brief version of some of the following material, see Avery Jones *et al.* (2006, p. 245).

[10] United States (1962, p. 4199); see also the 1930 meeting United States (1962, p. 4207), where the same text is unusually repeated almost verbatim. The 1928 model 1a provision is found at United States (1962, p. 4162).

The Committee was of opinion that, without going into these questions, one could solve the problem by determining the category in which income derived from authors' or inventors' rights should be placed for the purpose of the application of the model conventions.

This would obviously make it possible to bring such income under the system contemplated for income of a similar nature in the model conventions, and it would thus have the effect of preventing such income from being taxed simultaneously in more than one country.[11]

Specifically for current purposes, three categories were distinguished and positions developed: for payments to individual authors or inventors; payments to the heirs/ donees of authors or inventors; and income of enterprises (referred to as grantees) acquiring rights from authors and inventors in relation to patents or copyrights which they exploit in their businesses.[12] For payments received by the individual author or inventor in respect of their rights, most countries categorised them as 'professional earnings' and the 'Committee considered that this system was fair and consistent with the economic nature of income of that kind', so that the business profits rule applied. For payments received by those to whom the rights descended on death or gift, some countries still treated them as professional earnings while others treated them as income from movable capital. In conclusion on this situation, the Committee stated:

Whether the income in question is regarded as professional earnings or income from movable capital in the international sphere, by following the rules laid down in the model conventions one always find [sic], that the right of taxation belongs to the country in which the heir or assign is domiciled.[13]

This is very surprising, especially for countries which classified the income as from movable capital. As already noticed, it was unclear whether model 1a dealt with the issue at all and the Committee had previously expressly decided not to base its conclusions on this debated issue. Model 1b gave

---

[11] United States (1962, p. 4208).

[12] There was a fourth category dealing with cases where authors' or inventors' societies collected royalties on behalf of the owners which would nowadays be covered by the beneficially owned language of the royalty article. The Fiscal Committee concluded that the country where such a society was based should collect tax only on the commission if any earned from the collection activity, not on the royalties themselves, United States (1962, pp. 4208–9). Another of the issues that the 1928 committee left over for future decision was the 'measures for the avoidance of the double taxation of trusts and companies possessing a large number of transferable securities', which may be a similar issue, United States (1962, p. 4189).

[13] Ibid., p. 4208.

the exclusive taxing right to the residence country, as it clearly had an other income article based on residence only taxation; it was the model most favourable to residence taxation and, in effect, represented the UK and US position.[14] Model 1c, which is the only one to expressly mention movable capital, provided:

> The income from movable assets shall be taxable in the State in whose territory the creditor has his fiscal domicile, i.e., his normal residence, the term 'residence' being understood to mean a permanent home.
>
> When the other Contracting State levies a tax, by means of deductions at the source, on income from capital originating in the territory of that State, the right to this taxation shall not be affected by the rule in sub-paragraph I. In this case the State of domicile which in addition to its ordinary direct tax, levies a special tax on income originating in the other State, shall refrain from levying that tax or shall deduct therefrom the tax paid in the other State.
>
> In order to avoid or to mitigate the effects of such double taxation as is not, under the various fiscal systems, prevented by the provision of the previous sub-paragraph, the Contracting States shall come to an agreement, if necessary, to allow either the remission, in respect of the tax levied by the State of domicile, of the whole or part of the tax deducted by the State of origin, or a refund, upon production of proper evidence by the State of origin, of the whole or part of the tax collected by it by means of deductions.[15]

The last paragraph effectively leaves it up to negotiation apparently outside the treaty as to whether the residence or source country will give way if there is a tax at source leading to double taxation. The 1928 Commentary provides:

> Draft Bilateral Convention No 1c, like the immediately previous one, does not distinguish between impersonal and personal or between schedular and general taxes. It retains, as regards taxation at the source, the main provisions of Draft No 1a, and does not differ essentially from it except as regards the taxation of income from movable capital. As regards the latter, it provides that the tax shall in principle be levied by the State of domicile. If the State of origin also levies a tax by deduction at the source, the State of domicile is under obligation either not to levy a special tax upon the same income or to deduct from such tax the amount paid in the other State.

---

[14] See Graetz and O'Hear (1997, pp. 1066–89).
[15] United States (1962, p. 4174). The Commentary is at *ibid.*, p. 4175. In the event, it was model 1c that was most influential on subsequent tax treaties and models.

> Further, it is agreed that, if part of the income is still subject to double taxation, the Contracting States may, where circumstances require, take special steps either to deduct from the tax levied by the State of domicile the whole or part of the tax deducted by the State of origin or to grant a refund by the State of origin of the whole or part of the tax levied by deduction at the source.

It is hard to reconcile the conclusion on the second category of heirs or donees of the author or inventor with this Commentary. Perhaps the Committee is intending to state the factual position that arises for movable property in the form of patents or copyrights based on countries' replies. It is very difficult to know, as only summaries of the replies are provided and the member of the Committee who made the summaries then provided brief notes of conclusions. On the critical question of the taxation of foreigners receiving payments for patents or copyrights, only a few countries are mentioned in the notes, even though it is clear elsewhere in the summaries that other countries, such as the UK, levied tax on royalties by deduction at the source. One sympathises with the member who had to prepare the summaries and notes, as he indicates that countries had misunderstood various parts of the questionnaire, a not uncommon occurrence in such exercises.

For enterprises in the third category of grantees, the discussion demonstrates very clearly the underlying assumptions of the time about patents and copyrights:

> . . . it should be observed that the income received by the grantee is entirely different in nature from that received by the author himself or his heirs or assigns. The income received by the latter, whether in the form of a transfer fee paid once for all or in the form of royalties or shares, follows the rules for the income from authors' rights referred to . . . above, and is therefore taxable in the country in which the intitulee is domiciled. The income received by the grantee, on the other hand, will always be in the nature of industrial or commercial income, and will be taxed as such in the international sphere, according to the rules established for the taxation of the income of undertakings operating in the territory of one or more countries. In most of these cases the authors' rights and patents become part of the assets of the grantees' undertaking and the income derived therefrom cannot be separated from the aggregate income of the undertaking. This applies, for example, in the case of a publisher who buys a writer's work in order to publish a book and place it on sale; and it applies also to a manufacturer who buys a patent to use it in manufacturing his goods.

There are also cases, however, in which income from authors' rights and patents is distinguishable from the grantee's other income. We may mention the case of a publisher who buys the copyright of a musical composition in order to sell the performing rights to theatre and concert managers, or the case of a trader who buys patents from different inventors in order to sell them or lease the right of exploitation to a manufacturer or manufacturers.

... in both cases the income is industrial or commercial and should in principle be taxed as such.

The assumptions are that copyrights and patents belong to the individuals who write the work or make the invention or their heirs or donees and that enterprises acquire interests in such intellectual property from them. In most cases the grantee enterprises use the copyright or patent in their own business to produce products such as books or other goods which they sell. Less commonly, enterprises effectively trade in patents or copyrights by acquiring them and licensing or selling them to third (apparently unrelated) parties. In the first case, it has always been the position under tax treaties that the income from selling the books or other goods is business profits. In the second case, the analogy of trading in a similar way to selling goods is relied on to produce the same outcome. The assumptions that underlie the analysis are very different to the position nowadays, when most intellectual property is generated within and owned by multinational corporations (with some book authors probably the main exception) and most transactions in the property occur within such groups, that is, between related corporations rather than unrelated third parties. The implications of this change are explored in passing at various points.

The questionnaire did not draw any distinction between the two cases but simply asked what is the fiscal system applied to author's rights and patents when collected by grantees and what is the character of the income (from transferable securities, from the exercise of any trade or profession or from any other claim or source – movable property is not mentioned as such). The notes drawn from the summaries of the replies again do not cover all countries, do not draw the distinction, and indicate that seven countries treat the income as business profits and six as income from movable property (including one that uses both categories depending on the circumstances). Again, it is difficult to reconcile the conclusions with the information received in reply to the questionnaires and no reason is given for ignoring domestic classification despite the fact that the 1928 models are very much based on the character of income given by the source country (as in model 1c and its Commentary, quoted above).

There are several features of this history and subsequent events which indicate that the issue was a contentious one. The debate about whether the issue was already decided by the 1928 models was clearly heated – the arguments and issues are set out at length in the record of both the 1929 and 1930 meetings. It is noteworthy from the reference to 'first reading' in the conclusions above that they were only provisional, which is confirmed by the fact that, at the 1931 meeting, the Committee 'declared these principles adopted at second reading', noting by way of support that they had been approved in various quarters including the International Chamber of Commerce. This apparent adoption of legislative-like procedures suggests their controversial nature as does the unwillingness to reopen some of the debates about assigning taxing rights surrounding the 1928 models (the Committee approach as noted above was to decide the matter by analogy 'without going into these issues').[16] Finally, the decisions are hard to reconcile both with the 1928 models themselves and with the material that was received in response to the questionnaire.

A modern reader may suspect that there was an agenda here to push through a conclusion. As noted above, the Fiscal Committee was relatively small and it was fairly unrepresentative compared to the committee that produced the 1928 models covering mainly large and European countries – Belgium, France, Germany, Italy, Netherlands, Spain, Switzerland, UK and US. Based on the general approaches of these countries over the years, it is likely that opposition mainly came from Italy and Spain. The Netherlands, UK and (less strongly) US preferred residence only taxation and the principles adopted certainly favoured this approach.

In contrast to this after-the-fact political explanation, it may be that the issue was technical. One of the arguments for the principles is to prevent the income being simultaneously taxed in two countries as it is expressed in the quotation of conclusions above. The concern seems to be that differing classifications of the income may produce the effect that one country will apply one treaty provision and the other country will apply another, with the consequent possibility of double taxation. Such problems of conflicts of qualification have recently been reduced by developing principles for when the characterisation in one country gives

---

[16] See Graetz and O'Hear (1997). It may be that the formality of the procedures was simply a reflection of the committee's processes at the time. Similar procedures appear for another difficult issue left over from 1928, agency permanent establishments.

way to the other,[17] but no such thinking prevailed at this time. Another alternative technical purpose may have been to ensure that royalties were covered by treaties without an other income article so that the matter did not default to domestic tax law or to the need for some further agreement if model 1c were being followed.

An ambiguity between politics and technics runs through the whole history of this area. In retrospect, if the political explanation is adopted that there is a hidden agenda to achieve residence only taxation of royalties (which expression is used here to express the rule of taxation only in the country of residence unless there is a PE to which royalties are attributable), it is likely that the politics have been badly mishandled by those seeking this end. On the other hand, if the technical explanation is adopted, then it may be that the problem has gone away through the other income article in modern treaties but without any harm to anyone and some benefit for those who do not accept residence only taxation.

The Fiscal Committee did not in the immediate context of settling the principles to be applied to royalties adopt model language. However, at its 1931 meeting, where the principles were confirmed, another topic on the agenda was the possibility of a multilateral tax treaty based on the League's work. The 1930 meeting had appointed a subcommittee to look into the issue and it produced a draft which the 1931 meeting supplemented with a further two drafts. Two of the drafts included an article reading:

> Authors' rights and income from patents shall be taxable only in the State of fiscal domicile of beneficiaries. If, however, they are collected by persons to whom these rights have been assigned for a consideration, or fall on any other grounds into the category of industrial or commercial income, they shall be taxable as such under the conditions laid down in Article 4 [on business profits of PEs].[18]

Although the Committee decided that there was not sufficient support to proceed with a multilateral tax treaty, this language clearly reflects the outcome of the royalty work and is the origin of the residence only taxation in the current OECD model.

There is no separate definition here of what is covered by the article, and indeed the word royalties is not mentioned. For the origin of the royalties definition we need to look elsewhere. In terms of the Fiscal Committee, it is not necessary to look far. In this period the League was also involved in its

---

[17] As a result of OECD (1999) but the analysis is still controversial.
[18] United States (1962, pp. 4235 and 4238). The third draft was to similar effect though in slightly different language.

major project of the 1930s, the development of the current transfer pricing rules dealing with attribution of profits to PEs and taxation of associated enterprises. In 1933 the first draft was put forward and it defined the income subject to the business profits article at some length by inclusion and exclusion. One of the categories generally excluded was:

> Rentals or royalties arising from leasing personal property or from any interest in such property, including rentals or royalties for the use of, or for the privilege of using, patents, copyrights, secret processes and formulae, goodwill, trade marks, trade brands, franchises and other like property, provided the enterprise is not engaged in dealing in such property.[19]

This language is clearly the origin of the modern tax treaty definition of royalties. As with much of the League of Nations work, the language came from elsewhere as elaborated below.

If we turn to actual treaties, the word 'royalties' seems to appear first in a 1921 treaty between Germany and Czechoslovakia (at least in the official League of Nations English translation):

> It is agreed that the provisions of this Treaty shall not affect the laws in force in the Contracting States regarding the special taxation of royalties and commissions.[20]

This exclusion is interesting in the light of the later debate of whether the 1928 models covered royalties at all. In the 1930s and early 1940s there are many treaties dealing with royalties either under that name or using language more in accord with the 1931 multilateral drafts. Among European countries, it seems that Belgium was the first to deal expressly with the issue in language closer to the 1931 League drafts (or perhaps more accurately the 1930 League principles as the earliest treaties also date from 1931):

> Copyright fees and patent fees shall be taxable in the country in which the recipients have their fiscal domicile. Should such fees constitute income derived from an industrial or commercial undertaking, they shall be taxable under the conditions laid down in Article 7.[21]

---

[19] *Ibid.*, p. 4244.

[20] The term 'royalties' appears in the tax treaty context in relation to minerals as well as intellectual property and it is not clear from the text in this case which it is though the association with commissions suggests the latter.

[21] Belgium–France 1931. See also Belgium–Italy 1931 and Belgium–Luxembourg 1931 (copyright only). The tax treaties referred to in this article have been drawn from the treaty database Tax Analysts (electronic), generally based on the English texts/translations

Another early (1931) adopter was Sweden, which developed its own language:

> Royalty paid for the use of immovable property or for working mines or other mineral deposits shall be taxable in the State where the immovable property, mine or mineral deposit is situated.
>
> Other royalty shall be taxed in accordance with the provisions of Article 3 [residence only taxation].
>
> Charges payable periodically for the use of patents, models or the like shall be assimilated to royalty.[22]

Next in line seems to be France, which likewise had its preferred language:

> The taxation of receipts from copyright or from the sale or concession of licences to use patents, trade-marks, models, processes or formulae of manufacture shall be subject to the terms of Article 11 [residence only taxation], provided such receipts do not constitute income from an industrial or commercial enterprise, in which case they shall be taxable in accordance with the rules laid down in Article 3 [business profits of a PE].[23]

Hungary also seems to have pursued a separate article on the issue.[24] What is common about all these cases is that they provide exclusive residence taxation (usually with a PE exception) and are closer to the 1931 League language (or 1930 principles) without the effective definition of royalties found in the League context of industrial and commercial profits. The Swedish and French treaties lend credence to the view that the concern was simply to make sure that both countries were applying the same articles to the income, i.e., a technical explanation of the royalty article. In the case of Belgium, it may have been a means of ensuring that domestic law did not apply.

---

of the treaties. Most of the translations of old treaties at least are drawn from official sources such as the publications of the League of Nations and the United Nations. For these publications and other information on the tax treaty activities of these organisations, see Chrétien (1954, pp. 5–116). These Belgian treaties seem to be based on model 1c and not to have an other income article.

[22] Sweden–Finland 1931. See also Sweden–Denmark 1932 and Sweden–Netherlands 1935. All of these treaties have an other income article giving exclusive taxing rights to the residence country. For Sweden–US 1939 see below.

[23] France–Switzerland 1937. See also France–Sweden 1936, which follows this language rather than the Swedish preference above. Both of these treaties have an other income article with exclusive residence taxation. Conversely, in Belgium–France 1931 Belgium seems to be the leader as noted above. For France–US 1932 and 1939 see below.

[24] Hungary–Netherlands 1938, Hungary–Switzerland 1942.

The US is clearly the origin of the language that came to be included in the modern royalty definition, which is not surprising since Carroll, who was mainly responsible for the 1930s work on transfer pricing which produced the wording, was from the US. Naturally, he reached out to the familiar language of US law which had been enacted in 1921 as part of the original development of the US international tax rules.[25]

In one sense, however, the US role in the inclusion of a royalty article in tax treaties was simply reactive. The first US tax treaty was with France in 1932. On the US side, the main purpose of the treaty was to deal with the French tax on dividends paid by US parent corporations out of French based profits of subsidiaries. France wanted the treaty to remove the US tax on royalties received by French authors; the US was prepared to agree only if France gave up its tax on patent royalties received by US corporations. The treaty provides on royalties:

> The following classes of income paid in one of the contracting States to a corporation of the other State, or to a citizen of the latter State residing there, are exempt from tax in the former State:
> (a) Amounts paid as consideration for the right to use patents, secret processes and formulas, trade marks and other analogous rights;
> (b) Income received as copyright royalties . . .

The treaty also includes the League-style language in relation to industrial and commercial profits, though without the proviso in relation to dealing in the property.[26] The US treaty with France of 1939 goes further towards the later language in the royalties article (and its own domestic legislation), including combining the position of patents and copyright rather than dealing with them in separate paragraphs. The US–Sweden treaty of 1939 is a combination of the preferred US and Swedish language:

---

[25] The US Revenue Act of 1921, s. 217(a)(4) provides a US source rule as follows: 'Rentals or royalties from property located in the United States or from an interest in such property including rentals or royalties for the use of or for the privilege of using in the United States patents, copyrights, secret processes and formulas, good will, trade-marks, franchises and other like property.' In turn, this language codified the practice that had been generated in the US on earlier income tax legislation which did not contain explicit source rules: Graetz and O'Hear (1997, pp. 1057–9).

[26] US–Canada 1942 also has the industrial and commercial profits language but no article on royalties. The US–France 1932 treaty also seems to be the first that includes an associated enterprises article in the modern form which first appeared in the Fiscal Committee 1933 draft; it did not include the equivalent modern language for attribution of profits to PEs that also originated in the 1933 draft; US–Canada 1942 seems to be the earliest treaty with this language.

> Royalties from real property or in respect of the operation of mines, quarries, or other natural resources shall be taxable only in the contracting State in which such property, mines, quarries, or other natural resources are situated.
>
> Other royalties and amounts derived from within one of the contracting States by a resident or by a corporation or other entity of the other contracting State as consideration for the right to use copyrights, patents, secret processes and formulas, trade-marks and other analogous rights, shall be exempt from taxation in the former State.

There is no other income article in these treaties and the purpose was clearly to prevent the application of domestic law (the US having levied a withholding tax on royalties for many years).

The only country that seems to have negotiated during this period for source taxing rights over royalties in a separate treaty article is Romania:

> Copyrights and the proceeds of the sale or granting of licenses for the exploitation of patents, trade marks, models, manufacturing processes and formulae are taxable in the State in which they are payable.[27]

It thus seems likely that the purposes of royalties articles in treaties in the 1930s were mainly technical. There is no strong evidence of countries struggling to retain source taxing rights and having to give them away in order to achieve a treaty. Some major countries, such as Germany, which had a large treaty network, did not include articles on royalties in its treaties and was apparently content to allow the matter to be dealt with by other articles. The German preference seems to have been to include an other income article with exclusive residence taxation or something to similar effect.[28]

7.2 Mexico and London models and treaty practice

When the Fiscal Committee's activities moved to the Americas during World War II, the European influence was much less and the Latin American countries, which preferred source only taxation, predominated. Not surprisingly, the Mexico model of 1943 adopts source taxation of royalties in part (excluding payments for copyright):

---

[27] Romania–France 1942; compare Romania–Italy 1938 (to be settled by special agreement), Romania–Hungary 1932 (patents only taxable in country in which patents are issued).

[28] For examples from this period, see Germany–Romania 1937 and Germany–Yugoslavia 1940, which follow the pattern set in the treaties of the 1920s.

1. Royalties from immovable property or in respect of the operation of a mine, a quarry, or other natural resource shall be taxable only in the contracting State in which such property, mine, quarry, or other natural resource is situated.

2. Royalties and amounts received as a consideration for the right to use a patent, a secret process or formula, a trademark or other analogous right shall be taxable only in the State where such right is exploited.

3. Royalties derived from one of the contracting States by an individual, corporation or other entity of the other contracting State, in consideration for the right to use a musical, artistic, literary, scientific or other cultural work or publication shall not be taxable in the former State.[29]

The Europeans, no doubt, would have preferred to return to their predominant practice of residence only taxation but, as the Mexico model could not be undone without considerable political difficulty, the London model, in which the Latin American influence was more muted as the Europeans again predominated, adopted the Mexico model approach with the qualification that source taxation was only permitted in the case of royalties paid between associated enterprises and on condition that taxation was on a net basis. Paragraph 2 of the Mexico Model became:

2. Royalties derived from one of the contracting States by an individual, corporation or other entity of the other contracting State in consideration for the right to use a patent, a secret process or formula, a trade-mark or other analogous right, shall not be taxable in the former State.

3. If, however, royalties are paid by an enterprise of one contracting State to another enterprise of the other contracting State which has a dominant participation in its management or capital, or *vice versa*, or when both enterprises are owned or controlled by the same interests, the royalties shall be subject to taxation in the State where the right in consideration of which they are paid is exploited, subject to deduction from the gross amount of such royalties of all expenses and charges, including depreciation, relative to such rights and royalties.[30]

The Commentary explained the outcome as follows:

In the same way as other income from real property, which is governed by Article II of the Model Convention, royalties received by a person, as owner or possessor of real property in consideration of the right to use or exploit natural deposits and resources situated on the surface or in the subsoil of his property, such as mines, quarries, wells, springs, waterfalls, forests, are taxable in the country where the property is situated . . .

[29] United States (1962, pp. 4384–6).   [30] *Ibid.*, p. 4385.

The second paragraph of Article X refers to royalties from scientific, industrial and commercial property, such as patents, secret processes and formulae, trade-marks and trade-names. The Mexico Convention, applying the principle of immediate economic origin, placed them under a single rule according to which the royalties are taxable in the country where the patent or other similar right to which they correspond is exploited. As a result, the returns of patents and similar rights always remained taxable in the country where the rights were used, whether the proprietor exploited them himself or through a lessee.

Following a similar line of reasoning to that which inspired the new wording of Articles VIII and IX of the London draft [under which dividends and interest are only taxable in the country of residence], royalties from patents and similar rights are made taxable in the new version of paragraph 2 of the article under consideration exclusively in the country to which the grantor belongs. A restriction to that principle is, however, made by the new paragraph 3 in case the concession has taken place between inter-related enterprises. In that case, the royalties become taxable in the country where the rights are exploited subject to deduction of 'all expenses and charges including depreciation relative to such rights'.

The fourth paragraph of Article X in the London draft is identical with the third paragraph of the Mexico version. Copyright royalties from artistic and scientific productions, wherever earned, remain exclusively taxable in the country where the recipient has his fiscal domicile or permanent establishment. The specific purpose of this rule is to facilitate cultural exchanges.[31]

The 1933 language referring to – and in a sense effectively defining – royalties in the area of industrial and commercial profits disappears from the Mexico and London models but the language in the area of intellectual property for royalties is to the same effect.

A number of issues are raised by these developments. The association of royalties from mining and intellectual property in the same article was probably intended by the drafters of the Mexico model to bolster the case for taxing the latter (apart from copyright) at source for no-one was likely to question source taxation of mining royalties. This association was suggested by past Swedish treaty practice, which included both together in the same article. The question it raises is what of rentals for tangible movable property. It will be noted that these were included in the 1933 provision relating to industrial and commercial profits as they subsequently came to be in the royalty definition. It is natural to treat such property the same

[31] *Ibid.*, p. 4347.

as immovable property and intangible property used in a country if the latter two are amalgamated.

The separation of patent and copyright royalties into different rules was not in accord with previous practice or the 1930 principles of the Fiscal Committee. A very few previous treaties dealt explicitly only with patent royalties or only with copyright. The effect in such cases could have been to produce separate rules for each category, depending on what the rest of the treaty provided. The US-France treaty of 1932 had them in separate subparagraphs because of the history of the treaty, explained above, but with the same rule (hence their combination in the 1939 treaty). The justification of residence only taxation for copyright on the basis of cultural exchange resonated with some countries into modern times. It seems an unlikely way for countries that feel culturally dominated by other larger countries to redress the balance; indeed freeing such royalties from source tax may well produce the opposite effect as it will encourage inflows of foreign culture as much as outflows of local culture. The Mexico model also led to the result that the royalty article did not cover copyright comprehensively, which is difficult to justify, especially from a modern perspective in which software is protected by copyright.

The introduction of the qualification in the London model in relation to associated enterprises and net taxation was a significant departure from previous treaty practice and work of the Fiscal Committee. In terms of modern conditions, however, it was a potentially telling blow against tax planning that involved stripping income from a source country by payment of royalties between associated parties, especially as source taxation of royalties is not restricted by a rate limitation, only by a requirement of net taxation. It has not survived directly, though it may indirectly be the origin of the special relationship rule in the royalties article that restricts residence only taxation under that article to the arm's-length amount of royalties. Net taxation of royalties has not generally survived at tax treaty level. The only modern tax treaty rule about deductions relates to the payer of the royalty, not the payee in the form of the deduction non-discrimination rule that requires the deductibility of the arm's-length amount of royalties paid to non-residents to the same extent as royalties paid to residents. The effect of the modern rules is very different when combined with zero taxation or a rate limit in the royalties article, as the modern rules encourage the practice against which the London model was apparently directed.

To this point two other significant issues in the light of subsequent developments have not been raised; first, the treatment of know-how, which is at the border between property and services; and secondly, the meaning of 'use' and in particular the distinction between sale and use of intellectual property. They do not figure in the League of Nations discussions of the period covered so far but they loom large in modern times. With respect to the first, it will be noted that modern words in the royalty definition generally associated with know-how, payments 'for information concerning industrial, commercial or scientific experience' do not appear in any of the previous model or actual treaty language. Nonetheless it is arguable that under many of the formulations quoted above, know-how could be covered either in the reference to 'secret processes and formulae' or by the words 'analogous right' or variants of each.[32] There is clear evidence in some negotiations between the US and France in the 1950s that it was considered that know-how was already covered by the 1933 League wording which, as noted above, originated in the US. France wished to negotiate a protocol to the US–France 1946 estate tax, treaty but the US was not willing to do so unless France gave up the application of its turnover tax, which around this time morphed into the new invention of the VAT to US film companies and patent owners. Accordingly, the US and France negotiated a *procès-verbal* as to how France would apply its domestic turnover tax law in which it was stated:

> With respect to the royalties which they receive in connection with the licensing of the rights to exploitation in France of inventions, American licensors will enjoy a regime identical to that which is in effect for French licensors. Turnover taxes . . . will consequently not be applicable to royalties received by American enterprises which license the use of an 'invention' in France and which can, with respect to that invention, qualify as inventors. It is agreed that the term 'invention' includes, whether registered or not: patents, copyrights, trademarks, manufacturing processes or formulas (know-how).[33]

With respect to the second issue, the language employed by the Fiscal Committee and in many treaties was more or less clear that all

---

[32] Where the second phrase is 'other like property', this argument can be turned on its head. In many countries, including Australia, know-how is not property though it is legally protected by the law relating to confidential information. If an *ejusdem generis* interpretation is adopted for these words in the definition, it may be suggested that the first phrase must encompass property and so exclude know-how. This is a doubtful use of the *ejusdem generis* rule of construction and in any event seems too technical and out of place in a treaty context.

[33] Tax Analysts (electronic, document no. 95-30025). Around this time France entered into similar agreements with many other European countries containing the same language. A similar position is taken in the US Treasury Technical Explanation to the tax treaty negotiated in the 1950s between the US and India which did not enter into force, Tax Analysts (electronic, document no. 2000-28062).

payments with respect to patents and copyrights were covered, whether they involved licences or assignments. The current language of payments 'for the use of, or the right to use' any copyright etc. has its origins in the 1933 Fiscal Committee (and US) language, although the word used there was 'privilege' rather than 'right'. The current 'right to use' language started to appear in the tax treaties of the 1930s and appears in the Mexico and London models. Questions of which treaty provision covers assignments of intellectual property are raised clearly by the US–Sweden and US–France 1939 treaties, which have a provision on gains from the sale or exchange of capital assets as well as a royalties article. As the result was likely the same under both articles, however, it was not likely to be a practical issue.[34] Under the London model, the point seems to be squarely raised for the first time in a way which matters, as it permits the taxation of certain patent royalties at source but has residence only taxation for capital gains apart from immovable property and PE assets. Recent developments have been much concerned with the meaning of use and the distinction between use and sale.

7.3   OEEC work and treaty practice

The League of Nations mandate in the tax treaty area passed to the United Nations but nothing of significance for the development of model tax treaties happened there for a decade.[35] In the meantime, countries were busy negotiating and renegotiating tax treaties to suit the conditions that prevailed after World War II. In particular, the UK, which previously had not negotiated treaties based on League of Nations models, rapidly began to develop a substantial tax treaty network. Countries had too many models after the work of the League of Nations to produce international uniformity and developed countries felt that more work was required to deal with the issue. The recently formed OEEC took up the work in 1956.[36] The OEEC Fiscal Committee formed Working Party No. 8 (WP8)

---

[34]   The issue was the subject of litigation under US domestic tax law of the time, see *Wodehouse v US* (1949) 337 US 369 (USSC). Although Wodehouse resided in France at the relevant time, the US–France 1932 treaty only applied to French citizens and Wodehouse was a British citizen. The US–France 1939 treaty covered residents of France but only for years after those in issue in the case. The final language of the OECD definition of royalties may have its origin in the US but it is different so that US case law is not directly relevant. In particular, it is a 'means' kind of definition and is meant to be a treaty exclusive definition.
[35]   For a benign view of the UN work, see Chrétien (1954).
[36]   van den Tempel (1967, p. 7). Van den Tempel was chair of the OEEC/OECD Fiscal Committee and recounts the OEEC and OECD work leading to the 1963 OECD draft model.

to deal with royalties on 7 June 1957, composed of delegates from Germany and Luxembourg who produced a draft article in their first report of 12 February 1958 as follows:

1. Royalties and other amounts received as consideration for the use of, or the right to use any patent, licence to use a patent or other intellectual property (licence d'exploitation), copyright, design or pattern, trade mark or similar right (except a right to work natural resources) or manufacture process shall be taxable only in the State of which the taxpayer is a resident.
2. There shall be treated as royalties all rents and amounts similarly received as consideration for the renting of cinematograph films (including cinematograph files intended to be exhibited on television), for the use of industrial, commercial or scientific equipment and for the supply of information concerning industrial or commercial experience.
3. Where any royalty or amount mentioned in paragraphs 1 and 2 exceeds an adequate consideration, then the State of which the taxpayer is a resident shall be entitled to tax only so much of it as represents an adequate consideration.
4. Paragraphs 1 to 3 shall also apply to amounts received as consideration for the sale or disposal of any property mentioned in those paragraphs.
5. Paragraphs 1 to 4 shall not apply where a person who is a resident of one of the States possesses in the other State a permanent establishment or a fixed place of business which is used for the performance of professional services and any income aforementioned is derived from that establishment or place of business. In such case the other State shall have the right to tax such income.[37]

The articles attached at the end of the report demonstrate the variety of 1950s treaty practice including how some countries[38] continued their 1930 practices in relation to royalties despite the significant changes in the Mexico and London models. The attached Norway-UK 1951 treaty demonstrates the UK practice of combining interest and royalties in a single article along with other matters referred to below.

The Observations in the report (as substantially developed in later revisions) formed the basis of the later Commentary, parts of which are still used to this day.[39] After introducing the topic with a statement of the

[37] FC/WP8 (58)1. Document numbers are in accordance with the OEEC/OECD numbering system.
[38] Denmark–Sweden 1953 follows Swedish practice from the 1930s, see above; likewise, France–Switzerland 1958 follows earlier French practice, see above.
[39] Much of the Commentary as it became after the work of WP8 appears for the first time in the third (revised) report of WP8, see n. 47 below.

various situations covered in terms reminiscent of the 1930 League Fiscal Committee and recounting the League of Nations history, WP8 noted that recent tax treaties of OEEC countries followed residence only taxation. Although the draft article is expressed in the report to be following the London model (presumably based on the excessive royalty provision), really it is a reversion to the League 1930 principles. It was immediately clear that the denial of source taxing rights was going to be an obstacle as the Luxembourg delegate who helped prepare the report entered a reservation to the effect that while residence only taxation may be appropriate in a multilateral treaty, Luxembourg would not want to take this position in bilateral negotiations.

The denial of residence country taxation for amounts in excess of an arm's-length amount was a variation of the practice of the UK which had included a provision about excessive royalties in virtually all of its many treaties from Australia-UK 1946 onwards and the practice had spread to several other countries. WP8 assumed that the excess would be recharacterised in a way which would lead to a denial of a deduction (presumably as a dividend or return of capital) and not be taxed as a royalty so that it was unnecessary to add anything about the consequences of the provision.[40] This is different from the London model, under which royalties paid to associated enterprises were subject to unlimited net tax at source as royalties.

The draft includes equipment leasing and renting of films. There were by this time many treaties which included equipment leasing in the royalties article, starting it seems with the Netherlands–US 1948.[41] While equipment leasing is now included as seemed a likely result of the Mexico and London models as discussed above, mining royalties are expressly excluded and left to be dealt with under the immovable property article, the Swedish practice in that regard not being widely adopted. The inclusion of rental of films was by this time very common in treaties, having started it seems with the UK–US 1945 treaty (though the strong UK preference during the period was to make express provision excluding film rental from the royalties article or including it in industrial and commercial profits).[42] The reference to television in relation to films picks up the recent German practice starting with Canada–Germany 1956. Television

---

[40] The UK practice of the time was more in line with the modern form of the article, which is to remove the source country treaty limit under the royalty article on the excessive part.

[41] There seem to be at least twenty treaties up to the beginning of 1958 including the language.

[42] For the UK–US treaty of 1945 in this regard, see Avery Jones (2007, p. 231).

also made an appearance in many 1950s treaties in relation to the entertainers article.

By contrast, the wording in relation to know-how seems new. The language of secret processes and formulae referred to above that might cover know-how is omitted, though the words 'similar right' still appear and there is a reference to manufacture process in para. 1. The modern wording for know-how seems to first appear in an international setting in the WP8 report. The France–Germany 1959[43] tax treaty signed some eighteen months after the report of WP8 contains the wording apparently for the first time in an actual treaty but, as the German delegate for WP8 was very likely the German treaty negotiator with France, it is not possible to be sure which came first or whether there is some other origin for the language. The kind of payment that is envisaged is additional advice in relation to the supply of a patent for which an additional payment is made. The way it is described in the report might be thought to involve show-how as opposed to know-how, which is generally seen as the communication of existing knowledge rather than services to assist in using a patent.

The explanation given for the change is to avoid any dispute as to whether it is business or professional income or royalty. This is the same kind of technical explanation as was suggested above as a possibility for the League of Nations provisions. In reading the OEEC/OECD materials from the period, one gets the same ambiguous feelings. Is it politics or technics? As will be seen below, there are certainly elements of politics. On the other hand, WP8 and many of the OEEC delegates seem to be seeking the 'correct' technical solutions to structural issues. Despite the debate over source taxation that followed, some countries which later asserted strong source taxing rights over royalties in their treaties were happy to give them up in treaties negotiated during this period.[44]

The express coverage of assignments as well as licences clearly resolves one of the issues about the meaning of use referred to above. As there is no taxation of royalties at source under the draft in the absence of a PE, it

---

[43] The French text refers to 'la fourniture d'informations concernant des expériences d'ordre industriel, commercial ou scientifique', which is translated in this way into English in Tax Analysts (electronic, document nos 96-11284 and 93-30068). This language is different to the current French language OECD Model which is translated into English the same way. Other variants referring to experience in the royalties context are found in Finland–Switzerland 1956 and Austria–France 1959.

[44] One such country is Australia, which was not a member of the OECD until 1971. In its four treaties negotiated up to 1960 with the UK, the US, Canada and New Zealand, Australia ceded source taxing rights over many royalties. It only found its passion for source taxation with Australia–UK 1967.

is not clear that the addition makes much difference, but the possibility of tax at source under the Luxembourg reservation does, depending on whether there is a capital gains article and what it says. At the time of this report there was no OEEC work on capital gains (Working Party No 19 on capital gains being set up in November 1961) and no report on the issue was published by the OEEC or OECD prior to the 1963 OECD draft model. The provision seems to be a variant of UK practice that appears in many of its treaties from Netherland–UK 1948 onwards and spread to some other countries. France–Switzerland 1952, which is annexed to the report, uses different language to the same effect.

After the production of the initial report, the method of proceeding was to circulate it to OEEC members and to receive comments by way of documents,[45] meetings of WP8 and meetings of the full OEEC Fiscal Committee.[46] Several other reports including revised versions of the original report were produced in this way.[47] Towards the end of the process, a joint effort of working parties occurred to achieve consistency of structure and language across the dividends, interest and royalties articles given that they used a number of common ideas.[48] The final report of WP8 was published in 1961 as part of the fourth and final report of the Fiscal Committee under OEEC auspices.[49] The OEEC became the OECD in late 1961. The Fiscal Committee continued its work and produced the 1963 draft model, which brought together and revised the material in the four OEEC reports as well as providing new work, for example, in relation to the capital gains article. The ensuing discussion includes the more important issues that were dealt with in the royalties area following the order of discussion of the article above.

---

[45] Comments were included in the following documents: TFD/FC/38 (Switzerland, 6 May 1958); TFD/FC/48 (Portugal, 19 November 1958); TFD/FC/57 (Belgium, 2 December 1958); TFD/FC/55 (Italy, 19 January 1959); TFD/FC/80 (note of secretary of Fiscal Committee 16 November 1959); TFD/FC/102 (Switzerland, 5 October 1960 on interest and royalties).

[46] Meetings of the Fiscal Committee that dealt with the issue are as follows: FC/M(58)3 (8th session, 5–7 May 1958); FC/M(60)2 (17th session, 29 March–1April 1960); FC/M(605 (20th session, 6–9 September 1960); FC/M(60)6 (21st session, 25–28 October 1960); FC/M(61)1 (22nd session, 17–20 January 1961); FC/M(61)2 (23rd session, 7–10 March 1961); FC/M(61)3 (24th session, 18–21 April 1961).

[47] Further reports of WP8 are: second report FC/WP8 (58)2 (3 September 1958); supplement to second report FC/WP8 (58)3 (10 November 1958); aide-memoire FC/WP8 (58)4 (19 December 1958); second aide-memoire FC/WP8 (60)1 (3 May 1960); revised third report FC/WP8 (61)1 (27 February 1961); revised fourth report FC/WP8(61)2 (4 April 1961).

[48] TFD/FC/98 joint meeting of WP8, WP11, WP12 and WP15 (9 June 1960).

[49] OEEC (1961) in United States (1962, p. 4621).

Source taxation proved to be the most contentious issue in the development of the royalties article and led to a unique solution in the tax treaty field that comes nearest to the often expressed desire of the creators of model treaties to achieve a multilateral solution. The source issue was raised in various ways but the major questions were whether there was to be source taxation in the absence of a PE,[50] whether there was to be any limit on such source taxation and what the limit might be.

Belgium agreed with Luxembourg that residence only taxation was not appropriate in a bilateral context and produced various arguments for source taxation, such as the lack of balance that arises if income flows are unequal between countries (though it agreed that this could be met by looking across the deal struck in relation to different income flows under different articles and was not purely a royalties issue), and avoidance problems that arise if there is no tax at residence[51] or the payment is between related parties. On the other hand, it acknowledged that a source tax on a gross basis, while convenient, could lead to grossing up of the royalty payment by the amount of the tax and shifting the burden back to the payer. In its view, a net basis was the appropriate way to tax royalties and it is difficult to get agreement on the rate limit if a gross basis tax is used.[52]

Portugal, in its comments on the original draft, argued for source taxation, on familiar sovereignty grounds and was in favour of exclusive source taxation, as taxation on a residence only basis permits fictitious changes of residence or assignment of the intellectual property to a resident of another country – a variant on the avoidance concerns of Belgium. For this reason, it rejected the argument most often heard from the UK that

---

[50] There was some debate as to how the PE exception would be expressed assuming there was to be no force of attraction. The draft went through a number of versions on this issue but, as it is tied up also with how the similar exception is drafted in the dividends and interest articles, it will not be pursued here. Even at the very end at the 23rd session of the Fiscal Committee, Belgium in particular was concerned about the expression; it was agreed at this session that the property giving rise to the income must be part of the PE assets.

[51] This issue arose at various points. The UK requested a subject to tax provision but WP8 in its second report rejected such a test as out of keeping with the general structure and 'economy' of the model. At Fiscal Committee 23rd session it was agreed that the Commentary would not specify whether the residence only tax was conditional on tax being levied but would state that the matter can be settled in bilateral negotiations, see United States (1962, p. 4681) for the Commentary eventually published on this issue.

[52] Belgium raised its position at the 8th session of the Fiscal Committee and followed it up with a document setting out its views. It suggested additions to the PE exception to cover the lack of a residence tax and related parties.

the expenses giving rise to the intellectual property (especially of research) are incurred in the country of residence which accordingly should have the taxing rights.

Very early in the process, head counts began to be taken, as it seemed unlikely that consensus could be achieved. At the first count, seven countries favoured residence only taxation, with France also inclining this way though prepared to concede source taxation on a bilateral basis. Portugal favoured source only taxation, with which five other countries agreed, though they would concede residence taxation if necessary. Only two or three countries were happy with a gross basis limit.[53] At the Fiscal Committee, the original numbers were that four countries did not tax royalties at source under domestic law (based on the argument that this encouraged development) while the other countries did. All countries seemed to tax royalties on a residence basis, though the positions of Spain and Portugal were not clear. Under tax treaties, two countries wanted exclusive source taxation and seven exclusive residence taxation (the UK in particular raising the issue of net versus gross basis taxation and the problem of recovery of expenses) and the rest a mixture of the two. The Fiscal Committee accordingly asked WP8 to produce a draft permitting both residence and source taxation.[54]

WP8 in turn conceded the multilateral/bilateral distinction drawn by Luxembourg and Belgium and redrafted the article to include source taxation subject to a 5 per cent limit of the gross amount of the royalty which was to be relieved from double taxation in the residence state.[55] The first meeting on the redraft was inconclusive. The UK repeated its position on residence only taxation and raised the additional point that an OEEC model permitting source taxation of royalties would create difficulties in negotiating treaties with non-OEEC members (which it was heavily engaged in, especially with current and former colonies). Several countries agreed with the UK that 5 per cent was the maximum source tax that was acceptable (Ireland, Greece, Luxembourg, Germany and Switzerland). Austria was not prepared to accept such a low limit while Denmark, the Netherlands and Sweden thought 5 per cent was too high. Ireland considered that any source rate should be lower than that

---

[53] WP8 aide-memoire.   [54] Fiscal Committee 17th session.
[55] WP8 second aide-memoire. There is no source rule in this draft but such a rule appears in WP8 third report, which had reverted to residence only taxation; the source rule was deleted at Fiscal Committee 23rd session at the suggestion of Switzerland but a suggestion that such a rule be included where there is source taxation under the treaty was included in the Commentary, see United States (1962, pp. 4684–5).

permitted for dividends and interest. The UK was unhappy at the outcome of the meeting.[56]

Two more meetings were required before the matter was resolved. At the first, the countries restated their positions and sounded out the possible rules of the game for a compromise. It was made clear to delegates that a Council Recommendation (which was how the work would be promulgated on its completion) was not legally binding on member countries. It was also generally accepted that any limit stated in a model would not preclude countries negotiating lower rates on a bilateral basis. Austria, which was one of the countries insisting on source taxation, made the point that dividends, interest and royalties needed to be looked at together in bilateral negotiations and that it may be possible to have an initially high gross source tax (10 per cent was its preferred position) that could be phased down over time under the treaty. Italy also considered 5 per cent too low.[57]

At the next meeting there was a head count again. At this stage there were only five countries insisting on across the board source taxation: Austria, Greece, Portugal, Spain and Turkey. Switzerland moved that the committee revert to a residence only draft and Sweden suggested the proviso that the Commentary would permit up to 5 per cent gross tax at source. The Chair suggested that any deal struck would be included in the Council Recommendation (which is the unique part of the royalties story).[58] That is, the Recommendation would recognise that certain specified countries had the right to a 5 per cent rate limit and that the other countries would undertake to negotiate reciprocal tax rate limits with them on that basis. At the vote nine countries were in favour, two against (Belgium and Luxembourg) and six abstained (the five countries insisting on source taxation plus France).[59] Although there were further meetings when attempts were made to undo the two basic elements of the deal (a model with residence only taxation of royalties and a Council Recommendation under which if countries wishing source taxation would undertake to accept 5 per cent, other countries would undertake to accept this rate on a reciprocal basis), in the event the deal stuck and led to the following part of the Council Recommendation:

---

[56] Fiscal Committee 20th session.   [57] Fiscal Committee 21st session.

[58] The only other special deal that made its way into a recommendation was the special position of Greece with respect to shipping, OEEC (1959) in United States (1962, p. 4511 at p. 4559), but this did not involve any (non-binding) reciprocal undertakings as in the royalties case.

[59] Fiscal Committee 22nd session.

Notwithstanding the provisions relating to royalties in the Annex to this Recommendation, the other Member countries declare that they are prepared in bilateral Conventions and subject to reciprocity to concede to Greece, Luxembourg, Portugal and Spain a right to impose tax at 5 per cent on the gross amount of royalties, to which rate these four countries declare that they are prepared in such Conventions to limit their tax at the source where the recipient of the royalties has not in their respective territories a permanent establishment with which the right or property giving rise to the royalties is effectively connected.[60]

Although source taxation was the major issue, many other concerns were aired and their resolution significantly affected the ultimate outcome in a number of areas. There were technical issues around how the residence only principle was to be expressed.[61] Italy generally wished to apply force of attraction to PEs and tried unsuccessfully to achieve this in the model article for royalties. Eventually, Italy had to satisfy itself with a reservation on this issue.[62] The debate around the excessive royalties provision, by contrast, was much more intense and involved considerable shifts in position.

In lieu of the draft provision above, Austria wished the model to contain the London model provision, which gave unlimited source taxing rights on a net basis over patent royalties paid to an associated enterprise.[63] WP8 rejected this approach for several reasons. First, it confused the treatment of head offices and PEs with that of parents and subsidiaries and contradicted the underlying structure of tax treaties since the late 1920s of treating separate companies as separate taxpayers for treaty purposes, even when the companies were associated. Further, the base erosion argument

---

[60] United States (1962, pp. 4699–700). Luxembourg joined the group while Austria and Turkey could not accept the 5 per cent rate and entered reservations setting out 10 per cent and 20 per cent rate limits respectively. The difference is that these countries had no undertaking that other countries would accept these rates. Unsuccessful attempts were made at Fiscal Committee 23rd and 24th sessions to backtrack on residence only taxation and inclusion of the undertakings in the recommendation.

[61] WP8 in its second report used 'recipient' instead of 'taxpayer' in the provision to make clear that the residence of the person entitled to the royalty is determinative not the residence of the collector of the royalty. The issue was taken up again in the late 1960s eventually leading to the beneficial owner terminology in the 1977 model. See also n. 12 above. Concerns over this issue led to further changes to the text of the OECD model more recently in 1997.

[62] United States (1962, p. 4684). Italy raised the issue in Fiscal Committee 8th and 20th sessions, and in its written comments on WP8's work. Force of attraction was rejected by WP8 in its second report as contrary to modern treaty practice and in any event within the mandate of the working party dealing with business profits.

[63] Fiscal Committee 8th session.

that if a country grants a deduction to one taxpayer it should be able to tax the recipient of the payment, was considered too broad and would apply to many payments which it was generally accepted are not taxable in the country of the payer. WP8 considered that excessive royalties could be recharacterised under domestic law and were not special to the associated enterprises area; accordingly, it dropped the provision as unnecessary, though in a long annex discussing the issue it included a simplified version of the original draft.[64]

Switzerland was also concerned about the area but its issues were different. It considered that the excessive royalties rule should be confined to special relationships along the lines of the provision that first appeared in the Switzerland–UK 1954 treaty and a few other treaties during that period. It considered that the problem of excessive royalties only arose in practice between related parties and the rule should be so limited to prevent unwarranted use of it by countries. The UK was happy with this limit but Italy was not. The Swiss considered that it should be expressly stated that the excess was to be treated and taxed under the treaty as a distribution if the excessive royalties provision was contained in the model, although it agreed with WP8 that the matter could be handled under domestic law. In the result, its desire for a special relationship provision based on its treaty practice was satisfied but without any conclusion as to the nature of the excess.[65]

The more important issue that Switzerland raised was the deductibility of royalties to the payer in the source country. It argued that the royalties article should expressly confirm deductibility to which WP8 replied that its members 'know of no current Convention containing such a clause'.[66]

---

[64] WP8 second report: 'The provisions of this Article shall not apply to any part of the royalties or other payments which exceeds an adequate consideration.' It took some time to resolve the issue as it became entwined with the suggestions made by Switzerland.

[65] The provision was reinstated in the WP8 third report: 'Where, owing to a special relationship between the payer and the recipient or between either of them and some other person, the amount of the royalties paid, having regard to the use or right for which they are paid, exceeds the amount which would have been agreed upon by the payer and the recipient in the absence of the relationship, the provisions of this Article shall apply only to the last-mentioned amount. In that case, the excess part of the payment shall remain taxable according to the Contracting States' own laws, due regard being had to the other provisions of this Convention.' At Fiscal Committee 23rd session comments were made by Switzerland and Belgium and the Chair requested another redraft taking account of the Belgian concerns. The WP8 fourth report contains the provision in exactly the same terms which is more or less its modern form. Like the PE provision, this issue was also affected by the drafting of the similar provision in the interest article.

[66] WP8 supplement to second report.

Switzerland persisted, but the Fiscal Committee considered that it raised broader issues (such as the deductibility of other amounts like interest) and so the matter was left open. In reply, Switzerland produced a draft that is the origin of the non-discrimination deduction provision.[67] In the event, the provision did not appear in the royalties article. One proposal for the Commentary included a statement that if a country introduced a rule denying deductions for royalties paid to non-residents after entering into a treaty with residence only tax, this action would be considered contrary to the treaty but the statement was watered down in the final version to an exhortation to allow deductions.[68] It was not until 1977 that Switzerland succeeded in having their suggested provision included in the OECD model.[69] As noted above in relation to the London model on this topic, the Swiss proposals may be thought in the event to have encouraged tax planning through the payment of deductible royalties, whereas the Austrian preference may have significantly reduced such avoidance.

Some debate revolved around the definition of royalties, although generally these were more matters of drafting than substance. The combining of the first two paragraphs of the original WP8 draft into a single definition occurred relatively late in the process.[70] Greece was the only country to question the inclusion of equipment leasing, which may be thought surprising in the light of the subsequent efforts to eliminate it.[71] The exclusion of mining royalties was first moved to a separate paragraph

[67] 'Interest (royalties) paid by a resident of a Contracting State to a resident of the other Contracting State may be deducted from the gross income of the first-mentioned under the same conditions as and to the extent that such deduction is permitted where the recipient is a resident of the same State as the payer. Such deduction shall not be precluded by reason merely that the tax payable by the recipient on such interest (royalties) is reduced in accordance with this Article or that there is a special relationship between the payer and the recipient of the interest (royalties).'

[68] Fiscal Committee 20th session; Switzerland's comments of 5 October 1960 contained the draft; after inconclusive debate at Fiscal Committee 21st session the WP8 third report included the proposed Commentary as to the effect of changing domestic law which was retained in WP8 fourth report but modified in the published version United States (1962, pp. 4680–1).

[69] Article 24(5) in van Raad (1987, p. xxviii). Switzerland is also responsible for the ownership non-discrimination provision which it was successful in having included in the early OEEC/OECD reports and models: see Lang (2007, p. 106).

[70] WP8 third report.

[71] WP8 aide-memoire. OECD (1985, pp. 1–28) (reports on equipment leasing and container leasing) proposed removal of equipment leasing from the model which occurred in 1992. US lessors in particular were insistent on this change from a relatively early stage.

and then eliminated as unnecessary.[72] Similarly, the know-how material went though some redrafting. The Fiscal Committee produced a redraft early on that restored secret processes and formulas to the first paragraph of WP8's draft but left the second paragraph referring to information intact.[73] When the combination occurred, nothing was done to indicate which part of the definition covered know-how, though it probably did not matter much – the main issue was what constituted know-how and this had been left to the Commentary which was silent until 1977 and subsequently.

The main issue of substance was the ongoing attempt by the UK to remove film rentals from the definition. The underlying concern of the UK was source taxation of royalties. The UK persistence on the issue was the tip of the modern iceberg that inexorably drifts away from application of the royalties article. If source taxation of royalties is inevitable, then the strategy of countries which do not like it is to take income out of the article by revision of the article or interpretation to other, more helpful, residence only taxation articles (such as – in the absence of a PE – business profits, capital gains and other income). In this case the UK unsuccessfully attempted the revision route. It stated its position early in the process and maintained it to the end. All that was achieved was an acknowledgement in the Commentary that the matter could be dealt with bilaterally.[74] In terms of drafting, film rentals were moved from para. 2 to para. 1 of the original WP8 draft and the 'modern' reference to television was removed.[75]

---

[72] The move to a separate paragraph occurred in WP8 second report and a reference to the coverage by the article on immovable property was added in WP8 third report. Switzerland suggested at Fiscal Committee 23rd session that it be removed and this occurred in WP8 fourth report along with an annotation in the Commentary referring to the immovable property article.

[73] Fiscal Committee 8th session. To confuse matters, the UK suggested at Fiscal Committee 20th session that the Commentary should make clear that the reference to similar property or right covered secret processes or formulae. One of the Swiss suggested redrafts included the revolutionary idea that the word 'know-how' expressly appear in para. 1 of the WP8 draft; it also threw in technical experience for good measure and left the para. 2 reference to information intact.

[74] The UK position was stated at Fiscal Committee 8th session and repeated in many subsequent sessions. Essentially, it was that films have high levels of expenses which makes gross taxation inappropriate and that the income was more commercial in nature. The issue hung around through many documents and meetings until the second last meeting of the Fiscal Committee (23rd session) on royalties when the Commentary solution was adopted, see United States (1962, p. 4682) for the Commentary as published by the OEEC.

[75] WP8 second report included films in para. 1 of the draft article and eliminated the television reference where matters remained until the two paragraphs were combined into a single definition in WP8 third report without changing the substance on this issue.

A similar but more successful erosion of the royalties article by Switzerland may be observed in the area of assignments of intellectual property. The original WP8 draft included assignments of intellectual property in the royalties article and indeed was improved by Swiss suggestions.[76] Once work was commenced on the capital gain area late in the development of the OEEC/OECD model, the Swiss suggested that assignments may more appropriately be dealt with in that article.[77] No change was made at the time because the capital gain article was not completed by the OEEC, but when it appeared in 1963, assignments of intellectual property had disappeared from the royalties article.[78] In terms of residence only taxation of royalties under the OEEC/OECD models, this change made no difference, but it was highly significant if there was source taxation of royalties received on intellectual property but not on capital gains on the alienation of intellectual property.

Conclusion

This is the end of our forty-year historical voyage, though the royalties article has already been travelling more than twice that time. The story of the following forty-plus years is mainly one of the OECD Commentary rather than the terms of the article; little has changed in the article from where we leave it. At the end of the journey we are still left with the question why there is a royalties article. It was probably born in technics but its endurance is a matter of politics. Those politics are still alive and well today and will be visited on another occasion. There will always be more history, borders and 'Why?'s for Tiley to visit.

[76] The Swiss suggestion 6 May 1958 of adding 'or right' after 'property' in the provision on disposal was picked up by WP8 second report and maintained thereafter.
[77] Fiscal Committee 23rd session.
[78] van Raad (1987, p. xviii). As will be apparent from the preceding discussion, the Swiss may lay claim to the greatest success in modifying the royalties article during the OEEC/OECD process up to 1963; while the UK was unsuccessful in the process in getting its way, UK treaty practice was the most influential in the original WP8 draft of the royalties article.

8

Land taxation, economy and society in Britain and its colonies

MARTIN DAUNTON

Introduction

In pre-industrial societies, the structure of land ownership and tenure is central to the fiscal capacity of the state, the structure of society and politics and the pattern of economic growth. Land is obviously visible and measurable, and can therefore be taxed more easily than the profits of trade or industry. But a number of questions immediately arise, not least because the claim of the state for taxes collided with the demands of the landlord for rent and of the occupier for subsistence and profit. The state might side with the landlords to collect taxes in return for support of their claims to greater power and authority; or the state might opt to back the proprietors, improving their security of tenure in return for taxation. Of course, in societies of small independent proprietors, these trade-offs did not apply and the state might prefer to have a direct relationship with owner-occupying yeomen or peasants.[1]

The choice was not only a matter of fiscal extraction, for it also had implications for economic growth. Which is more likely to lead to growth: small proprietors willing to invest their energy and capital in land; or economies of scale from large estates? Critics of small proprietors complained that they were inefficient, lacking sufficient capital and skill; and opponents of great estates argued that they led to exploitation and a society based on bitter conflict. These debates had implications for discussions of the fiscal capacity of the state, for assumptions about the growth potential of each form of tenure shaped expectations about the yield of taxes. The state might attempt to shift the nature of tenure towards large estates if

[1] For a controversial analysis of this trade-off, see Brenner (1976). Sean Eddie's doctoral thesis on Prussia in the late eighteenth and early nineteenth century focuses on this issue, and I have gained from discussions with him, and also with David Todd in relation to his work on the application of land taxes to Algeria in the nineteenth century.

it believed that the result would be economic growth and hence more revenue; or it might seek to create small proprietors if it felt such an outcome was more effective as a route to growth and higher tax yields. Of course, these choices rested on contested normative assumptions about social structure – and in some circumstances taxation could not only provide revenue for the state but could also be used as a mechanism for changing the form of society. Land taxation is far from a narrowly specialist concern: it is central to our understanding of the history of Britain and its colonies, as of other countries.

8.1 Nature of land taxation in Britain resting on the land tax

Let us start by considering the nature of land taxation in Britain which rested on the English land tax of 1694 and its extension to Scotland after 1707. In theory, the tax was not confined to land and also fell on personal property and income from office. Again in theory, it was levied at four rates of 1s., 2s., 3s. and 4s. in the pound, so that in principle tax revenue would rise in line with the income received by the taxpayer. In reality, the tax was confined to land and did not increase in line with rents which rose rapidly in the second half of the eighteenth century and in the early nineteenth century. The lowest rate of 1s in the pound was assumed to produce £500,000 rising to a maximum of £2 million at 4s. These aggregate sums were divided between counties and boroughs according to their contributions in 1693, rather than current regional prosperity. The commissioners of the land tax – members of the local landed community in each county – did make annual estimates of the rents of holdings in their districts in order to divide the county's contribution between the landowners, but these figures were not systematic and did not provide the state with an evaluation of the taxable capacity of the land. The commissioners were also responsible for the assessed taxes on items of conspicuous consumption such as male servants and riding horses which offered another way of taxing the more prosperous members of society by visible signs of affluence.[2]

Consequently, the land tax was a falling proportion of the revenue of the state and of the income of landowners over the next century, and the shortfall was made up by other taxes and in particular excise duties. In 1696–1700, the land and assessed taxes together accounted for

---

[2] On the operation of the land tax, see Ward (1953) and Ginter (1992) which stresses the problems in using the data given the manner in which it was compiled.

36.3 per cent of government income, with customs duties for 26.5 per cent and excise duties 26.1 per cent. By 1791–95, the proportions were respectively 16.0, 20.9 and 47.3 per cent.[3] The wars with revolutionary and Napoleonic France placed pressure on the tax system, and led William Pitt to search for new sources of revenue. In 1798, he introduced a measure to allow land owners to redeem the land tax, if they paid sufficient government stock into the sinking fund to produce a fifth more interest than the land tax. Hence to redeem a land tax of £100 a year, the owner would hand to the government stock producing an annual yield of £120. Pitt's aim was to reduce the burden of the national debt, but the terms were simply not attractive to landowners and the amount of tax redeemed was small. Consequently, Pitt introduced the income tax – or more strictly, the property and income tax – in 1799 as a temporary measure for the duration of the war. In effect, Pitt was aiming to restore the initial intention of the land tax of 1694 in extracting revenue from both real and personal property and from the income of offices.[4]

As the incidence of land taxation fell in the eighteenth century, so the concentration of land ownership rose, and small proprietors with freehold or some form of long lease with secure tenancies gave way to tenant farmers on short annual lets. The reasons for the rising level of concentration and change in tenure are much debated, and this is not the place to explore them.[5] The change was not to any appreciable extent caused by the tax system – but the failure of the land tax to capture the rising income of great landowners as rents increased in the later eighteenth and early nineteenth centuries exposed the injustice of the tax system and fuelled a radical critique of the British state which became increasingly strident after the demise of the income tax in 1816. Landowners ceased to pay tax on their rental income and the land tax was not revised, so that their liability to taxation was lower than ever. In 1811–15, land and assessed taxes were 11.1 per cent of the tax revenue of the central government, with income tax a further 19.8 per cent; customs duties amounted to 20.4 per cent and excise duties 39.8 per cent. In 1831–35, land and assessed taxes were only 10.5 per cent of the tax revenues of the central government and income

---

[3] Data from Daunton (2001, p. 35, table 2.1); see also O'Brien (1988) and O'Brien & Hunt (1993).

[4] Ward (1953, pp. 133–6); Beckett (1985); Beckett & Turner (1990); Cobbett (1812–1820, Vol. 23, 2 April 1798, Cols. 1360–76); United Kingdom (1870a, Vol. 1, pp. 317–18). On the nature of Schedule A in the revised income tax of 1803, and the early description of the tax, see Tiley (2004c, pp. 85–6).

[5] I have discussed these debates in Daunton (1995, chapter 3).

tax did not exist; customs duties were now 38.3 and excise duties 36.4 per cent of revenue.[6] Ricardo pointed to the economic consequences of the increase in rents over the late eighteenth and early nineteenth centuries. In his analysis, the economy would experience a 'stationary state', hitting a ceiling with no prospect for economic growth. As the population rose, so wages fell and prices rose: the labourers' income therefore fell back to subsistence level. Farmers were attracted by higher prices to move to marginal soils with higher costs and lower profits; farmers on better soils would make a higher profit, but would soon be obliged by competition for the land to pay higher rents so that their profits fell. Hence the major beneficiaries were the landowners who received higher rents and took a higher share of income. Consequently, the economy tended towards a stationary state as they took more rent and both rents and profits were squeezed. Ricardo argued that rent was therefore susceptible to taxation.[7] Commentators such as William Cobbett took a similar line from a sense of cultural loss, lamenting the erosion of the position of yeomen farmers who formed the basis of a society resting on independence. Not only were landowners failing to contribute to the costs of the state, but radicals complained that they were benefiting from sinecures and pensions. The result, so it seemed to many radicals, was a biased and unfair system of taxation which was subversive of political stability, social harmony and economic prosperity.[8]

In the early years of Victoria's reign, the Anti-Corn Law League and the Financial Reform Association claimed, with some justice, that the fiscal system was biased. As the Anti-Corn Law League argued, the land tax had not been changed since the 1690s, landowners were protected by the corn laws, and they were failing to contribute their fair share to the costs of government. Indeed, the Financial Reform Association argued in 1860 that the restoration of the land tax to the real level of the 1690s – 4s. in the pound or 20 per cent on the annual value of all land, buildings, mines and dividends from government loans and public companies – would solve all fiscal problems, allowing a reduction in customs duties and the abolition of the income tax which hit more active, industrious forms of activity.[9]

Not only had the land tax been frozen, but real property was escaping from death duties in a way that radicals thought was grossly inequitable. In the early nineteenth century, there were two duties on personal property:

---

[6] Daunton (2001, p. 35, table 2.1).   [7] Ricardo (1951, chapter II, p. 204).
[8] Dyck (1992).
[9] Financial Reform Association (1859, p. 23); Tenant (1856, 1857, 1862, 1872); Greg (1860).

the probate duty of 1694, which fell on the estate left by the deceased, and the legacy duty of 1780, which fell on the recipient. Both excluded real property, which was justified as a way of balancing the contribution it was already making through the land tax. But the failure to increase the contribution from the land tax led Pitt in 1796 to propose an extension of the legacy duty to landed as well as personal property, at a rate varying according to the degree of relationship with the deceased. The legacy duty was strongly opposed by Charles James Fox for introducing the novel principle of a tax on capital which would 'enable the state to seize upon the whole property of the country'. A tax on land enflamed 'country' fears of the intentions of the executive. It was, claimed one alarmed MP, 'a political measure immoderately increasing the influence of the Crown, and full of danger in its obvious consequences to the constitution and freedom of the country'. The proposal to apply the legacy duty to real property only passed the Commons on the casting vote of the Speaker, and Pitt decided that the political dangers were too great to proceed. He withdrew the application of the legacy duty to land and so it only applied to personal property according to the degree of relationship to the person making the bequest.[10] Joseph Hume remarked in 1842 that the exclusion of land from the legacy duty in 1796 was 'class legislation', explained by the nature of the Commons as 'a jury of landowners, whose interests were opposed to those of the country at large'. The problem, as Hume saw it, was that the government was 'maintaining the interests of the landed proprietors in opposition to those of the country in general'. Even after the repeal of the corn laws in 1846, Richard Cobden continued to complain of the bias in the taxation system. 'Let us not boast of English freedom or of equality before the law, while this injustice remains', he complained. 'In what form could aristocratic privilege assume a more offensive and costly aspect than in that of a bold and palpable exemption from taxation.'[11]

In the opinion of the critics of the fiscal system, the bias in death duties connected with another bias in the income tax. 'Spontaneous' incomes from land (Schedule A of the income tax) and government bonds continued regardless of energy or health, and left an asset at death. 'Precarious' or 'industrious' incomes from trade, industry and the professions were dependent on the energy of the individual, and ceased on retirement or death. Consequently, the recipient of a precarious income needed to save

[10] Dowell (1884, Vol. 2, pp. 173–4); Buxton (1888, Vol. 1, pp. 117–18).
[11] Daunton (2001, pp. 227 and 229), quoting United Kingdom (1829–91, Vol. 62, 26 April 1842, Col. 1153); Financial Reform Association, *Financial Reform Tracts, Number 6, The National Budget for 1849* (London), pp. 8–12.

for old age or for his dependants after his demise. The advocates of differentiation argued that precarious incomes should pay a lower rate of tax to take account of the need to save – for practical reasons, not on actual savings but according to an estimate of what proportion of income an individual should save. By the early 1850s, radicals such as Hume, who had argued for a rigorous policy of retrenchment in order to abolish the income tax, were moving towards support of the income tax as a way of shifting the fiscal burden away from indirect taxes – always on condition that the income tax was differentiated to remove the bias between income from land and from trade. Their case was considered in a number of Select Committees in the 1850s and 1860s, before disappearing from the political agenda until its adoption by the Liberal government in 1907 as a differential tax between 'unearned' and 'earned' income.[12]

The great success of Gladstone's budget of 1853 was to marginalise both of these criticisms of the inequity of taxation of land. He was not willing to accept differentiation, which he saw as a claim for special treatment by merchants and manufacturers, akin to the demands of landowners for protection by the corn laws or of ship-owners for protection by the navigation laws. His aim was to purge the state of special privileges, and to ensure that the tax system was even-handed. He also feared that differentiation between types of income would lead to graduation between rich and poor, so turning the tax system into an instrument for class rivalry. Graduation was, he argued –

> [g]enerally destructive in its operation to the whole principle of property, to the principle of accumulation, and through that principle, to industry itself, and therefore to the interests of both poor and rich ... it means merely universal war, a universal scramble among all classes, everyone endeavouring to relieve himself at the expense of his neighbour, and an end being put to all social peace, and to any common principle on which the burdens of the State can be adjusted.

He was therefore firmly committed to a flat-rate tax for different types and levels of income, while making two concessions to deal with the bias perceived by critics of the tax system. The first was a tax-break on the actual sums used to purchase life insurance rather than a lower rate on all precarious income. The concession contained the demands for differentiation, and, because it was available to any taxpayer who purchased life

---

[12] Daunton (2001, pp. 91–7).

insurance, it was not divisive between classes.[13] The second change was to death duties.

Gladstone countered the claim that the income tax was unfair between spontaneous and precarious income by offering compensation through changes in the death duties which was, he felt, safer than changes in the income tax, with the danger that it would become an instrument of class conflict. Such an outcome was less likely to occur with respect to death duties which could be justified as a means of creating a more active and dynamic use of wealth by preventing mere passive enjoyment of inheritance. As he pointed out in 1853:

> The greatest mischief of taxes upon property is the liability of a constant recurrence of those struggles of classes which are often associated with them. But in carrying into effect this increase in the legacy duty, you have this great advantage, that the liability to pay occurs only once within the limitation which the laws of a higher power have ordained, that it only occurs once, on the death of a man . . . this is a most weighty consideration for those whose duty it is to inquire how they can best neutralise the social dangers incident to all questions connected with the taxation of property.

Real property should therefore be brought within the reach of death duties with the introduction of a new succession duty. However, he did not accept that it should pay at the same level as personal property, for reasons that connected with another vexed issue: the incidence of local property taxes or rates.

Gladstone argued that land and houses paid the land tax and inhabited house duty (albeit at a modest rate), as well as the income tax on the flow of rental income. In addition, real property was liable to the local rates, and he argued that real property should therefore pay the succession duty on less onerous terms. His solution was to apply the legacy duty to real property by charging the successor to real property on the life interest rather than the full capital value, with a right to pay over four years; by contrast, personal property paid on the full capital value at once. His aim was to adjust the burden of death duties on real and personal property to take account of the impact of local rates on the former, as well as using death duties on both real and personal property to provide some compensation for precarious income. It was certainly not to impose a higher burden on land as peculiarly susceptible to taxation.[14]

[13] Daunton (2001, pp. 97–103).
[14] Discussion of death duties from Daunton (2001, pp. 230–3); Gladstone's quote is from United Kingdom (1829–91, Vol. 125, 18 April 1853, Col. 1395).

These measures largely removed the attack on landed property as a matter of high politics for the next thirty or so years. Attention focused on somewhat narrow, technical issues relating to the local rates which were another form of tax on real property. The Local Taxation Committee was formed by landed and agricultural interests in 1869 to argue that they were over-taxed by the rates, and to urge that the cost of various national or 'imperial' services should be transferred to the central government. In 1872, the Commons passed a motion that additional burdens should only be imposed on the rates on condition that the central government contributed. At this stage, there was no clear ideological split between parties, and many senior Liberals could accept that land was over-burdened by local taxation. However, some admitted that the burden was being shifted from the land back to the houses erected on it, and they came up with some modest policy proposals. In 1870, George Goschen presented a report to Gladstone's first ministry, arguing that real property was not overtaxed in general compared with other countries, but that the share of taxation taken by land was falling while that taken by houses was rising. At this stage, thinking on the incidence of the tax was uncertain, and the furthest he was willing to go was to suggest an explicit division of the tax between owner and occupier, with a separate representation for landowners on local bodies. He was far from admitting the suggestion of Ricardo that land was peculiarly liable to taxation.[15]

The case for an increase in the taxation of land was made by J. S. Mill, who followed his father James and Ricardo in arguing that rent comprised an increasing share of income created by the efforts of the rest of society and that it should therefore be appropriated by society. As Mill remarked in 1871:

> Land is limited in quantity while the demand for it, in a prosperous country, is constantly increasing. The rent, therefore, and the price, which depends on the rent, progressively rises, not through the exertion of expenditure of the owner, to which we should not object, but by the mere growth of wealth and population. The incomes of landowners are rising while they are sleeping, through the general prosperity produced by the labour and outlay of other people.

Mill would leave landowners with their existing 'unearned' increment but would remove any further gains. As we shall see, radical critics of

---

[15] Daunton (2001, pp. 290–1); United Kingdom (1870, Vol. 1, pp. 317–18); United Kingdom (1870b, pp. 19–20) and Goschen (1872, p. 204); Daunton (1983, pp. 224 and 226); Offer (1981, chapter 11).

landowners were to go further in the 1880s, but at this stage few followed Mill's radical proposals.[16]

The focus was on another question: the power of great estates to dominate the urban land market, so forcing up prices and imposing leaseholds which were criticised as the root cause of slums. Why should house owners maintain their properties in the final years before leases expired and they returned the houses to the ground landlord without compensation? Radical Liberals pressed for legal reforms to create an active land market and to allow the enfranchisement of leases – issues that were addressed at inordinate length by the Select Committee on Town Holdings.[17] The issue became much more central and divisive in the 1880s, when the entire question of the tax burden on real property was re-opened, and policy moved beyond the uncertainties of Goschen in 1870 and the concerns of the Select Committee on Town Holdings. The debate was transformed by the appearance of Henry George's *Progress and Poverty*, which gave a new force to Ricardo's notion of rent and Mill's proposals to tax the unearned increment. The book appeared in the US in 1880, and by the mid-1880s was having a serious impact on debates in Britain and (as we shall see) in the white settler colonies.[18]

The debate over George and unearned increment connected with a continued concern with local taxation. In 1885, Gladstone proposed an increase in the succession duty on real property, but the Commons rejected his suggestion on the grounds that real property should not be taxed any more until it was relieved of the burden of rates for national services such as education. In 1888, the Conservative Chancellor, George Goschen (who had left the Liberal party over home rule) handed the revenue of various duties over to local government, including half the proceeds of the probate duty, in order to reduce the pressure on local rates. Consequently, a duty on personal property was being used to subsidise the rates on real property – and he then increased the succession duty on real property in order to preserve balance. Goschen argued that he was rebalancing the fiscal constitution to be fair between all types of property. Liberals were not convinced, and the issue was now taking on a clear ideological and party political dimension compared with earlier discussions. His Liberal opponents argued that he was actually creating an imbalance for in relieving real property of local rates, he had removed any need for it to have

[16] Offer (1981, pp. 182–3).
[17] Daunton (1983, pp. 224–30); Reeder (1961); United Kingdom (1886–90).
[18] George (1880); Offer (1981, chapter 12).

preferential treatment in national taxation. Gladstone agreed, and now pressed for the same level of death duties on both real and personal property. In fact, Goschen only made the situation worse (as far as the Liberals were concerned) in his new estate duty of 1889, which imposed a higher rate on personal than on real property – and, in 1895, the Conservatives made a further concession to land by reducing the local rates on agricultural land. Goschen had moved from his position as a Liberal in 1870, when he felt that real property was not over-taxed, and that land should bear more of the incidence compared with houses; as a Conservative he was taking the opposite position and relieving land of taxation. The lines were drawn for a battle over the taxation of land.[19]

Many Liberals started to move in a more radical direction than Gladstone. His aim was to create balance in the fiscal constitution between land and personal property, and his disagreement with Goschen was over how precisely that should be done. He did not wish to launch an attack on landowners and the unearned increment. But it was possible for younger and more radical Liberals to make two further, connected, steps. One was to argue that the incidence of local rates did not stay with the owners of the land but fell on tenants and occupiers through increased rents; the other was to extend Ricardo's and Mill's claims that land had a particular capacity to bear tax so that it should be paying much more than in the past. The case was made by W. H. Dawson in 1890:

> The well-being of the working-classes in particular – like the interests of society in general – require (1) that the unearned value of land – that value which is created by the operation of purely social causes – shall be diverted from its present channel in such a way that the community as a whole shall share in it; and also (2) that the incidence of local taxation shall be so modified that the owners of the land upon which towns are built shall bear a considerable share of the parochial expenditure which tends to maintain and increase the value of the land.

Many in the Liberal party moved away from Gladstone's desire to ensure that taxation on land was proportionate, to argue that land values were socially created by the activities of other members of the community who took initiatives to build houses or factories, and by collective spending on the infrastructure. Hence there should be an increase in the tax burden on real property. The change was apparent in the formulation of William

---

[19] Daunton (2001, pp. 233–7 and 290–7).

Harcourt's graduated estate duty of 1894 and, much more, Lloyd George's land campaign from 1909, which imposed new taxes on land values.[20] The debates over the taxation of land connect with another issue: how efficient was Britain's highly distinctive tripartite tenurial system of large landed estates, tenant farmers and landless labourers, which was consolidated in the course of the eighteenth century? Unlike in post-revolutionary France or in areas of recent white settlement in the British colonies, there were few small owner-occupying farmers; most of the land was managed by substantial tenant farmers who provided livestock and machinery. In the eighteenth century, some farmers still held land on long leases for terms of years or a number of lives, with a relatively modest annual rent and periodic 'fines', as lives fell in or the lease was renewed. As a result, these farmers had some form of 'ownership' or expectation of succession, and the prospect of gain from rising prices and profits.[21] They lost ground and, by the nineteenth century, the great majority of farms were held on annual tenancies with a full market rent paid in cash, and tenants had lost most of their rights to the land. Most of the land was owned by substantial landowners – the great aristocratic and gentry estates, and the holdings of the Church and charitable foundations.

Contemporaries were divided on the benefits and drawbacks of this distinctive tenurial system for economic growth and the distribution of welfare between the various parties. Was the British tenurial system a model of efficiency, or a pathological deformation? Perhaps the tenurial system in Britain and Ireland rested on the abuse of power rather than the natural workings of economic efficiency and harmony. On this view, land had been 'stolen' from the people by the dissolution of the monasteries, by the appropriation of clan lands by chieftains in Scotland, by the dispossession of the Irish, and by parliamentary enclosure. Critics were concerned that political power and the legal impediments to a free market in land led to dispossession of sturdy yeomen farmers and an independent peasantry, creating impoverished landless labourers and forcing people into unhealthy and demoralising towns. The change in the tenurial system to short tenancies and rack rents, in their view, allowed great landowners to pass the risks of agriculture – disease, poor weather or falling prices – onto their tenants who were obliged to pay a sizeable rent and to support the leisured existence of their landlords. Land should now be restored

---

[20] Daunton (2001, pp. 233–55); Daunton (1983, pp. 227–8) quoting Dawson (1890). On death duties, see Daunton (2001, chapter 8) and on the land campaign, see Offer (1981, Part V).

[21] This is explained in Daunton (1995, pp. 52–7 and 61–87).

to the people by a new, just, use of political power. The problem, in the eyes of the radicals, was that the blessings of a free market had not been extended to land, where arcane legal practices hindered transfer and sale. Some recent historians agree with the critique. Allen, for example, emphasises the importance of the 'yeoman's agricultural revolution' of the early eighteenth century, compared with the 'landlord's agricultural revolution' of the later eighteenth century. Similarly, Offer points to the costs of sustaining the manor house and church as a burden on English farmers in the nineteenth century which made them uncompetitive in the production of wheat with recent areas of settlement where these costs did not apply.[22]

Of course, defenders of the existing tripartite structure took a different view, arguing that the division of responsibility between landlord and tenant lead to efficiency rather than exploitation, allowing an escape from the Malthusian trap of immiseration and famine. Landowners could reinvest in agricultural improvements and reorganisation of efficient holdings, freeing farmers from the need to find capital to buy land, so that they could concentrate on the provision of animals, fertilisers and machinery in comparison with their counterparts in France or Germany who used any spare resources to buy more land which was farmed in small, uneconomic units. As Alfred Marshall pointed out in 1883, 'it requires as much capital to buy twenty acres as it does to farm a hundred'. Some observers argued that the real difference lay not in the scale of farms or the tenurial structure, so much as in attitudes. One French commentator, Leonce de Lavergne, pointed out that large estates existed elsewhere in Europe without the benefits found in England. He felt that the vital point was how the estates were worked: in many cases, large European landlords relied on share-cropping or *metayage* rather than the English practice of leasing farms for cash rents. Further, the scale of the market led to a highly commercialised attitude to farming, making it 'a branch of industry'. On this view, large estates were efficient not merely because of size but also because their owners were imbued with a commercial ethos.[23]

The debates took a new turn at the end of the nineteenth century, when the onset of agricultural depression cast doubt on the supposed efficiency of the tripartite system, for landlords experiencing falls in their rental incomes were now less able to invest in change. The benefits of

---

[22] Allen (1992); Offer (1989, chapter 8).
[23] Overseas visitors were intrigued, admiring and repelled by the British system: see Thompson (2002, pp. 127–8 and 133).

specialised small owner-occupiers in Denmark or the Low Countries, or of family farms in the mid-west of America, became more apparent, strengthening the demands of radicals for a fundamental change in the tenure of land. The virtues of owner-occupying farms also appealed to the right. As Lord Salisbury, the Conservative prime minister, pointed out in 1892, 'a small proprietary constitutes the strongest bulwark against revolutionary attack'. Similarly, Christopher Turnor, a farmer and member of the Unionist Social Reform Committee, argued in favour of small farms in 1911, pointing out that the use of intensive techniques as in Denmark could double the output of food and provide security in a future naval war.[24]

These issues within Britain were central also in Ireland, India, the white settler colonies and Africa. Land taxation was inseparable from normative assumptions about the preferred social structure and expectations about economic growth. Should large estates be encouraged as efficient and as a source of political and social stability, with the state entering into an alliance with the owners? Or should small owner-occupiers be encouraged to create a greater sense of independence and dynamism in a society based on a sense of ownership and participation? The fundamental issue was: what was the best form of taxation and the optimal form of land ownership for social justice and economic growth? Had British history in the eighteenth and early nineteenth centuries offered a path to emulate or to shun? The debates were central to the history of the British empire, taking the metropolitan controversies in new directions, as can be seen from two case-studies of India and New Zealand.

8.2 Nature of land taxation: the case of India

In India, the British faced an existing system of land tenure and fiscal extraction, with a large indigenous population without formal political rights in shaping policy. The key problem was how to move from a complex hierarchy of rights where proprietorship and revenue extraction were overlapping and multiple, and the solutions proposed reflected assumptions about the most desirable pattern of land ownership and understandings of the course of growth, both of which were influenced by English precedents, mediated by administrative and political expediency in India.

---

[24] Thompson (2002, p. 133): on Salisbury and Conservatives, see Offer (1981, pp. 152–7, 354 and 380) and Fforde (1990). The issue is also discussed in Levy (1911): see p. 95 for the quote from Salisbury.

The permanent settlement in Bengal in 1793 offered one solution. The *zamindars* possessed a clear right of ownership that was linked with collection of revenue for the government. Payments were fixed and failure to pay meant loss of proprietorship. An alliance was created between the East India Co. and *zamindars* against peasants, so creating intermediaries to contain revolt against taxation. The *zamindars* might be seen as equivalent to large aristocratic landowners in England who would encourage agricultural development and provide a force for stability in rural society.[25]

The English land tax was itself a form of 'permanent settlement', as it had been fixed in the 1690s and formed a decreasing proportion of income from the land as rents rose in the later eighteenth century. By analogy, the *zamindars* might react in the same way as large English landlords, investing their profits in order to encourage growth and prosperity. However, the permanent settlement also had a serious disadvantage: the East India Co., and later the Crown, did not share in the profits of agriculture as the value of land rose, and taxes had to be imposed on other groups in society which might be viewed as inequitable and a source of political controversy, as had happened in Britain. In other words, land tenure and the tax system were linked with visions of growth based on a particular view of the English agricultural revolution and the benefits of great estates or of their drawbacks. English landowners were criticised by radicals as parasites, expropriating common land, increasing rent levels, and ignoring their social obligations. Similarly, the *zamindars* were open to criticism for extracting more rent without reinvesting and without fulfilling their obligations to maintain water supplies and other communal services.

The outcome of these criticisms was a temporary settlement in the North West Provinces in 1833, which allowed renegotiation of the government's claim to revenue, so ensuring that revenue rose in line with rents and land values, or according to the needs of the government. However, the temporary settlement also created practical problems, for renegotiation led to tensions and involved closer company or crown involvement in fiscal extraction. Hence the British government in India shifted back to the use of permanent settlement on the grounds that it led to growth and minimised resistance.

Not everyone agreed that the use of settlement was desirable, not least James Mill, who was responsible for the revenue letters from the Board of Control in London to the government of India. He followed Ricardo

---

[25] Contrast Travers (2004).

in arguing that rent was an unearned income from land, offering the best source of revenue without distorting the allocation of labour and capital. Consequently, Mill argued that in districts not covered by the permanent settlement, taxation should be based on the share of rent in the total produce of land. By levying a tax directly on the cultivator, exploitative middlemen could be removed, and by varying the tax by the quality of land, the unearned surplus or Ricardian rent produced by superior land could be captured. The task was entrusted to R. K. Pringle, who set to work recording the extent of each holding, its quality, and estimating the net produce left after all costs had been met, including a reasonable return to family labour and capital; the government should then claim 55 per cent as its share. It was implemented in 1828, without success, for the collection of data was flawed and the revenue demand was too high. The solution was to adjust Pringle's approach, without abandoning the search for Ricardian rent.[26]

The adjustment formed the basis of the *ryotwari* system which asserted the rights of cultivators or peasants (*ryots*) who paid taxes direct to the government. From 1835, the Bombay Survey and Settlement evolved as a means of preventing exploitation of cultivators by tax farmers, and encouraging increases in productivity and efficiency through incentives to the cultivators to accumulate capital and increase their revenues. The land was surveyed to establish occupation and soil quality; and rather than make unrealistic calculations of the amount of net produce, payments were assessed according to the condition of the occupier and the amount paid from the area in the past. The *ryot* would then be assured the payment of the same amount for a defined period before a new settlement was implemented – a highly complex and time-consuming exercise. In theory, all land belonged to the state, but the *ryot* had security of tenure so long as he paid tax to the government, with the right to sell and bequeath the land. The amount of tax varied with the quality of land, so that inefficient *ryots* would be encouraged either to improve their techniques to pay the tax, or transfer their holdings to someone who could. The Bombay Revenue and Settlement thus rested on a particular vision of the connection between tenure and economic growth.[27]

Whether the system had the desired effect is another matter, for contrary to the intentions of the reformers, the tax might act as a disincentive

---

[26] Stokes (1959, pp. 93–102); McAlpin (1983, pp. 108–9). For a denial of the importance of Ricardian Rent in practice, see Mann (1995).
[27] McAlpin (1983, pp. 110–13).

by imposing a high charge on the cultivator; and the intrusion of tax collectors might generate tension. Perhaps the tax system was securing revenue at the expense of growth. In 1901, the Famine Commission complained that the proponents of the *ryotwari* system 'expected the accumulation of agricultural capital: but their plans did not promote thrift, nor did they conduce to the independence of the *ryot*. They looked for the capitalist cultivator; and we find the *sowkar's* serf.'[28]

Many Indian nationalists complained that the burden of the land revenue rose as a proportion of output over time with serious economic consequences. The reality was different, particularly when the amount of land tax collected per acre is compared with the amount of output sold to pay the tax. In the Bombay Presidency, the nominal tax per acre was reduced in the initial settlement and continued to fall during its term; although the amount was increased at re-settlement, it remained lower than before the initial settlement. Changes in prices meant that the tax demand varied in real terms as a proportion of income: prices rose over this period, so the real value of the tax declined to a greater extent.[29] The land tax remained the major source of central government revenue, although it did decline as a proportion of net revenue from 52.8 per cent in 1865 to 48.1 per cent in 1895 and 40.1 per cent in 1910 – a much higher proportion than in Britain or, as we shall see, in New Zealand.[30] The decline accelerated after the war, as a result of political protest such as the Bardoli campaign in the Bombay Presidency against reassessment of the land settlement that led to refusal to pay. The problem facing the government was how to find an alternative. Excise duties were unpopular and led to nationalist unrest; customs duties could be justified in India as protective of local industries, though they were opposed by British exporters; the income tax was disliked by British residents and by *zamindars* who saw it as a way of circumventing the permanent settlement. As far as the land tax was concerned, India offered an arena for debates over the virtues and shortcomings of the English tenurial system, with divergent outcomes in different parts of the Raj.[31]

8.3 Nature of land taxation: the case of New Zealand

In the case of white settler colonies, land offered another form of revenue – from land sales. Of course, the price charged for land would affect the

---

[28] Quoted in Bagchi (1990, p. 40).   [29] McAlpin (1983, pp. 198–202); Travers (2004).
[30] Thomas (1939, p. 500).   [31] Charlesworth (1984, pp. 522–3).

social structure of these new societies: low land prices would encourage small farmers, akin to the peasant proprietors or yeoman of the English past and the French present; high land prices would lead to larger estates more akin to the pattern in Victorian Britain. The decision reflected normative assumptions about social structure – and also the needs of the government for revenue. In a newly settled society, the government needed to raise large loans for capital expenditure on the infrastructure of roads, railways and harbours, and the ability to secure loans on good terms depended on a steady flow of income. In the case of New Zealand, the Treaty of Waitangi allowed the Maori some rights in land, and gave the government the sole right of purchase of any land they wished to sell. The aim was to protect the Maori from exploitation but the government also hoped to sell the land to settlers at a profit. Obviously, the greater the net profit received by the government, the less need there would be to impose high taxes. As far as the settlers were concerned, they would prefer the government's profit margin to be maintained by paying a low figure to the Maori rather than charging a high price to them. For their part, the Maori did not accept the government's assumption that the indigenous inhabitants owned only a small part of the land; and even if they were willing to sell, they resented the appropriation of a large part of the value of the land as a form of taxation to subsidise white settlers.

Territorial revenue (largely land sales and also timber licences and an assessment of stock) rose from 17.3 per cent of central government revenue in 1850 to 62.0 per cent in 1854 – an exceptionally high level. In the 1850s as a whole, the figure was 44.7 per cent. Clearly, land revenues were crucial to the large-scale investment in the infrastructure of New Zealand and its ability to raise loans on the London market. The land rush of the 1850s also had long-term consequences for the future of tax policy. The Governor, George Grey, reduced the price of land in 1853, from £1 to £3 to 5s. or 10s. – and the result was not the creation of small family farms so much as the purchase of vast sheep runs by a few rich men, often absentees. Apart from territorial revenues, the central government was heavily dependent on customs duties which accounted for 84.6 per cent of revenue in 1850 and 36.0 per cent in 1854; in the 1850s as a whole, the figure was 47.7 per cent. Other forms of revenue were obviously minor.[32]

---

[32] See Goldsmith (2007, chapter 1). I am grateful to Dr Goldsmith for allowing me to see and cite his study. The figures come from New Zealand (1893) and New Zealand (1858–, annual figures for 1853–59).

The situation was unstable. The Maori resented the sale of their lands, and also complained that they were paying a large part of the customs duties without representation.[33] In 1860, they rose against the settlers – with the result that the costs of government increased considerably, and the London money market was reluctant to lend. Further, the net proceeds of land sales went to the recently created provincial governments from 1856 which left the central government in straitened circumstances. In 1864, customs duties were increased but it was soon clear that more taxes were needed, not least from 1870 in order to fund Julius Vogel's programme of heavy investment in the infrastructure designed to encourage immigration, economic growth and future tax revenues.

The result was deep controversy between the advocates of death duties, stamp duties, income tax, retrenchment, or the confiscation of Maori land. In 1866, legacy, succession and probate duties were introduced which fell more heavily on personal property. They were replaced in 1875 by a new estate duty on both real and personal property, graduated from 1 to 10 per cent according both to the degree of kinship and the size of the estate. Hence a child who inherited between £100 and £1,000 paid 1 per cent, while a brother paid 2.5 per cent; on estates over £20,000 the proportions rose to 2 per cent and 5 per cent. The bias in favour of land was removed.[34]

Increasingly, attention turned to the need to tax land. The issue had appeared in New South Wales in 1860, when a land tax was proposed with the ambition of stopping the emergence of large estates when lands were thrown open for sale. The large graziers or squatters were opposed by an alliance of settlers with urban interests who wished to open land to small farmers and to challenge the power of the squatters.[35] An important figure in the case of New Zealand was George Grey, the Governor of New Zealand from 1845 to 1853 and 1861 to 1868. Grey sympathised with the Irish peasantry since his early days as an officer in Ireland; and as governor in South Australia he opposed the existing policy of land settlement for recreating the faults of the English class system at the expense of the labourers. As we have noted, in his first period as governor in New Zealand, he aimed to replace large settlers with small farms by reducing land prices, though without success. During his residence in Britain between 1868 and 1870, he developed radical views on the land question, arguing that English landowners in Ireland should be dispossessed and that the great landed aristocracy of England had expropriated the land of the people.

---

[33] Sinclair (1957, p. 42).   [34] Goldsmith (2007, chapter 2).   [35] See McMichael (1984).

He was convinced by J. S. Mill's argument that land values were 'unearned'. He returned to New Zealand in 1870, and he entered politics in 1874 with a mission to transform the tax system from its dependence on customs duties to a tax on land and incomes, and to introduce a policy to favour small-holders against the owners of the great sheep runs. Above all, Grey attacked the emergence of a landed class in New Zealand as in Britain, pointing to the 'gigantic evil of an aristocracy with enormous tracts of land, unfairly acquired in many instances'. Expropriation of land by force from the Irish, through the clearances in Scotland or by parliamentary enclosure in England, were being repeated in New Zealand, and should be stopped before the new country sank into the ways of the old world. Grey became Prime Minister in 1877, and a start was made on implementing his policies by John Ballance, who became Treasurer in 1878.[36]

The state of Victoria set a precedent in 1877, introducing the first land tax in Australia with the intention of breaking up large estates above 640 acres. New Zealand followed in 1878–9, when Ballance introduced a land tax. However, Ballance diverged from Victoria, for New Zealand had incurred larger loans, especially during the premiership of Vogel, and needed more money. The land tax applied to smaller holdings than in Victoria, on the unimproved value of land worth more than £500. The income tax was charged on the actual income of land; the tax in New Zealand was charged on the value of the land before any improvements were made and regardless of whether it produced revenue, at a flat rate of 1d in pound. His strategy was to exempt small holders and any improvements to land created by the energy of the owners: he aimed to tax increases in the value of land apart from improvements by the owner. Above all, he aimed to tax the unearned increment from large, idle holdings which produced no revenue but were rising in value because of public investment. Underlying the tax was the assumption that, whilst landowners were not paying their fair share of taxes, they were taking the benefits of public works in increased land values. His vision for New Zealand was a denser settlement of independent small holders. In the same spirit, he proposed a tax on the profits of joint-stock companies: by contrast, income from trade and industry undertaken by family firms or partnerships was not taxed. In the absence of an income tax, earnings from personal exertion (that is, salaries, professional fees or the profits of trade and industry) were untaxed, going much further than the advocates of differentiation in Britain in the 1850s and 1860s. The New Zealand tax of 1879 did not

[36] Goldsmith (2007, chapter 3); Rutherford (1961); see also Belich (2006).

tax income from employment at all, whereas landed property was taxed even if it produced no income.

Of course, Ballance's approach was challenged as inequitable between urban and rural interests. Why should urban traders escape any direct taxation of their income, whereas landowners paid tax even if their land produced no income, and was heavily mortgaged to urban lenders? The company tax was abandoned, but the land tax was passed – just as depression hit. Land prices collapsed, and so did the revenue from sales, from £1.51 million in 1871 to £270,000 in 1879. Meanwhile, the government faced a large deficit. The opponents of Grey and Ballance – led by Harry Atkinson, who served on several occasions as premier and Treasurer – argued that the answer was to increase customs duties, and to replace an inequitable land tax with a general property tax on both real and personal property, which was introduced in 1879 on assets of £500 and above. Not everyone was convinced, for, as Ballance pointed out, professional incomes escaped taxation; and assets of the same value paid the same tax despite very different yields. The issue remained highly contentious, and Ballance returned to the issue on his return to office.

Above all, Ballance's ambition was to increase the density of settlement, creating a class of yeomen farmers and to break up the great estates which reached levels of concentration even exceeding Britain. Liberals complained of idle land in the hands of monopolists whilst farmers' sons were forced to migrate or move to towns. In 1885, Ballance introduced a Land Act in order to encourage settlement by offering leases of small holdings of crown land and by making government loans available. He believed that large pastoral farms blocked economic progress and prevented access to land by new settlers; unlike many contemporaries, he did not argue that the Maoris should surrender their land in order to encourage settlement. Above all, in the election of 1890, he campaigned for radical land reform, arguing for a tax on the 'unearned increment', and advocating Henry George's policies as a means of 'bursting up the great estates'. He returned to power as both premier and Colonial Treasurer, working with John MacKenzie, the Minister of Lands from 1891 to 1900, to implement his proposals. As Ballance explained in 1891, 'our taxation is intended to relieve the springs of industry and to encourage *bona fide* settlement of the country'.

The Liberal government re-introduced the flat-rate land tax of 1d. in pound on land valued above £500, supplemented by a new graduated land tax on estates with an unimproved value above £5,000. Ballance aimed to break up the large estates through the graduated tax – though it is doubtful if the rate was high enough to force landowners into selling. He also introduced a progressive income tax in place of the property tax. The shift from the property tax to income tax reduced the number of people liable to pay, especially in the towns, and meant that no tax was paid in the absence of profit; it also reached professional men. Further, the government changed the method of disposing of land by the Land Act of 1892. McKenzie's policy was not to sell the freehold of land, with the danger that it would fall into the hands of monopolists, but rather to offer perpetual leases with an initial term of 999 years at 4 per cent of the capital value which would never be reassessed. Clearly, this policy was welcomed by small farmers and it assisted the government policy of increasing the density of development by removing costs of entry into farming. However, it did nothing to appropriate the unearned increment. In 1894, the Land for Settlements Act allowed the government to purchase land from large estates for settlement, with the threat of compulsion against those who did not sell voluntarily. The great estates were in retreat – and McKenzie also appropriated land from the Maoris for small farmers, somewhat ironically in view of his early experience with the clearances in Scotland.[37]

The tax system was still highly dependent on indirect taxes, which did not impress supporters of George and advocates of free trade. In 1899/1900, customs and excise amounted to 75.6 per cent of tax revenue; stamp and death duties for 9.7 per cent, land and property tax for 13.4 per cent and income tax for 4.5 per cent. Not surprisingly, William Pember Reeves, a leading social reformer and politician who later became Director of the LSE and a key interpreter of New Zealand social policies in Britain, complained in 1902 that the revenue from the land tax was 'almost ludicrously small' compared with the customs, and that too little was being done to break up the great estates. The top rate of land tax was raised in 1903 – and did lead to the break-up of large estates by the expedient of division within families in order to evade the highest rate. In 1907 and 1912, the top rate of land tax was again raised, in the hope that the imposition would now lead to estates being broken up, and in 1909, the death duty was also increased to foster more equal distribution of wealth.[38]

The tax system of New Zealand had therefore adopted the radical position of James and John Stuart Mill to a greater extent, and at an earlier

---

[37] See his collection of essays in Ballance (1887); McIvor (2004); McIvor (1989); Hamer (1988); Goldsmith (2007, chapter 3); Bassett (2004); Brooking (2004).
[38] Goldsmith (2007, chapters 4 and 5).

date, than in the metropole. The shortcomings – as they were seen – of the large estates and a hierarchical social structure were avoided. Growth was linked with yeoman farmers and a wide distribution of property which would also create justice and social harmony. The experience of New Zealand was eagerly seized upon by Liberal land reformers in Britain as a sign of what could be achieved by legislative action.[39]

Conclusion

These changes in taxation policy have been explained in their political and ideological contexts – of assumptions about economic growth, about the desired social structure, about the capacity to bear taxation and the social origins of income and wealth. Of course, they also had important legal implications. The imposition of taxes on real and personal property at different rates posed complicated legal questions about the precise line between the two, or the status of settled personal property to which the heir did not have an absolute right.[40]

The definition of real and personal property or of precarious and spontaneous incomes was not easy. In both India and in New Zealand, the property rights of indigenous people had to be defined in ways that were understandable to the British rulers or settlers. As Peter Harris has shown in the case of the income tax, parliamentary draftsmen and legislators often 'lifted' the statutes from Westminster. But, in the process, the law was adjusted and changed under the pressure of political expediency, fiscal need and ideological ambition. Historians often complain that lawyers are insufficiently interested in these extra-legal influences; equally, historians are ignorant of the nuances of legal reasoning. An increased exchange of ideas and information between the two disciplines of law and history is needed, and the conferences of the Centre for Tax Law at the University of Cambridge have been a model of what can be achieved.

---

[39] See Edmund Rogers' forthcoming PhD thesis on the uses made of the white settler colonies in British debates on social policy.
[40] See the interesting discussion in Mandler (2001).

9

Meade and inheritance tax

JOHN AVERY JONES

Lady Bracknell. . . . *What is your income?*
Jack. Between seven and eight thousand a year.[1]
Lady Bracknell. [Makes a note in her book.] In land, or in investments?
Jack. In investments, chiefly.
Lady Bracknell. That is satisfactory. What between the duties expected of one during one's lifetime, and the duties exacted from one after one's death,[2] *land has ceased to be either a profit or a pleasure. It gives one position, and prevents one from keeping it up. That's all that can be said about land.*

Introduction

John Tiley's first experience of tax was updating *Beattie's Estate Duty* and his most recent article is on the history of death duties.[3] I want to continue that topic and look at inheritance tax in the light of the proposals of the Meade Committee, on which I had the privilege to serve, knowing Tiley's enthusiasm for recommending the Committee's Report to his students. My timing is bad, as the 'Mirrlees Review',[4] popularly known as Son of Meade, is currently in progress. I am glad that the topic of inheritance taxes is still on the Review's agenda, in spite of the international trend away from such taxes, and indeed it received a boost in Professor Alan Auerbach's IFS 2006 annual lecture,[5] given on the same day as the launch of the Mirrlees Review.

---

[1] *The Importance of being Earnest*, Act 1. Note the measurement of wealth in terms of income leading to equating absolute ownership with a life interest. However, Cecely Cardew had 'about a hundred and thirty thousand pounds in the Funds' (Act 3, scene 1).
[2] *The Importance of being Earnest* opened in February 1895. The audience would have appreciated this topical reference to estate duty introduced in 1894, which is unfortunately lost on today's audiences.
[3] Beattie and Tiley (1970); Tiley (2007).
[4] For details of the Mirrlees Review see www.ifs.org.uk/mirrleesreview.
[5] Auerbach (2006).

I should start with a word about donor- or donee-based taxes on the transfer of wealth, a distinction that figures large in Tiley's historical article on death duties as for some periods we have had both in force at the same time.[6] I remember when I was a very young man, Professor Stanley Surrey, the great American tax scholar, saying to me that he did not see any difference between them. Fortunately, I stopped myself in time from explaining the difference to him, and instead I asked him why. The answer was essentially the same as Meade's: that while it may not make any difference with a donor-based tax whether one leaves property to a rich or poor donee, it certainly makes a difference on the next transfer, assuming that the tax is progressive; with a donee-based tax it makes a difference on the first transfer as well. In the long run, there is therefore less difference between them than appears at first sight. But it is true that a donee-based tax contains more incentive to pass on wealth to a poor donee because the present is certain, and the future is uncertain because the poor donee may build up wealth or the rich donee may lose it, in which case the second-generation effect may turn out to be the opposite from what was expected. We, and most of those common law countries that still have death duties have generally[7] adopted donor-based taxes, which is perhaps more consistent with freedom of testamentary disposition, Ireland's capital acquisitions tax being an exception, while most civil law countries, which have forced heirship, have donee-based taxes, which is more consistent in taxing the donees on what they are entitled to receive. The difficulty of fitting trusts into a donee-based tax has encouraged donor-based taxes in common law countries, since the essence of a trust is that it is a mechanism for putting off the decision about who is the real donee, at least in terms of capital. Indeed, the trust may be the cause of the difference. The use, the forerunner of the trust, made the former common law forced heirship of land untenable, thus leading to freedom of testamentary disposition,[8] and thus indirectly to the need for donor-based taxes.

---

[6] Legacy duty and succession duty were donee-based; probate duty (1694–1894), account duty (1881–1894), settlement estate duty (1894–1914), temporary estate duty (1889–1894), estate duty (1894–1974), capital transfer tax (1974–1986) and inheritance tax (1986–) were, or are, donor-based.

[7] Though not exclusively.

[8] Strictly, it was the intended, but unsuccessful, abolition of the use by the Statute of Uses 1535 that led to pressure for the Statute of Wills 1540 abolishing forced heirship of land, but this was restoring the position to what could previously be achieved by means of the use.

9.1 Summary of Meade's transfer tax proposals

Meade's simplest proposal for a transfer tax was called a 'linear annual wealth accessions tax' or LAWAT.[9] It is a donee-based tax and, unlike an ordinary wealth tax, which makes no distinction between inherited and created wealth, it taxes only inherited wealth. The tax on the donee is the present value of an annuity equal to the payments of a notional flat-rate wealth tax from the donor's 85th birthday to the donee's 85th birthday.[10] If one assumes that the donor has built up the wealth himself, the effect is that the wealth is tax-free until he is 85, whether he continues to own it or passes it on to the donee. Alternatively, if the donor inherited the wealth, at the time he inherited it, he paid to frank the notional wealth tax up to his 85th birthday. Either way, there is no additional tax until the donor's 85th birthday. There is no discouragement to passing on wealth because, whenever it is passed on, there is no additional tax for the period up to the donor's 85th birthday. Because the start of the calculation is deferred until the donor's 85th birthday, the earlier the wealth is passed on, the lower the tax.

In more detail, the donee calculates a notional annual wealth tax on the inheritance received and calculates the present value of an annuity of the amount of the notional wealth tax on the gift from the donor's 85th birthday to the donee's 85th birthday (that is, the present value of an annuity equal to the notional wealth tax to the donee's 85th birthday minus the present value of an annuity to the donor's 85th birthday). Because the tax is not progressive, one cannot have a lifetime nil-rate band, although there can still be an annual exemption, and the notional wealth tax rate scale can have a nil rate band. There are some administrative advantages; one does not need to keep cumulative lifetime figures as each gift is treated separately. A disadvantage of LAWAT is that it is difficult to deal with changes in the rate of notional wealth tax. The donor may have franked the wealth at one rate on receipt and the donee still has the benefit of a credit for this period even though the rate may have increased in the meantime. But Meade considered that some rough justice must be accepted under this proposal. At the time of Meade, before the personal computer, the

---

[9] I can disclose that the Meade Committee pronunciation was 'LARWAT' (rhyming with lard and cat), and the same for PARWAT.

[10] I expect that if the Committee were writing today this would be a higher age because life expectancy at age 65 has increased by about three years since then (for some figures, see Banks and Blundell (2005, p. 37)), but I shall keep to the original proposal. The fixed-term annuity is chosen because valuation depends only in the discounting rate and is much easier than the valuation of life annuities.

calculations were not easy. I remember calculating the tables in the Report on what was in those days quite an advanced programmable calculator. Today all one needs to do is to enter something like 'PV(discount rate, number of years, annual wealth tax payments)' into a spreadsheet.

One does not need to know how LAWAT is calculated;[11] one only needs a rate schedule for the tax, such as the following illustrative one taken from the Report.

Age of donor (years)

Age of donee (years)	0	5	15	25	35	40	45	50	55	60	65	70	75	80	82.5	85
	Rate of LAWAT (%)															
0	–	–	2	3	5	6	8	9	11	13	16	19	22	26	28	31
5	–	–	1	3	5	6	7	9	11	13	15	18	22	26	28	30
15	2	1	–	1	3	5	6	8	10	12	14	17	21	25	27	29
25	3	3	1	–	2	3	5	6	9	10	13	16	19	23	25	28
35	5	5	3	2	–	1	3	4	6	8	11	14	17	21	23	26
40	6	6	5	3	1	–	1	3	5	7	10	13	16	20	22	25
45	8	7	6	5	3	1	–	2	4	6	8	11	15	19	21	23
50	9	9	8	7	4	3	2	–	2	4	7	10	13	17	19	21
55	11	11	10	9	6	5	4	2	–	2	5	8	11	15	17	20
60	13	13	12	10	8	7	6	4	2	–	3	5	9	13	15	17
65	16	15	14	13	11	10	8	7	5	3	–	3	6	10	13	15
70	19	18	17	16	14	13	11	10	8	5	3	–	3	7	10	12
75	22	22	21	19	17	16	15	13	11	9	6	3	–	4	6	9
80	26	26	25	23	21	20	19	17	15	13	10	7	4	–	2	5
82.5	28	28	27	25	23	22	21	19	17	15	13	10	6	2	–	2
85	31	30	29	28	26	25	23	21	20	17	15	12	9	5	2	–

Thus if a donor aged 65 made a gift to a donee aged 40 the rate of LAWAT payable by the donee would in accordance with the table be 10 per cent. This is calculated as the difference between the present value of an annuity from the donee's 40th to 85th birthday (24.52), and the present value of an annuity from the donor's 65th to 85th birthday (14.88) equals 9.64, rounded to 10.[12] If the donee were older than the donor there would be a refund, or possibly no tax would be charged.[13]

[11] The formulae are set out in Meade (1978, pp. 338–43, Appendix 15.2). The discount rate used in the table is 3 per cent.

[12] The rounding is for simplicity of illustration; the tax could be based on rates calculated to several decimal places.

[13] Meade (1978, p. 331) to avoid an avoidance possibility with spouses.

LAWAT is based on a linear notional wealth tax. Its progressive equivalent is 'progressive annual wealth accessions tax' ('PAWAT'). Because it is progressive it treats the donor and donee, who may have different rates of notional wealth tax, separately. The principle is similar. The difference from LAWAT is that when the donor passes the asset on he obtains a refund of the remaining part of the tax that he paid[14] from the date of the gift to his 85th birthday, which could be either on the basis of the highest marginal rate that he paid, giving the most incentive to pass on inherited wealth quickly to a donee who has not received any inheritance, or at the average rate, which avoids complications about changes in the rate and adjustments to the brackets for inflation; and the donee pays to frank the notional wealth tax for the whole period from the date of the gift until the donee's 85th birthday. Because the donor and donee are treated separately, one can now have a progressive wealth tax schedule which takes into account all the lifetime receipts of gifts by the taxpayer. If, therefore, the donor has paid tax on inherited wealth at a high rate, he will obtain a refund of this tax as soon as he makes a gift himself, and the difference in tax will be the greatest if the donor passes it on quickly to a donee who has received no gifts. There is therefore an incentive to pass on inherited wealth to those who have inherited less in the past, which might be thought to be the essence of an ideal acquisitions tax. In contrast to LAWAT, however, there is no incentive to pass on saved wealth because, if the donor continues to hold it, the wealth remains free of tax until passed on, but under PAWAT it is taxed in the hands of the donee when passed on. It would be possible to deal with this by giving the donee a rebate on a gift of saved wealth calculated at a notional rate (up to the amount of tax paid by the donee), or to give the donee a discount of the tax payable which depended on the age of the donor.

Unlike LAWAT, one cannot just have a rate schedule; one must do the calculations for each party. I make no apology for quoting the following from the Report because no one can match James Meade's ability to make the complicated seem simple.[15]

When in 1977 Mr Smith, aged 45, inherits £500,000 he will, according to the progressive tax schedule shown in Table 15.1,[16] be liable for an underlying annual wealth tax of £4,250 a year, as is shown by the following calculation:

[14] If he built up the wealth himself, the refund will be nil.
[15] There is a more complicated example including a succession of gifts, changes in the rate schedule and indexation for inflation in Meade (1978, pp. 344–6, Appendix 15.3).
[16] Not set out in full here but part can be seen from the next table.

Slices of the £500,000 inheritance (£)	Rate of equivalent annual wealth tax (%)	Amount of annual wealth tax (£)
50,000	0	0
50,000	$\frac{1}{2}$	250
400,000	1	4,000
Total 500,000		4,250

From the table of annuity multipliers [see Table below] it can then be calculated that the value in 1977 of an annuity of £4,250 for the next forty years, until Mr Smith's 85th birthday, is £4,250 × 23.11 = £98,217; and this is therefore the PAWAT payable by Mr Smith on receipt of the inheritance.

Table of annuity multipliers[17] (i.e. the present value of an annuity of £1 for a number of years up to the taxpayer's 85th birthday)

Age of taxpayer (years)[18]	Annuity multiplier
0	30.63
5	30.20
15	29.12
25	27.68
35	25.73
40	24.52
45	23.11
50	21.49
55	19.60
60	17.41
65	14.88
70	11.94
75	8.53
80	4.58
82.5	2.37
85	0

When in 1992 at the age of 60 Mr Smith makes the gift of £100,000 to his son, he will be passing on £100,000 which has been franked for annual wealth tax for the remaining twenty-five years up to his 85th birthday. Mr

[17] Based on a discount rate of 3 per cent a year.
[18] Age of donee (for tax paid on gifts received); age of donor (for tax refund on gifts made).

Smith has a claim to a repayment of PAWAT, which 'defranks' the £100,000 from his annual wealth tax liability for the coming twenty-five years; but his son is now liable to PAWAT, which will frank this £100,000 for the son's underlying liability to annual wealth tax for the next sixty years, i.e. until the 85th birthday of the son who is now aged 25.[19]

The Committee also had a third proposal for the taxation of wealth transfer that was not favoured. This was 'age gap annual wealth accessions tax' ('AGAWAT'). It was also progressive including all receipts of gifts. The donee pays tax calculated on a similar basis to PAWAT but for the period from the date of the gift to the donor's present age. This created problems with routing gifts via a younger poor relative. The donee may not intend to hold the wealth for the period until he is the same age as the donor, and there is no incentive to hand-on wealth. I shall not therefore consider this proposal further.

9.2 Adopting LAWAT

We are now living in a different world from Meade's so far as progression is concerned. When the Committee was sitting the then new capital transfer tax had a rate scale rising from 0 to 75 per cent in eighteen bands, and income tax had a rate scale from 34 to 83 per cent in ten bands (on top of which was the investment income surcharge of up to 15 per cent). Such progression and high rates are now a thing of the past, which makes LAWAT more of a possibility.

Capital transfer tax excelled over estate duty in its treatment of spouses. Estate duty at best required payment of duty on the first spouse's death and exempted the assets from duty on the second spouse's death if the survivor was not competent to dispose of the capital,[20] that is had only a life interest; and otherwise fully taxed the estates of both spouses. Capital transfer tax, and now inheritance tax, operates the other way round by exempting the transfer from tax on the first death, which is clearly much more socially desirable. Spouse exemption was not in fact new in 1974; it was merely an example of history repeating itself. A spouse exemption had operated under legacy and succession duty until 1909,[21] when, instead of exemption, spouses were put into the lowest rate category with children.

LAWAT gave no relief for inter-spousal transfers. Because the tax is age-related, there is a potential problem if there were an exemption that a

[19] Meade (1978, pp. 322–3).   [20] Finance Act 1894, s. 5(2).
[21] Finance (1909–10) Act 1910, s. 58(2).

donor would tend to make a gift to the older spouse who could then pass it on tax-free to the intended younger spouse.[22] The lack of an exemption might not matter much because if the spouses were the same age there would be no tax; if the donee were younger by a small number of years there would be a small amount of tax; and if the donee were older there would be a repayment of tax, or no tax. But PAWAT is much more complicated. On marriage each spouse may have received gifts in the past and they may not be the same age. One could average both the previous receipts and their ages to give such attributes to the tax unit, which would be used for gifts and receipts in the future while they were married. The tax unit would have to be disaggregated again on the death of the first to die or on divorce. The Report did go into this in more detail,[23] but I think that I have said enough to show that it is unworkable, or at least extremely complicated, in practice, probably even more so now with the greater incidence of divorce. If one could ignore the potential avoidance by making gifts to the older spouse, one could have a spouse exemption with LAWAT.

As Meade demonstrates throughout, one should in any case not look at taxes in isolation. Particularly with the Committee's favoured expenditure tax, which might be described as a miser's charter,[24] at the time there seemed to be a greater need to tax the accumulation of wealth by an annual wealth tax. An annual wealth tax has the opposite effect to LAWAT and PAWAT, by not differentiating between inherited and created wealth, which is at its most serious with the building up of a business, although the effect is lessened if one had an expenditure tax rather than an income tax because under the former one can plough back profits before paying tax on them. But that does not remove the problem entirely and the Committee's suggestion was that on business assets the wealth tax should be allowed to accumulate with interest and be paid on transfer of the business, which

---

[22] See Meade (1978, p. 327).

[23] Meade (1978, p. 347, Appendix 15.4). It also highlighted (on p. 329) an avoidance possibility between spouses.

[24] The expression was used within the Committee but I do not think was used in the Report. In an expenditure tax savings are not taxed but income not saved (and any dis-savings) are taxed. We are far nearer to an expenditure tax now than when Meade was sitting. Housing and pensions already have expenditure tax treatment (or better in the case of the lump-sum pension) and now £181 billion is in ISAs (or its predecessor PEPs) (at November 2006; HM Revenue & Customs, *National Statistics*, Table 9.6) which has expenditure tax treatment. See Meade (1978, ch. 8) for the equivalence of giving relief on investment and tax on disinvestments (as for pensions) or taxing the income used for investment and giving relief on disinvestments (as for ISAs), coupled in both cases with no tax during investment.

again makes more sense under an expenditure tax because the funds needed to pay such liability could be accumulated tax-free. One of the Committee's favoured combinations to accompany an expenditure tax was a LAWAT with a low threshold, to provide a discrimination against inherited wealth, accompanied with an annual wealth tax with a high threshold and a progressive rate structure on the largest fortunes as a main weapon to encourage the wide dispersion of wealth.[25] But, as with progression, the world has moved on and one would not contemplate a wealth tax today. Many of the countries which used to have one have abolished it. I do not think that this affects the merits of LAWAT on its own. The great advantage that LAWAT has over PAWAT is that wealth that the donor has created remains tax-free until the donor's 85th birthday, whereas under PAWAT tax is payable by the donee immediately it is passed on.

9.3 Trusts

It is clear from Tiley's most recent article on the history of death duties that he prefers donee-based death duties. The Meade proposals are necessarily donee-based taxes. An important question is whether donee-based taxes can be made to work for trusts? The Irish experience is that they can, and we did tax life interest trusts under legacy duty and succession duty.

The donee-based legacy and succession duties dealt with life interest trusts by equating life interest trusts to annuities,[26] and taxed annuities according to their value as set out in a table[27] in the Schedule to the Act in a similar way to the table for writing down the cost of short leases for

---

[25] Meade (1978, pp. 363, 516 and 518).
[26] Legacy Duty Act 1796 (36 Geo 3 c.52), s. 12: '... all Persons who, under or in consequence of any such Bequest, shall be entitled for Life only, or any other temporary Interest, shall be chargeable with the Duty in respect of such Bequest, in the same Manner as if the annual Produce thereof had been given by way of Annuity ...' Succession Duty Act 1853, s. 21: 'The Interest of every Successor, except as herein provided, in Real Property, shall be considered to be of the Value of an Annuity equal to the annual Value of such Property, after making such Allowances as are herein-after directed, and payable from the Date of his becoming entitled thereto in possession, or to the Receipt of the Income or Profits thereof during the Residue of his Life, or for any less Period during which he shall be entitled thereto ...'
[27] Legacy Duty Act 1796 (36 Geo 3 c.52) Schedule; Succession Duty Act 1853, Sch. 1. The two schedules are different. For example, the value of an annuity of £100 for a 65-year-old is £776.2.0 for legacy duty and £821.12.6 for succession duty, presumably reflecting changed actuarial expectation of life between the two dates.

capital gains tax, which is also based on the value of an annuity.[28] No serious attempt was made to tax discretionary trusts until 1969 for estate duty.[29]

The first time life interest trusts were taxed on the full capital by donor-based taxes was the 1881 provision applying when the settlor had made a settlement on himself for life or had the power to claim the capital, which Tiley will remember became the obscure s. 2(1)(c) of the Finance Act 1894,[30] famously described in Parliament at the time as a cross-reference 'to an Act which was amended by another Act which was to be amended by this Act'. The first general charge on the capital supporting life interests was the 1894 estate duty s. 2(1)(b): 'Property in which the deceased or any other person had an interest ceasing on the death of the deceased, to the extent to which a benefit accrues or arises by the cesser of such interest . . .' This equates a right to income with the capital, as no doubt Lady Bracknell was doing in the quotation with which I started. When wealth was in land, spending capital was more difficult: either one had to sell a piece of land, which was not easy, or borrow. Normally, therefore, ownership gave only a right to income. The Settled Land Act obscured the difference between absolute ownership and a life interest; the land was in the name of the tenant for life and therefore under his control, like absolute ownership, but if he sold the land or mortgaged it the proceeds went to the trustees, like a life interest. It is perhaps not surprising that estate duty equated the two, but this seems less appropriate today when most capital is not land and spending capital in the form of financial assets is much easier.

Apart from the specific reference to trusts in connection with PAWAT,[31] which was because of the difficulty of applying a progressive tax based on

[28] Taxation of Chargeable Gains Act 1992, Sch. 8. See Richardson (1967) for the derivation of the table, on the inaccuracies of which Richardson said: ' . . .one hesitates to accuse Our Masters of trying to construct a Table to five-figure accuracy with the aid of four- or five-figure logarithms (instead of six- or seven-), but that is what it looks remarkably like.' I am sure Tiley will remember using logarithms at school even if this reference is meaningless to most readers.

[29] Finance Act 1969, s. 36. Legacy duty applied to discretionary trusts by treating every distribution as a legacy: *Attorney General v Wade* [1910] 1 KB 703 (KBD).

[30] 'Property which would be required on the death of the deceased to be included in an account under section thirty-eight of the Customs and Inland Revenue Act, 1881, as amended by section eleven of the Customs and Inland Revenue Act, 1889, if those sections were herein enacted and extended to real property as well as personal property, and the words "voluntary" and "voluntarily" and a reference to a "volunteer" were omitted therefrom . . .'

[31] Meade (1978, pp. 329 and 348). It proposed that the donor should receive a repayment when the trust was set up, and the donee should pay tax on receipt of a distribution of capital from a trust based on his net cumulative total of gifts received at the time of receipt but based on his age at the date on which the trust was set up. This equates to charging

age to the beneficiary of a trust, the Meade Committee looked at trusts generally,[32] the taxation of which would be much simpler under their expenditure tax proposals as one could ignore trusts as being no different from a savings vehicle, the income of which was not taxed.[33] While the asset remained in trust, no expenditure could occur. But I do not think there is a specific reference to the treatment of life interest trusts under LAWAT or PAWAT. The Committee approved for wealth tax[34] the existing capital transfer tax (now inheritance tax) approach of treating the life tenant as owner of the trust capital, although the scope of this approach was somewhat reduced in 2006.[35] I suspect that the Committee would not have ignored the existence of a life interest for LAWAT and PAWAT and only taxed distributions of capital in the way discussed for PAWAT but how should this be done?[36]

9.4 Combining the legacy and succession duty approach to trusts with Meade's LAWAT

The treatment of life interest trusts in legacy and succession duty by equating them to annuities has something in common with the Meade proposals, which tax the donee of an absolute interest on the value of an annuity, although not one based on the income but on a notional wealth tax (which might be considered part of the income). Could one not combine the two ideas and also tax the recipient of a life interest trust in the same way as property owned outright in LAWAT by taking the capital of the trust, applying a notional wealth tax to it, and capitalising the notional wealth tax as an annuity with the tax being paid by the trust? With LAWAT, absolute ownership is treated more like a life interest, because the tax liability is based on a notional annual wealth tax for a fixed period

tax when the trust was set up. There is an obvious danger to the Revenue of making an immediate repayment to the settlor and receiving a deferred receipt from the beneficiary. This could be avoided either by not repaying the settlor but adding the repayment to the trust in the form of a tax credit accumulating at interest which could be used to pay the beneficiary's tax; or alternatively, at the time the trust was set up, an advance payment of tax could be charged (possibly at the same rate as the settlor's repayment so that no net payment would be made) and the beneficiary's receipt on distribution from the trust would be grossed-up by this advance payment.

[32] Meade (1978, ch. 19).   [33] *Ibid.*, p. 407, method 3.

[34] *Ibid.*, p. 409. The possibility of valuing the life interest itself was discussed. This had been suggested in the Green Paper on Wealth Tax but with a preference for treating the capital as belonging to the life tenant (United Kingdom (1974, para.16)) and expanded on in 'Trusts: Memorandum submitted by the Board of Inland Revenue' in United Kingdom (1975, p. 166, paras.10–11).

[35] Finance Act 2006, Sch. 20.   [36] See the summary in the text above.

approximating to one's life, rather than being based on market value of the asset which is the capitalised income in perpetuity. Effectively, one would retain the equivalence of life interests with absolute ownership but the other way round: absolute interests would be taxed more like life interests. By changing the tax treatment of absolute ownership in this way, indirectly this would be a much fairer way of taxing life interest trusts and one that works with a donee-based tax.

Legacy duty and succession duty provide a precedent for taxation of life interests based on the value of an annuity,[37] and so the idea cannot be ruled out under the Principle of the Dangerous Precedent, if I may quote a Cambridge book that will be familiar to Tiley.[38]

There is also a more recent precedent taxing discretionary trusts on a similar basis in the original 1965 capital gains tax provisions for taxing non-resident trusts set up by UK resident and domiciled settlors.[39] The 1965 Finance Bill provided for the gains accruing to the trustees to be apportioned in such manner as is just and reasonable between persons having interests in the settled property, whether the interest be a life interest or an interest in reversion *or an interest under a discretionary trust*. The words in italics were deleted as a result of debate in Parliament and a new sub-s. (3) added to deal with discretionary trusts:

> (3) For the purposes of this section–
> (a) if in any of the three years ending with that in which the chargeable gain accrues a person has received a payment or payments out of the income of the settled property made in exercise of a discretion he shall be regarded, in relation to that chargeable gain, as having an interest in the settled property of a value equal to that of an annuity of a yearly amount equal to one-third of the total of the payments so received by him in the said three years . . .

The drafting was somewhat vague; for example, it does not state how long the annuity is assumed to last, which would make it impossible to value.[40] But the precedent exists.

---

[37] See text above.

[38] 'The *Principle of the Dangerous Precedent* is that you should not now do an admittedly right action for fear you, or your equally timid successors, should not have the courage to do right in some future case, which, *ex hypothesi*, is essentially different, but superficially resembles the present one. Every public action which is not customary, either is wrong, or, if it is right, is a dangerous precedent. It follows that nothing should ever be done for the first time.' Cornford (1908, ch. 7).

[39] Finance Act 1965, s. 42. The provision is mentioned in Meade (1978, p. 404).

[40] As Lord Fraser pointed out in *Leedale v Lewis* [1982] STC 835 (HL) at p. 841h.

(If I might be allowed to digress I should point out that the House of Lords later decided that discretionary trusts were dealt with by the just and reasonable apportionment among beneficiaries having interests in the settled property, which in the context included discretionary beneficiaries.[41] This caused something of a scandal when the amendment made in Parliament was pointed out[42] and the law was changed by the Finance Act 1984.[43] It was a case that would never have happened after *Pepper v Hart*[44] and indeed may have contributed to the abolition of the Hansard rule, for which we had to wait another ten years.)

Now that we have computers and cannot complain of the difficulty of calculating the value of an annuity for a fixed term, perhaps the time has come to dust off LAWAT, which seems the preferable alternative, particularly as we now have a flat rate of inheritance tax above the nil rate band rather than the eighteen rate bands that existed when the Committee was sitting. I therefore propose a LAWAT with life interest trusts treated in the same way as property owned outright.

[41] *Leedale v Lewis* [1982] STC 835.
[42] See Avery Jones (1983) arguing for a relaxation of the Hansard rule.
[43] Finance Act 1984, s. 70 and Sch. 14.   [44] [1993] AC 593 (HL).

10

Taxation, human rights and the family

PHILIP BAKER

Introduction

Is it really worth having all this fuss and bother about the Human Rights Bill?
Over the years the Convention has been interpreted to require United Kingdom
courts to change their practices in various ways at the personal level, but what
about protecting a person from an unjustified demand for tax?[1]

In the realm of taxation, has the incorporation of the European
Convention on Human Rights[2] (hereafter 'the Convention') into United
Kingdom domestic law by the Human Rights Act 1998 been all 'fuss and
bother'? Now that almost ten years have passed since the 1998 Act, what
answer should one give to the question posed by Professor Tiley in 1998?[3]

This short chapter cannot possibly seek to assess the impact of the
European Convention on Human Rights on all aspects of the UK taxation
system.[4] Rather, this chapter seeks to examine only a narrow area: that is

---

[1] Tiley (1998b, p. 269). This quotation is taken from the opening of a case note on *National &*
Provincial Building Society v United Kingdom (No. 21319/93) (1998) 25 EHRR 127 (ECtHR).
The case note concludes as follows: 'What lessons are to be learnt? The first must be that
while the European Court of Human Rights is a tribunal to which tax-related issues can
properly go, there is strong resistance to doing anything which might obstruct the fiscal
intentions of the contracting States ... The 1997 case shows that the Court of Strasbourg
will not encourage them [the judges] to hasty action, but if political controls are ineffective
in this country, why can we not look to the judges for protection? Is this not what the
Convention is meant to be about?'

[2] To give the Convention its full title, it is the 'Convention for the Protection of Human
Rights and Fundamental Freedoms', signed at Rome on 4 November 1950 (ETS No. 5).

[3] The author has had the pleasure of leading discussion groups with Tiley on Taxation and
Human Rights as part of the Cambridge LLM over the past several years. He would also
like to pay particular tribute to Tiley's contribution to the academic discipline of tax law,
and to the fact that Tiley first introduced him to the study of tax law in the Cambridge Tax
Policy Seminar in 1977–78.

[4] For a more general review of the impact of the Convention on tax matters, including a
review of the case law of the European Court of Human Rights, see Baker (2000).

the impact of the Convention on the taxation of the family or, more correctly, how the Convention has been applied in tax cases involving personal and family status before the European Court of Human Rights. Taxation and the family is, of course, a particular area of interest of Tiley,[5] and, as will be seen below, some of his comments on the discriminatory nature of UK tax provisions have proved to be quite prophetic.

The primary focus of this chapter, therefore, is on challenges which have been brought to certain provisions of UK and other countries' tax laws involving issues of personal and family status before the European Court of Human Rights in Strasbourg. The chapter will seek to show that, though the overall results may have been relatively meagre, it has been worth all the fuss and bother about the Human Rights Act.

10.1 The bases in the Convention for challenging tax rules based upon personal status

By way of background, it is worth reminding ourselves that there are three principal provisions in the Convention which may be relevant to taxation rules where personal or family status is a factor in the rule. These are the Articles of the Convention relating to the prohibition of discrimination, the right to respect for private and family life, and the right to marry.

Article 14 of the Convention provides:

> **Prohibition of Discrimination**
> The enjoyment of the rights and freedoms set forth in this Convention shall be secured without discrimination on any ground such as sex, race, colour, language, religion, political or other opinion, national or social origin, association with a national minority, property, birth or other status . . .

This non-discrimination provision is a 'non-free-standing' provision, which on its terms relates only to discrimination in the enjoyment of the rights and freedoms contained in the Convention. It is necessary, therefore, for a claimant to base his or her claim on Art. 14 in association with another substantive provision of the Convention. In the field of taxation, it is now well established that discriminatory tax provisions can be

---

[5] See, for example, his recent article Tiley (2006b).

challenged on the basis of a combination of Art. 14 together with Art. 1 of the First Protocol, which secures the protection of property.[6] The discriminatory challenges are not restricted, however, to the specific statutes mentioned in Art. 14, which includes discrimination on grounds of sex, race, birth 'or other status' and would therefore embrace discrimination on any ground related to personal status.

Article 8 of the Convention provides:

> **Right to respect for private and family life**
> 1. Everyone has the right to respect for his private and family life, his home and his correspondence.

Article 8 introduces a qualified right, where the infringement may be justified by the government concerned on the grounds contained in Art. 8, para. 2. In the taxation field, Art. 8 has primarily been raised in connection with surveillance and information gathering activities by revenue authorities. However, it has also been mentioned in cases involving taxation and the family.

Finally, Art. 12 provides:

> **Right to Marry**
> Men and woman of marriageable age have the right to marry and to found a family, according to the national laws governing the exercise of this right.

Perhaps it is something of a reflection of the ingenuity of tax lawyers that this Article has also been raised in tax cases concerning family status, but without any notable success.

10.2 Discrimination on grounds of marital status

The scene for this discussion is largely set by two early cases decided by the old European Commission of Human Rights, *Hubaux v Belgium*[7] and

---

[6] See *Darby v Sweden* (No. 11581/85) (1991) 13 EHRR 774 (ECtHR), which has been cited in a number of subsequent cases where challenges have been brought to discriminatory tax provisions.

[7] (No. 11088/84), Commission decision of 9 May 1988 (ECmHR). (This decision and some of the others mentioned below are not published, but the text can be found on the European Court of Human Rights' 'HUDOC' website: http:/cmiskp.echr.coe.int/tkp197/search.asp?skin-hudoc-en.

Lindsay v United Kingdom.[8] These applications were both registered with the Commission on the same date, 16 August 1984.[9]

The *Hubaux* case concerned complaints against the Belgian system of aggregating the income of husbands and wives for tax purposes. The taxpayer argued that by virtue of the system of aggregating income, he was liable to a higher overall tax charge than if he and his wife had remained separate. The claim was based upon Art. 14 (combined with Art. 1 of the First Protocol), Art. 8 (by itself and also combined with Art. 14) and also Art. 9 ('freedom of thought, conscience and religion' – making reference to the religious nature of marriage as a sacrament). The Commission declared the application inadmissible as married couples and co-habitees were not in a comparable position.

In *Lindsay* the taxpayer complained of the UK system of aggregating the income of husbands and wives.[10] The taxpayer based his complaint on Art. 8, Art. 12, Art. 14 (combined with Art. 8) and Art. 14 (combined with Art. 1 of the First Protocol). The Commission invited the parties to a hearing[11] but then dismissed the complaint on the grounds that married persons and co-habitees are not in a comparable position, and that the rules applied by the UK for the taxation of married couples were within the wide 'margin of appreciation' which a state enjoys in tax matters.

There has been no serious attempt to challenge the *Hubaux* and *Lindsay* cases since they were decided in 1986 and 1988. It seems generally to be accepted that, where taxation issues are concerned and during the subsistence of the marriage, married persons and co-habitees are not in a comparable position.[12] The only case since 1988 was *Catharine Feteris-Geerards v Netherlands,*[13] which concerned the wife of the well-known

---

[8] (No. 11089/84) (1987) 9 EHRR CD555 (ECmHR).

[9] There is no explanation as to why these two cases, raising a similar issue, were registered on the same day with consecutive Registry numbers. There does not seem to have been any planned attempt to test the application of the Convention to tax rules which applied differently to married couples. The two cases were introduced to the Commission on different dates, 4 June 1984 in the case of *Linsday,* and 17 July 1984 in the case of *Hubaux.* It may simply be that in the Registry it was appreciated that these cases raised similar issues, and it was decided to give them consecutive numbers and register them on the same date.

[10] The complaint related specifically to the year of assessment 1982/83, which preceded separate taxation of husbands and wives, and when the highest income tax rate was 75 per cent. Regarding the taxation of husbands and wives, see discussion below at Chapter 11.

[11] It is interesting to note the UK government was represented by (inter alia) Alan Moses and Brian Cleave; the taxpayer by David Pannick.

[12] But see the discussion of the *Burden* case below.

[13] (No. 21663/93), Commission decision of 13 October 1993 (ECmHR).

Dutch tax lawyer (with a strong interest in human rights issues) Maarten Feteris, who represented his wife in the case. In the claim, complaint was made of a Dutch rule under which certain tax deductions were allocated between the spouses on the basis that they were allocated to the spouse with the higher income. The basis of the complaint was Art. 14 (combined with Art. 1 of the First Protocol). The Commission dismissed the claim as follows:

> Having regard to all the rights and obligations which characterise marriage . . . noting that Article 8 of the Convention protects family life, and given the Contracting States' wide margin of appreciation in the field of taxation as to the aims to be pursued and the means by which they are pursued, the Commission accepts that a married couple may in some respects be treated as an economic unit, also taking into account the desirability to keep rules concerning the determination of taxable income simple and practical . . . In these circumstances the Commission is satisfied that there was an objective and reasonable justification for the transfer of tax deductible amounts to the spouse with the higher income.

While these cases may now be regarded as slightly dated, they present a clear obstacle to anyone seeking to argue that tax rules which might treat a married couple adversely by comparison with co-habitees could be regarded as in breach of the Convention. However, final examination of these cases should, perhaps be deferred until after a fuller consideration of other cases involving discrimination on grounds of personal or marital status.

10.3 Discrimination on grounds of sex

One area where taxpayers have had some success – at least from a theoretical point of view – in challenging substantive tax rules is where those rules make an arbitrary distinction between taxpayers according to whether they are male or female. Perhaps the best illustration of this is the case of *van Raalte v Netherlands*.[14] Under the former Dutch rules relating to child benefit contributions, an unmarried and childless woman over the age of 45 years was not required to pay the contribution. However, a man in similar circumstances was required to pay. Mr van Raalte complained of this overt discrimination against men.[15] The Dutch government noted that there was a biological reason behind the distinction in that women

---

[14] (No. 20060/92) (1997) 24 EHRR 503 (ECtHR).

[15] It is interesting to note that Mr van Raalte was represented by Professor Maarten Feteris.

over the age of 45 were unlikely to have children, and pointed to the wide margin of appreciation enjoyed by states: aside from that, the government did not seek to justify the legislation but pointed out that the exemption for women had been abolished with effect from 1 January 1989.

The European Court of Human Rights held that there had been a violation of Art. 14 (taken together with Art. 1 of the First Protocol), but denied Mr van Raalte any financial compensation. In an aspect of the decision which has been revisited more recently,[16] the Court held that, if the exemption for women had not existed, Mr van Raalte would still have had to pay the contribution. This, of course, highlights one of the dangers of a taxpayer who complains of discriminatory tax provisions. The government concerned may simply remove the discrimination by removing the exemption or advantageous treatment for the other social group. This is not exactly an encouragement to taxpayers who wish to challenge discriminatory tax provisions.

Other challenges based upon tax provisions which discriminate on grounds of sex have been brought against the UK.

Helen MacGregor v United Kingdom[17] concerned the additional personal allowance for a taxpayer whose spouse was incapacitated, under s. 259 of the Taxes Act 1988. The legislation applied only to a man with an incapacitated wife, and not to a woman with an incapacitated husband. The Commission found the claim admissible based upon Art. 14 (combined with Art. 1 of the First Protocol). A friendly settlement was reached and so no final decision on the merits was issued. The legislation was subsequently amended[18] and finally repealed.[19]

In the National Insurance Contribution context, in the case of *Walker v United Kingdom*,[20] the taxpayer complained that he had to continue to pay contributions until the state retirement age of 65 for men, while a woman could cease paying contributions at the state retirement age of 60. The complainant was a man over 60, and if he had been a woman he could have ceased to pay contributions. After finding the complaint admissible,[21] the Court concluded that a linkage of payment of National Insurance Contributions to the state pensionable age should be regarded as pursuing a legitimate aim and as being reasonably and objectively justified. The Court had previously concluded that the UK's plan to equalise

---

[16] See the discussion of Widowers' Bereavement Allowances below.
[17] (No. 30548/96), Commission decision of 3 December 1997 (ECmHR).
[18] By Finance Act 1998, s.26.   [19] By Finance Act 1999, ss. 33, 139 and Sch. 20.
[20] (No. 37212/02), Court judgment of 22 August 2006 (ECtHR).
[21] See the admissibility decision of 16 March 2004, (2004) 39 EHRR SE4.

the pension age for men and women in the year 2020 was within the margin of appreciation.[22] There was accordingly no violation of Art. 14. One might conclude at this point that even tax measures that discriminate on grounds of sex may fall within the margin of appreciation enjoyed by governments. Following the *van Raalte* case, a taxpayer who successfully complains of discrimination on grounds of sex in the granting of a tax exemption to one sex but not to another may not receive any financial compensation for that claim. The argument may be that the grant of the exemption is anomalous, and that to award pecuniary compensation would be to extend the anomaly.

10.4 The Widower's Bereavement Allowance cases[23]

A discussion of tax measures which discriminate on grounds of sex leads to a discussion of the widower's bereavement allowance cases, which have now, one suspects, by and large come to their final conclusion.

In 1980, the Chancellor of the Exchequer, Sir Geoffrey Howe, introduced an additional allowance for a widow following the death of her husband. At the time, such an additional allowance could be justified on the basis that, under the system of taxation of the income of husbands and wives at that time, the death of a husband would deprive the widow of the benefit of his higher personal allowance. At the time, Tiley wrote and, with remarkable foresight, referred to the possible discrimination against widowers that this involved.[24]

In the late 1990s, a number of widowers sought an allowance equivalent to that granted to widows and, when they were refused, took their claims directly to Strasbourg. In two cases, *Crossland v United Kingdom* and *Fielding v United Kingdom*, after the claims had been found to be admissible,[25] a friendly settlement was agreed and the UK government paid the equivalent of the value of the bereavement allowance to the claimants. Other widowers sought to claim a similar settlement, and when such claims were rejected an action was brought in the UK courts, which led

---

[22] See *Stec v United Kingdom* (Nos. 65731/01 and 65900/01) (2006) 43 EHRR 47 (ECtHR, GC).

[23] Strictly speaking, discussion of a 'widower's bereavement allowance' is inaccurate: there was only ever a bereavement allowance under Taxes Act 1988, s. 262, which was available to widows only. However, it is convenient to refer to these claims as claims for a widower's bereavement allowance.

[24] Tiley (1980, p. 218).

[25] *Crossland v United Kingdom* (No. 36120/97), Decision of 9 June 1999 (ECtHR); *Fielding v United Kingdom* (No. 36940/97), Decision of 9 June 1999 (ECtHR).

ultimately to the decision of the House of Lords in *R v HM Commissioners of Inland Revenue, ex parte Wilkinson.*[26]

By the time of the House of Lords case, the UK government had conceded that the grant of the allowance to widows and not to widowers was discriminatory and contrary to Art. 14. However, the government contended successfully that, by virtue of s. 6 of the Human Rights Act 1988, they could not grant the allowance to widowers without contravening primary UK legislation. More practically, they argued – and Lord Hoffmann accepted in the leading speech – that there was no obligation to compensate widowers for any pecuniary loss: the retention of the widows' allowance after the introduction of separate taxation was an anomaly and it would be to extend this anomaly if widowers were to be given compensation. In essence, the argument was that the correct response to this discriminatory provision was to remove the allowance for all taxpayers following the introduction of separate taxation, and therefore widowers were not entitled to a financial payment.

On the same date, the House of Lords held that widowers were, however, entitled to claim compensation for certain social security benefits – the Widow's Payment and Widowed Mother's Allowance.[27]

Following the refusal of the UK government to make payments similar to those paid to Messrs Crossland and Fielding, a large number of widowers lodged claims directly with the Court in Strasbourg for compensation for the failure to grant them a widower's bereavement allowance. After the two House of Lord cases, the UK government offered to settle the claims of widowers for the social security benefits (Widow's Payment and Widowed Mother's Allowance), but offered no payment in respect of the Widower's Bereavement Allowance. Finally, in the case of *Hobbs and Others v United Kingdom*,[28] the Court in Strasbourg reached the same conclusion as Lord Hoffmann in the House of Lords. That is, that the widow's bereavement allowance was an anomaly and that widowers were not entitled to any compensation despite the admitted breach of Art. 14.

Again, one might make the point that there is little encouragement for taxpayers who would wish to challenge discriminatory tax rules in this saga of the widower's bereavement allowance. At the end of the day, with the exception of Messrs Crossland and Fielding, other widowers received no compensation for the failure to extend to them the

---

[26] [2005] UKHL 30 (HL).
[27] See *R v Secretary of State for Work and Pensions, ex parte Hooper* [2005] UKHL 29 (HL).
[28] (Nos. 63684/00, 63475/00, 63484/00 and 63468/00) (2007) 44 EHRR 54 (ECtHR).

bereavement allowance despite the fact that it was accepted that the tax allowance had been operated on a discriminatory basis. It might have been true that the better response of the UK government when faced with the discriminatory allowance after the introduction of separate taxation was to remove the allowance. Nevertheless, this was not done, and the widowers were discriminated against for a number of years. This leaves a theoretical situation under which discriminatory tax measures may be challenged. However, if compensation is unlikely to be paid at the end of the day, one wonders how many taxpayers would bother to bring a challenge.

10.5 Discrimination on grounds of former marital status

The question of deductibility of maintenance payments to a former partner (or for the benefit of a child of a former relationship) is also a topic on which Tiley has written.[29] This is also a topic where a taxpayer has had somewhat more success – see *P. M. v United Kingdom*.[30]

This case concerned qualifying maintenance payments under the Taxes Act 1988, s. 347B. Where qualifying maintenance payments were made for the benefit of any child of the family, they were deductible by the payer but only if there had been a prior marriage (whether the marriage was subsisting or had been dissolved or annulled). In *P. M.'s case*, the taxpayer had lived in a stable relationship with his partner, but they had never married. They had a daughter and, after their separation, the taxpayer undertook to pay maintenance for his daughter. He was denied a deduction for the maintenance payment on the grounds that he and the girl's mother had never been married. The Strasbourg Court accepted the taxpayer's claim for compensation on grounds that the provision was discriminatory between parties to a former marriage and parties who had never been married. The Court dealt with the comparison with married couples as follows:

> . . . This is not a situation where the applicant seeks to compare himself to a couple living in a subsisting marriage (see for example, *Lindsay v United Kingdom*, cited above, where married and unmarried couples, taxed differently, were not found to be in a comparable position), but one where

---

[29] See Tiley (1985b).

[30] (No. 6638/03) (2006) 42 EHRR 45 (ECtHR). The author should disclose that he was involved in assisting in the presentation of P.M.'s case to the European Court of Human Rights.

the married father has separated or divorced and is also living apart from the
child of the family. Other persons, not parents, are not covered by the child
support provisions and are generally in a different situation. This applicant
differs from a married father only as regards the issue of marital status and
may, for the purposes of this application, claim to be in a relevantly similar
position.

   28 The justification for the difference in treatment relied on by the Government is the special regime of marriage which confers specific rights and
obligations on those who choose to join it. The Court recalls that it has in
some cases found differences in treatment on the basis of marital status has
had objective and reasonable justification (see, for example, *McMichael v
United Kingdom*, judgment of 24th February 1995, Series A, no. 307-B, §
98, concerning legislation which did not grant automatic parental responsibility to unmarried fathers who inevitably varied in their commitment
and interest in, or even knowledge of, their children). It may be noted however that as a general rule unmarried fathers, who have established family
life with their children, can claim equal rights of contact and custody with
married fathers (see *Sahin v Germany* [GC], number 30943/96, s.94, ECHR
2003–VIII). In the present case the applicant has been acknowledged as the
father and has acted in that role. Given that he has financial obligations
towards his daughter, which he has duly fulfilled, the Court perceives no
reason for treating him differently from a married father, now divorced
and separated from the mother, as regards the tax deductibility of those
payments . . .

   There are a number of comments one might make on this judgment.

   First, the UK government could not realistically say here that the tax
deductibility of qualifying maintenance payments for previously married
couples was anomalous and should not have been extended to couples
that were never married.

   Secondly, the judgment implicitly recognises the continuing force of
the old case law to the effect that a state may tax married couples differently
from unmarried persons during the subsistence of the relationship. The
new point added by *P. M.'s case* is that the difference in tax treatment may
no longer be justified once the relationship has ended.

   Thirdly, the essence of the decision is that, once a relationship has
ended, the parties to that relationship may be in a similar position whether
they were previously married or not. The obligations of mutual support,
or support for children of the relationship, may be the same regardless of
whether there was a previously subsisting marriage or not. This raises the
interesting question as to whether on the termination of a relationship on

death, married and previously unmarried couples should be regarded as being in a comparable position.[31] Assuming that there is a similar legal duty (or possibly a recognised moral duty) to make adequate provision for the maintenance of a dependent – whether a spouse, civil partner or not – then it may be that other dependents can claim to be in an objectively similar position to a spouse or civil partner.

10.6 Discrimination on grounds of existence of a family unit

We come finally to the most recent issue before the European Court of Human Rights regarding UK taxation and family units. On 12 December 2006, the Strasbourg Court issued its judgment in the case of *Burden and Burden v United Kingdom*,[32] but the case has subsequently been referred to the Grand Chamber, and at the time of writing that hearing is pending.

The applicants were unmarried sisters aged 88 and 81 respectively at the time of the judgment. They had lived together all their lives and were currently living in a house built on land inherited from their parents. They were concerned that, when either of them was to die, the survivor would have to sell the house in order to pay inheritance tax.[33]

Had they been a married couple, or a homosexual couple who had formed a civil partnership,[34] then there would have been an inheritance tax exemption on the death of the first to die. In effect they argued that there was discrimination against them because of the failure to extend the exemption regime to them as a family unit.

---

[31] Which in turn raises the interesting question of whether the Special Commissioners' decision in *Holland v IRC* [2003] STC (SCD) 43(Sp. Com.), which concerns the application of the inheritance tax inter-spousal exemption to unmarried couples, should be reconsidered in the light of the decision in *P. M. v United Kingdom*. This issue is not considered further here.

[32] (No. 13378/05) (2007) 44 EHRR 51 (ECtHR).

[33] There is a very puzzling aspect to this case. If one examines the financial figures set out in the case, it appears that on the death of the first of the two sisters there should have been sufficient other assets held by that sister to pay any inheritance tax without recourse to selling the house (particularly given the availability of the instalment option). Perhaps there are other facts that have not been made clear in the judgment. Certainly, one has to accept that the two sisters were sufficiently concerned that the inheritance tax bill on the death of the first sister to die would necessitate sale of the property, and this worry was sufficient to allow them to claim victim status to pursue their claim.

[34] It is a fair point to make that the extension of the tax treatment of spouses to civil partners in a homosexual relationship may also be seen as a change to the tax system brought about as a result of the Human Rights Act. One cannot conclusively say this, though, as it may be seen as much as a reflection of a change in societal norms.

By a majority of four votes to three, the Court held that there had been no violation of Art. 14. The judgment recognised that the decision not to extend the exemption beyond married couples and civil partners fell within the wide margin of appreciation of the UK government.

What will be the final outcome of the case remains for the judgment of the Grand Chamber. If the taxpayers are successful then there is, in effect, a very significant new restriction on the margin of appreciation enjoyed by states in the field of taxation. UK tax legislation has already seen an extension of the treatment of married couples to civil partners. This case would require a similar treatment to be extended to others – perhaps not simply siblings but also close friends – who had effectively formed a single family unit and should be taxed as such.

Conclusion

This short chapter has sought to consider the somewhat limited jurisprudence where the European Court of Human Rights has considered the impact of the Convention on taxation rules which employ criteria based on personal or family status. As has been seen, a number of those cases arise from provisions contained in UK tax legislation.

In many respects, this brief discussion of taxation, human rights and the family ends with matters up in the air pending the judgment of the Grand Chamber in the *Burden* case. This chapter has charted the somewhat mixed fortunes of taxpayers who have sought to rely upon provisions of the Convention to challenge legislation which discriminates on grounds of sex.

In terms of Tiley's initial question, '*Is it really worth having all this fuss and bother about the Human Rights Bill?*', the jury is still out. In the nine years since the Human Rights Act incorporated the Convention into UK domestic law, there have been a few victories for taxpayers. The greater impact of the Convention may exist, however, rather more in the way that the government chooses to tax the family in the future. It may be that we shall see less discriminatory provisions and a more equal treatment of family units going forward. If that is correct, then the 'fuss and bother' would have been worthwhile.

11

Family connections and the corporate entity: income splitting through the family company[1]

DAVID OLIVER AND PETER HARRIS

Introduction

This book has been structured along the lines of two themes that (amongst others) inspire the writings of John Tiley. The first of these themes, avoidance, essentially involves using tax law in a manner that is contrary to legislative intent. The second of these themes, taxation of the family, involves proper identification of the tax subject and so is one of the fundamental structural features of the income tax. It is, therefore, not surprising that John is interested in a case such as *Jones v Garnett*,[2] which involves something of an intersection between these two themes.[3] *Jones v Garnett* involves the family business with, like so many avoidance cases, an artificial entity (a company) inserted between the business and the family members. This paper takes a conceptual and retrospective look at the taxation of the family company and how it may be and has been used to determine the allocation of income to the tax subject identified by the legislature.

Jones v Garnett is in many ways a classic fact pattern for a family company. Two family members (Mr and Mrs Jones) owned equally the shares in a private company, Artic Systems Ltd. They both worked for the company but unequally, Mrs Jones working as an administrator for around five hours per week. Both drew small wages, particularly Mr Jones. In accordance with tax advice, they relied for their family income on the distribution of dividends not wages. From a tax perspective, the importance

[1] This paper relies in part on Archives of the Inland Revenue on various Finance Bills, which are in the possession of the Centre for Tax Law, Law Faculty, University of Cambridge. John Tiley rescued these archives from potential oblivion and we hope he will feel that we have made good use of them in this paper.
[2] [2007] UKHL 35 (HL).
[3] Tiley (2006b) discusses *Jones v Garnett* at the Court of Appeal level.

of this simple structure is flexibility. It potentially enabled the Joneses to determine all of the fundamental features of a payment, the building block that makes up the income tax base. It enabled them to determine: (i) who derived the income, whether Mr Jones, Mrs Jones or the company; (ii) the amount of income derived, the transfer pricing issue; (iii) the time at which income is derived, particularly in their control over the payment of dividends from the company; and finally (iv) they also controlled the type of income derived, whether wages, dividends or even capital gains.[4]

Despite each of these four fundamental features playing a tax role in the context of the family company, each of the latter three feed off the first, which is the primary focus of this paper. The ability to determine the allocation of income between related tax subjects is often referred to as 'income splitting'. The ability to income split is essentially a function of identification of the tax subject, discussed below in the first section of this chapter. Section 11.2 then proceeds to consider the simple use of a company to split wage income between family members. Section 11.3 considers the primary feature at issue in the *Jones v Garnett* case, income splitting between family members through the distribution of dividends by the family company. But where the company retains its profits, the split is more accurately between the family members and the company. This is considered in section 11.4. The retention of profits may increase the value of shares, which raises the issue of income splitting between family members at the point a company is sold. This is considered in section 11.5.

11.1 Relevance of the tax subject

Income splitting is a function of the identification of the tax subject. If the family were identified as the tax subject there would be no question of income splitting between family members. It would not matter who in the family derived the income, as it would all be aggregated before tax rates were applied. While this may be viewed as in some sense neutral, it would do nothing to encourage social independence through the equal allocation of resources between family members. Rather, it would encourage the family to rely on the individual with the greatest earning capacity. Practically, the difficulties with the family as the tax subject are in identifying who is within and who is outside the family and the tax consequences

---

[4] For the sake of simplicity, unless otherwise noted, in this paper 'income' includes capital gains. Broadly, like other types of income, capital gains represent an increase in wealth.

of joining and leaving the family. In an environment of increased family breakdown and reconstitution, this might be particularly problematic.[5] The benefit of family taxation is that it recognises the economic reality that families act as a single economic unit.[6] Any attempt to tax the individuals of a family seeks to draw artificial economic lines between people that pool economic resources. In the context of progressive taxation, separate taxation of family members encourages family members to derive their income equally, as this will produce the lowest amount of tax. This raises the problem of the tax effect of dealings between family members as they somewhat naturally engage in transactions that tend to even out the levels of taxable income of each member. The more progressive the income tax the greater the incentive to engage in income averaging transactions.

Similar problems and options arise in the context of corporate groups (a 'family' of companies). At one extreme, group members may be separately recognised and this system causes complexities when group members deal with each other. At the other extreme, only the group may be recognised for tax purposes, i.e. consolidation. As with the taxation of a family, a pure consolidation regime involves complexities when members join or leave the group. The family company is at the intersection of these two different types of families (individuals and companies). There is no reason why a family company could not also be included within a broad concept of 'family', if that were chosen as the tax subject. The result would be a peculiar form of consolidation. The US has this peculiar form of consolidation under its check-the-box regime. Under this regime many forms of entity may elect to be treated as transparent, with the result that for tax purposes their activities are attributed to their owners.[7]

The UK has never identified the family as the tax subject in income taxation. However, it did go part of the way in the context of spouses. Under the original income tax of 1799, a wife's income was simply allocated to

---

[5] For some statistics on constitution of the family in the UK, see Bowler (2007). For an economic analysis of policy issues in taxing the family see Apps and Rees (2007) and the references cited therein.

[6] As an example, in the early days of the National Socialist government in Germany and at a time of high unemployment the government legislated to tax the family as a single economic unit. This point was recalled on 12 November 2002 by Manfred Mössner from the University of Münster at one of the regular Tax Workshops arranged in Cambridge by Tiley. Mössner suggested that at that time if a family had one wage earner it was fortunate and if it had more than one wage earner it was doubly fortunate and this measure was well received.

[7] See Title 26 Code of Federal Regulations § 301.7701–1 and following. Although this treatment has only been in place since 1996, it is similar to the treatment under the first US federal income tax during the civil war, see Harris (1996, pp. 79–80).

her husband.[8] This was consistent with the common law at this time under which on marriage the wife's property became that of her husband.[9] The equivalent rule in the 1803 income tax was isolated in the rules following Schedule D.[10] In the 1806 income tax it was more sensibly located in the general rules preceding the rules for each Schedule and the exception for women traders extended to any other entitlement 'to any property or profits to her sole or separate use'.[11] It was similarly located in the 1842 income tax.[12] In 1882 married women became capable of holding property and contracting as a *femme sole*.[13] But for married women living with their husbands, the income tax law did not follow suit. In 1894 it became possible for husband and wife to claim an additional allowance for the wife if she had income from a profession, employment or vocation, extended to trades in 1897.[14]

The situation was different for children, who have always been tax subjects in their own right.[15] The same is true of corporations and companies, which had been treated as separate taxpayers for centuries before the income tax.[16] But this would have been of limited relevance before the advent of the registered company in 1842 and its subsequent popular adoption by families.[17]

---

[8] Income Tax Act 1799 (39 Geo. 3 c. 13), s. 41 stated: 'Income of any Married Woman, living with her Husband, shall be stated and accounted for by her Husband . . .'

[9] Baker (2002, pp. 484–7). See also the judgment of Baroness Hale in *Jones v Garnett* [2007] UKHL 35 (HL) at para. 58 referring to *Blackstone's Commentaries*.

[10] Income Tax Act 1803 (43 Geo. 3 c. 122), s. 45. Its location seems to have had something to do with the addition that 'any married Woman acting as a sole Trader by the Custom of any City or Place . . . shall be chargeable . . . as if she was actually sole and unmarried . . .' Baker (2002, p. 484) notes that under the custom of some cities and boroughs such a woman might be considered to own property. Under the 1803 income tax any such custom was subject, nevertheless, to the general rule attributing the wife's income if she was living with her husband. The woman sole trader addition to the 1799 provision might have been influenced by the intervening decision of Lord Eldon in *Beard v Webb* (1800) 2 Bos. & P. 93, 126 ER 1175 (Exch), which discussed at length the legal position of a married woman carrying on a sole trade in the City of London.

[11] Income Tax Act 1806 (46 Geo. 3 c. 65), s. 56.

[12] Income Tax Act 1842 (5&6 Vic. c. 35), s. 45.

[13] Married Women's Property Act 1882, s. 1.

[14] Finance Act 1894, s. 34(2) and Finance Act 1897, s. 5, respectively. See the interesting discussion in Daunton (2001, pp. 218–21), suggesting that the initial resistance to extending the treatment to trades related to the risk of income splitting between husband and wife.

[15] Although parents and guardians were residually liable for their tax, e.g. see Income Tax Act 1842 (5&6 Vic. c. 35), s. 173.

[16] See Harris (2006) and particularly at pp. 49–50 with respect to the direct tax of 1450.

[17] Popular adoption is clear by the time of the celebrated case of *Salomon v A Salomon & Co Ltd* [1897] AC 22 (HL).

In any case, the incentive to income split would have been minimal before World War I. Tax rates were low (typically less than 10 per cent) and the only form of progression was through the personal allowance system.[18] This situation changed dramatically with the introduction of Super-tax in 1911.[19] As progressive tax rates rose, so did the incentive to income split.[20] This had an effect both in the context of families and family companies. For centuries families had used settlements and covenants to allocate rights between family members.[21] Covenants in particular had been recognised as early as the beginning of the income tax as an effective way of assigning income. Interest and annuities were generally deductible under the residual income tax of the Triple Assessment of 1798, as they were under the income tax of 1799.[22]

Things became somewhat more complicated with the introduction of deduction at source in 1803. Tax was to be deducted at source from 'Annuities, yearly Interest of Money, or other annual Payments', either by denying a deduction for such payments in the context of a trade or by requiring actual deduction and remittance to the Revenue.[23] At first blush it is not obvious how this can give rise to an income split, particularly in the context of a generally flat rate income tax. However, there was progression in the form of exemption and abatements. A person receiving annual payments that were within the thresholds of exemption or abatement could claim a refund of tax deducted at source.[24] So a person with a low level of income could reclaim tax paid by deduction at source by a person with a higher amount of income.

---

[18] Allowances for children, in addition to for low income, were available under the early income tax until 1806, e.g. Income Tax Act 1803 (43 Geo. 3 c. 122), s. 195. They reappeared with the introduction of Super-tax in 1911, Finance Act (1909–10) Act 1910, s. 68.

[19] Finance (1909–10) Act 1910, s. 66. Super-tax was replaced with Sur-tax in Finance Act 1927, Part III.

[20] When Super-tax was introduced, the income tax rate was just under 6 per cent with an additional 2.5 per cent Super-tax. By the end of World War I, both these rates were 30 per cent.

[21] See Baker (2002, ch. 16).

[22] Triple Assessment Act 1798 (38 Geo. 3 c. 16), Sch. Part II, para. 1 and Income Tax Amendment Act 1799 (39 Geo. 3 c. 22), Sch. A General Deductions, paras. 1 and 4. These rules followed that in the land tax, under which debts were deductible in calculating the chargeable amount of debts and movables; for example, Land Tax Act 1797 (38 Geo. 3 c. 5), s. 3.

[23] Income Tax Act 1803 (43 Geo. 3 c. 122), s. 208, which became Income Tax Act 1842 (5&6 Vic. c. 35), ss. 100 and 102.

[24] Income Tax Act 1803 (43 Geo. 3 c. 122), ss. 199 and 200, which became Income Tax Act 1842 (5&6 Vic. c. 35), ss. 163–5.

Subtler was the question of whether the person making the annual payment could reduce their income by the amount paid. This would be relevant only where that person's income without the deduction was too large for the exemption or abatement but with the deduction they would be entitled to an exemption or abatement. Thus arose the distinction between the aggregate amount of a person's income under the Schedules and that person's 'aggregate profits' or 'aggregate income' (later 'total income') for the purposes of calculating exemption or abatement.[25] A classic example was an average person paying interest on a mortgage. Such a person might have aggregate income under the Schedules above the exemption threshold but if a deduction were granted for the interest the person might fall within the exemption threshold.

The wording of the exemption in the 1842 income tax was similar but added a qualification. Persons could claim a repayment of tax –

> except so much of such Duties as the Person claiming such Exemption shall or may be entitled to charge against any other Person, or to deduct or retain from or out of any Payment to which such Claimant may be or become liable . . .[26]

Clearly this exception was to prevent the person paying, say, the mortgage interest, who was required to deduct tax from that interest and pay it to the Revenue, from making a repayment claim in respect of tax deducted from the interest paid to the bank. But in the context of such a system, it seems clear that in determining the person's entitlement to an exemption, that person's own aggregate income should be reduced by the interest paid. And it seems this is how the Revenue administered the claim for exemption.[27]

---

[25] Income Tax Act 1803 (43 Geo. 3 c. 122), s. 193 referred to 'the aggregate annual Amount of his, her, or their Profits'. The Income Tax Act 1805 (45 Geo. 3 c. 49), s. 180 replaced 'Profits' with 'Income'. The wording of Income Tax Act 1806 (46 Geo. 3 c. 65), s. 173 was somewhat different.

[26] Income Tax Act 1842 (5&6 Vic. c. 35), s. 163.

[27] Murray and Carter (1895, p. 187) note that: 'It was during the year 1876–7 that, for the first time, facilities were given to persons desirous of claiming exemption or abatement, by providing a form of claim in the form of return itself, instead of leaving persons to apply specially to the assessor or surveyor for a form . . .' At pp. 198–9 they reproduce the relevant part of the form for 1891/92 with a heading 'Particulars of my TOTAL INCOME'. Nos. 1 and 2 of this part of the form required particulars of income. No. 3 required 'Particulars of DEDUCTIONS FROM INCOME, such as GROUND RENT, INTEREST, &c.' See also the form at pp. 244–5. At p. 195 they provide a clear example of calculating the exemption for a person paying mortgage interest. See also Stopforth (1987, p. 418), quoting evidence given to the 1851 Select Committee.

This somewhat implicit process became very important with the intro-duction of Super-tax in 1911. Super-tax was charged according to a per-son's 'total income'.[28] For this purpose –

> the total income of any individual from all sources shall be . . . estimated in the same manner as the total income . . . for the purposes of exemptions or abatements under the Income Tax Acts . . .[29]

These mechanisms together with the use of the family company (not subject to Super-tax) made income splitting a relatively straightforward matter.[30]

This situation did not last very long. The 1920 Royal Commission con-sidered whether a husband and wife should be taxed separately. It also considered the possibility of using the family as the tax subject, rather than its individual members. The conclusion was some change in the allowances area but otherwise no change.[31] Further, it heard evidence with respect to the avoidance of Super-tax and made specific and consecutive recommendations in the areas of retained profits of closely held compa-nies and settlements without specifically connecting these two areas or the tax subject issue. With respect to settlements, the Commission limited the issue to 'alienation of income by means of deeds' for the benefit of infant children, although its recommendations were slightly wider than this.[32] The recommendation with respect to undistributed profits is fur-ther discussed below at 11.4.

These recommendations were adopted in a broadly consistent form (but in reverse order) in 1922. This year saw the introduction of what became know as the settlement provisions and the introduction of the allocation of retained profits of a family company to its controllers for Super-tax purposes in consecutive provisions of the Finance Act 1922.[33] As commonly happens when reviewing historical provisions, the proximity

---

[28] Finance (1909–10) Act 1910, s. 66(1).

[29] Finance (1909–10) Act 1910, s. 66(2). The subsection went on at para. (d) to state that 'any deductions allowable on account of any annual sums paid out of the property or profits of the individual shall be allowed as deductions in respect of the year in which they are payable . . .'

[30] For example, see the example from *The Accountant* of 6 June 1914 discussed in Stopforth (1987, p. 419). Also see the facts in *Wiggins v Watson's Trustees* [1934] AC 264 (HL) and *IRC v Payne* (1940) 23 TC 610 (CA).

[31] United Kingdom (1920, paras. 248–71).

[32] *Ibid.*, para. 576 and see Stopforth (1987, pp. 420–1).

[33] Finance Act 1922, ss. 20 and 21, respectively. The former was interpreted by the House of Lords in *Wiggins v Watson's Trustees* [1934] AC 264 (HL).

of these provisions to each other highlights their conceptual connection.[34] Both involved the reattribution of income for Super-tax purposes. They also highlight that, at least in an historical context, the settlement provisions were not intended to deal with income splitting between family members and their company.

None of these features directly affected the identification of the tax subject but were, rather, qualifications to it. There were different developments in the context of families of companies. As mentioned, historically each company was considered a separate taxpayer, whether a member of a corporate group or not. This changed in 1915 when the UK introduced a consolidation regime in the context of Excess Profits Duty. The Finance (No. 2) Act 1915 taxed a parent and its wholly owned subsidiaries as if the subsidiary 'were a branch' of the parent.[35] The Revenue explained the purpose of this provision as follows:

> [T]o secure that where a parent company carries on its business in part through subsidiary companies, and one company makes excess profits while the other sustains a deficiency, the deficiency may be set off against the excess, and duty my be charged only on the balance, if any.[36]

This form of consolidation (with a nine-tenths ownership requirement) was adopted again when Excess Profits Duty was reintroduced in the form of National Defence Contribution in 1937, later Profits Tax.[37] In particular, s. 22 of the Finance Act 1937 (the Act which introduced National Defence Contribution) provided that where a resident body corporate was a subsidiary of another resident body corporate ('the principal company') then the principal company could elect for the subsidiary to be grouped with it so that profits or losses arising to the subsidiary from its trade or business were to be treated as arising from the trade or business carried on by the principal company. Section 42 of the Finance Act 1938 lowered the nine-tenths threshold by providing that a body corporate was deemed to be a subsidiary of another body corporate if and so long as not less than three-quarters of its ordinary share capital was owned by that other

---

[34] For another example of this sort of connection in the context of double tax relief, see Harris (1999).

[35] Finance (No. 2) Act 1915, Sch. 4, para. 6.

[36] Archives of the Inland Revenue on the Finance (No. 3) Bill 1915, Excess Profits Tax, p. 274A.

[37] Regarding the introduction of National Defence Contribution and its conversion into Profits Tax, see section 11.3 below.

body corporate.[38] The election was irrevocable but of course the grouping would cease if the subsidiary company ceased to be a subsidiary within the definition.[39]

Even after the introduction of consolidation in the context of National Defence Contribution members of corporate groups continued to be taxed separately under income tax. The *Tucker Committee* considered the matter in 1950. It briefly outlined a number of different methods of taxing corporate groups and felt that some relief from separate taxation was justified in the context of losses and the transfer of stock between group members. The consolidation regime (then used in the context of Profits Tax) was dismissed because of, amongst other things, complications arising in 'cases of companies coming into or leaving a group'.[40] Instead, it took the advice of the Inland Revenue and proposed for income tax a contribution regime (involving subvention payments deductible to the group member payer but assessable to the group member recipient).[41] This proposal was enacted in s. 20 of the Finance Act 1953.

When Profits Tax and income tax on companies were merged into corporation tax in 1965, the contribution regime of the income tax was adopted rather than the consolidation regime of the Profits Tax.[42] The Revenue later explained this choice as follows:

> One of the main reasons for the decision was the practical one that 'full grouping' might well give rise to substantial delays in settling group liabilities. The group assessment would have to await the settlement of the tax position of every single member. Some minor point affecting one company might hold up the settlement of a considerable total liability.[43]

Corporate groups were not satisfied with the total adoption of the subvention system in 1965, preferring the consolidation system under the Profits Tax. The preference seems to have arisen from the difficulties associated with need to make a subvention payment and, in particular, the

---

[38] This definition is echoed today in the Taxes Act 1988 definition of '75% subsidiary' for, inter alia, group relief purposes; see Taxes Act 1988, ss. 832(1) and 838(1)(b).

[39] There was a different compulsory consolidation system based on a 90 per cent threshold under the Excess Profits Tax that applied during the Second World War. Generally, see United Kingdom (1951, paras. 289–95).

[40] United Kingdom (1951, para. 291).

[41] This type of group relief is still used in some Scandinavian countries. The Finnish contribution regime was subject to challenge under EC law in Case C-231/04 *Oy AA* [2007] ECR 00 (ECJ).

[42] Finance Act 1965, Sch. 15, para. 10.

[43] Archives of the Inland Revenue on the Finance Bill 1967, Vol. 1, p. 92.

interaction of company law and the possible existence of minority share-holders. So in 1966 the Inland Revenue further investigated 'some system of grouping of the profits and losses of members of a group'. But the Revenue continued to be of the view that consolidation was 'not feasible'. Timing continued to be a problem and further it would be difficult to determine how much of a loss belonged to a company if it 'left the group'. The introduction of capital gains tax in 1965 caused further perceived difficulties:

> It would not be possible to allow capital 'losses' of one company against the capital gains of another without complex provisions to prevent manipulations leading to substantial loss of tax.[44]

One can only speculate at what is being referred to here, but it is likely to involve companies joining and leaving groups in order to move capital losses or gains and the problems associated with gains and losses on the sale of subsidiaries. The subvention payment system was replaced by the current system of group relief in 1967, which was viewed as avoiding 'both the problems of "full grouping" and the disadvantages of the subvention payment system'.[45]

So by 1970 the only formal aggregation of family income of either families of individuals or families of companies continued to be that of husband and wife living together and this situation pertained until 1973.[46] As Tiley notes:

> Under the law prevailing until 1973, a wife's income was simply treated as that of her husband. This meant that her income was added to his and so taxed at the cumulative rate appropriate to their joint income; however, in practice, the provision of an additional personal relief for married women (the wife's earned income relief) and the practice of having a long band of income taxed at what we now call basic rate reduced the financial injustice.[47]

---

[44] *Ibid.*, p. 93.
[45] *Ibid.* The group relief system was inserted by Finance Act 1967, s. 20.
[46] Regarding the joint taxation of husbands and wives, see Income Tax Act 1918, General Rule 16, Income Tax Act 1952, s. 354 and Taxes Act 1970 s. 37.
[47] Tiley (1999, p. 131). A married man was entitled to an enhanced personal relief, which had its origins in Finance Act 1918, s. 27 that became Income Tax Act 1918, s. 13. Finance Act, 1897, s. 5 (discussed above) became Income Tax Act 1918, s. 21. Both provisions were replaced with the revision of personal allowances in Finance Act 1920 (which changed the differentiation system based on total income into a deduction for earned income), the former continuing as s. 18(1) and the latter appearing to morph into the wife's earned income relief in s. 18(2). Section 18 became Income Tax Act 1952, s. 210 and then Taxes Act 1970, s. 8.

The change in 1973 enabled a wife to elect to be taxed separately on her earned income, but such an election resulted in the loss of the wife's earned income relief.[48] Further, the election did not affect the wife's investment income. It was not taxed separately until the general move to separate taxation of husband and wife that took effect in 1990.[49] There were and are further qualifications to this treatment in the form of transferable allowances and tax credits but these are not relevant for present purposes.[50]

The settlement provisions enacted in 1922 had always had the potential of allocating to a parent the income of any disposition for the benefit of a child.[51] Between 1968 and 1972 the Labour government took the added step of allocating all the unearned income of an unmarried child to their parents.[52] By contrast, the attribution of accumulated profits to shareholders of closely held companies for Sur-tax purposes, also introduced in 1922, continued even after companies ceased to be subject to income tax in 1965 and through to 1988.[53] Although apportionment ceased from 1989, in 2000 a special regime was introduced for individuals deriving what would otherwise be employment income through a company. The effect of this legislation is to treat the income as if it were derived directly by the individual. It is further discussed in section 11.2 below.

11.2 Working for the family company

Perhaps the most straightforward method of income splitting between family members in the context of a family business is for the business to simply hire the services of a family member. This simple method need not involve the use of a company as, for example, a sole trader parent or partnership between parents may hire the services of other family members. As Tiley notes:

---

[48] See Finance Act 1971, s. 23.

[49] Taxes Act 1970, s. 8 had become Taxes Act 1988, s. 279, which was repealed by Finance Act 1988, s. 32, and see Tiley (1999, p. 131).

[50] Generally, see Tiley (1999) and Tiley (2005b, pp. 152–8).

[51] Finance Act 1922, s. 20 became Income Tax Act 1952, Part XVIII Chapter III, then Taxes Act 1970, Part XVI, then Taxes Act 1988, Part XV and now Income Tax (Trading and Other Income) Act 2005, Part 5, Ch. 5.

[52] Finance Act 1968, s. 15, which became Taxes Act 1970, ss. 43–8. Also see Tiley (1999, p. 137).

[53] Finance Act 1922, s. 21 became Income Tax Act 1952, Part IX, Ch. III and, particularly s. 245. Section 245 became Finance Act 1965, s. 78 then Taxes Act 1970, s. 296, replaced by Finance Act 1972, s. 94 and Sch. 16 and then became Taxes Act 1970, Part XI, Ch. III.

Income splitting between spouses may be practised if, for example, the wife runs a business and employs her husband in it; the money paid to the husband will be deductible in computing the profits of the wife's business and will be taxable to the husband as employment income. Such arrangements must, of course, be genuine and are closely scrutinised by the Inland Revenue.[54]

Tiley makes a similar comment in the context of the hiring of children.[55] While not essential for income splitting in this way, the introduction of a company does increase the number of options (and number of persons) available for income splitting as the controllers may also be hired by the company and family members may also be appointed as directors rather than just employees or independent contractors.

When a family company hires a family member, there are two primary issues; how much may be deducted by the company and how much must be included in the income of the family member. For present purposes it will be assumed that these are of equal amount (i.e. the amount of deduction and the amount of income) but this need not be the case as the rules for deductibility are not the same as those for inclusion in income. The deduction and inclusion is straightforward if the remuneration is a market or arm's-length amount for the services rendered. However, if it is not clearly arm's length then there are two possibilities. The first is that the wages are below an arm's-length amount. This is most likely to be the case with the dominant earner in the family who might otherwise be taxable at the higher rate. The second is that the wages are below an arm's-length amount. This is most likely to be the case with subsidiary earners in the family who might otherwise not use the benefits of their exemption limit and lower rate thresholds.

The facts of *Jones v Garnett* appear to provide an example of the first possibility and maybe the second possibility. Despite working full-time for the company, Mr Jones for the years in question (1996–2000) drew, on average, £7,000 as wages. By contrast, the company he worked for, which relied nearly solely on his efforts to produce its profits, averaged more than £57,000 as profits subject to tax for the same years. Mrs Jones, who worked around five hours a week, by contrast averaged £3,000 in wages for the same period, perhaps not an excessive amount by market standards but substantially more per hour than Mr Jones was earning. Why didn't the Revenue challenge the level of these wages? Could they safely be described, in Tiley's words, as 'genuine'?

[54] Tiley (1999, pp. 133–4).   [55] *Ibid.*, p. 136.

The issue is essentially one of transfer pricing. The UK does have transfer pricing rules but they have never, since their modern introduction in 1951, applied in the context of family members or family members and their family company, even since the reforms of 2004, which expanded their domestic application.[56] In the absence of such rules, HMRC is left scrambling for other rules that might be used to attack what is essentially a transfer pricing issue.[57] There are two types of rules that HMRC has tried to apply that are further considered in what follows. The first is whether the payment by the company to the family member is deductible under the 'wholly and exclusively' test in s. 74(a) of the Taxes Act 1988. The second is whether the settlements legislation may apply. In either case the rules were not designed to deal with what is often a straightforward transfer pricing issue and, at least at one level, it seems rather bizarre that HMRC is forced to rely (or thinks it can rely) on these rules to deal with the issue.

Deduction of remuneration

Under s. 74(a) of the Taxes Act 1988, the expenditure by the family company on, say, wages of a family member is only deductible if it is 'wholly and exclusively' for the purposes of the company's trade. One of the bizarre consequences of seeking to use this rule as a transfer pricing rule is that even if it is effective, it is only one-sided. The rule may possibly deny a deduction for excessive remuneration but cannot increase the remuneration of someone like Mr Jones, who appears to have been working at an undervalue. Nevertheless, the Revenue have on occasion sought to rely on this provision to deny a deduction for excessive remuneration.

In the leading case of *Copeman v Flood*, a company, the shares of which were held by five members of the family (husband, wife and three children)

---

[56] International transfer pricing rules, of a type, were introduced by Finance (No. 2) Act 1915, s. 31(3) but this provision only applied outside the Commonwealth. When the UK began concluding double tax treaties after World War II, an issue arose as to whether the transfer pricing rule in double tax treaties (as implemented in domestic law) could impose a charge to tax. The Law Officers advised the Revenue that it could not. The result was Finance Act 1951, s. 37 to support such a charge. Archives of the Inland Revenue on the Finance Bill 1951, pp. 125–7. The extension to certain domestic transactions was effected by Finance Act 2004, ss. 30–7. See also the explanatory memorandum cited in Oliver (1998), which discusses this issue.

[57] This discussion should not be taken to suggest that applying transfer pricing rules within a family is a straightforward matter or that it is appropriate. Such an application raises many difficulties, some of which are discussed further in section 11.4 below.

who were also directors of the company, paid in the year in question to each of the directors a sum of £2,600 as directors' fees.[58] As a result a gross profit of £15,623 was turned into a loss of some £300. The inspector challenged the deductibility of the payment to two of the directors, the daughter aged 17 and a son aged 23, putting forward the view that, having regard to their age and duties, the whole of the payments to them could not be regarded as laid out 'wholly and exclusively' for the purposes of the trade. He suggested a deduction of £78 for the daughter (who had no business experience) and £350 for the son. The daughter's duties consisted principally in answering telephone calls by farmers to the private residence in the evenings enquiring about the price for their pigs, which would have been settled by the directors in conference each evening. The son's duties mainly consisted in calling on farmers to buy pigs from them.

The General Commissioners held that they could not interfere with the company's prerogative to pay such sums as it saw fit as directors' remuneration. On appeal to the High Court, Lawrence J held that the decision did not address the question as to whether the sums in question were wholly and exclusively laid out for the purpose of the company's trade and remitted the case to the Commissioners to find as a fact whether the sums were wholly and exclusively laid out etc. and, if not, how much, if any, was wholly and exclusively laid out. We do not know what decision the General Commissioners came to on that point since such decisions were and continue to be unreported except where there is an appeal.

A different form of development in this regard began to occur when Excess Profits Duty was introduced in 1915. The Finance (No. 2) Act 1915 provided:

> Any deduction allowed for the remuneration of directors . . . of a trade or business shall not, unless the Commissioners of Inland Revenue . . . otherwise direct, exceed the sums allowed for those purposes in the last pre-war trade year . . . and no deduction shall be allowed in respect of any transaction or operation of any nature, where it appears, or to the extent to which it appears, that the transaction or operation has artificially reduced the amount to be taken as the amount of the profits of the trade or business for the purposes of this Act.[59]

The Revenue later explained the purpose of the first part of this provision as follows:

---

[58] (1940) 24 TC 53 (KB).   [59] Finance (No. 2) Act 1915, Sch. 4, para. 5.

This provision . . . arises from the fact that in the case of private limited companies the whole or the major part of the profits are often, for legitimate reasons, paid away as remuneration of directors who are virtual owners of the company. It makes small difference to the recipient in these cases whether the profits are received in the form of dividends or fees, but if any profits received in the later form were allowed to be treated as a deduction in computing the sum chargeable, that sum would not reflect the excess profits realised and the object of the Excess Profits Duty would be defeated.[60]

The second part of the provision looks very much like a general anti-abuse rule. It was designed to counteract –

[v]arious devices . . . open to the taxpayer for reducing the 'profits' of the chargeable period, such as paying away abnormal sums as directors' fees, creating special charges for interest on borrowed money . . . or manipulating valuations of stock.[61]

Technical difficulties with this provision caused an addition in 1916 to effectively deny a deduction for directors' fees in the case of companies controlled by their directors (by treating the company as a firm).[62] A simpler rule was adopted in Corporation Profits Tax, introduced in 1920. The 1916 rule was adjusted so as to deny a deduction for directors' fees exceeding £1,000 per annum. The first part of the 1915 provision was not repeated but the second part (the anti-abuse rule) was repeated.[63]

When in 1937 Excess Profits Duty was reintroduced in the form of National Defence Contribution, a modified version of the 1916 provision was inserted.[64] The 1937 provision contained specific restrictions on the deductibility of directors' remuneration in the case of director controlled companies, with an overall provision that in no case should the deduction exceed £15,000.[65] There was an exception for the remuneration of a 'whole-time service director', defined to mean a director who is required to devote substantially the whole of his time to the service of the company

---

[60] Archives of the Inland Revenue on the Finance Bill 1916, Excess Profits Duty, p. 12.
[61] Archives of the Inland Revenue on the Finance (No. 3) Bill 1915, Excess Profits Duty, p. 38.
[62] Finance Act 1916, s. 49.
[63] Finance Act 1920, s. 53(2)(c) and (d), respectively. Interestingly, s. 53(2)(b) denied a deduction for interest and royalties paid by a company to its controllers.
[64] The version in the Bill as introduced was more closely modelled on the 1916 provision and the Revenue notes on the clause made the connection clear. The provision was modified at the committee stage. Archives of the Inland Revenue on the Finance Bill 1937, pp. 254–5 and 425–6.
[65] Finance Act 1937, Sch. 4, para. 11.

in a managerial or technical capacity and is not the beneficial owner of more than 5 per cent of the ordinary share capital of the company.[66] The 1937 legislation contained the anti-avoidance rule from the Finance (No. 2) Act 1915 but it appeared in isolation (as under the Corporation Profits Tax).[67] The Revenue's explanation of this provision was virtually the same as that provided in 1915 (quoted above), with a subtle but important adjustment. The explanation began:

> '[v]arious devices are open to the taxpayer for reducing the profits of the chargeable period, such as paying away abnormal sums to relatives engaged in the business . . .'[68]

The change from 'directors fees' to 'abnormal sums to relatives engaged in the business' may reflect an increasing concern with the type of arrangement in issue in *Copeman v Flood*. The lack of a similar provision in the income tax seems to reflect a concern for greater revenue exposure in the context of National Defence Contribution (as with Excess Profits Duty and Corporation Profits Tax before it).[69]

One way to escape the restrictions in Finance Act 1937 would be to cause the company to cease to be a director-controlled company by directors transferring their shareholdings to family members who were not directors. This ploy (amongst others) was attacked in 1951 (after National Defence Contribution had been morphed into Profits Tax, see section 11.3 below) by a broader anti-avoidance provision which included the transfer or acquisition of shares in a company where the main benefit which might have been expected to accrue from the transaction or transactions in the three years immediately following the completion thereof was the avoidance or reduction of liability to Profits Tax.[70]

---

[66] This exception was inserted at the report stage. The exception was inserted to cater for the remuneration of an 'employee' that is, for 'administrative convenience, given a seat upon the Board of Directors'. Such remuneration was viewed as an 'ordinary expense'. Archives of the Inland Revenue on the Finance Bill 1937, pp. 627 and 631.

[67] Finance Act 1937, Sch. 4, para. 10. The rule was extended to cover not only reduction in profits but also the creation or increase of a loss.

[68] Archives of the Inland Revenue on the Finance Bill 1937, p. 425.

[69] National Defence Contribution was based on profits as computed according to income tax principles, with certain adjustments, as for example in relation to directors' remuneration. Accordingly, in order to be deductible that remuneration had to satisfy not only the specific limitation in Finance Act 1937 but also the 'wholly and exclusively' test, as later held in *Copeman v Flood* (1940) 24 TC 53 (KB), i.e. the remuneration had to satisfy two tests for the purposes of National Defence Contribution.

[70] Finance Act 1951, s. 32. The 'main benefit' test was first used in the anti-avoidance rule in the Second World War Excess Profits Tax due to practical difficulties in applying a 'main

The absolute limitation on the deductible amount of directors' remuneration continued throughout the life of the Profits Tax regime until it was replaced in the Finance Act 1965 with corporation tax. The limitation nevertheless survived because for corporation tax purposes the profits of companies were to be computed on the basis of income tax principles, with some adjustments, and one of the adjustments provided by the Finance Act 1965 concerned a limitation on the deduction of directors' remuneration in the case of a close company, i.e. a company under the control of five or fewer persons. This gave it a wider application than the Profits Tax restriction, which had applied only to director-controlled companies and not to income tax payable by companies.[71] The exclusion for whole-time service directors continued and specific limits were introduced for a so-called full-time working director, that is, a person who would be a whole-time service director but for owning 5 per cent or more of the ordinary share capital.[72] The overall limitation, as for Profits Tax, was set at 15 per cent of the profits (before deducting the remuneration) but was relaxed to allow a right of election to calculate the profits on the basis of a three-year average so as to allow for fluctuating or cyclical results.

These restrictions on the deduction of directors' remuneration were abolished in 1969, leaving the 'wholly and exclusively' test as the sole limitation on the deduction of remuneration paid by family companies to family members.[73] This test was again the subject of litigation in the context of remuneration paid to family members in 1981 in the case of *Dollar v Lyon*.[74] The taxpayers (a husband and wife) carried on a trade as farmers (though not through a company). They paid their children (aged around 14, 11, 9 and 7 at the time) for help on the farm the minimum agricultural wage prescribed by statute for fifteen hours work per week. They were paid £2 per week in cash and the balance in National Savings Certificates purchased in their names at the end of the year. The General Commissioners held that only the cash payment of £108 to the eldest child was wholly and exclusively expended for the purpose of the trade, the other payments being in the nature of pocket money.

Vinelott J in the High Court dismissed the taxpayer's appeal. He found the idea 'strange and unconvincing' that a child of 8 would enter into a

purpose' test. See Finance Act 1941, s. 35, as amended by Finance Act 1944, s. 33 and Archives of the Inland Revenue on the Finance Bill 1951, pp. 105–8.

[71] Finance Act 1965, s. 74.

[72] This itself echoed a relaxation in the Profits Tax restriction towards the end of the Profits Tax regime.

[73] Finance Act 1969, s. 28.   [74] [1981] STC 333 (Ch D).

contract of employment with their parents, although he simply dismissed the appeal for lack of evidence to this effect. The most surprising feature of this judgment is the lack of reference to any previous decided cases, demonstrating the dearth of authority in this area.

In the result, the case law and experience in this area is uncertain and unsatisfactory. Of the two cases of some relevance, one is extreme (*Dollar v Lyon*) and the other (*Copeman v Flood*) was remitted without any clear guidance. The fact that specific provisions were inserted in the Excess Profits Duty, National Defence Contribution, Profits Tax and corporation tax suggest that as a general rule there is a wide discretion in family companies to determine the level of remuneration of working family members. Further, to the extent that the 'wholly and exclusively' requirement does place some limitations on income splitting in this area, it is useless in a case such as *Jones v Garnett* where the remuneration was at an under rather than overvalue.

The attraction of income splitting through employment by the family company has varied over time. When employment income was taxed at a lower effective rate than investment income, owing to the existence of earned income relief, it was more attractive.[75] But in the modern environment, when earned income is taxed at the same rate as investment income *and* attracts a National Insurance liability, it is seen to be less favourable. Hence the structure in *Jones v Garnett*, where Mr Jones was happy to work at what may be viewed as an undervalue so as to inflate the family company's profits. As discussed in section 11.4, this has been particularly emphasised in recent years due to a low corporate tax rate.

In 2000 this incentive *not* to derive earned income through a company was addressed as part of the extension of the IR 35 provisions. The Finance Act of that year introduced legislation aimed at individuals deriving what would be employment income through intermediaries including private companies.[76] The effect of this legislation is to ignore the company and allocate the income directly to the individual provided that they have

---

[75] Differentiation (earned income relief) was first introduced by Finance Act 1907, s. 19, which applied a lower rate to earned income within a certain threshold. From Finance Act 1920, a taxpayer was entitled to a deduction from their earned income. This remained the treatment until earned income relief was replaced with an additional rate for investment income in 1973: Finance Act 1972, s. 66. The additional rate was repealed in 1984: Finance Act 1984, s. 17. It must be kept in mind that for a large part of this period the income of wives (even earned income) was allocated to their husbands, see section 11.1 above.

[76] Finance Act 2000, s. 60 and Sch. 12, now Income Tax (Earnings and Pensions) Act 2003, Part 2, Ch. 8.

a material interest in the company (more than 5 per cent).[77] While the legislation has an important role to play in limiting the potential to income split through family companies, it does not apply in a situation where if the income were derived directly it would be from independent services. It is not clear whether this legislation might have applied in *Jones v Garnett* but the facts predated the introduction of this legislation.[78]

Settlements legislation

If the 'wholly and exclusively' limitation does not apply and the IR 35 provisions are not available, might the Revenue be able to apply the settlements legislation to income splitting through working for the family company? The application of this legislation is limited by the judicial concept of 'bounty'. In the context of the first possibility under consideration (a family member working for the family company at an undervalue), the initial beneficiary of the bounty will be the company. The company might retain the bounty, distribute it as dividends or find a way to disburse the bounty in a deductible form such as by paying excessive remuneration to another family member. The later option, which might be viewed as the same as the second possibility under consideration (a family member working for the family company at an overvalue), is considered here. The dividend option is considered under section 11.3 and the retention option under section 11.4 below.

The settlements legislation cannot apply to a company simply employing a family member at an overvalue. In such a case it would be the company that created the possible settlement (the employment) and provided the element of bounty (the overpayment). Even if the application of the settlements legislation in these circumstances could create a charge to income tax on the settlor (the company), companies are not subject to income tax.[79]

Question whether the settlements legislation could apply to a person providing services at an undervalue to a company where the company used

---

[77] Note the echoing of the lower than 5 per cent holding requirement of a whole-time service director originally introduced by Finance Act 1937, Sch. 4, para. 13 (discussed above).

[78] The Special Commissioners' decision notes that during the period in question Mr Jones worked through three different agencies for four different clients: [2005] STC (SCD) 9 (Sp. Com.) at para. 16.

[79] Taxes Act 1988, s. 6(2). It would seem to require rather bizarre circumstances for the Revenue to seek to apply the settlements legislation to a non-resident company, which might be subject to income tax. An interesting, though purely historical, question is whether the settlements legislation might have applied to a company as settlor when resident companies were still subject to income tax, i.e. before 1965.

the bounty to over-remunerate another member of the family working for the company. The facts of *Jones v Garnett* might provide an example of such a situation, particularly if Mrs Jones had derived her return purely as remuneration rather than as a mixture of remuneration and, predominantly, dividends. As a result of the House of Lords decision in this case, there seems no reason why this would not be a settlement. However, as in the case itself, the question would turn to whether the exception for outright gifts between spouses would apply.[80]

There seem to be serious doubts as to whether this exception could apply. First, there is the issue as to whether the contract of employment in the hands of the employee could amount to a 'gift' of 'property'. Secondly, even if such a contract could amount to a 'gift' and 'property', is it 'made by one spouse to the other'? It is the family company that makes the contract.[81] Thirdly, it may be that the contract of employment (at least the bit at an overvalue) is 'substantially a right to income'. If the exception would not be available, the situation sits at curious odds with the result in the case itself, where the exception applied to the issuing of shares to Mrs Jones. This is particularly so considering the additional risk that the company may not be able to deduct the excess remuneration under the 'wholly and exclusively' test and the potential for double taxation.[82]

Where the bounty (the excessive remuneration) is to a family member other than a spouse, it seems that the settlements legislation cannot apply unless the family member is an unmarried child of the person providing the services at an undervalue.[83]

11.3 Distributions of the family company

The Joneses' only engaged in a minimal (if any) amount of splitting their income through the use of wages derived from the company. The majority of the split was through the use of the shareholding in the company and dividends paid on that shareholding. The dividend income received was more than £25,000 for each of them for the years in question. To achieve

---

[80] Income Tax (Trading and Other Income) Act 2005, s. 626.

[81] Lord Hoffmann in the House of Lords rejected a similar argument by the Revenue that the company issued the shares to Mrs Jones and so there was no gift by Mr Jones: [2007] UKHL 35 (HL) at para. 28.

[82] This potential arises irrespective of the application of the settlements legislation.

[83] Income Tax (Trading and Other Income) Act 2005, ss. 626 and 629. Some situations involving spouses may not be caught in any case because the settlor will not have a retained interest. See definition of 'spouse' in s. 625(4), which is not expressly adopted for the purposes of the spouse exception in s. 626.

this effect, the Joneses had to ensure the company was profitable and this was secured by Mr Jones working at an apparent undervalue. The split was achieved by a dual reallocation of income and simultaneous dual recharacterisation of income. The potential remuneration for the labour of Mr Jones was turned into profits in the hands of the company. The company profits were turned, to the extent of half, into dividends in the hands of Mrs Jones. As Tiley notes, in principle, family members are free to 'divide assets between them as they wish . . .'[84] Even where income is joint income of spouses, it is treated as several and divided according to the interests in it.[85]

But it is only logical to seek to split income in this way where distributed corporate profits are subject to substantial relief from economic double taxation. If corporate profits are subject to full taxation in the hands of the company and distributed profits are subject to full taxation in the hands of the shareholder, without relief for one tax against the other (the 'classical' system), then the incentive to income split through the use of dividends is reduced. When the classical nature of the corporate tax system is high, it might be expected that families will predominantly attempt to income split through the use of wages. In the face of full dividend relief, dividends provide a useful method of income splitting between family members that are treated as separate taxpayers.

Traditionally, the UK has been a dividend relief country. After an initial brief flirt with a dividend deduction system, in 1803 the income tax settled on dividend relief in the form of a dividend tax credit by way of the mechanism of deduction of tax at source.[86] This was a system of full dividend relief and would remain in place until 1965. However, classical elements were added in the form of other corporate taxes that were not credited to shareholders. This started with Excess Profits Duty in 1915[87] and was continued between 1920 and 1924 with Corporation Profits Tax.[88] Full dividend relief returned until the introduction of National Defence Contribution in 1937,[89] supplemented with Excess Profits Tax in 1939.[90] Profits Tax followed in 1947, which only applied to corporations.[91]

---

[84] Tiley (1999 p. 134).   [85] Income Tax Act 2007, ss. 836 and 837.
[86] Income Tax Act 1803 (43 Geo. 3 c. 122), ss. 127 and 193.
[87] Finance (No. 2) Act 1915, ss. 38–45. Excess Profits Duty applied to all trades and business meeting certain criterion and not just corporations.
[88] Finance Act 1920, s. 52.   [89] Finance Act 1937, ss. 19–25.
[90] Finance (No. 2) Act 1939, Part III.
[91] Finance Act 1946, ss. 36 and 44 (renaming 'National Defence Contribution' as 'Profits Tax') and Finance Act 1947, s. 31 (exempting individuals and partnerships from Profits Tax).

Throughout these additional charges, corporations remained subject to income tax, which was fully credited to shareholders on distribution.[92] It is only during the Profits Tax era that there was a clear impediment to an individual seeking to income split through the payment of dividends by the family company.[93]

In 1965 the income tax and Profits Tax applicable to corporations was replaced with corporation tax.[94] This tax was not creditable to shareholders and so the result was a full classical system. In such a context, there was increased impetus for family members to seek to income split through wages paid by family companies rather than through dividends distributed by them. A dividend tax credit system was reintroduced in 1973, with the credit typically fixed at the basic rate of income tax.[95] The form of the system changed from 1999 but for present purposes its substance remained.[96] Accordingly, the level of dividend relief varied at times depending on the relationship between the corporate tax rate and the basic rate of income tax.[97]

The level of dividend relief became particularly high for companies with small profits (many family companies would fall into this category). Provision for a lower rate for such companies was made with the introduction of the new dividend relief system in 1973.[98] In that year the small

---

[92] From 1947, when the rate of profits tax increased from 5 per cent to 25 per cent, a corporation was not subject to profits tax to the extent that its profits were apportioned to individual shareholders for Sur-tax purposes under Finance Act 1922, s. 21 or the provisions that replaced it; Finance Act 1947, s. 31. As subsequent distributions from previously attributed profits were exempt in the hands of shareholders, e.g. Finance Act 1922, s. 21(4), the result seems to have been that these shareholders were fully relieved from Profits Tax and any economic double taxation. The same system applied with respect to the earlier Corporation Profits Tax; Finance Act 1922, s. 21(5).

[93] Generally, see Harris (1996, pp. 73–9 and 89).

[94] Finance Act 1965, ss. 46–89 and Sch. 11–20.

[95] Finance Act 1972, Part V. The exceptions were financial year 1973 (when the basic rate was 38.75 per cent and the tax credit was 30 per cent of the grossed up amount) and financial year 1993 (when the basic rate was 25 per cent and the tax credit was 22.5 per cent of the grossed up amount). From 1993 to 1998, dividends were subject to the lower rate of 20 per cent instead of the basic rate and the dividend tax credit was pegged to that lower rate.

[96] Finance (No 2) Act 1997, ss. 30–6 and Finance Act 1998, ss. 30–2 and Sch. 3. The new system reduced the tax credit to one-ninth of the distribution but reduced dividend tax rates to 10 per cent (lower rate shareholders) and 32.5 per cent (higher rate shareholders).

[97] The classical nature of the system was most substantial from 1979 to 1982 when there was 22 per cent between the corporate tax rate (52 per cent) and the basic rate (30 per cent). Dividend relief was highest for 1991 and 1992 when there was 8 per cent between the corporate tax rate (33 per cent) and the basic rate (25 per cent).

[98] Finance Act 1972, s. 95.

profits rate was 42 per cent instead of 52 per cent, which substantially increased the level of dividend relief for these companies.[99] But, interestingly, increasing the level of dividend relief was not the reason for the introduction of the lower rate. Rather, it was the situation of small companies *not* distributing dividends that prompted the relief. The Revenue noted that small companies –

> because of their size found it more difficult to raise capital than larger companies, and therefore [are] required to retain more of their profits; 'Such companies . . . benefit less from the reduction in the rate of tax on distributed profits than they would lose on paying a higher rate of tax on their retentions'.[100]

There was a substantial drop in the small profits rate to 30 per cent for financial year 1983. This pegged the small profits rate to the basic rate of income tax and meant that the level of dividend relief for these companies became 100 per cent. A classical element returned when the dividend tax credit rate was reduced in 1993 but the small profits rate remained at 25 per cent (the basic rate). However, since 1993 the small profits rate further reduced and from 2000 it became possible to get in excess of full dividend relief for profits derived through a small company.[101]

As noted above, before 1973 the incentive to income split within a family was retarded by the fact that a wife's income was attributed to her husband. From 1973 it was possible for a wife to be taxed separately on her earned income, which would have provided the possibility of income splitting by employing the wife in the family company. There would be no general incentive to income split between husband and wife in the form of distribution of dividends until the introduction of full separate taxation of spouses in 1990. This separation combined with the application of the small profits rate to most family companies (thereby typically producing full dividend relief) would make income splitting through the family company in the form of dividends more beneficial than ever before. Indeed, for a number of years, including those in issue in *Jones v Garnett*,

---

[99] Finance Act 1974, s. 10.
[100] Archives of the Inland Revenue on the Finance Bill 1972, Vol. 1, p. 551, quoting the Select Committee in United Kingdom (1972). The cost of the reintroduction of dividend relief in 1973 was partly offset by a general increase in the rate of corporation tax.
[101] This occurred with the introduction of the starting rate, which was 10 per cent for 2000 and 2001, and nil until it was abolished in 2006. In any case, from 2002 the small profits rate was 19 per cent, which of itself produced somewhat more than full dividend relief.

it has been more beneficial for the spouse with the lower income to derive dividends through a family company rather than wages from it.[102] To a more limited extent, the same is true of the family member making the major contribution to the company.

The major weapon for the Inland Revenue against income splitting through the use of a company and the distribution of dividends is the settlement provisions. Before 1990 there are a number of examples where the courts were willing to apply the provisions to corporate structures involving what might be considered to be a family company. An early example is *Copeman v Coleman*, where the father's business was incorporated in 1933 and in 1937 preference shares were issued to his children.[103] Dividends were declared and the children claimed a refund of excess dividend tax credits. Lawrence J had no difficulty in finding that the settlement provisions attributed the dividends to the father.[104]

Crossland v Hawkins involved an actor providing his services through a company.[105] The shares in the company were held by a trust for the benefit of the actor's children. Profits from the provision of the actor's services were distributed as dividends in 1956 and applied to the children's benefit by the trustees. The children claimed a refund of excess dividend tax credits. The Court of Appeal applied the settlement provisions to treat the dividends as the income of the actor. A more direct case was *Butler v Wildin*, where, as in *Copeman v Coleman*, the children were issued the shares directly.[106] This was not a classic case of providing services through a company but rather one of land development where the father and his brother took all the risk and co-ordinated matters. The children claimed a refund of excess dividend tax credits on dividends declared in 1985. Vinelott J had no difficulties in attributing the dividends to the father under the settlement provisions.

Post-1990 there are two examples of the Revenue seeking to apply the settlement provisions to income splitting through the distribution of dividends to spouses. The first was *Young v Pearce*, where two husbands arranged for their trading company to issue preference shares to their wives in 1990, i.e. the year in which spouses began to be taxed separately

---

[102] This is because National Insurance Contributions are imposed on wages but not dividend income. The situation became particularly advantageous when, from 2000, the small profits and starting rates of themselves produced more than full dividend relief.

[103] (1939) 22 TC 594 (KB).

[104] For background to this case and the way in which companies were being used to income split between family members see Stopforth (1992, pp. 103–4).

[105] (1960) 39 TC 493 (CA).   [106] [1989] STC 22 (Ch D).

from their husbands.[107] Dividends were distributed in 1990 to 1992 on the preference shares, which were sufficient to ensure that the wives would not be in a position to claim excess dividend tax credits. Nevertheless, the Revenue sought to apply the settlement provisions and allocate the dividends to the husbands. Vinelott J had no difficulty in applying these provisions. In particular, the wives had not paid full value for the preference shares and these shares constituted wholly or substantially a right to income.

The second post-1990 application is *Jones v Garnett*, the facts of which are outlined above. The importance of this case is that Mrs Jones paid full value for her shares and made a substantial contribution to the company. This case highlights the difficulties caused by the 1990 change to separate taxation of spouses. The only obvious amendment made to the settlement provisions as a result of this change was to exclude outright gifts (that are not wholly or substantially a right to income) from the scope of the provisions.[108] There were two core issues in this case. The first was whether the settlement included not just the issue of shares and appointment of Mr Jones as director but also included Mr Jones working at an undervalue. The second was whether ordinary shares are wholly or substantially a right to income. The Court of Appeal answered 'no' to both these issues but the House of Lords answered 'yes' to the first and 'no' to the second.

11.4 Retained profits of the family company

Companies are artificial persons and may act only through individuals. In the case of a family company, this will usually involve acting through family members. It follows that in the typical case all the profits of a family company are in some shape or form derived from the family members that set it up and operate it, whether through the labour of family members, their capital or the opportunities they provide. In such a case it would be difficult to apply transfer pricing style provisions between a family company and its family members. Family members would not work at an undervalue for third parties and they would not risk their capital and transfer their opportunities unless they were to derive the profits. So a

---

[107] [1996] STC 743 (Ch D).
[108] See Tiley (2006b p. 298) and references cited therein discussing Finance Act 1989, s. 108. This provision is now Income Tax (Trading and Other Income) Act 2005, s. 626.

market value rule could result in virtually all the profits of the family company being allocated to family members.

Where the family company distributes its profits, it naturally falls out of the picture and the analysis focuses on how the dividends are distributed between family members compared to their contribution to the company. However, where the company retains its profits the investigation is rather one of enquiring whether or not the company's retained profits might be allocated to family members irrespective of distribution (as might be the case if transfer pricing rules were applied to their full extent).

If the corporate tax rate is at or near the highest individual marginal tax rate, it matters little whether there is an allocation of retained profits of the family company to the family members. There is no opportunity for tax deferral and families may be expected to ensure that the company derives or retains few profits (and the company would be funded with loans or equity contributions). If there is dividend relief, the family company may simply distribute all of its profits (see section 11.3). If there is a classical system, it might be expected that the family company will have few profits because of deductible payments made to family members whether through wages (see section 11.2), interest or otherwise. But if the corporate tax rate is substantially less than that of dominant family members, there will be an incentive to shelter corporate profits from taxation through retention in the family company.

As mentioned above, until 1911 there was no difference between the tax rate applicable to individuals and that applicable to companies.[109] However, Super-tax changed this because companies were not subject to it. Retaining profits in a company, therefore, would enable high rate tax-payers to avoid the imposition of the higher Super-tax rates. For example, in 1914 the income tax rate increased to 8.33 per cent and the highest rate of Super-tax rose to 8.89 per cent, meaning a high rate individual could reduce their tax by half by retaining profits in a company. The distortion remained broadly similar until rates peaked in 1920 at 30 per cent income tax and 30 per cent Super-tax. The situation began to concern the Chancellor as early as March 1914.[110] Josiah Stamp (then first class inspector of the Revenue) recorded a note of a meeting with the Chancellor of 30 March:

---

[109] Taxpayers could ensure the use of personal allowances buy drawing sufficient wages from the company or causing it to pay sufficient dividends and reclaim the dividend tax credits.

[110] Interestingly, the US had introduced a rule to deal with this problem in its 1913 income tax; Tariff Act of 1913, 38 Stat. 114, chap. 16, Section II.A, Subdivision 2.

The Chancellor informed me that he wanted some information on Income Tax matters that it was inadvisable to discuss on the telephone. He and Mr Masterman had had brought to their notice several cases of *private* Companies ('firms' to all intents and purposes) in which the proprietors were evading Super-tax by keeping down the declared dividends to a low figure and investing the profits in the name of the Company . . .

He asked what method I should suggest for treating these companies as firms. I suggested that, without reflection, a division of the total Income Tax assessment, after prior allocations, in the ration of the shares in question, might meet the case. He asked for a scheme and a statement of the probable yield to be furnished to him.[111]

There follows a note pointing out the similar income tax treatment of firms and companies but how this differed when it came to claiming abatements and the imposition of Super-tax. The note pointed out that, at that time, dividends received from small companies were at a disadvantage, as they were not earned income (subject to lower rates at the time), whereas the profits of a firm might be. The note continued to consider problems of an apportionment of profits for Super-tax where the company had issued varying interests such as debentures, preference shares, ordinary shares or deferred shares. It concluded that '[i]t is therefore not practicable to represent the interest of any individual in a Company in every case by a simple fraction of the total capital'. Nevertheless, the note proceeded to provide three examples of a rule that might be used for apportionment purposes. The note made a rough estimate of the loss of Super-tax through retention at £99,000.

Subsequent correspondence thought the proposals gave rise to 'grave administrative problems' and if put into effect would have to 'give the Special Commissioners power to determine *ad hoc* the interest of the shareholder concerned . . .'[112] The Revenue finally corresponded to the Chancellor, Mr Lloyd George, on this matter by letter of 28 April 1914. It concluded:

I am not prepared with any workable scheme for getting over the difficulties, so that I hope that your Budget speech will not announce that you are dealing with this subject.[113]

Here it seems the matter lay until the Royal Commission of 1920. The Commission noted:

[111] Archives of the Inland Revenue on the Finance Bill 1914, Vol. 1, p. 175.
[112] *Ibid.*, pp. 184–8.   [113] *Ibid.*, p. 218.

In the case of what is known as a 'one man company,' where practically all the shares are held by one shareholder, it will pay that shareholder . . . to refrain from declaring a dividend and to allow the profits of his company to remain undistributed. When this plan is adopted it is sometimes varied by the shareholder borrowing from his company the money he needs for his current expenditure . . . held by the Special Commissioners not to be taxable income in his hands . . .[114]

The recommendation was to attribute the retained profits to the shareholders for Super-tax purposes. The legislature acted on this recommendation in s. 21 of the Finance Act 1922 (contemporarily known as the 'one man company provisions'). Section 21 gave the Special Commissioners power to attribute the undistributed profits of a company to its members where they considered that it had 'not distributed a reasonable part of its income . . .' Subsequent distributions of attributed profits were exempt in the hands of shareholders.

The section applied to any company incorporated in the UK since 5 April 1914, with not more than fifty shareholders, which had not issued any of its shares as a result of a public invitation to subscribe for shares and which was under the control of not more than five persons.[115] In Sch. 1 to the Finance Act 1922, the Special Commissioners were instructed to make the apportionment 'in accordance with the respective interests of the members'.[116] While the Special Commissioners had power to enquire as to the beneficial owner of any shares, it does not seem that there were any particular rules that would prevent splitting the attribution by having children hold shares. Here the Revenue would have had to rely on the settlement provisions.[117]

---

[114] United Kingdom (1920, para. 575).
[115] By the time of the consolidation in 1952, the public invitation requirement had become 'a company in which the public is not substantially interested': Income Tax Act 1952, s. 256(1). Note how both this concept and the 'control of not more than five persons' requirement are carried through to the current close company regime: Taxes Act 1988, ss. 414 and 415. Further, the controlled foreign company legislation (which like Finance Act 1922, s. 21 apportions corporate income to shareholders) also inherited the public quotation exception: Taxes Act 1988, s. 748(1)(c) and Sch. 25, para.13.
[116] This rule has a number of similarities with the 1913 US rule referred to above, although the US rule was not limited to corporations controlled by a limited number of shareholders.
[117] This was not a problem in the case of spouses. *IRC v Latilla-Campbell* [1951] AC 421 (HL) held that corporate income apportioned to a wife as shareholder under Finance Act 1922, s. 21 was assessable on the husband under the normal rules attributing income of a wife to her husband (as to which see section 11.1 above). Incidentally, the company whose income was apportioned in this case was F. P. H. Finance Trust Ltd, see text at n. 122.

Things began to be tightened in 1936, when a distinction was made between investment companies and other companies.[118] In 1937 legislation, in the case of an investment company, the Special Commissioners were given a right to disregard the interests of members and rather have regard to rights on winding up.[119] This was tightened further in 1939 to allow the Special Commissioners to make an apportionment to a person that was not a member of an investment company but who was likely to be able to secure that income or assets of the company would be applied to their benefit.[120] This would certainly have been targeted at income splitting through a family company and looks to have been the response of the Revenue to structures such as that in *Chamberlain v IRC* (discussed below).[121] It did not, however, apply to trading companies.

The distinction between investment companies and trading companies gave rise to the interesting case of *F.P.H. Finance Trust Ltd v IRC*.[122] In this case the company had, in the particular accounting period, a small amount of investment income but had suffered a much larger trading loss. The Revenue argued that since its only 'income' was investment income it was an investment company. The House of Lords (Lord Russell of Killowen dissenting) rejected the argument, Viscount Maugham commenting that –

> the sub-section uses the present tense 'consists' and says nothing as to the length of time during which the income has been received by the company. I cannot think that the definition is framed so that a company may be 'an investment company,' say, in January, when its trading business is going badly, but it is not an investment company, say, in March, when its trading business has recovered.[123]

---

[118] Finance Act 1936, s. 20. Some amendment had been made to the 1922 legislation by the Finance Act 1927, ss. 31 and 32.

[119] Finance Act 1937, s. 14(3).   [120] Finance Act 1939, s. 15.

[121] The Archives of the Inland Revenue on the Finance Bill 1939 contain twenty-eight pages (pp. 12–39) on how the Bill sought to prevent 'avoidance of Sur-tax through the use of "one-man" companies in this country'. It continued on p. 12 to note that: '[i]n some cases such avoidance has been found associated with companies carrying on a genuine trade or business, but, particularly in recent years, the characteristic type of company has been an investment company existing for no other reason than tax avoidance.' In seeking to justify the broad discretion given to the Special Commissioners, the Revenue suggested, at p. 36, that 'in the interests of justice to all taxpayers avoidance of taxation must be suppressed, however drastic the remedy may be'.

[122] [1944] AC 285 (HL).

[123] *Ibid.* at pp. 304–5. Lord Atkin, at p. 307, likewise thought that 'the application of the definition requires the examination of the company's activities over a period of certainly more than one year, and that there was no evidence to support the finding that in April

For present purposes, there was only one amendment of interest as these attribution rules made their way through the Income Tax Act 1952, the Finance Act 1965 and the Taxes Act 1970 (discussed above in section 11.1). It involves the jurisdictional scope of the provisions. As noted, the 1922 provision only covered companies incorporated in the UK and so a foreign corporation was excluded even if resident in the UK. When this provision was consolidated in the Income Tax Act 1952, Wheatcroft commented that the exclusion of companies incorporated abroad –

> is not specifically stated in s. 255(1) which only 'includes' the bodies incorporated in the U.K. but formerly 'company' was primarily defined as a company within the Companies Acts . . . and although this was not repeated in I.T.A, 1952, there is a presumption that no change was intended as that statute was a consolidating statute.[124]

Wheatcroft added that the company would be 'brought within the ambit of the settlement provisions relating to transfers of income abroad . . .' and so the exemption would be of 'little use to the tax avoider'.[125]

On the introduction of corporation tax on companies, in place of income tax and Profits Tax, by the Finance Act 1965 the concept of the so-called 'surtax direction' was continued, with greater sophistication, in the close company apportionment provisions of that Act.[126] The 1965 provisions applied to any company under the control of five or fewer participators or of participators who were directors and not falling within certain exclusions, one of which was a company not resident in the UK.[127] Thus the parameters of the legislation moved from the place of incorporation of the company, in the 1922 legislation, to the place of residence. The Finance Act 1965 apportionment rules continued into the 1970 consolidation.[128] The attribution was partly relaxed in 1980 with respect

1938 this was an investment company. The opposite view that a company, while still continuing its ordinary trading, may be an investment company one year and a non-investment company the next, popping in and out of the Inland Revenue pigeon-holes as trade was bad or good, seems to me inconsistent with the language used and from a business point of view to be deprecated.'

124 Wheatcroft and Bramwell (1963–, para. 1–1266, n. 14 (release 20:1-ii-67)). Wheatcroft cites *Howard de Walden v IRC* (1941) 30 TC 345 (HL), which was a case in which the House of Lords refused to apply the attribution rules to a foreign company.

125 *Ibid.* at note 15. Those settlement provisions appeared in Income Tax Act 1952, s. 412(7) (now Income Tax Act 2007, Part 13, Ch. 2). They date from Finance Act 1936, s. 18 and Finance Act 1938, s. 28 but are outside the scope of this paper.

126 Finance Act 1965, s. 78.   127 Finance Act 1965, Sch. 18, para. 1(1).

128 Finance Act 1965, s. 78 became Taxes Act 1970, s. 296, replaced by Finance Act 1972, s. 94 and Sch. 16 and then became Taxes Act 1970, Part XI, Ch. III.

to trading income due to the general fall in the highest personal marginal tax rate under the new Conservative government.[129] It was removed entirely in 1989 after the highest personal marginal rate was again reduced to its current level of 40 per cent.[130] In the original Finance Bill for that year, special provisions were included relating to a new type of close company to be known as a close investment holding company. Such a company was to be subject to special rules to neutralise the tax advantages otherwise occurring on the abolition of the apportionment rules. These were dropped and all that remained was a provision preventing a close investment holding company taking advantage of the small companies rate of corporation tax[131] and a provision restricting the refund of excess dividend tax credits on distributions of such companies.[132]

Outside of this attribution regime, Sur-tax provided a general incentive for companies to retain their profits. Indeed, between 1947 and 1956 this incentive was added to through relief from the full rate of Profits Tax for companies that retained their profits. Retention was emphasised further with the introduction of corporation tax and the classical system in 1965. The reintroduction of dividend relief in 1973 eased a little this incentive toward retention by increasing the corporate tax rate and reducing the amount of tax collected on distribution.

At present the corporate tax rate of 28 per cent is substantially lower than the highest individual marginal rate of 40 per cent. But in the context of family companies, often the most relevant rate is that applicable to companies with small profits. This rate is currently half the highest individual marginal rate (similar to that which prompted the attribution regime in 1922), although set to rise to 22 per cent in the next few years. This creates a powerful incentive to retain profits in a company, unless they can be distributed to basic rate shareholders. More than this, it creates a substantial incentive to split income not just between family members but also between family members and the family company. For most family members, their basic rate tax band ends at about £40,000 but with the family company it ends at £300,000 and even then only goes up to 30 per cent and not 40 per cent. Family members can use

---

[129] See Finance Act 1980, s. 44.

[130] Finance Act 1989, s. 103. Also see Tiley (2005b, p. 958).

[131] See Taxes Act 1988, s. 13A. The forethought present here is slightly ironic given more recent controversies over access to the small companies rate.

[132] Finance Act 1989, s.106 (repealed on the abolition of the refund of tax credits).

the family company to pay them income up to their basic rate tax band and then shelter the remainder from higher rate tax by retaining it in the company.

Since the end of direct attribution in 1989, the only possible weapon that the Revenue has to challenge this form of income splitting is again the settlement provisions; but is this really available to them? Could the settlement provisions be applied to the retained profits of a family company? As pointed out in section 11.1, it seems unlikely that they were intended to apply in such a situation since when they were introduced in 1922 they were accompanied by the rule attributing retained profits for Super-tax purposes. Further, the amendments to the attribution rules in 1939 (discussed above) seem to have been particularly targeted at income splitting through retained profits in a family company and they lasted until the end of attribution in 1989. There is no case in which the Revenue has sought to apply the settlement provisions to retained profits of a company and the issue raises a number of uncertainties.

The first uncertainty is whether a family member working at an undervalue for their company can amount to an arrangement, and therefore potentially a settlement.[133] While the ad hoc nature of the services provided in *Jones v Garnett* raised some difficulty in this regard,[134] if there is an express arrangement for the provision of the services, particularly if it is fixed for a number of years, this should be capable of constituting a settlement: *Crossland v Hawkins* and *IRC v Mills*.[135]

However, there would still need to be an element of bounty for the arrangement to constitute a settlement. Is it possible to confer bounty on an artificial person such as a company? Companies are separate legal persons and this would support an argument that they can be the beneficiary of bounty. If this is accepted then there may be a settlement and issues move to the operative provisions of the Income Tax (Trading and other Income) Act 2005 (ITTOIA), s. 624(1). There is no attribution to the family member settlor unless the income arising under the settlement (in the current case the company profits arising from the exploitation of the family member's services) arises from 'property in which the settlor has an interest'. Technically, the income of the settlement would arise from the provision of the family member's services. Could that

---

[133] ITTOIA, s. 620(1).
[134] The Court of Appeal thought that on the facts it could not, whereas the House of Lords said that it could.
[135] (1960) 39 TC 493 (CA) and [1975] AC 38 (HL), respectively.

constitute 'property' and, if so, would the family member have an 'interest' in it?

It is submitted that a formal agreement to provide services, such as those in *Crossland v Hawkins* and *IRC v Mills*, may constitute property. An ad hoc arrangement such as that in *Jones v Garnett* is more difficult and seems unlikely to meet the threshold of 'property'. However, even in a case like *Jones v Garnett*, if there is a 'settlement', the investment of the retained profits by the family company would constitute 'property' and so income arising from this retention might be covered even if income arising from the direct exploitation of the services is not.

As for the retention of an 'interest' in the property, if the separate entity approach of the company is adopted it may be argued that the company is the only person with an interest in its property. It is fundamental to company law that only the company has an interest in its property. The shareholders have no interest in company property.[136] However, ITTOIA, s. 625(1) extends the meaning of an interest in property to any circumstance in which the property or any related property 'will, or may, become' payable to the settlor. There seems little doubt that a family member that is a shareholder would have an interest in the company's property based on this extension, at least because of the possibility of distribution or liquidation.

These issues are highlighted by the difficult case of *Chamberlain v IRC*.[137] In that case, the Revenue needed to establish that the 'income arising under the settlement' was the income of an investment company (the shares in which were held by trusts for the benefit of the taxpayer's children). This meant that 'the property comprised in the settlement' had to be the property held by the company (shares in another company). The House of Lords held that the property properly comprised in the settlement was the funds invested by the trusts (i.e. the shares in the investment company) and not the assets of the investment company itself. This is understandable in a situation in which the trusts seem to have paid at least a genuine price for the shares in the investment company and the taxpayer and his brother retained shares in the investment company. Further, the taxpayer and his brother did not work at an undervalue for the investment company, at least not directly. The situation under consideration is far from the facts of *Chamberlain v IRC*, which seems

---

[136] *Macaura v Northern Assurance Co Ltd* [1925] AC 619 (HL).
[137] (1943) 25 TC 317 (HL). This case was decided under Finance Act 1938, s. 38, which incorporates differences from the present legislation. The case is analysed by Vinelott J. in *Young v Pearce* [1996] STC 743 (Ch D) at pp. 751–4.

no comprehensive bar to the application of the settlement provisions to retained profits of a family company.

11.5 Disposal of shares in the family company

The final situation for consideration is an extension of the situation considered in section 11.4. If there is an incentive to retain profits in the family company, that incentive may be countered by the need of family members for cash. Instead of paying out dividends, the family company may retain its profits and the family members sell their shares outside the family (the presumed scenario). This can achieve an effective income split between family members such as where the corporate profits are attributable to a family member working at an undervalue but the shares are held by other family members who derive gains on the disposal of shares. Assuming the purchaser causes the company to distribute the retained profits, this situation encompasses the classic dividend strip. This may be the 'full strip' (bond-wash) such as where the purchaser strips the profits and then sells the shares back to family members or the family members may decide to part with the company permanently.

Whether there is an incentive to engage in this sort of transaction rather than other forms of income splitting involves the interaction of a number of factors. The first is any incentive towards retention (considered in s. 11.4). The second (related to the first) is the tax treatment of the family member if they did derive dividends (considered in section 11.3). The third is the comparative tax treatment of the family member if they sell their shares, for present purposes assumed to be a capital receipt. The fourth is the comparative tax treatment of the purchaser with respect to the receipt of the dividends. A final matter to consider is the tax treatment of the purchaser if they later decide to further sell the shares.

Until the introduction of Super-tax in 1911, there would have been some but not a great incentive to dividend strip. The tax rate of the company was at least as high as that of the shareholder. Further, shareholders were not taxable on the receipt of dividends as the company's tax liability franked the dividend (the situation was different for foreign securities). Capital gains on the disposal of shares were not taxed and so there was some symmetry between the treatment of dividends and gains on the disposal of shares. However, a lack of symmetry might arise in two respects. The first was for those persons that could claim a refund of excess dividend tax credits. These would be individuals entitled to exemption or abatement but potentially more importantly exempt institutions. The second was for financial institutions that purchased the shares and held them on revenue account. Such an institution would not be taxable on any dividend received (for the same reason as other shareholders) but might claim a loss on the loss of value caused by the dividend distribution when the shares were further sold.

The introduction of Super-tax would have added to this incentive. The tax issues surrounding the purchaser remained but now there was an added benefit for the seller. Like income tax, Super-tax only applied to income and not capital gains. So it became possible to avoid Super-tax by retaining profits in the company and selling the shares instead of distributing dividends. The apportionment rules introduced in 1922 and discussed in section 11.4 above would have addressed some of these issues but not, for example, the problem of losses incurred by a financial institution on disposal of shares after the strip.

The matter was first addressed in 1927 by, on determination by the Special Commissioners, deeming income on stocks and securities to accrue day-to-day over a year and on sale part of the sale proceeds might be treated as that income and fall into total income.[138] However, the provision only applied for the purposes of Super-tax and not standard rate income tax. At this time the Revenue had –

> no definite information as to the extent to which this form of avoidance is practised, but it is obvious that its potentialities are great and it is known that, in certain cases, very large amounts of stock have been sold and re-bought in this way, presumably with a view to avoiding Super-tax.[139]

It seems that the Revenue misjudged the situation somewhat because by 1937 the Revenue was noting that 'bond-washing'[140] might result in a loss of both Sur-tax and income tax at the standard rate –

> the income tax that has been lost in recent years has been practically all at the standard rate . . . and it is estimated that the annual loss of tax at the standard rate is in the neighbourhood of £m.1.[141]

There was some problem with the sale of foreign securities to foreigners but '[t]he bondwashing with financial concerns at home is of much

---

[138] Finance Act 1927, s. 33.
[139] Archives of the Inland Revenue on the Finance Bill 1927, p. 74.
[140] This was the generic term and covered not only the stripping of dividends from shares but also interest from bonds.
[141] Archives of the Inland Revenue on the Finance Bill 1937, p. 150.

greater importance . . .'[142] The essential problem was with the deduction claimed by the washer (stripper) on disposal. Section 12 of the Finance Act 1937 addressed the situation by treating the original owner as if they had continued to be the owner of the securities. A restriction on this provision was that it required a pre-existing arrangement to reacquire the securities. A supplementary provision was introduced in the following year to similarly treat someone who sold the right to dividends on shares (without selling the shares) as continuing to derive the dividends.[143]

It was not until 1955 that the situation was perceived to have deteriorated again to a situation in which action was required. Section 4 of the Finance (No. 2) Act 1955 took action against 'dividend stripping' transactions. These are transactions involving the buying of shares, distribution of profits accumulated prior to the purchase and subsequent sale of the shares. They are distinguished from 'bond-washing' by the absence of an agreement to return the shares to the seller. The rules were targeted at 'financial concerns', where the risk was with the potential deduction of the loss on the subsequent disposal of shares, and at exempt institutions (including superannuation funds and charities), where the risk was with claims for refund of dividend tax credits.[144] The effect of the section was to bring the dividend into charge without dividend tax credits for financial concerns (so as to offset the subsequent loss) and, in the case of exempt institutions, just to bring the dividend into charge.

These 1955 measures were found not to cover all possibilities for dividend stripping and were supplemented in 1958[145] and again in 1959.[146] Nevertheless, there was concern and in 1960 the legislature changed track from the existing practice of attempting to 'stop dividend stripping and bond washing by specific legislation directed at particular devices as they come to light'. Rather, the government decided to introduce 'a general anti-avoidance provision against the avoidance of tax by transactions in securities'.[147] The Revenue suggested that such an approach could be justified by reference to general anti-abuse rules in Australia and New Zealand and Canada.[148] There was further reference to the general anti-avoidance

---

[142] Ibid., p. 151.
[143] Finance Act 1938, s. 24. The provision reversed, in part, the decision in Paget v IRC (1938) 21 TC 677 (CA). See also Tiley (2005b, p. 1049).
[144] Archives of the Inland Revenue on the Finance Bill (Nos. 1 and 2) 1955, pp. 96–7.
[145] Finance Act 1958, ss. 18–19.   [146] Finance Act 1959, ss. 23–6.
[147] Archives of the Inland Revenue on the Finance Bill 1960, pp. 114–15.
[148] Regarding the general anti-avoidance rules of Australia and New Zealand and their English origins, see Harris (2007a) and Harris (2007b) and the references cited therein.

provision in the Profits Tax (s. 32 of the Finance Act 1951, discussed in section 11.2 above) with the suggestion that as a result the proposed provision (particularly as a result of its narrower scope) did not 'break new ground'.[149] Section 28 of the Finance Act 1960 empowered the Commissioners to counteract tax advantages arising from certain transactions in securities. Importantly, it targeted not just the stripper but could also apply to the family member selling to the stripper, ensuring they were taxable including subject to Sur-tax.

Moreover, it impacted also on those disposals which did not envisage a dividend-strip. As already discussed, the retention of profits within the company deferred the taxation of those profits in the hands of the shareholder until such time as they were distributed by way of dividend. We have seen how the legislature sought to limit this effect by the provisions on close-company apportionment, but to the extent that these provisions did not apply, the sale of shares in a company would be treated as a capital sum and would be subject only to capital gains tax, after 1965, and to no such taxation before that. It was this circumstance which was addressed by circumstance D in s. 28 of the Finance Act 1960. This applied where a person receives a consideration which represents the value of assets which are available for distribution by way of dividend, e.g. retained profits within the company, and receives the consideration in such a form that he does not pay or bear tax on it as income. An assessment could be made to counteract the tax advantage obtained. There was an exclusion for disposals made for bona fide commercial reasons or in the ordinary course of making or managing investments and a clearance procedure.

The provisions only applied to companies under the control of not more than five persons and any other company which did not satisfy the condition that its shares or stock are authorised to be dealt in on a stock exchange in the UK, and are so dealt in (regularly or from time to time). This limitation is narrower than it looks at first sight. First, in the case of a company under the control of five or fewer persons there is no exclusion for such a company which is quoted on the stock exchange or in which the public are substantially interested; secondly, any unquoted company will fall within the second definition. However the provision would not apply to any company which was under the control of one or more companies to which the provision would not apply, e.g. the subsidiary of a quoted

---

[149] Archives of the Inland Revenue on the Finance Bill 1960, pp. 117–18.

company not under the control of five or fewer persons would not be within the provision.

The classic example of the application of this provision is the *Cleary* case.[150] Two sisters each owned one-half of the share capital of two companies, M Ltd and G Ltd . They each sold the shares which they held in M Ltd to G Ltd for cash and each received £60,500 being the full value of the shares as ascertained on a valuation of them.[151] They thereafter continued to own all of the issued shares in G Ltd, which now held the shares in M Ltd previously held by the sisters. The difficulties in interpreting the statute are illustrated by the fact that the Special Commissioners, the High Court and the Court of Appeal each came to a different conclusion or to the same conclusion but for different reasons. As Lord Upjohn put it:

> [T]he draftsman has paid no attention to the proper use of language, in relation to companies and their finances, which has been accepted by lawyers and accountants alike for a very long time. For example, in para. (i) he has treated profits, which are 'sums in account' (£180,000 in this case) on the left-hand side of the balance sheet, as synonymous with 'other assets', which are physical or realisable assets on the right-hand side of the balance sheet. He seems to think 'income' and 'reserves', which are really sums in account, are properly described as 'other assets'. This gives rise to a degree of difficulty in the construction of the section.[152]

Finally, the House of Lords upheld the decision of the Court of Appeal holding that the price of the shares was 'received in connection with the distribution of profits' of G Ltd, and that the respondents obtained a tax advantage.

Some sympathy for the taxpayer was expressed in both the Court of Appeal and the House of Lords, where Lord Upjohn, for example, said: 'This may seem a harsh conclusion, as indeed it is, but this is a matter for Parliament.'[153]

The next major development to have impact in relation to dividend stripping was the introduction of capital gains tax, first for short-term

---

[150] *Cleary v IRC* [1968] AC 766 (HL).

[151] An important issue for capital gains purposes and death duty/capital transfer tax purposes in relation to the family company is the valuation of shareholdings in the company. For example, how can allowance be made for the absence of a quoted share price as a comparable or to what extent should shares held by other family members be taken into account in determining the size of holding to be valued? We have regarded this as outside the scope of this paper.

[152] *Cleary v IRC* [1968] AC 766 (HL) at pp. 790–1.   [153] *Ibid.*, at p. 791.

gains in 1962 and then generally from 1965.[154] This introduction would potentially remove the benefit of the family member selling to the stripper. The family company would be subject to tax on its retained profits and then the family member would be subject to capital gains tax on gains on disposal of shares including any part of the gain attributable to increases in the value of the shares resulting from the retention of the profits. This can result in an element of double taxation. The higher the rate of capital gains tax the greater the incentive to seek to income split through mechanisms other than the sale of shares (e.g. the methods considered in sections 11.2 and 11.3).

During the early years capital gains tax was set at a rate of 30 per cent, before 1978 with a potential reduction under the 'half-income rule'. As basic rate income tax could reach 41.25 per cent before progression, deriving capital gains could still be more beneficial than deriving income. This was recognised in the Finance Act 1966, with an extension of the circumstances in which the general anti-dividend stripping rules in the Finance Act 1960 could apply to the selling family member.[155]

When the tax laws were consolidated in 1970, the various rules applying to transactions in securities were amalgamated in Part XVII, Chapter I encompassing the general anti-abuse rule enacted in 1960 and Chapter II the remaining provisions.[156] These were transferred, subject to various amendments (that are not relevant for present purposes), to the 1988 consolidation and, at least the general anti-abuse rule implemented in 1961, to the Income Tax Act 2007.[157]

Two other developments in the context of capital gains tax are worthy of mention. In 1988 the rate of capital gains tax was aligned with the top rate for income tax. This would reduce the incentive to dispose of shares in family companies pregnant with profits (indexation was a counter factor). It will be recalled that this was the time that the attribution regime was removed for profits in closely held companies. 1997 saw the introduction of taper relief and the increase in taper for business assets means that many family members might secure a 75 per cent reduction in their chargeable

---

[154] Finance Act 1962, Part II, Ch. II and Finance Act 1965, Part III, respectively. A wife's capital gains were attributed to her husband in a manner similar to that in the income tax; Finance Act 1965, Sch. 10, para. 3(1).

[155] Finance Act 1966, s. 39.

[156] Taxes Act 1970, Part XVII. The exception was Finance Act 1927, s. 33, which became Taxes Act 1970, s. 30. This rule and the 1937 and 1938 rules had been consolidated as Income Tax Act 1952, ss. 30, 469 and 470, respectively.

[157] Taxes Act 1988, Part XVII, Chs. I and II. The general anti-abuse rule is in Income Tax Act 2007, Part 13, Ch. 1.

gains when disposing of shares in the family company. The result is an effective maximum tax rate of 10 per cent. This relief has once again provided an incentive to dispose of shares in a family company rather than distribute profits. Further, because of the abolition of attribution in 1988 the incentive applies to more family companies than ever, enticing them to run the gauntlet of the highly complex anti-abuse provisions.[158]

Despite the elaborateness of the anti-abuse provisions just considered, they would not of themselves appear to entitle the Revenue to attribute a capital gain made by one family member on sale of shares in the family company to another family member (e.g. one working for the company at an undervalue). However, the capital gains tax legislation has its own pared down version of the income tax settlement provisions.[159] As under income tax, a settlor has an interest in a settlement if property comprised in the settlement will or may become payable for the benefit of the settlor or the settlor's spouse.

There is no exception for 'outright gifts' between spouses as under the income tax but this is apparently not necessary. The provision requires a chargeable gain to accrue to trustees of the settlement from the disposal of settled property. There is no definition of 'trustee' or 'settlement'. There is a definition of 'settled property' but that requires that property be held on trust (not defined).[160] It would appear to require extreme facts in a situation of the type under consideration to reach a conclusion that the family member disposing of the shares in the family company held them on trust for another family member (e.g. the one working for the family company at an undervalue). In any case, there would be a need to show that the settlor or their spouse could benefit from property comprised in the trust. This would not obviously be the case where the shares are held by, for example, children.

Conclusion

The UK income tax system has at various times, to a great or lesser extent, encouraged (consciously or unconsciously) family members to split income, whether through the use of a family company or otherwise.

---

[158] The more public part of this incentive is the current debate over the tax treatment of private equity funds. For example, see Silsby and Smith (2007). The reintroduction of a flat rate capital gains tax (18%) in 2008 reduces but does not eliminate the incentive to derive capital gains.

[159] Taxation of Chargeable Gains Act 1992, s. 77. This provision was inserted at the same time as separate taxation of spouses was introduced by Finance Act 1988, s. 109 and Sch. 10.

[160] Taxation of Chargeable Gains Act 1992, s. 68.

It has no comprehensive rule against income splitting between family members and yet it is clear that the Revenue have serious concerns as to whether and in what circumstances it might be appropriate. What the system does have is a mismatch of rules that may apply in different contexts depending on the type of income splitting engaged in. These range from the 'wholly and exclusively' requirement in the context of payments by the family company to the potential application of the dividend stripping provisions. Two rather effective rules (in their context) were the attribution of profits of close companies to their shareholders and the attribution of a wife's income to her husband. Both expired at the end of the 1980s. The current key weapon in the Revenue's arsenal, indeed in many cases its only weapon, is the settlements legislation.

In this regard and with respect to the 1990 move to separate taxation of spouses, Tiley notes:

> To allow [one spouse] to transfer, for example, earnings or dividends to [the other spouse], would simply have enabled taxpayers who were not minded to act on a commercial basis to rearrange their income to take the best advantage [from; sic.] the availability of personal allowances and lower ends of the progressive rate structure. The 1988 principles were after all based on separate taxation not aggregation followed by income splitting. Section 660A(6), now s. 626, is the resulting compromise; the transfer of assets is permitted to be effective for income tax purposes between spouses living together but it must be real.[161]

As an express exclusion from the settlement provisions, Tiley is correct. But what is clear from the House of Lords judgment in *Jones v Garnett* is that the settlement provisions cannot be effectively used to prevent all forms of income splitting between family members, particularly through the use of a company. These provisions were largely designed to prevent the transfer of income from capital[162] where the transferor could possibly benefit from that income in the future or where the transfer was made to minor children. They were not so clearly designed to cover the splitting of remuneration for services, especially through the legal construct of the company or general splitting between spouses. In particular, they were not designed to cover income splitting with the family company in the form of retained profits nor, despite the width of the anti-dividend stripping rules, sale of shares by a family member.

---

[161] Tiley (2006b, p. 299).

[162] 'Alienation of income by means of deeds' is the 1920 Royal Commission's phrase; United Kingdom (1920, para. 576).

As their name suggests, the settlement provisions belong to an era in which the wealthy divided their wealth and income between family members through the use of trusts. In the current services era, these provisions are looking substantially archaic. They currently cause unnecessary uncertainty with respect to the taxation of everyday events, such as those areas covered by this paper.[163]

Whether income splitting between family members is appropriate in order to achieve fairness or whether it must be prevented to enhance fairness and which is the better economic approach is a complex question to which there is no clear answer. The government's present position is that 'individuals involved in these arrangements should pay tax on what is, in substance, their own income and that the legislation should clearly provide for this'.[164] The problem is that families share resources. While it may be clear what a family's 'own income' is (assuming one can identify what is and what is not a family), it cannot be clear what is and what is not a particular family member's 'own income'.

Economists teach us that we simply must account for household production in determining tax policies relating to families.[165] The pay-off for one family member in what is a single economic unit (the family) engaging in market activities is often the provision by another family member of household production. Due to different faculties of family members, some households have greater flexibility in balancing that division between family members than others. It is not at all clear that those families with greater flexibility in this division should be rewarded by paying comparatively less tax. Families share production, they share resources and income, it is arguable that the 'own income' of a family member is their share of 'family income', rather than what can be an even more arbitrary figure determined by a fiction that family members deal with each other at arm's length.[166]

In an area as critical and fundamental as this, the government stands to be crticised no matter which way it moves. But it is useful briefly to consider the options open to it. One option, which may be viewed as

---

[163] The government has acknowledged this in the Ministerial Statement of 26 July 2007 following the House of Lords decision in *Jones v Garnett*. The statement acknowledged 'the need for the Government to ensure that there is greater clarity in the law regarding its position on the tax treatment of "income-splitting"'. United Kingdom (2007).

[164] United Kingdom (2007).   [165] For example, Apps and Rees (2007).

[166] Conceptually, there is an analogy between splitting income between family members and using formulary apportionment for attributing income to members of a corporate group (family of companies).

the existing system, is to do nothing and allow family members to adjust their situations to income split, if they can. The apparent unfairness of this system is that some families, particularly those with family businesses, are in a better position to achieve 'self-help' income splitting than others. The same can be true of those with capital income, subject to the settlements legislation. The families with least flexibility in this regard are those where the family's income is derived predominantly by one family member from employment.

A second option is to aggregate family income and either tax the family or apportion the income between family members according to some formula and tax them.[167] This has some potential to create fairness between families, though it is not clear that it will produce the most effective economic outcome. It also raises the difficult issue of identifying who is in and who is out of a family. Diametrically opposed to this formulary apportionment system is the system which the government seems to currently prefer. This is to impose transfer pricing rules to arrangements between family members to get at what is a market value allocation of income between them. The problem with this system is that it has a high compliance cost and relationships and activities within a family and the manner in which a family decides who will engage in market activities very often have no market equivalent. This system also takes no account of the family production payoff in deciding 'whose income' it is.

A final option worth consideration is to accept that none of these approaches produces fairness. Rather, the fairness might be in making income splitting available to all economic units. This could be achieved by primarily accepting individual taxation but, as in the first option, permitting families to arrange their affairs so as to engage in income splitting, e.g. as the Joneses did. The government's position is that this is not fair to those families that cannot so arrange their affairs. But instead of seeking to stop the likes of the Joneses from income splitting, the government might grant those families that cannot a right to elect to pool their income and then split it out according to a formulary apportionment. The result would be something like the US's tick-the-box regime for companies. That system has caused dramatic difficulties in the international field but rarely is criticism levied at it from a domestic fairness perspective. Certainly, it should not be dismissed as a possibility because of its international problems. Families differ from companies in at least one important respect; families are real and so less mobile than companies.

---

[167] 'Family' or household income is already amalgamated for the purposes of the family tax credit rules.

It is hoped that the government will take time to analyse and weigh these options carefully (as well as any others that come to light), including the economics and the implications for simplicity and fairness. At the least, it should make a clear and reasoned decision. As noted, the government stands to be crticised no matter which way it moves. But at least that criticism should be based on a simple difference of opinion. The current problem is that it is not clear from the legislation that the legislature has an opinion at all and that causes unacceptable uncertainty. It is hoped that the government will take time in the consultation process following *Jones v Garnett* to formulate a clear policy on all the issues covered by this paper and, in particular, the issue of transfer pricing between family members. As a bare minimum, if income splitting within a family and through a family company is not to be tolerated, it is time the settlement provisions were morphed into something more fit for purpose. In December 2007 the UK government released a consultation document and draft legislation to prevent income splitting through company distributions.

EPILOGUE
ESTABLISHING THE FOUNDATIONS OF TAX LAW IN UK UNIVERSITIES

JUDITH FREEDMAN

If G. S. A. Wheatcroft initiated the academic teaching of tax law in UK universities, then John Tiley ensured its continuation. Professor Tiley has been the face of UK academic tax law for the past thirty years, both in domestic and international arenas. At home he has dealt with other law teachers who were dubious about the role of taxation in the curriculum, with the professions and with government. At an international level he has ably represented the UK in gatherings of tax teachers.[1] It seems inconceivable that he will cease making a contribution to teaching and writing on his retirement, but this marks a suitable point at which to assess the position we have reached with tax teaching in the UK and to consider the future.

In his own fascinating survey of the development of UK tax law teaching, '50 years: Tax, Law and Academia', written to celebrate the fiftieth anniversary of the *British Tax Review*, Tiley concluded the state of the tax academy is mixed and that, whilst –

> there is every reason to think that tax can and will survive as an area of study in which both research and teaching of the highest quality can be carried on in our universities . . . its place can, at times, seem precarious.[2]

It is hard to argue with his conclusion without seeming complacent (and complacency would certainly be misguided) but Tiley is over-modest in his article about his own contribution and about the progress he has

---

[1] Professor Tiley was President of the Society of Public Teachers of Law in 1995–6. The fact that a tax lawyer was elected to this prestigious role was both a personal tribute and represented a certain degree of recognition of tax law as a discipline. He was also a founding member of the European Association of Tax Professors (EATLP) and has served on the Academic Committee as the UK representative and latterly the Vice Chair of the Academic Committee. He is a member of the Tax Law Review Committee of the Institute for Fiscal Studies and the Steering Committee providing strategic guidance on the Government's Tax Law Rewrite project.

[2] Tiley (2006a, p. 248).

fronted over the last two decades. Without his vision and his seminal contributions to the literature, there might well be no tax being taught in the UK law schools today. Now, however, the question is not, as it used to be, whether tax law has a place in the legal curriculum at all but rather how it might best be taught and studied, and whether standards can be maintained and suitable staff and students recruited. These are difficulties still and, it seems more so for tax law than in other areas of law, but at least tax law is widely accepted as both an undergraduate and graduate subject in the law school curriculum.[3] According to a 2001 survey, tax law is now in the curriculum of around half the UK universities teaching law.[4] There is some cause for concern that retiring tax lawyers will not be replaced in some universities,[5] but, equally, since 2001 there have been new appointments in tax law at a number of law schools and, in welcome developments, some universities are employing more than one tax law specialist[6] and interdisciplinary tax research and activities are expanding.[7]

There are new challenges facing law generally as a discipline in UK higher education and research and these include plans to fund universities in different ways in the future. The approaches to be used are still under discussion. We have yet to complete the 2008 Research Assessment Exercise, based on peer review, which is currently the basis for research funding.[8] It seems likely, however, that the post-2008 methods will rest more heavily than at present on funding delivered through the research councils. This presents real difficulties for law, since there is no dedicated law research council, and legal research has to be fitted, sometimes uneasily, into the criteria of either the Economic and Social Research Council (ESRC) or the Arts and Humanities Research Council (AHRC). According to the AHRC website:

---

[3] See Park (1997).
[4] Figures taken from a survey by A. Miller, cited in Tiley (2006a, p. 233).
[5] See Kerridge (2001). Kerridge, writing in 2001, had a pessimistic view of the future of tax law in the UK universities. It would clearly be wrong to assume that there will not be setbacks and there is much more work yet to do with some law schools.
[6] Notably, Cambridge, KCL, QM and LSE in London, Oxford and Warwick.
[7] For example, the Tax History Conference at the Cambridge Centre for Tax Law. The long-running interdisciplinary tax seminar at the LSE run by the economics and law departments, has been joined by activities between the Said Business School, Economics and Law at the Oxford University Centre for Business Taxation and between accountants and lawyers at Warwick University. The Tax Research Network runs an annual interdisciplinary conference.
[8] For further information see www.hefce.ac.uk/research/assessment/.

Law may include doctrinal, theoretical, empirical, comparative or other studies of law and legal phenomena. The AHRC shares with the ESRC responsibility for studies in law. The AHRC focuses on studies where the focus is on the content or procedures of the law. The ESRC has an interest in funding socio-legal studies, which reflect a focus on the socio-economic impact of the law and the legal system.[9]

At first glance this might seem to cover just about everything an academic lawyer might want to do, but the problem is that lawyers are being asked to specify a methodology for their work in order to obtain funding, and this methodology tends to be judged by analogy with methodologies in other disciplines. The template offered by the research councils suggests a scenario in which law must adopt one or other methodology. It could be argued, however, that this creates an unnecessary straightjacket for legal research. Surely any project with a focus on the socio-economic impact of the law should *also* be concerned with the content and procedures of the law? Is that not the point of a lawyer undertaking such an exercise, as opposed to a sociologist or an economist? The stated approach of the research councils (although perhaps not the practice) not only seems to misunderstand legal research but might also result in the subordination of law to other disciplines in the case of interdisciplinary or multi-disciplinary work, since those other disciplines have a more obvious methodological categorisation and the lawyers may just be required to follow suit.

In reality what appears to be happening now is that much academic legal research is embracing 'a pluralism of methodological approaches', in the phrase of McCrudden,[10] and that this may produce its own unique methodology; one that does not fit neatly into the divide agreed upon by the research councils.

These general comments on legal studies apply very strongly in the field of taxation. Tiley's work might be said to be the epitome of the 'hybrid methodology'. His textbook, *Revenue Law*,[11] contains doctrinal analysis of case law and statute at the highest level but at the same time draws upon a wide range of literature taken from history, philosophy, political science, economics and accounting. These are not simple cross-references: this

---

[9] www.ahrc.ac.uk/about/subject_coverage/respanel8.
[10] See McCrudden (2006, p. 642). McCrudden argues that those engaging in doctrinal legal analysis are now much more frequently than before ready to support, and sometimes to test, their doctrinal or theoretical models by drawing on social science influenced information, resulting in this 'methodological pluralism'.
[11] First published by Butterworths in 1976. See now Tiley (2005b).

literature is used to throw light on the legal discussion in a way which is totally natural and integrated. This achieves a healthy pluralistic approach to teaching and research.[12]

McCrudden poses the question of whether 'methodological pluralism' is strength or a weakness. Could it show a 'desire to derive comfort by leavening legal research with undigested parts of other more prestigious disciplines?' In his view this is not the case: rather, it shows 'a mature openness to other disciplines that demonstrates self-confidence'.[13] The fact is, of course, that it depends on how well it is done. There is a danger for tax lawyers that if they attempt to adopt a pluralistic approach they will become second tier social scientists and that they will risk 'alienating many of the practitioners and policymakers who constitute the natural audience for their work'.[14] On the other hand, lawyers have much to contribute by ensuring that those from other disciplines take into account and properly understand legal systems, rights and obligations, relationships, organisations and procedures and consider value systems. The lawyers in turn have much to learn about aims and objectives, economic efficiency, cause and effect and likely behavioural responses from other social sciences. In the area of taxation, lawyers must engage with economists, accountants, political scientists, sociologists and historians and this must be a two-way process. Only then will a unique form of pluralistic legal methodology result rather than a second-rate hotchpotch. There is still much tax writing that is very descriptive (or as Brooks has put it, 'no better than the average manual on how to operate a power tool'[15]) or where the references to context and the literature from other disciplines are superficial, but at its best a pluralistic methodology transcends the limitations of its constituent parts.

In the US, methodological pluralism is rather more problematic for legal academics, who are under greater pressure than in the UK to be part of a 'school of thought' or academic grouping. There is a lively debate in the tax literature about the relative merits of doctrinal law, law and economics and critical tax theory.[16] In North America, tax lawyers are far more likely to have economics training than in the UK and thus this is a dominant school in terms of research, although much of the teaching is quite doctrinal and vocational in orientation. There is little doubt that the degree of learning in economics in the US produces very sophisticated

---

[12] For a more detailed case in favour of such an approach to tax research by this author, see Freedman (2004b).
[13] McCrudden (2006, p. 645).   [14] Livingston (1998, p. 367).   [15] Brooks (1985, p. 446).
[16] See Mehrotra (2005), citing proponents of the various approaches.

scholarship at a level which has not been achieved by UK tax lawyers often (if at all), and that those of us working in the UK have much to learn from this literature. Yet it should be noted that this level of sophistication may have its drawbacks.

Livingston has argued that, whilst the traditional tax law literature, using economic concepts, was good legal scholarship, providing the bridge between theory and practice which only academic lawyers can provide, as the economic concepts become more sophisticated and complex, economics is coming to dominate tax law.[17] As McCrudden points out, some might think this is no bad thing.[18] If, however, we believe that an understanding of law has something distinctive to offer to tax studies, complete domination by economics will represent a serious loss to the academic tax community and also to practitioners and policy makers. Livingston's answer is that tax lawyers should aim for an 'eclectic, interdisciplinary scholarship' that borrows from several fields without being dominated by any and which is also well grounded in non-tax legal scholarship.[19] In other words, he is recommending the type of pluralism of methodological approaches described and applauded by McCrudden and seen in some of the best academic tax literature.

This type of engagement with other disciplines is not easy. Given the pressures on academics to publish, the easiest route by far is to stick to one's own discipline and publish in journals recognised within that discipline. Working with colleagues from other disciplines can be frustrating and time consuming and may lead to output that is hard to place in recognised law reviews. Sometimes lawyers may feel that they are talking a different language from other social scientists; sometimes it is worse than that and the words used appear to be the same but then are discovered to have a different meaning. This does not mean we should give up on interaction and pluralism: in fact is shows how vital it is if we are to produce research which makes a real contribution to the understanding of the role, function and operation of taxation.

This takes us back to Tiley's work. To this author, as a young lecturer thrust into teaching tax for the first time at the LSE in 1982, Tiley's *Revenue Law* was very simply a life-saver. When Butterworths decided to turn the book into a practitioner volume in 1984, tax law teaching seemed to have been seriously threatened. No university subject can thrive without a good textbook and the alternatives available at that time were not

---

[17] Livingston (1998).   [18] McCrudden (2006, p. 641), citing Posner (1987).
[19] Livingston (1998, p. 406).

adequate for a graduate university course. As Kerridge put it, the absence of a new edition of Tiley had a 'measurable negative impact'.[20] The key problem was the removal of just that material which had transformed the book from pure doctrinal analysis to something far more worthy of university study. The excision of this material not only left a lacuna but transformed the fundamental nature of the doctrinal material. The publishers were persuaded to produce a *Policy Supplement* from the parts removed from the practitioner version and for a while gave this to students free of charge. The economics of this were puzzling. Presumably, some kind of market research supported the removal of this material for practitioners but, if that was the case, it must have been flawed research because, for practitioners who really want to understand the law and be able to apply it, as for students, 'the historical, comparative and policy material is not something which supplements the technical material – it is absolutely essential'.[21]

Fortunately, in 2000, the publisher Richard Hart came to the rescue and, after a long gap, the fourth edition and then, soon after, the fifth edition of *Revenue Law* were published.[22] The book is now daunting in terms of physical size and content and, as Kerridge points out, it is not a beginner's book, but it is a treasure trove for any serious student of taxation and the range of material covered is breathtaking.[23] It is not overtly interdisciplinary and Tiley's work has generally been sole authored or written with other lawyers.[24] His textbook, however, draws on a wide range of material. It provides a very solid starting point not only for teaching but also for future research. Tiley's aim in writing the book was not only to provide a suitable textbook for university students but also to 'raise the status and standing of tax law in law faculties'.[25] No-one with access to the book could doubt that tax law is a suitable subject for university study.

Wheatcroft laid the foundations for tax law in the UK; Tiley has built soundly upon them and has influenced many others to take up this

---

[20] Kerridge (2001, p. 284).   [21] Kerridge (2001, p. 283).   [22] Tiley (2005b).
[23] It is 1,471 pages long. This growth in the book matches the increasing complexity of tax law and the mass of legislation that is enacted on a yearly basis. This continues to increase. BBC News online reported on 6 September 2007 that the legislation published in Tolley's *Yellow Tax Handbook* has grown from 5,952 pages in 2001 to 10,500 pages in 2007 (although the number of pages in 2007 has in fact been kept down to under 10,000 by using a smaller print size!).
[24] Although he has recently engaged increasingly with historians and has organised tax history conferences at the Cambridge Centre for Tax Law.
[25] Tiley (2005b, p. v).

fascinating subject and to develop it yet further. The future of tax law in the UK universities cannot be disentangled from that of other legal subjects but some of the issues which face it are even more acute. If it is difficult to recruit good legal academics in view of salaries and competing attractions, then those with an interest in taxation are going to be particularly difficult to attract and retain. If there is a danger that legal scholarship will be subordinated to other, more dominant methodologies such as economics then this is a particular danger for tax law which is so heavily inter-linked with economics.

How can these very real problems be tackled by those who follow Tiley? First and foremost we need to encourage students to study tax law, not only at graduate level but also at undergraduate level. Much of the recent effort in the UK universities has concentrated on specialist master's degrees in taxation and these will of course produce the future teachers and researchers we need, but before they take a specialist course in taxation law, students need to know that they are interested in the subject. Few enough UK students take master's courses in law and only a tiny proportion of them take the tax courses because, unlike students from other jurisdictions where tax law is more frequently taught to undergraduates and even sometimes mandatory,[26] they have often not had any experience of tax law before taking their graduate degree. An undergraduate introduction to tax law will be the best way to attract UK students to the graduate courses as well as ensuring a wider understanding of taxation law amongst lawyers generally. Thus this is a plea to tax law teachers not to concentrate on graduate tax courses at the expense of undergraduate offerings.

Secondly, we need to encourage some of these students to go on to write doctorates in taxation law. This requires funding, as Tiley points out,[27] as well as a pool of master's students upon which to draw.

Thirdly, the development of sustainable long-term tax teaching and research programmes requires acceptance that this cannot be achieved by a lone scholar, however good he or she might be. University law departments need more than one full-time tax lawyer if the subject is to be

---

[26] This should not be taken as a recommendation that tax law should be mandatory for undergraduates.

[27] Tiley (2006a). Tiley refers to the very welcome funding for doctoral students that has been made available by the Chartered Institute of Taxation. In addition, there are some doctoral studentships at the Oxford Centre for Business Taxation funded by the One Hundred Group and law students may apply to the AHRC for studentships through the normal channels. All these sources are very competitive.

developed at both graduate and undergraduate level. Part-time help from practitioners has proved invaluable over the years and many of these part-timers have made major contributions to the development of the subject, but professional curriculum development requires full-time and special-ist lecturers in the modern university environment, although in a subject like tax, practitioner input will always be very important. Some progress has been made in this direction but of course there is much more to do.[28]

Finally, the students and the scholars we appoint need to develop their subject in a way that will win the respect of their colleagues in law faculties as well as those working on taxation in other disciplines and in practice. This is an exceptionally demanding task for the lawyers and demands patience and understanding from those in other disciplines too, but the result should be an enrichment of tax research generally.[29] Tax law aca-demics have to be recognised as being engaged on work which is not a second-tier version of some other discipline but a discipline with its own unique contribution to make. The structure of research funding in the UK needs to recognise this. Success will not be achieved by subordinating tax law to other disciplines but only by persuading those working in those other disciplines, and especially economics, to engage with us, to teach us their skills but also to be prepared to learn about ours. Tiley's *Revenue Law* would be a very good place for them to start.

---

[28] KPMG not only created a post at Cambridge but also one (which this author is fortunate enough to hold) at Oxford: it is unlikely that either would have been created without Tiley's work and reputation. Oxford is about to create a second post with generous financial help from McGrigors, Solicitors. Other universities, including the London colleges and Warwick, have also expanded their complement of tax law teachers in recent years.

[29] The author is grateful for the assistance and patience of economists at the Institute for Fiscal Studies and at the Oxford Centre for Business Taxation, with whom she is working.

REFERENCES

Allen, R. C. (1992), *Enclosure and the Yeoman: The Agricultural Development of the South Midlands, 1450–1850* (Oxford: Oxford University Press)

American Bar Association Section of Taxation (2007), 'Economic Substance Codification: ABA has "Substantial Reservations"', *Tax Notes* 115: 389–96

Apps, P. and Rees, R. (2007), *The Taxation of Couples*, IZA Discussion Paper No. 2910 (Bonn: Institute for the Study of Labor) at http://papers.ssrn.com/sol3/papers.cfm?abstract_id = 1000899

Aprill, E. P. (2001), 'Tax Shelters, Tax Law, and Morality: Codifying Judicial Doctrines', *SMU Law Review* 54: 9–35

Arnold, B. J. (2004), 'Tax Treaties and Tax Avoidance: The 2003 Revisions to the Commentary to the OECD Model Convention', *Bulletin for International Fiscal Documentation* 58(6): 488–511

Arnold, B. J. (2006a), 'Confusion Worse Confounded: The Supreme Court's GAAR Decisions', *Canadian Tax Journal* 54: 167–209

Arnold, B. J. (2006b), 'The Supreme Court and the Interpretation of Tax Statutes – Again', *Canadian Tax Journal* 54: 677–84

Arnold, B. J. and Wilson, J. R. (1988), 'The General Anti-Avoidance Rule – Part II', *Canadian Tax Journal* 36: 1123–85

Atiyah, P. S. and Summers, R. S. (1987), *Form and Substance in Anglo-American Law* (Oxford: Clarendon Press)

Auerbach, A (2006), 'The Future of Capital Income Taxation', *Fiscal Studies* 27: 399–420

Avery Jones, J. F. (1983), 'The *Leedale* Affair', *British Tax Review* 1983: 70–2

Avery Jones, J. F. (2007), 'The History of the United Kingdom's First Comprehensive Double Tax Agreement', *British Tax Review* 2007: 211–54

Avery Jones, J. F. *et al.* (2006), 'The Origins of Concepts and Expressions Used in the OECD Model and their Adoption by States', *Bulletin for International Taxation* 60: 220–54

Bagchi, A. K. (1990), 'Land Tax, Property Rights and Peasant Insecurity in Colonial India', *Journal of Peasant Studies* 20: 1–49

Baker, J. H. (2002), *An Introduction to English Legal History*, 4th edition (London: Butterworths)

Baker, P. (2000), 'Taxation and the European Convention on Human Rights', *British Tax Review* 2000: 211–377

Ballance, J. (1887), *A National Land Policy Based on the Principle of State Ownership* (Wellington: Lyon and Blair)

Baltus, F. (2006), 'Les "Pratiques Abusives" en Matière de TVA', *Journal de Droit Fiscal* 80: 338–60

Bank, S. A. (2001), 'Codifying Judicial Doctrines: No Cure for Rules but More Rules?', *SMU Law Review* 54: 37–45

Banks, J. and Blundell, R. (2005), 'Private Pension Arrangements and Retirement in Britain', *Fiscal Studies* 26: 35–53

Bankman, J. (2004), 'The Tax Shelter Problem', *National Tax Journal* 57: 925–36

Bassett, J. (2004), 'Atkinson, Sir Harry Albert (1831–1892)', in *Oxford Dictionary of National Biography* (Oxford: Oxford University Press), online edition: www.oxforddnb.com/view/article/844

Beale, L. M. (2006), 'Tax Advice Before the Return: The Case for Raising Standards and Denying Evidentiary Privileges', *Virginia Tax Review* 25: 583–669

Beatson, J. (2006), 'Unlawful Statutes and Mistakes of Law: Is there a Smile on the Face of Schrödinger's Cat?', in A. Burrows and A. Rodger (eds.), *Mapping the Law* (Oxford: Oxford University Press), pp. 163–80

Beattie, C. N. and Tiley, J. (1970), *Beattie's Elements of Estate Duty*, 7th edition (London: Butterworths)

Beckett, J. V. (1985), 'Land Tax or Excise: The Levying of Taxation in Seventeenth- and Eighteenth-Century England', *English Historical Review* 100: 285–308

Beckett, J. V. and Turner, M. E. (1990), 'Taxation and Economic Growth in Eighteenth-Century England', *Economic History Review* 43: 377–403

Belich, J. (2006), 'Grey, Sir George (1812–1898)', in *Oxford Dictionary of National Biography* (Oxford: Oxford University Press), online edition: www.oxforddnb.com/view/article/11534

Birks, P. (2005), *Unjust Enrichment*, 2nd edition (Oxford: Oxford University Press)

Bittker, B., McMahon, M. and Zelenak, L. (2002), *Federal Income Taxation of Individuals* (New York: Warren, Gorham & Lamont)

Bowler, T. (2007), *Taxation of the Family*, Tax Law Review Committee Discussion Paper No. 6 (London: Institute for Fiscal Studies)

Brenner, R. (1976), 'Agrarian Class Structure and Economic Development in Pre-industrial Europe', *Past and Present* 70: 30–75

Bridgland, N. (2006), 'The EU Code of Conduct to Eliminate Harmful or Potentially Harmful Business Tax Regimes: The Future', *Tax Planning International European Union Focus* 8(1): 8–11

Brooking, T. (2004), 'McKenzie, Sir John (1839–1901)', in *Oxford Dictionary of National Biography* (Oxford: Oxford University Press), online edition: www.oxforddnb.com/view/article/34752

Brooks, N. (1985), 'Future Directions in Canadian Tax Law Scholarship', *Osgoode Hall Law Journal* 23: 441–75

Bulkeley, W. M. (2007), 'IBM's Under-the-wire Tax Break', *Wall Street Journal*, 7 June 2007, p. A3

Buxton, J. (1888), *Finance and Politics: An Historical Study. 1783–1885*, 2 vols. (London: John Murray)

Canada (1988), *Explanatory Notes to Legislation Relating to Income Tax*, June (Ottawa: Department of Finance)

Canellos, P. C. (2001), 'A Tax Practitioner's Perspective on Substance, Form and Business Purpose in Structuring Business Transactions and in Tax Shelters', *SMU Law Review* 54: 47–72

Charlesworth, N. (1984), 'The Problem of Government Finance in British India: Taxation, Borrowing and the Allocation of Resources in the Inter-war Period', *Modern Asian Studies* 19: 521–48

Chirelstein, M. A. and Zelenak, L. A. (2005), 'Tax Shelters and the Search for a Silver Bullet', *Columbia Law Review* 105: 1939–62

Chowdry, M. (2004), 'Unjust Enrichment and Section 80(3) of the Value Added Tax Act 1994', *British Tax Review* 2004: 620–37

Chowdry, M. (2005), 'The Revenue's Response: A Time Bar on Claims', *Law Quarterly Review* 121: 546–50

Chrétien, M. (1954), 'Le rôles des organisations internationals dans le règlement des questions d'impôts entre les divers états' *Recueil des Cours* 86-II: 1–116

Cobbett, W. (1812–1820), *The Parliamentary History of England, From the Earliest Period to the Year 1803*, Vols. 13–36 (London: Longman & Co.)

Cooper, G. S. (2001), 'International Experience with General Anti-avoidance Rules', *SMU Law Review* 54: 83–130

Cooper, G. S. (2006), 'The Emerging High Court Jurisprudence on Part IVA', *University of Sydney Law School Legal Studies Research Paper Series*, No. 06/09 at http://papers.ssrn.com/sol3/papers.cfm? abstract_id = 919480

Cornford, F. M. (1908), *Microcosmographia Academica* (Cambridge: Bowes & Bowes), available at www.cs.kent.ac.uk/people/staff/iau/cornford/cornford.html

Daunton, M. (1983), *House and Home in the Victorian City: Working-Class Housing, 1850–1914* (London: Edward Arnold)

Daunton, M. (1995), *Progress and Poverty: An Economic and Social History of Britain, 1700–1850* (Oxford, Oxford University Press)

Daunton, M. (2001), *Trusting Leviathan: The Politics of Taxation in Britain, 1799–1914* (Cambridge: Cambridge University Press)

Dawson, W. H. (1890), *The Unearned Increment: Or, Reaping without Sowing* (London: Swan Sonnenschein & Co.)

Degadt, C. and van Hoorebeke, A. (2006), 'New Belgian Anti-Abuse Measures: Belgian Legislator adopts Halifax Doctrine', *Tax Planning International European Union Focus* 8(10): 14–15

Dodge, D. (1988), 'A New and More Coherent Approach to Tax Avoidance', *Canadian Tax Journal* 36(1): 1–22

Douma S. and Engelen, F. (2006), 'Case Note: *Halifax plc and Others v. Commissioners of Customs and Excise*: The ECJ Applies the Abuse of Rights Doctrine in VAT Cases', *British Tax Review* 2006: 429–40

Dowell, S. (1884), *A History of Taxation and Taxes in England from the Earliest Times to the Present Day*, 4 vols (London, Longmans & Co)

Dunbar, D. (2006), 'Judicial Techniques for Controlling the New Zealand General Anti-Avoidance Rule: The Scheme and Purpose Approach, from *Challenge Corporation* to *Peterson*', *New Zealand Journal of Taxation Law and Policy* 12: 324–96

Dyck, I. (1992), *William Cobbett and Rural Popular Culture* (Cambridge: Cambridge University Press)

Edelman, J. (2005), 'Limitation Periods and the Theory of Unjust Enrichment', *Modern Law Review* 68: 848–57

European Commission (1997), 'Towards Tax-Coordination in the European Union – A Package to Tackle Harmful Tax Competition', 1 October 1997, COM (97)495 final

de la Feria, R. (2006a), 'The European Court of Justice's Solution to Aggressive VAT Planning – Further Towards Legal Uncertainty?', *EC Tax Review* 15: 27–35

de la Feria, R. (2006b), 'Giving Themselves Extra VAT? The ECJ Ruling in *Halifax*', *British Tax Review* 2006: 119–23

Fforde, M. (1990), *Conservatism and Collectivism, 1886–1914* (Edinburgh: Edinburgh University Press)

Financial Reform Association (1859), *Report on Taxation. Direct and Indirect. Adopted by the Financial Reform Association, Liverpool, and Presented at the Annual Meeting of the National Association for the Promotion of Social Science Held at Bradford, Oct. 1859* (Liverpool)

Freedman, J. (2004a), 'Defining Taxpayer Responsibility: In Support of a General Anti-Avoidance Principle', *British Tax Review* 2004: 332–57

Freedman, J. (2004b), 'Taxation Research as Legal Research', in M. Lamb, A. Lymer, J. Freedman and S. James (eds.), *Taxation: An Interdisciplinary Approach to Research* (Oxford: Oxford University Press), pp. 13–34

Freedman, J. (2005), 'Converging Tracks? Recent Developments in Canadian and UK Approaches to Tax Avoidance', *Canadian Tax Journal* 53(4): 1038–46

Galle, B. (2006), 'Interpretative Theory and Tax Shelter Regulation', *Virginia Tax Review* 26: 357–403

Gammie, M. (1997), 'A Perspective from the United Kingdom', in G. S. Cooper (ed.), *Tax Avoidance and the Rule of Law* (Amsterdam: IBFD Publications), pp. 181–218

Gammie, M. (2005), '*Barclays* and *Canada Trustco*: Further Comment from a UK Perspective', *Canadian Tax Journal* 53(4): 1047–52

Gammie, M. (2006), 'Sham and Reality: The Taxation of Composite Transactions', *British Tax Review* 2006: 294–317

Gergen, M. P. (2002), 'The Logic of Deterrence: Corporate Tax Shelters', *Tax Law Review* 55: 255–86

Ginsburg, M. (1985), 'The National Office Mission', *Tax Notes* 27: 99–102

Ginter, D. E. (1992), *A Measure of Wealth: The English Land Tax in Historical Analysis* (London: Hambledon Press)

Glenn, H. (2007), 'IRS Official, Practitioners Pan Economic Substance Doctrine Codification', *Tax Notes* 115: 888

Goldsmith, P. (2007), *We Won; You Lost. Eat That! A Political History of Tax in New Zealand Since 1840*, unpublished manuscript

Goschen, G. J. (1872), *Reports and Speeches on Local Taxation* (London: Macmillan and Co.)

Granwell, A. and S. McGonigle (2006), 'US Tax Shelters: A UK Reprise?', *British Tax Review* 2006: 170–208

Graetz, M. J. and O'Hear, M. M. (1997), 'The "Original Intent" of US International Taxation', *Duke Law Journal* 46: 1021–109

Greg, W. R. (1860), 'British Taxation', *Edinburgh Review* 111: 254

George, H. (1880), *Progress and Poverty: An Inquiry into the Cause of Industrial Depressions and of Increase of Want with Increase of Wealth. The Remedy* (New York: D. Appleton & Co.)

Gunn, A. (2001), 'The Use and Misuse of Antiabuse Rules: Lessons from the Partnership Antiabuse Regulations', *SMU Law Review* 54: 159–76

Gustafson, C. H. (1997), 'The Politics and Practicalities of Checking Tax Avoidance in the United States', in G. S. Cooper (ed.), *Tax Avoidance and the Rule of Law* (Amsterdam: IBFD Publications), pp. 349–76

Halperin, D. (1995), 'Are Anti-abuse Rules Appropriate?', *Tax Lawyer* 48: 807–16

Hamer, D. (1988), *The New Zealand Liberals: The Years of Power* (Auckland: Auckland University Press)

Harris, P. (1996), *Corporate/Shareholder Income Taxation and Allocating Taxing Rights Between Countries: A Comparison of Imputation Systems* (Amsterdam: IBFD)

Harris, P. (1999), 'An Historic View of the Principle and Options for Double Tax Relief', *British Tax Review*, 1999: 469–89

Harris, P. (2000), 'Origins of the 1963 OECD Model Series: Working Party 12 and Article 10', *Australian Tax Forum* 15: 3–223

Harris, P. (2006), *Income Tax in Common Law Jurisdictions: From the Origins to 1820* (Cambridge: Cambridge University Press)

Harris, P. (2007a), 'Fair in Love but not Taxation: The English Origin of the Australasian General Anti-Avoidance Rule – Part I', *Bulletin for International Taxation* 61(2): 65–83

Harris, P. (2007b), 'Fair in Love but not Taxation: The English Origin of the Australasian General Anti-Avoidance Rule – Part II', *Bulletin for International Taxation* 61(3): 109–25

Harvard Law Review Association (2004) 'Developments in the Law – Corporations and Society: V. Governmental Attempts to Stem the Rising Tide of Corporate Tax Shelters', *Harvard Law Review* 117: 2249–71

Herman, T. (1999), 'Tax Report', *Wall Street Journal*, 10 February 1999, p. A1

HM Revenue & Customs, *National Statistics* at www.hmrc.gov.uk/stats/

Hoffmann, L. (2005), 'Tax Avoidance', *British Tax Review* 2005: 197–206

International Fiscal Association (2002), *Form and Substance in Tax Law*, Cahiers de Droit Fiscal International, Vol. 87a (The Hague: Kluwer)

Kay, J. (1979), 'The Economics of Tax Avoidance', *British Tax Review*, 1979: 354–65

Kerridge, R. (2001), '*Revenue Law* by John Tiley', *British Tax Review*, 2001: 283–7

Korb, D. (2007), 'What a Difference Two Years Make! Remarks at the 2007 University of Southern California Tax Institute', *Tax Notes Today*, 2007 TNT: 16–65

Lang, M. (2006), 'Rechtsmissbrauch und Gemeinschaftsrecht', *Steuer und Wirtschaft International* 16: 273–85

Lang, M. (2007), 'Non-Discrimination: What Does History Teach Us?', in *Fiscalité et enterprise: politiques et pratiques: Mélanges en l'honneur de Jean Pierre Le Gall* (Paris: Dalloz), pp. 103–8.

Lavoie, R. (2001), 'Deputizing the Gunslingers: Co-Opting the Tax Bar into Dissuading Corporate Tax Shelters', *Virginia Tax Review* 21: 43–99.

Leclercq, L. (2007), 'Interacting Principles: The French Abuse of Law Concept and the EU Notion of Abusive Practices', *Bulletin for International Taxation* 61(16): 235–44

Levy, H. (1911), *Large and Small Holdings: A Study in English Agricultural Economics* (Cambridge: Cambridge University Press)

Livingston, M. (1998), 'Reinventing Tax Scholarship: Lawyers, Economists, and the Role of the Legal Academy', *Cornell Law Review* 83: 365–436

Locher, P. (2007), 'Rechtsmissbrauchsüberlegungen im Recht der direkten Steuern in der Schweiz', *Archiv für Schweizerisches Abgabenrecht* 75: 675–700

McAlpin, M. B. (1983), *Subject to Famine: Food Crises and Economic Change in Western India, 1860–1920* (Princeton: Princeton University Press)

McCarthy, H. L. (2007), 'Abuse of Rights: The Effect of the Doctrine on VAT Planning', *British Tax Review* 2007: 160–74

McCrudden, C. (2006), 'Legal Research and the Social Sciences', *Law Quarterly Review* 122: 632–50

McDaniel, P., McMahon, M. Simmons, D. and Abreu, A. (2004), *Federal Income Taxation, Cases and Materials*, 5th edition (New York: Foundation Press)

McInnes, M. (2003), 'Interceptive Subtraction, Unjust Enrichment and Wrongs – A Reply to Professor Birks', *Cambridge Law Journal* 62: 697–716

McIvor, T. (1989), *The Rainmaker: A Biography of John Ballance* (Auckland: Heinemann Reed)

McIvor, T. (2004), 'Ballance, John (1839–1893)', in *Oxford Dictionary of National Biography* (Oxford: Oxford University Press), online edition: www.oxforddnb.com/view/article/1225

McMichael, P. (1984), *Settlers and the Agrarian Question: Capitalism in Colonial Australia* (Cambridge: Cambridge University Press)

Makkus, E. and de Preter, J. (2006), 'Abuse of Rights: The End of VAT Planning?', *Tax Planning International European Union Focus* 8(3): 15–17

Mandler, P. (2001), 'Art, Death and Taxes: The Taxation of Works of Art in Britain, 1796–1914', *Historical Research* 74: 271–97

Mann, M. (1995), 'A Permanent Settlement for the Ceded and Conquered Provinces: Revenue Administration in North India, 1801–33', *India Economic and Social History Review* 32: 245–69

Murray, A. and Carter, R. N. (1895), *A Guide to Income-Tax Practice* (London: Gee & Co.)

Meade, J. S. (1978), *The Structure and Reform of Direct Taxation: report of a committee chaired by J. E. Meade* (London: George Allen & Unwin)

Mehrotra, A. J. (2005), 'Teaching Tax Stories', *Journal of Legal Education* 55: 116–25

Morse, S. C. (2006), 'The How and Why of the New Public Corporation Tax Shelter Compliance Norm', *Fordham Law Review* 75: 961–1018

Moss, M. and Gillham, G. (2006), 'Controlled Foreign Companies Legislation and the Abuse of Law', *Tax Planning International Review* 33(12): 3–7

Neville Brown, L. (1994), 'Is there a General Principle of Abuse of Rights in European Community Law?', in D. Curtin and T. Heukels (eds.), *Institutional Dynamics of European Integration, Essays in Honour of Henry G. Schermers*, vol. II (Dordrecht/Boston/London: Martinus Nijhoff), pp. 511–26

New Zealand (1858–), *Statistics of New Zealand for 1853, 1854, 1855, and 1856 (1857, etc.) . . . Compiled from official records* (Auckland)

New Zealand (1893), 'Statistical Summary of the Colony of New Zealand for the Years 1840–1852 (inclusive)', in *The New Zealand Official Year Book* (Wellington: Government Printer)

Nutt, A. (2007), 'O'Connor Cites Justice Gains in Combating Tax Shelters', *Tax Notes* 115: 697

O'Brien, P. K. (1988), 'The Political Economy of British Taxation, 1660–1815', *Economic History Review* 41: 1–32

O'Brien, P. K. and Hunt, P. A. (1993), 'The Rise of the Fiscal State in England, 1485–1815', *Historical Research* 66: 129–76

OECD (1963), *Draft Model Double Taxation Convention on Income and Capital* (Paris: OECD)

OECD (1985), *Trends in International Taxation* (Paris: OECD)

OECD (1992–), *Model Tax Convention on Income and on Capital*, Committee on Fiscal Affairs (Paris: OECD)

OECD (1998), *Harmful Tax Competition – An Emerging Global Issue* (Paris: OECD)

OECD (1999), *The Application of the OECD Model Tax Convention to Partnerships* (Paris: OECD)

OECD (2000), *Issues related to Article 14 of the OECD Model Tax Convention* (Paris: OECD)

OEEC (1958), *The Elimination of Double Taxation: Report of the Fiscal Committee of the OEEC* (Paris: OEEC)

OEEC (1959), *The Elimination of Double Taxation: 2nd Report by the Fiscal Committee of the OEEC* (Paris: OEEC)

OEEC (1961), *The Elimination of Double Taxation: Fourth Report of the Fiscal Committee of the OEEC* (Paris: OEEC)

Offer, A. (1981), *Property and Politics, 1870–1914: Landownership, Law, Ideology and Urban Development in England* (Cambridge: Cambridge University Press)

Offer, A. (1989), *The First World War: An Agrarian Interpretation* (Oxford: Clarendon)

Oliver, J. D. B. (1998), 'Ship-money', *British Tax Review* 1998: 1–3

Park, A. (1997), 'Tax Law in and after the Wheatcroft Era', in R. Rawlings (ed.), *Law, Society, and Economy* (Oxford: Clarendon Press), pp. 131–45

Pearlman, R. A. (2002), 'Demystifying Disclosure: First Steps', *Tax Law Review* 55: 289–324

Pedroli, A. (2007), 'L'elusione fiscale nel diritto italiano', *Archiv für Schweizerisches Abgabenrecht* 75: 701–26

Posner, R. A. (1987), 'The Decline of Law as an Autonomous Discipline 1962–1987', *Harvard Law Review* 100(4): 761–80

van Raad, K. (1987), *1963 and 1977 OECD Model Income Tax Treaties and Commentaries* (Deventer: Kluwer)

Raskolnikov, A. (2006), 'Crime and Punishment in Taxation: Deceit, Deterrence, and the Self-Adjusting Penalty', *Columbia Law Review* 106: 569–642

Reeder, D. A. (1961), 'The Politics of Urban Leaseholds in Late Victorian England', *International Review of Social History* 6: 413–30

Ricardo, D. (1951), *On the Principles of Political Economy and Taxation*, in P. Sraffa and M. H. Dobb (eds.), *The Works and Correspondence of David Ricardo* (Cambridge: Cambridge University Press), vol. 1

Richardson, J. W. (1967), 'Correspondence', *British Tax Review* 1967: 153

Ridsdale, M. (2006), 'Halifax and others v. Commissioners of Customs and Excise (Case C-255/02)', *Tax Planning International Review* 33(3): 10–11

Rostain, T. (2006),'Sheltering Lawyers: The Organized Bar and the Tax Shelter Industry', *Yale Journal on Regulation* 23: 77–120

Rousselle, O. and H. M. Liebman (2006), 'The Doctrine of Abuse of Community Law: The Sword of Damocles Hanging over the Head of EC Corporate Tax Law?', *European Taxation* 46: 559–64

Rush, M. (2006), *The Defence of Passing On* (Oxford: Hart Publishing)

Rutherford, J. (1961), *Sir George Grey, 1812–1898: A Study in Colonial Government* (London: Cassell)

Schizer, D. M. (2006), 'Enlisting the Tax Bar', *Tax Law Review* 59: 331–72

Schler, M. L. (2002), 'Ten More Truths About Tax Shelters: The Problem, Possible Solutions, and a Reply to Professor Weisbach', *Tax Law Review* 55: 325–95

Schön, W. (1996), 'Gestaltungsmissbrauch im Europäischen Steuerrecht', *Internationales Steuerrecht* 5(2): Appendix

Schön, W. (2000), 'Tax Competition in Europe – the Legal Perspective', *EC Tax Review* 9: 90–105

Schön, W. (2002), 'Der "Rechtsmissbrauch" im Europäischen Gesellschaftsrecht', in R. Wank *et al.* (ed.), *Festschrift für Herbert Wiedemann zum 70. Geburtstag* (Munich: C. H. Beck) p. 1271 *et seq.*

Schön, W. (2006a), 'The Mobility of Companies and the Organizational Freedom of Company Founders', *European Company and Financial Law Review* 3: 122–46

Schön, W. (2006b), 'State Aid in the Area of Taxation', in L. Hancher, L. T. Ottervanger and P. J. Slot (eds.), *EC State Aids*, 3rd edition (London: Thomson/Sweet & Maxwell, London), pp. 241–76.

Sheppard, L. (2007), 'Bad LILO Facts Make Good Law?', *Tax Notes* 114: 733–41

Silsby, W. and Smith, I. (2007), 'BATR (Badger and Toad Relief)', *Taxation* 160(4115): 39–42

Silverman, M., Lerner, M. and Kidder, G. (2006), 'The Economic Substance Doctrine: Sorting Through the Federal Circuit's "We Know It When We See It" Ruling in Coltec', *The Tax Executive* 58: 423–41

Simmonds, S. (2007), 'Government Continues Winning Streak in Shelter Litigation', *Tax Notes* 115: 913

Simpson, P. (2006), 'Case Note: *Cadbury Schweppes plc v. Commissioners of Inland Revenue*: the ECJ Sets Strict Test for CFC Legislation', *British Tax Review* 2006: 677–83

Sinclair, K. (1957), *Origins of the Maori Wars* (Wellington: New Zealand University Press)

Stratton, S. (2007), '*Black & Decker* to Settle; Bigger Case on Horizon', *Tax Notes* 114: 980

Stevens, R. (2005), 'Justified Enrichment', *Oxford University Commonwealth Law Journal* 5: 141–50

Stokes, E. (1959), *The English Utilitarians and India* (Oxford: Clarendon Press)

Stopforth, D. (1987), 'The Background to the Anti-Avoidance Provisions Concerning Settlements by Parents on their Minor Children', *British Tax Review* 1987: 417–33

Stopforth, D. (1992), '1922–36: Halcyon Days for the Tax Avoider', *British Tax Review* 1992: 88–105

Surrey, S. S. (1969), 'Complexity and the Internal Revenue Code: The Problem of the Management of Tax Detail', *Law & Contemporary Problems* 34: 673–710

Tailby, C. (2006), 'Halifax – A Basis for Optimism?', *The Tax Journal* 833(17 April): 4–6.

Tax Analysts (2007), 'Senate Finance Tax Counsel Says Codification of Economic Substance Likely', *Tax Notes Today* 2007 TNT: 97–3

Tax Analysts (electronic), *Worldwide Tax Treaties* (Falls Church: Tax Analysts), available at www.taxanalysts.com

van den Tempel, A. J. (1967), *Relief from Double Taxation* (Amsterdam: IBFD)

Tennant, C. (1856), *The People's Blue Book: Taxation As It Is and As It Ought to Be*, 2nd edition (1857), 3rd edition (1862), 4th edition (1872) (London: Longmans, Green & Co)

Thomas, P. J. (1939), *The Growth of Federal Finance in India* (Madras: Oxford University Press)

Thompson, F. M. L. (2002), 'Changing Perceptions of Land Tenures in Britain, 1750–1914', in D. Winch and P. K. O'Brien (eds.), *The Political Economy of British Historical Experience, 1688–1914* (Oxford: Oxford University Press), pp. 119–38

Tiley, J. (1980), 'Widowhood Anomalies', *British Tax Review* 1980: 216–18

Tiley, J. (1985a), 'An Academic Perspective on the *Ramsay/Dawson* Doctrine', in J. Dyson (ed.), *Recent Tax Problems* (London: Stevens & Sons), pp. 19–27

Tiley, J (1985b), 'Section 52 and Maintenance Payments', *British Tax Review* 1985: 329–33

Tiley, J, (1987a), 'Judicial Anti-avoidance Doctrines: The U.S. Alternatives – Part I', *British Tax Review* 1987: 180–97

Tiley, J. (1987b), 'Judicial Anti-avoidance Doctrines: The U.S. Alternatives – Part II', *British Tax Review* 1987: 220–44

Tiley, J. (1988a), 'Judicial Anti-Avoidance Doctrines: Some Problem Areas', *British Tax Review* 1988: 63–103

Tiley, J. (1988b), 'Judicial Anti-Avoidance Doctrines: Corporations and Conclusions', *British Tax Review* 1988: 108–45.

Tiley, J. (1989), 'Case Comment, *Craven (Inspector of Taxes) v. White (Stephen)*', *British Tax Review*, 1989: 20–8

Tiley, J. (1990), 'Double Taxation – Visiting Academics', *Cambridge Law Journal* 49: 225–8

Tiley, J. (1992), 'Trading Tax Matters in the House of Lords', *Cambridge Law Journal* 51: 443–6

Tiley, J. (1995), 'Taxation – Exploring the New Approach', *Cambridge Law Journal* 54: 258–61

Tiley, J. (1998a), 'Away from a Virtuous Tax System', *British Tax Review* 1998: 317–47

Tiley, J (1998b), 'Human Rights and Taxpayers' *Cambridge Law Journal* 57: 269–73

Tiley, J. (1999), 'United Kingdom', in M. T. Soler Roch (ed.), *Family Taxation in Europe* (London: Kluwer Law International), pp. 129–50

Tiley, J. (2001), 'First Thoughts on *Westmoreland*', *British Tax Review* 2001: 153–8

Tiley, J. (2004a), 'Tax Avoidance Jurisprudence as Normal Law', *British Tax Review*, 2004: 304–31

Tiley, J. (2004b), 'United Kingdom', in H. Ault and B. Arnold (eds.), *Comparative Income Taxation: A Structural Analysis*, 2nd edition (Amsterdam: Kluwer Law International), pp. 115–36

Tiley, J. (2004c), 'Aspects of Schedule A', in J. Tiley (ed.), *Studies in the History of Tax Law* (Oxford, Hart Publishing), pp. 81–97

Tiley, J. (2005a), 'Barclays and Scottish Provident: Avoidance and Highest Courts; Less Chaos but More Uncertainty', *British Tax Review* 2005: pp. 273–80

Tiley, J. (2005b), *Revenue Law*, 5th edition (London: Hart Publishing)

Tiley, J. (2006a), '50 years: Tax, Law and Academia', *British Tax Review* 2006: 229–48

Tiley, J. (2006b), 'Tax, Marriage and the Family', *Cambridge Law Journal* 65: 289–300

Tiley, J. (2007), 'Death and Taxes', *British Tax Review* 2007: 300–19

Tiley, J. and Jensen, E. (1998), 'The Control of Avoidance: The United States Experience', *British Tax Review* 1998: 161–85.

Travers, T. N. (2004), '"The real value of the lands": the *Nawabs*, the British and the Land Tax in Eighteenth-century Bengal', *Modern Asian Studies* 38: 517–38

Trombitas, E. (2004), 'The Abracadabra Effect and Tax Avoidance – Comments on Inland Revenue's Exposure Draft INA0009: Interpretation of Sections B61 and 6B1 of the Income Tax Act 2004 – Part 1', *New Zealand Journal of Taxation Law and Policy* 10(4): 353–89

Trombitas, E. (2005), 'The Abracadabra Effect and Tax Avoidance – Comments on Inland Revenue's Exposure Draft INA0009: Interpretation of Sections B61 and 6B1 of the Income Tax Act 2004 – Part 2', *New Zealand Journal of Taxation Law and Policy* 11(1): 37–68

United Kingdom (1801–), *Parliamentary Papers* (Blue Books) (London: HMSO)

United Kingdom (1829–91), *Hansard's Parliamentary Debates*, 3rd Series (London: Baldwin and Cradock)

United Kingdom (1870a), *Report of the Commissioners of Inland Revenue: 13th Report*, in United Kingdom (1801–), 1870 [C.82-I] XX. 377

United Kingdom (1870b), *Report of G J Goschen . . . on the Progressive Increase of Local Taxation*, in United Kingdom (1801–), 1870 (470) LV.177

United Kingdom (1886–90), *Report and Proceedings, Select Committee on Town Holdings*, in United Kingdom (1801–), 1886 (213) XII.367, 1887 (260) XIII.41, 1888 (313) XXII.1, 1889 (251) XV.1, 1890 (341) XVIII.1, 1890–91 (325) XVIII.15, 1892 (214) XVIII.613

United Kingdom (1920), *Report of the Royal Commission on the Income Tax*, in United Kingdom (1801–), 1920 Cmd. 615 XVIII.97

United Kingdom (1951), *Report of the Committee on the Taxation of Trading Profits*, in United Kingdom (1801–), 1950–51 Cmd. 8189 XX.1

United Kingdom (1972), *Reform of Corporation Tax*, in United Kingdom (1801–), 1971–72 Cmnd. 4955 XXXIX.1

United Kingdom (1974), *Wealth Tax*, in United Kingdom (1801–), 1974 Cmnd. 5704 XVII.525

United Kingdom (1975), *Minutes of Evidence of Select Committee on a Wealth Tax*, in United Kingdom (1801-), 1974–75 (696-II) XVIII.785

United Kingdom (1994), *Restitution: Mistakes of Law and Ultra Vires Public Authority Receipts and Payments*, Law Commission Report No. 227 (London: The Stationery Office)

United Kingdom (2007), 'Treasury: Small Businesses and Settlements Legislation', Written Ministerial Statement of 26 July by Angela Eagle, available at www.theyworkforyou.com/wms/?id = 2007-07-26a.89WS.5

United States (1962), 'Model Tax Conventions', in Joint Committee of Internal Revenue Taxation, *Legislative History of United States Tax Conventions* (Washington: US Government Printing Office), vol. 4, available at http://setis.library.usyd.edu.au/oztexts/parsons.html, items 3 and 4

United States (1982), *Legislation Relating to Tax-Motivated Corporate Mergers and Acquisitions: Hearings Before the Subcommittee on Select Revenue Measures of the House Committee on Ways and Means*, 97th Cong., 2d Sess. 90

United States (2004), 'American Jobs Creation Act of 2004: Conference Report, Statement of Conference Managers', H. R. Rep. No. 108–755 at http://waysandmeans.house.gov/Links.asp?section = 1639

United States (2005), 'Summary of Joint Committee Staff "Options to Improve Tax Compliance and Reform Tax Expenditures"' JCX-19-05R, 12 April 2005 at www.house.gov/jct/x-19-05r.pdf

Vanistendael, F. (2006), '*Halifax* and *Cadbury Schweppes*: One Single Theory of Abuse in Tax Law?', *EC Tax Review* 15: 192–5

Vinther, N. and Werlauff, E. (2006), 'Tax Motives are Legal Motives – The Borderline between the Use and the Abuse of the Freedom of Establishment with Reference to the *Cadbury Schweppes* Case', *European Taxation* 46: 383–6

Virgo, G. (1993), 'The Law of Taxation is Not An Island – Overpaid Taxes and the Law of Restitution', *British Tax Review* 1993: 442–67

Virgo, G, (2004), '*Deutsche Morgan Grenfell*: Restitution of Tax Paid by Mistake', *British Tax Review* 2004: 8–14

Virgo, G. (2005), '*Deutsche Morgan Grenfell*: the Right to Restitution of Tax Paid by Mistake Rejected', *British Tax Review* 2005: 281–6

Virgo, G. (2006), *The Principles of the Law of Restitution*, 2nd edition (Oxford: Oxford University Press)

Waincymer, J. (1997), 'The Australian Tax Avoidance Experience and Responses: A Critical Review', in G. S. Cooper (ed.), *Tax Avoidance and the Rule of Law* (Amsterdam: IBFD), pp. 247–306.

Ward, W. R. (1953), *The English Land Tax in the Eighteenth Century* (London: Oxford University Press)

Ward, D. A., Avery Jones, J. F. et al. (1985), 'The Business Purpose Test and Abuse of Rights', British Tax Review 1985: 68–123

Ward, D. A. and Cullity, M. C. (1981), 'Abuse of Rights and the Business Purpose Test as Applied to Taxing Statutes', Canadian Tax Journal 29(4): 451–75

Weisbach, D. A. (1999), 'Formalism in the Tax Law', University of Chicago Law Review, Vol. 66, pp. 860–86

Weisbach, D. A. (2001), 'The Failure of Disclosure as an Approach to Tax Shelters', SMU Law Review 54: 71–82

Weisbach, D. A. (2002), 'Ten Truths about Tax Shelters', Tax Law Review 55: 215–53

Wheatcroft, G. S. A. and Bramwell, R. M. (eds.), (1963–), British Tax Encyclopedia (London: Sweet & Maxwell)

Wolfman, B. (1981), 'The Supreme Court in the Lyons Den: A Failure of Judicial Process', Cornell Law Review 66: 1075–102

Wolfman, B. (2004), 'Why Economic Substance is Better Left Uncodified', Tax Notes 104: 445

Wolfman, B., Holden, J. P. and Harris, K. L. (2006), Standards of Tax Practice 2006 Supplement (Falls Church: Tax Analysts)

Lord Wright of Durley (1939), Legal Essays and Addresses (Cambridge: Cambridge University Press)

Yin, G. K. (2001), 'Getting Serious about Corporate Tax Shelters: Taking a Lesson from History', SMU Law Review 54: 209–37

Zelenak, L. (2001), 'Codifying Anti-avoidance Doctrines and Controlling Corporate Tax Shelters', SMU Law Review 54: 177–93

Zimmer, F. (2002), 'General Report', in International Fiscal Association (2002), pp. 19–67

TABLE OF CASES

TABLE OF ABBREVIATIONS

EC	European Communities
ECJ	European Court of Justice
EU	European Union
GAAR	General anti-avoidance rule
IRC	Internal Revenue Code (US)
IRS	Internal Revenue Service (US)
OECD	Organisation for Economic Co-operation and Development
OEEC	Organisation for European Economic Cooperation
UK	United Kingdom
US	United States of America

INDEX